Praise for *The Human Ri*

"Alfred de Zayas offers us an invaluable insider's account of how the global system created after World War II to protect human rights is brazenly manipulated by the United States Government and others for geopolitical ends. De Zayas is a human rights leader of remarkable insight, experience, wisdom, and integrity, whose account is both searing and hugely constructive. He makes vividly clear why we must, and how we can, truly champion peace and human rights."

JEFFREY D. SACHS, professor at Columbia University

"Alfred de Zayas is an experienced human rights scholar, knowledgeable and straightforward. Worth reading in depth."

PROFESSOR MARC BOSSUYT, Antwerpen, former President of the Belgian Constitutional Court and member of the UN Sub-Commission on Promotion and Protection of Human Rights

"Alfred de Zayas provides a candid view of the 'human rights industry' from the perspective of someone who has been inside the system for almost five decades. Like the whistleblowers he cites in the book's dedication, Alfred is willing to provide a glimpse into the good and bad of the UN's growing human rights industry."

CURTIS DOEBBLER, Research Professor of Law at the University of Makeni (Sierra Leone), representative of the NGO International-Lawyers.org to UN Headquarters

"This book is a long-overdue critique of the human rights system by someone who truly values human rights and who has a unique and valuable perspective as a human rights practitioner for 50 years. As Zayas so eloquently explains, the human rights system has sadly become a business, motivated by the drive for the approval of its rich and self-interested (Western) patrons. The result is a system infected by unfairness and double standards—the very opposite of what we would want from a system which purports to protect the most basic rights of humanity. However, this is not a fatalistic or cynical critique like some. Rather, it is a hopeful work which offers constructive criticism and concrete suggestions for making the system one that works for everyone and upholds the very values it was created to promote. I highly recommend this book for experts, practitioners, and lay readers alike."

DANIEL KOVALIK, Professor of International Human Rights at the University of Pittsburgh School of Law, and author, *No More War: How the West Violates International Law by Using "Humanitarian" Intervention to Advance Economic and Strategic Interests*

More praise ...

"This book reveals the inner-workings of the United Nations by that rare public servant willing to shine a light on corruption and failure as well as courage and success. It also gives us an honest and expert survey of nonprofit organizations and media outlets that report on human rights. Most importantly, it provides a detailed plan to reform a system currently preverted by the power of certain governments rather than shaped by the interests of those most in need."

DAVID SWANSON, Executive Director, World Beyond War

"Human rights veteran Zayas formulates a courageous critique and viable proposals to improve the system and to preserve the essence of the Universal Declaration of Human Rights, threatened by politicization and corporate interests."

GILLES-EMMANUEL JACQUET, professor,
Geneva School of Diplomacy and International Relations

"There is a human right to truth. Zayas shows us that History and Law can be instrumentalized and turned into fake history and fake law. This book by a veteran human rights scholar documents the hijacking of the human rights system by governments, corporations, and lobbies. Zayas is not only a distinguished professor of law, he is also a historian whose books have helped correct the politicized historical record. This new book raises important ethical questions that deserve answers. A 'must read.'"

DR. FRANZ SEIDLER, professor emeritus,
Universität der Bundeswehr, Munich

"Professor de Zayas raises important issues about the politicization of the UN Human Rights Office and the Human Rights Council. He formulates pragmatic proposals for the reform of UN human rights institutions in the spirit of the UN Charter. The book is supported by hundreds of credible sources and calls for serious debate."

PROFESSOR TIAN LI, Director of the Center for Human Rights and
Peaceful Development, and Associate Professor of School of Law,
Shandong University, China

"Alfred de Zayas is among the most acute observers of the United Nations and in particular of the Geneva human rights arena. For a good forty years, he has followed, analyzed, and unveiled the apparent as well as the deep trends and hidden influences which shape the agenda of governmental and non-governmental organizations. His present work is a masterpiece. Anyone who wants to understand how non-profit NGOs became a big business and how they have been weaponized by the West at the expense of justice and equity will cherish this book."

GUY METTAN, independent journalist, author, and
former director of Geneva Press Club

"This book is an eloquent indictment of international crimes and the corruption of vital international institutions. It is a plea for the reversal of these negative and dangerous trends for the good of humanity. It exposes the disease and what can be done to start the remedy and cure. Coming from an experienced UN insider, this is an essential book for all who care about human rights and peace."

RICK STERLING, journalist and board chair of the
Mt. Diablo Peace & Justice Center

"Alfred de Zayas has done it again, calling on human conscience unequivocally and non-apologetically to rectify the dysfunctions of the UN system for the protection and promotion of Human Rights. Zayas wants it reoriented toward a just, equitable and sustainable development for all, not just the privileged. The promise of food security and planetary health will remain a mirage unless reforms are undertaken and the United Nations recommits to implementing the UDHR. The common heritage of mankind is threatened by the falsehoods that surround political discourse and lip-service to human rights. Sober reflections in all humility can restore our human dignity as we follow the plan of action proposed by Zayas. Only we can be the guardians of our Rights."

DR. MAWULI SABLAH, West Africa Regional Advisor for Health and
Nutrition, Catholic Relief Services, Burkina Faso

"A timely and necessary book. Alfred de Zayas is one of the world's deepest and most authoritative thinkers."

DR. ALAN MACLEOD, University of Glasgow Media Group,
editor, Mintpress

More praise ...

"At a time when corruption and newspeak seem to become the new normal, de Zayas remains an untiring voice of reason and decency."

MAX KERN, retired senior officer, International Labour Office, Geneva, chief of the freedom of workers section, in charge of verification of compliance with ILO conventions

"Zayas is a noted peace and human rights activist. His new book on the human rights industry reveals double-standards of the Human Rights Council, Inter-American Court and European Court of Human Rights. As a high UN official for decades, Zayas knows what he is talking about."

JOSÉ LUIS MAZÓN COSTA, Madrid-based human rights lawyer before the UN Human Rights Committee, ECHR, Spanish Supreme Court and Spanish Constitutional Court

"In this book an insider of the human rights system resolutely addresses some of the most uncomfortable truths of the 'industry.' With evidence that speaks for itself, he puts on the table an unspoken reality, showing that many actors are using Human Rights for geopolitical purposes and for totalitarian imposition of their values. Zayas manages to shed a light of hope and formulates sharp proposals aimed at restoring the institutions to their true purpose. Every person involved with Human Rights should read this and practice introspection."

LUIS ROBERTO ZAMORA BOLAÑOS, former Costa Rican Ambassador to Seoul, member of the International Association of Democratic Lawyers

"The world needs a better narrative. Alfred de Zayas offers an all-encompassing perspective for a world order, justly built upon human dignity and genuine compliance with the law of the precious International Bill of Human Rights. The book is an invitation to soul-searching."

MARJOLIJN C. SNIPPE, International lawyer, Board member World Federalist Movement in the Netherlands

"Alfred de Zayas provides the broadest authoritative assessment to date of the accelerating instrumentalization and weaponsization of human rights institutions and communications, resulting in thwarting universal ethics and mechanisms for democratic governance, justice and well-being worldwide. Beyond diagnosis, the book offers a prescription for an imperative take back of this heritage of the peoples of the world for the rights of all and thus peace and a just and equitable world order."

PATRICK TARAN, President of Global Migration Policy Associates

THE HUMAN RIGHTS
INDUSTRY

*Reflections of a Veteran
Human Rights Defender*

ALFRED DE ZAYAS

Clarity Press, Inc.

ISBN: 978-1-949762-52-5
EBOOK ISBN: 978-1-949762-53-2

In-house editor: Diana G. Collier
Book design: Becky Luening

Library of Congress Control Number: 2023935853

Clarity Press, Inc.
2625 Piedmont Rd. NE, Ste. 56
Atlanta, GA 30324, USA
https://www.claritypress.com

DEDICATION

This book pays tribute to true human rights defenders.

It commends the enormous courage of thousands of whistleblowers worldwide, women and men, who choose conscience and civic responsibility over personal convenience, risking their lives, liberty, and careers to serve democratic societies and open our eyes to corruption, lies, scams, cover-ups, and crimes perpetrated by governments, corporations and financial institutions.

Whistleblowers are true heroes of our time and deserve national and international solidarity. Some of them surely merit the Nobel Peace Prize.

It is obvious that government criminality is contrary to every notion of democracy and rule of law. It would end, if we could ensure transparency and accountability. Thus, we need more whistleblowers to reveal what crimes are being committed in our name. As history demonstrates, secrecy is a crucial facilitator of crime and corruption. Moreover, it is my conviction and hope that whistleblowers will also help us fix the human rights system that over the years has been hijacked for geopolitical purposes. Once again I propose, as I have done in my reports to the UN Human Rights Council and General Assembly, that a Charter of Rights of Whistleblowers be adopted in order to shield them from persecution and prosecution.

Among these paladins of truth, let us honour:

Julian Assange, Bill Binney, Joe Darby, Antoine Deltour, Thomas Drake, Sibel Edmonds, Daniel Ellsberg, Vera English, Perry Fellwock, George Galatis, Daniel Hale, Ian Henderson, John Kiriakou, Karen Kwiatkowski, Chelsea Manning, Cathy Massiter, Samuel Provance, Michael Ruppert, Keith Schooley, David Shyler, Karen Silkwood, Edward Snowden, Jeffrey Sterling, Linda Tripp, Mordechai Vanunu, Sherron Watkins, Jeffrey Wigand, Peter Wright . . .

- Julian Assange | since 2010 – Wikileaks founder published the Collateral Murder video showing United States soldiers fatally shooting 18 civilians from a helicopter in Iraq
- Bill Binney | 2005 – NSA spying on American public
- Joe Darby | 2004 – Abu Ghraib POW torture and cover-up
- Antoine Deltour | 2012 – Lux-leaks, tax evasion/avoidance by multinationals
- Thomas Drake | 2005–2011 – NSA violations of Article 4 U.S. Bill of Rights, Trailblazer Project
- Sibel Edmonds | 2002 – denounced FBI cover-ups, founder of National Security Whistleblowers Coalition
- Daniel Ellsberg | 1971 – released the Pentagon Papers about the U.S. war in Vietnam
- Vera English | 1990 – lab technician at nuclear facility, GE radioactive contamination
- Perry Fellwock | 1971 – former NSA analyst who disclosed mass surveillance
- George Galatis | 1996 – nuclear power plant Millstone's unsafe procedures
- Daniel Hale | 2014 – illegal drone warfare
- Ian Henderson | 2018 – OPCW inspector who revealed tampering with Douma evidence
- John Kiriakou | 2007 – CIA officer reveals waterboarding practices
- Karen Kwiatkowski | 2002 – retired U.S. Air Force lieutenant colonel – the source of Sy Hersh on Iraq
- Chelsea Manning | 2010 – released 75,000 documents to Wikileaks proving U.S. war crimes in Iraq and Afghanistan, convicted 2013 under the Espionage Act
- Cathy Massiter | 1984 – MI5 officer who disclosed government surveillance of trade unions

- Samuel Provence | 2003–2004 – Intelligence officer revealed torture in Abu Ghraib
- Michael Ruppert | 1996 – CIA involvement in drug trafficking
- Keith Schooley | 1992 – former stockbroker at Merryll Lynch, disclosed fraud and corruption
- David Shayler | 1997 – M15 targeted assassination plans
- Karen Silkwood | 1974 – nuclear power risks
- Jeffrey Sterling | 2002 and 2004 – CIA revelations on Operation Merlin
- Linda Tripp | 1998 – White House staff member, uncovered Monika Lewinski scandal
- Mordechai Vanunu | 1986 – revealed clandestine Israeli nuclear weapons program
- Edward Snowden | 2013 – revealed illegal surveillance by NSA, author of Permanent Record
- Sherron Watkins | 2002 – Enron scandal
- Jeffrey Wiegand | 1996 – nicotine levels in tobacco
- Peter Wright | 1988 – former MI5 science officer who disclosed security services plots, won case before European Court of Human Rights against UK in 1991

The above women and men are true patriots and should be recognized as crucial defenders of democracy and human rights.

"True patriotism springs from a belief in the dignity of the individual, freedom and equality not only for Americans but for all people on earth, universal brotherhood and good will."

ELEANOR ROOSEVELT

CONTENTS

PREFACE

"The World Economic Forum is increasingly
becoming an unelected world government that
the people never asked for and don't want."

ELON MUSK, JANUARY 18, 2023[1]

AMONG the institutions and organizations that shape our conscious-
ness, our perception of reality, our moral compass, we recognize our
families, teachers, universities, churches, mosques and synagogues,
books, the daily press, social media, television and the movie industry
and our public intellectuals.

There are many other "players" who in one way or another
impact public opinion, including our local and federal governments,
our clubs and sports organizations, corporations and their subtle and
not so subtle publicity. In a larger sense, our world is influenced by the
United Nations and its agencies, including UNESCO, UNICEF, WHO,
WTO, ILO, UNDP, UNEP, the World Bank (WB) and International
Monetary Fund (IMF), regional alliances including the Organization
of American States (OAS), the European Union (EU), the African
Union (AU), the North Atlantic Treaty Organization (NATO), as well
as the World Economic Forum (WEF), and the thousands of nongovernmental organizations.

All of these players impact the enjoyment of our civil, cultural,
economic, political and social rights. They can and do significantly
contribute to a democratic and equitable international order based on
human dignity and international solidarity. But they can be manipulated and hijacked by geopolitical interests, resulting in unjust distribution of wealth nationally and internationally, and a retrogression in
human rights.

This book endeavours to explore how the "narrative managers"
in governments, corporations, nongovernmental organizations and the
media shape our perception of human rights, and how imperialistic
fantasies, geopolitical agendas, the sequels of colonialism, and the
emergence of new forms of economic colonialism endanger the promotion and protection of human rights worldwide. The good news is

that we can do something about it. Our goal is to identify the problems and formulate a plan of action to make the system work better.

The title of this book has an evolutionary history and *raison d'être,* corresponding to my more than fifty years of involvement in the human rights field. For some readers the title could suggest unintended associations, convey a feeling of *déjà vu,* or induce a sense of resignation over how institutions and society in general actually function, which may be a profound disappointment to blue-eyed optimists.

We humans tend to opportunistically calibrate everything to our personal advantage—and often to the disadvantage of others. In this context I am always reminded of a favourite Terentius quotation, *homo sum, humani nil a me alienum puto.* I am human, so nothing human is really foreign to me.[2]

Over a period of fifty years of active participation in human rights endeavours (I used to go out in the cold and demonstrate for social causes even as a teenager), I experienced a spectrum of feelings toward the many challenges posed by the suffering of other human beings, by the needless wars and outbreaks of violence, by the tragedies visited on individuals and their families, by the concrete problems faced by communities, and by the ways in which society has tried to correct the dysfunctions of our socio-economic apparatus.

This book has had a long gestation and represents an attempt at a constructive criticism of the human rights promotion and protection system. It formulates a kind of roadmap, a call for action, so that human dignity can be incrementally enjoyed by all peoples in all corners of the planet.

An appropriate title for the book could have been *International Human Rights at a Cross-road,* but there are already such book titles around, or maybe *International Human Rights Monitoring Mechanisms,* or a variant thereof, but I am already the co-editor of a book with that title.[3]

As an alternative title I considered "The human rights family," since that is how we would like to understand human rights, as something familiar, inherent in the human species, something to be shared with our sisters and brothers the world over. Alas, families also have acrimonious disputes. This book endeavours to identify the sources of dispute and instead emphasize our commonalities, the convergence of the needs and aspirations of all human beings, the importance of civilized human relations.

Another possible title could have been *The Human Rights System*, but that title is already taken and, in any event, it would not reveal much about its probable content and the necessary criticism of that system's deficiencies. Yet another title could have been *The Human Rights Apparatus,* but that would generate an impression of emotionless automatism as in Charlie Chaplin's *Modern Times,* instead of the idea of innovative, vibrant collective work-in-progress.

During my five decades of involvement in various capacities in diverse human rights activities, I have had the privilege of learning side-by-side with brilliant academics, independent experts, makers and shakers, committed, altruistic, true heroes of human rights. I observed and participated in the development of constructive initiatives, but I also detected incoherence, inequity, abuse in the application of norms, discrimination among victims, intellectual dishonesty, narcissism and even cynicism. Whereas the human rights system is undoubtedly based on valid ethical principles, these principles can be betrayed by the "industry" that has emerged and threatens to penetrate all facets of genuine human rights activism.

It bears repeating that as social animals we carry with us certain predispositions, preferences, and prejudices. Similarly, every enterprise operated by humans is subject to being instrumentalized for ulterior purposes. Hence, it is not surprising that some human rights institutions lend themselves to "weaponization" against geopolitical rivals, frequently with the media acting as echo chambers. It is, however, crucial that the noble ideals associated with social progress and human dignity not be hijacked to serve selfish economic or political ends.

These considerations would justify two other titles highlighting the dangers: *The Human Rights Business,* which would emphasize the economic take-over of human rights programmes by corporations and special interests, or the simpler concept and my ultimate choice—*The Human Rights Industry*—which throws light on the functioning of this vast and essential enterprise that encompasses individuals, civil society, religious institutions, universities, think tanks, non-governmental organizations, inter-governmental organization, national human rights institutions and even corporate boardrooms.

Regardless of its title, this book is neither moralistic nor judg-mental, although it does identify generic problems including selec-tivity, double standards, and the misuse of values and principles for selfish purposes. It would be wrong to see the book as denigrating or denouncing our human rights institutions. Nor is it an exercise in bellyaching. Far from it. What this book does do is to take stock of the current situation, identifying deficiencies, and proposing how best to fix the problems that beset the system. We all should nurture an optimistic spirit and persevere in the hope of enhancing the enjoyment of human rights by all women and men on the planet. It proposes a plan of action to overhaul the system and repair what is dysfunctional. It discards cosmetic changes, "band aids," or superficial solutions, but seeks to formulate strategies to make the human rights institutions work more efficiently.

The book acknowledges the accomplishments of non-govern-mental organizations such as the Women's International League for Peace and Freedom, the International Peace Bureau, or the Geneva International Peace Research Institute. These and many other genuine NGOs are guardians of our human rights. The book also celebrates major achievements of the United Nations since the adoption of the Universal Declaration of Human Rights on December 10, 1948, and anticipates what human rights will look like in 2048, one hundred years after the adoption of this indispensable Magna Charta of humanity.

There is good reason for optimism. We now have a vast system of binding human rights treaties and expert Committees with jurisdiction over most States, we have national human rights institutions, we have a keener awareness of the problems. We observe that considerable progress in human rights terms has been achieved since 1948, partic-ularly in the advancement of women's rights, minorities' rights, the abolition of capital punishment and the expansion of local, regional, and international human rights courts.

Nevertheless, it is important to remind ourselves that progress is not inevitable, and that there can be retrogression in human rights. Indeed, we must recognize that there has already been such retrogres-sion with regard to many economic and social rights, while the wealth disparity in the world continues to grow, nationally and internation-ally. We must remind ourselves that human dignity and human rights are not commodities, but the heritage of every member of the human family. Among the entitlements of each person are certain fundamental rights and freedoms, both collective and individual, including the right to live in peace and dignity, which necessarily encompasses freedom from fear and want; the right to food, water, health, and shelter; the rights to one's identity, culture, and language; and the right to one's religion, convictions and expression.

It is worth remembering that the UN Division of Human Rights under Theo van Boven[4] advanced a holistic view of all human rights—civil, cultural, economic, political, and social—which are acknowledged as universal, interdependent, and interrelated. When in 1980 Theo hired me, I hoped to make a difference, help advance standard-setting, monitoring and implementation.

Today the donors dictate the agenda, and the mainstream media suppress legitimate dissent and non-conforming narratives—even reports from UN rapporteurs whose findings do not serve the desired political purposes. This is also due to lack in leadership in the human rights institutions.

Today under the banner of human rights Orwellian policies are defended, such as unilateral coercive measures that kill tens of thousands of innocent people every year worldwide—a form of State terrorism and a crime against humanity for purposes of Article 7 of the Statute of Rome.

Under the pretext of providing "humanitarian assistance," lethal military interventions are conducted, e.g., in Libya, an emblematic example of how the noble idea of the "responsibility to protect" was corrupted.

The epistemological onslaught sells interventionism and enforced regime change as "colour revolutions," which are not home-grown but serve the interests of foreign players and are often prepared by foreign NGOs and intelligence services through overt and covert activities. Thus, the so-called "Arab Spring" morphed into the Libyan winter and the Syrian chaos.

The propagandistic use of the words "human rights," "democracy," "rule of law," and "freedom" demeans them and subverts rational discourse. A "human rights industry" operates at all levels, transforming values through fake news and phoney narratives that in turn generate fake history, fake law, fake diplomacy, fake freedom, and ultimately fake democracy.

As I learned through experience, some UN "experts" and highly praised UN envoys are hardly independent, nor truly committed to human rights, but "establishment" types drawn from the same pool of former politicians who are faithful to their respective elites and enjoy the privileges of the institutionalized "revolving door." Many UN rapporteurs simply serve the human rights industry, in a manner inconsistent with their mandates and their code of conduct.[5] The question arises whether the Human Rights Council itself is at the service of the "status quo" and the geopolitical strategies of hegemons. The same applies to the Secretariat of many UN institutions whose career development is frustrated by the constant "parachuting" of former politicians and government officials into the senior management posts.

This book looks at the voting record in the General Assembly and Human Rights Council by China, Russia, the United States, Canada, Australia, Japan, UK, EU, OIC, Group of 77, Non-aligned Movement, etc. With growing alarm, we observe how States and some nongovernmental organizations betray their democratic responsibilities and basic liberal principles, brazenly lie, engage in evidence-free accusations and hyperbole, blackmail and bully weaker States. We witness how fake news is instrumentalized to concoct fake law. Indeed, there is a veritable war on truth and gradually we are slipping into a fake democracy.

Quis custodiet ipsos custodes?[6]—who will guard over the guardians?—when the mainstream media no longer performs the function of the watchdog, no longer alerts us to endemic—and specific—governmental abuses but acts like cheer leaders for the interests of the "elites" and transnational corporations, when they indoctrinate us into loving "Big Brother" ....

Who will guard over the guardians, when the executive, legislative and judicial institutions are progressively corrupted, when institutions like the Organization for the Prohibition of Chemical Weapons and many "independent commissions" work teleologically, tamper with the evidence and suppress crucial facts, when other supposedly objective organizations systematically disinform the public, disseminate fake news, and suppress dissent?

I have come to the conclusion that *only we, the people, can be the guardians of our rights*. It is our responsibility to reclaim democracy and our right to effective participation in public affairs, as stipulated in Article 25 of the International Covenant on Civil and Political Rights.

Multilateralism and international solidarity can and must be practiced by governments and non-State actors alike. Hence, the UN system as a whole must reject bloc confrontation, provocation, escalation of tensions, warmongering and xenophobia. It is not difficult to understand that there is only one planet Earth and it is the duty of states to devise a just *modus vivendi*. Only thus can enduring peace in the world—based on the principles of the sovereign equality of states and the self-determination of peoples—be ensured. States and NGOs must seek and practice international solidarity[7] if we want to achieve the Sustainable Development Goals[8] and reclaim our human dignity. While we recognize that we cannot eradicate evil in human behaviour, we must work hard to curtail the processes furthering human greed and arrogance.

This will require "conversion therapy." Military-first economies must be gradually transformed into human security economies. Today the greatest enemies of peace and prosperity are the military-industrial-financial complexes, mostly in the United States but elsewhere as well, which have undermined democracies throughout the world. Another major obstacle to progress in the human rights field is the nefarious impact of much of the corporate media, which relentlessly lie, distort the facts, and censor.

A better world is indeed possible.[9] This will demand intellectual and emotional honesty from each and every one of us. It will require a radical change of budgetary and other priorities as well as the freedom to seek and impart information as stipulated in Article 19 of the International Covenant on Civil and Political Rights.

A democratic and equitable international order will require a rediscovery of the spirituality of the Universal Declaration of Human Rights and a commitment to make those rights reality, as the San Francisco non-governmental organization Eleanor Lives proposes, together with a plan of action to reclaim the international bill of human rights[10] and establish an international court of human rights.

The chapters that follow will endeavour to give a bird's eye view of the manifold problems that plague the institutions that should be promoting and protecting the human rights of all, and not just the interests of the elites, who give lip service to human rights but actually prefer the "good old world" where the rich are rich, and the poor are poor.

Obviously, this book cannot be considered complete or comprehensive. It is an invitation to other hands-on human rights activists to take a closer look at how the system works and where the dysfunctions lie. It invites the members of bodies like the Human Rights Council and the Human Rights Committee to do an exercise of soul-searching, to see whether their actions serve human dignity, whether they can do better in the future.

This book gives examples that I consider representative of the challenges we face—not only snapshots, vignettes or episodes but cases and situations symptomatic of the problems that the human rights community faces.

Let us reject the binary approach to human rights—good countries vs. bad countries, democracies vs. autocracies. Such a Manichaean approach is both untenable and unhelpful, because the world is far more complex than we can grasp, there is always bad in the good and even some good in the bad. We are all in this together and must tackle global problems in international solidarity—with good will, faith and optimism.

This book salutes the work of the World Social Forum, which held its 14th session in Mexico City from 1 to 6 May. The Final Declaration reminds us that in a contradictory world situation, it is urgent to continue working for world peace and "to redefine an alter-globalisation proposal corresponding to the new situation; to understand the new contradictions of the world system; to start from the movements to resist, to define alternatives, to build a new project of emancipation. Another world is possible and together we must build it!"[11]

CHAPTER 1

AUTHORITY AND CREDIBILITY

Peace, development and human rights are essentially inter-related, inter-dependent and indivisible.

THEO VAN BOVEN

Whether our challenge is peace-making, nation-building, democratization or responding to natural or man-made disasters, we have seen that even the strongest amongst us cannot succeed alone.

KOFI ANNAN

THE UNITED NATIONS Charter and the Universal Declaration of Human Rights launched a universal movement toward the recognition of human dignity and the individual and collective rights that derive from it. The UN's labour in standard-setting has been phenomenal, as indeed concretized in nine core human rights treaties and the creation of numerous expert bodies charged with their implementation. The Commission on Human Rights and its successor, the Human Rights Council, have established working groups, commissions of inquiry, fact-finding commissions, and appointed independent experts and special rapporteurs to make sure that follow-up to the norms is being implemented. It can be said without fear of contradiction, that the UN's job of standard setting, which is ongoing, and its system of examination of State party reports before the expert committees and before the Universal Periodic Review of the Human Rights Council, have borne fruit and advanced the human rights of billions of human beings. Our goal is to make the UN and its procedures more effective and to remove the obstacles to the realization of civil, cultural, economic, social and political rights by all members of the human family. This chapter introduces the following four chapters which focus on four emblematic institutions of relevance to the promotion and protection of human rights: the Office of the UN High Commissioner for Human Rights, the Human Rights Council, the International Criminal Court, and the Organization for the Prohibition of Chemical Weapons.

The authority and credibility of every institution, whether domestic or international, judicial or quasi-judicial, executive or advisory, depends on its adherence to specific terms of reference laid down in its charter, constitution or statute. The purpose of this introductory chapter to the four chapters on institutions to follow is to explore the reasons why public trust in United Nations agencies, special procedures, working groups, rapporteurs and commissions as well as judicial and quasi-judicial institutions, including the International Criminal Court and the Organization for the Prohibition of Chemical Weapons, has declined. I shall also propose pragmatic recommendations as to how they might endeavor to win back and strengthen that trust.

Every institution seeking to establish its authority and credibility is bound by a code of deontology which it must observe in good faith, enabling it to be held accountable for *ultra vires* actions or pronouncements which contradict its own legality and legitimacy. When an institution becomes politicized and oversteps its mandate—and many do—it thereby sacrifices its authority and loses the confidence of those who hitherto have believed in it. Transparency and accountability are therefore of the essence.

Credibility also depends on the professionalism and impartiality of the institutions' secretariat,[1] on the commitment of its staff to that code of conduct. As a staff member myself, I had the honour of working with professionals of high ethical standards. As I have written elsewhere, my immediate superior and mentor, Justice Jakob Möller, was "integrity in person."

An institution, a function or a secretariat does not possess automatic authority and credibility by virtue of its title. This must be earned. Moreover, institutions must demonstrate that they can do more than just denounce violations of human rights, more than "name and shame" a targeted country or politician. First, clear standards must be set. Second, these standards must be made juridical and justiciable. Third, regional and international courts and tribunals must be competent to issue final judgments that are solidly based on the applicable standards, coherently argued, and above suspicion of partiality. It is this that makes the resolutions, decisions, rulings and judgments credible, and ultimately enforceable. And conversely, if not—not.

My long experience suggests that the UN secretariat is no different from the secretariat of any governmental office or private sector institution. Secretariat members are humans like the rest of us: some are idealists, some ideologues, some straight-arrows, others intriguers, some conscientious workers, others opportunists, some committed, others paper-pushers, some genuine, others hypocrites, etc. And as in all human institutions, we encounter peer pressure, groupthink, "comfort zones," jealousies, vendettas, and rationality and irrationality side by side.

Personally, as an old UN staffer and a believer in the legacy of Eleanor Roosevelt,[2] René Cassin and others, I feel personally offended, even hurt, when I realize that the image of the organization to which I devoted decades of my life is not what it should be and that it has lost much of the respect it once enjoyed, being considered by many as compromised. I feel saddened that some experts and officials have disappointed the expectations we placed on them, that an organization as such has not been true to its Purposes and Principles as laid down in the Charter's noble Preamble and its Articles 1 and 2. I feel saddened when an organization acquires a reputation for applying double standards—condemning some states while keeping silent about others in contradiction to the non-discrimination articles of all UN human rights treaties—or when an organization relies on public relations more than on honesty, as illustrated by a British USG's evidence-free statememts concerning Russian soldiers' alleged mass rape, during the Ukraine war, as discussed below. I mourn over the betrayal of ideals and values. Again and again the UN has abandoned the victims and danced to the tune of the powerful.

A great disappointment came in 2003, when the UN was unable to prevent the illegal U.S. invasion and bombardment of Iraq—when in spite of the Security Council's direct involvement in the search for weapons of mass destruction, the UN was forced to withdraw its weapons inspectors from Baghdad for their own protection, because it was apparent that the United States would bombard Iraq contrary to the wishes of a majority in the international community and absent any legality or legitimacy.

March 20, 2003 has gone down in history as the day when the U.S. and the "coalition of the willing" staged a coup d'état against humanity, a revolt against the UN Charter, international treaties and customary international law by invading and devastating a country that was not threatening any of its neighbours, that was cooperating with the United Nations and with resolutions of the Security Council. This happened notwithstanding the fact that two UN inspectors, Hans Blix[3] and Mohammed ElBaradei[4] had been investigating the non-existence of weapons of mass destruction. The inspectors had to be evacuated when it became apparent that the U.S. would attack without UN approval—in total disregard of the United Nations and the global majority. In a very real sense, the UN was shown to be "irrelevant." There was hardly an outcry in the General Assembly, in the International Court of Justice, in the UN Commission of Human Rights against the monstrosity that had occurred.

Admittedly, the then secretary general, Kofi Annan, did say that the invasion was contrary to the UN Charter, and when pressed by the media, he stated that it was in fact an "illegal war"[5]—but he said that only much later. Following the invasion, there was no Resolution from the General Assembly condemning the aggression, demanding an immediate stop to the operation and punishment of the aggressors, no subsequent demand for criminal prosecution of the air force commanders, of drones operators, of the soldiers using indiscriminate weapons in Baghdad, Mosul, and Fallujah, leaving a trail of radiation from depleted uranium weapons.[6] There was no accountability for terror bombings, indiscriminate killing of civilians, torture of prisoners of war in Abu Ghraib[7] and illegal CIA renditions to Guantanamo.[8] There was no resolution demanding that the U.S. and the "coalition of the willing" pay reparations to the tune of billions of dollars for the colossal destruction of Iraq and its infrastructures, including UNESCO world heritage sites.

The apologetics practiced by the mainstream media, the official denials, and the attempt by legal experts to "justify" what had happened and the looting that was still ongoing were articularly offensive to any person committed to human rights and the rule of law—were and continue to be. The U.S. government's "torture memos" are a blemish on the legal profession. Alberto Gonzalez and other senior U.S. lawyers actually argued that the detainees in Guantanamo and elsewhere should be considered as "unlawful combatants"—an improved term with no legal standing—in order that they might be deprived of protection under the Geneva Conventions. The memos written by John Yoo,[9] deputy assistant attorney-general in the Office of the Legal Counsel in the U.S. State Department were a disgrace for the profession.

The international community also witnessed the war crimes and crimes against humanity committed by NATO forces in Afghanistan, Libya, and Syria. All of them were accompanied by apologetics and cover-ups. Even though Wikileaks and other sources threw light on the crimes, the criminals remained unpunished. Only the whistleblowers were persecuted and prosecuted.

Compare this to the Russian invasion of Ukraine in February 2022—undoubtedly a gross violation of the UN Charter, in particular of Article 2(4). In this case the General Assembly duly condemned it[10] and urged Russia to pay reparations to Ukraine.[11] Unfortunately no such resolutions were ever adopted by the General Assembly in the case of NATO's bombardment of Yugoslavia in 1999, or the drone war against the peoples of Afghanistan and Iraq. What does this tell us about the authority and credibility of the GA, given its obvious selectivity in its condemnation of aggression and war crimes?

A recent *faux pas* by the UN Special Representative on sexual violence, Pramila Patten, a UK barrister, constitutes an embarrassment to the organization. A USG in such an important position must be very careful what he/she says. In October 2022, Ms. Patten made the claim, in an interview with the AFP, that the Russian Armed Forces were employing a deliberate "rape strategy." She is quoted as having said, *inter alia, "you hear women testify about Russian soldiers equipped with Viagra, it's clearly a military strategy,"* only to admit in November that she did not have any solid evidence to substantiate her previous statement.

The Russian government requested a correction, because such a statement was then picked up by the mainstream media worldwide and significantly magnified, thus feeding into an atmosphere of hatemongering against Russians, incompatible with Article 20 of the International Covenant on Civil and Political Rights. Such reckless statements by a senior UN official can be seen as constituting evidence of lack of objectivity and even direct incitement to hatred against Russians in general, bearing in mind that the recipients of the disinformation are common persons who already harbour prejudices and tend to generalize. A more circumspect USG would have remembered that this kind of false allegations of mass rape and distribution of Viagra to soldiers had already been disseminated by the mainstream media in the context of the earlier wars in Iraq and Libya.[12] Surely Ms Patten should also have been aware that more recently during the Ukraine war, a similar low-level propaganda had been peddled by a high-level Ukrainian parliamentary human rights minister, who invented rape stories and eventually had to resign because of her inability to substantiate any of her allegations concerning Russian mass rape.[13]

Russia has demanded a correction and or retraction from the UN for the accusations of Ms. Patten,[14] stating *"The allegations Ms. Patten has brought forward are of a very serious nature, which have the power to shape public discourse around the events in Ukraine." In fact, her words were "widely distributed amongst media outlets and social media, to create a misleading, if not entirely false, narrative."* As expected, no retraction has been forthcoming. Not surprisingly, Russian Foreign Ministry spokeswoman Maria Zakharova blasted the UN official's claims as going *"beyond the reach of reason."*[15]

What do citizens of the world make of such reckless narratives? Some will condemn all Russians for having elected Putin as their president. Others will reject Russian culture, including Tchaikovsky and Dostoyevsky. And yet other will turn their backs on the UN because of unprofessionalism. It is disconcerting to read statements in the social media such as "I mean, c'mon . . . who is going to expect an apology from an organization where the worst of the worst criminals of each country is carefully chosen to represent them. UN is a mafia. That's what they do to earn a living." Is this, then, what the noble idea and ideals of the UN have come to? U.S. linguist Professor Noam Chomsky gave an interview to *Democracy Now!* concerning the credibility of the United Nations and commented: "One important action that the United States could take is to live up to its own laws. Of course, it would be nice if it lived up to international law, but maybe that's too much to ask. . . ."[16]

Those of us who have worked for decades in the human rights field are dismayed by the loss of confidence that currently affects United Nations institutions, and the efforts by some governments and by some in the media to make the United Nations irrelevant.[17] We cannot let this happen. We must push back and vindicate the plan of action for humanity. While these efforts may only address the UN itself and not the principles imbedded in international law which have evolved over centuries, if we did not have the United Nations, the world would have to establish a similar organization to replace it to carry on the quest for peace and human rights. Even those States frequently the butt of its decisions—Russia and China—retain their support for the United Nations and take their grievances to it, rather than, as yet at least, advocating for its demise and/or proposing a replacement. That is why we should take a close look at the UN's institutions and ensure that they do what they are supposed to, that they regain their initial good reputation and make us look up to the Organization with renewed hope and optimism.

CHAPTER 2

THE OFFICE OF THE UN HIGH COMMISSIONER FOR HUMAN RIGHTS (OHCHR)

The High Commissioner for Human Rights shall: "...respect the sovereignty, territorial integrity and domestic jurisdiction of States ...promote the universal respect for and observance of all human rights ... Be guided by the recognition that all human rights—civil, cultural, economic, political and social—are universal, indivisible, interdependent and interrelated and that, while the significance of national and regional particularities and various historical, cultural and religious backgrounds must be borne in mind, it is the duty of States, regardless of their political, economic and cultural systems, to promote and protect all human rights and fundamental freedoms ... [and] a balanced and sustainable development for all people and of ensuring realization of the right to development. ... "

GENERAL ASSEMBLY RESOLUTION 48/141 OF DECEMBER 20, 1993

OVER ITS 77 YEARS of existence, the United Nations Human Rights Office has grown enormously from the modest secretariat[1] of the UN Division on Human Rights, which was established in 1946 under the Canadian John Humphrey (1905–1995), a distinguished Professor of law at McGill University in Montreal, and a true champion of human rights. Humphrey contributed considerably to the drafting of the UDHR and directed the Division for twenty years until 1966. I met him many times in Geneva, since he continued coming to attend meetings of the Commission on Human Rights well until the 1990s and readily shared his vision and friendship with younger colleagues.

Humphrey was followed by the Belgian, Marc Schreiber, and the Dutchman, Professor Theo van Boven[2] from the University of Maastricht, who hired me into the Division in 1980. To this day van Boven is remembered—deservedly—as a hero of human rights, who denounced racism, systematic torture and disappearances in many countries. Nonetheless—or accordingly—he was essentially fired by UN Secretary General Javier Perez de Cuellar under massive pressure from the U.S., because of van Boven's objective criticism of Western interventions and support of military juntas worldwide.

Theo was followed by the Austrian diplomat and legal scholar, Dr. Kurt Herndl, who served with distinction from 1982 until 1987 at the Assistant Secretary General level. This actually entailed a "promotion" of the Division, newly renamed the Centre for Human Rights, which Dr Herndl led for five years from 1982 to 1987. Thanks to his initiatives the function of UN Special Rapporteur against Torture and the UN Voluntary Fund for Advisory Services and Technical Assistance were established. Dr Herndl also set in motion the process for the preparation of the first model legislation on the implementation of a human rights convention, specifically, the Convention for the Elimination of All Forms of Racial Discrimination. In 1987 the Centre was again "promoted" and its new Director was the Swede, Jan Martenson, who was already Under-Secretary General for Disarmament. My most productive years in the Office were perhaps 1987–92, when we established a small think tank to come up with initiatives for approval by the General Assembly, including the World Conference on Human Rights, which was held in Vienna in June 1993. Martenson's successor in 1992 was the Frenchman, Antoine Blanca, who served for only a year and left the office in disarray, only to be followed by the hyperactive Senegalese, Dr. Ibrahima Fall, who directed the Vienna World Conference, which proposed the creation of the Office of the UN High Commissioner for Human Rights at the Under-Secretary General level.

The Office of the UN High Commissioner for Human Rights was established pursuant to General Assembly Resolution 48/141 of December 20, 1993 and commenced operations on April 5, 1994 under the first High Commissioner, Jose Ayala Lasso from Ecuador.[3]

There have been 7 High Commissioners and one Acting High Commissioner: Jose Ayala Lasso (Ecuador, 1994–1997), Mary Robinson (Ireland, 1997–2002), Sergio Vieira de Mello (Brazil, 2002–2003), Acting High Commissioner Bertrand Ramcharan (Guyana, 2003–2004), Louise Arbour (Canada, 2004–2008), Navi Pillay (South Africa, 2008–2014), Zeid Ra'ad Al Hussein (Jordan, 2014–2018), Michelle Bachelet (Chile, 2018–2022) and Volker Türk

(Austria, since September 2022–). From a very modest start, OHCHR now has 104 field presences worldwide.

One would like to believe that there is a certain presumption of authority and credibility that goes with the function of High Commissioner, but experience shows us that every HC must prove his/her mettle and earn his/her own laurels. A worthy High Commissioner must inspire the staff, must engage the secretariat in joint teamwork. An effective HC must be a consummate diplomat, not a political activist, not a judge who condemns States and Heads of State, but a philosopher HC who is result-oriented and has a genuine desire to convince governments that it is in their own best interest to make reforms so as to enhance the enjoyment of human rights by all persons under their jurisdiction.

A true HC is not a windbag, braggart, bull artist, trumpeter, but rather a perseverant international civil servant who is animated by a commitment to human dignity and is skillful in quiet diplomacy. He/she must be much more than just a "manager" or CEO of a human rights industry. Under no conditions should HCs confuse their functions with those of a prosecutor-general or high inquisitor. Their function is more in the line of a medical doctor, a surgeon-general who listens to all patients and tries to help and do no harm, who is skilful in preventing and curing disease. Ideally the High Commissioner's Office should complement the humanitarian work of the International Committee of the Red Cross, a truly professional organization that does not play politics and where the human being, the victim, is the only concern, notwithstanding his/her country of origin. Moreover, the performance of every High Commissioner must be judged not only by what he/she says, but by what he/she does, and not just by that, but by what he/she fails to do. Much of the legitimate criticism of HCs lies in the initiatives that they have taken or not taken, often for purely political reasons.

I had the honour of working closely with the first High Commissioner for Human Rights, José Ayala Lasso, and to accompany him on various missions. Ayala was a low-key High Commissioner, who did not like to grandstand. In Rwanda he did remarkable work during the genocide and its aftermath, but he did it discreetly and frequently at a personal risk. Somethings I think of Ayala as a kind of Raoul Wallenberg, who saved so many Hungarian Jews in 1944 before being arrested by the Soviets and made to disappear. Ayala had the intellectual honesty to denounce all violations of human rights, no matter by which country, no matter who the victims were, and to work indefatigably for reconciliation.

On two occasions he did something that could be termed "politically incorrect," since it concerned Germans who had suffered ethnic cleansing under the Poles, Czechoslovaks and Yugoslavs in the years 1945–48. Fifteen million ethnic Germans had been expelled from their homelands, only and exclusively because they were German. Their lands, where their ancestors had lived for 700 years, were taken away and they themselves were brutally expelled,[4] much like the Palestinians were expelled from their olive orchards in Palestine. It is to Ayala's credit that he had the courage to endorse the human rights claims of the German expellees. On May 28, 1995 he told the representatives of the expellees assembled at the *Paulskirche* in Frankfurt am Main:

> The right not to be expelled from one's homeland is a fundamental right. . . . I submit that if in the years following the Second World war the States had reflected more on the implications of the enforced flight and expulsion of the Germans, today's demographic catastrophes, particularly those referred to as "ethnic cleansing" in Yugoslavia, would, perhaps, not have occurred to the same extent.[5]

Ten years later in Berlin, Ayala returned to Germany to reaffirm the universality of human rights and the right to one's homeland, reiterating "Every person has the right to remain in peace, security and dignity in one's home, or on one's land in one's country. . . . Every person has the right to return voluntarily, and in safety and dignity, to the country of origin and, within it, to the place of origin or choice."[6] This took courage, because the German expellees to this day are not universally perceived as "consensus" victims. The curse of "collective guilt" hangs over all Germans of the war generation, and it was the 15 million Germans from the East who ended up paying the huge historical bill for the abhorrent Nazi crimes. And yet, these expellees were victims themselves, victims of racism, victims of collective punishment. I have known all High Commissioners personally and very much doubt that all of them would have had the courage to stand up for these "unsung victims." Alas, it is easier for High Commissioners and UN rapporteurs alike to go with the flow and grandstand for those victims who already have the blessing of Amnesty International and Human Rights Watch.

With High Commissioner Ayala Lasso at the
Holocaust Memorial in Berlin 2005

The present High Commissioner Türk started his tenure in September 2022. We must give him the benefit of the doubt and encourage him to do better than some of his predecessors. Yet, one of his first actions can be put in the category of a blunder—at least of etiquette. He penned an open letter to Elon Musk,[7] which can only be interpreted as a gratuitous warning formulated in a language that may betray that Türk too is tempted to serve Washington and Brussels. This suspicion resurfaces because of the tenor of his end-of-mission statement in Ukraine on December 7, 2022[8] and in his Human Rights Day statement of December 9, both of them failing to appeal for a de-escalation of that conflict, the need for disarmament, and a recognition of peace a human right. The High Commissioner's statement to the 52nd session of the Council on March 31, 2023 on the war in Ukraine disappointed because of its lack of balance and historical context, betraying an pronounced Western bias, not only in what it said, but in what it failed to say.[9]

At this stage of the Ukraine conflict, what was necessary was a strong appeal to negotiate without pre-conditions and a commitment to reconstruct and reconciliate. Although the blaming game is seldom constructive, it is necessary to recall the pre-history of the conflict and the 2015 Security Council Resolution 2202, endorsing the Minsk agreements.

It was the firm conviction of the Security Council that the situation in eastern regions of Ukraine can only be resolved through a peaceful settlement to the crisis. Resolution 2202: (a) Endorses the "Package of measures for the Implementation of the Minsk Agreements" adopted and signed in Minsk on February 12, 2015 (Annex I); (b) Welcomes the Declaration by the President of the Russian Federation, the President of Ukraine, the President of the French Republic and the Chancellor of the Federal Republic of Germany in support of the "Package of measures for the Implementation of the Minsk Agreements" adopted on February 12, 2015 in Minsk, and their continuing commitment therein to the implementation of the Minsk Agreements; and (c) Calls on all parties to fully implement the "Package of measures," including a comprehensive ceasefire as provided for therein."[10]

It is disappointing that neither Volker Türk nor Secretary General Antonio Guterres cite or remember Resolution 2202. Nor do they refer to General Assembly resolution 60/251 on the creation of the Human Rights Council, which calls on the Human Rights Council to eliminate double standards. The preamble of resolution 60/251 commits the Human Rights Council to ensure "universality, objectivity and non-selectivity in the consideration of human rights issues, and the elimination of double standards and politicization."[11]

Sometimes I think that the OHCHR is perfectly happy to live with double standards, because, as a friend said, "If they had no double standards, they would have no standards at all."

What should be expected from the High Commissioner is to offer his good offices as mediator, or to endorse the various blueprints for peace formulated by think tanks and NGOs like the International Peace Organization,[12] a strong appeal to all warring factions in Ukraine to negotiate an immediate cease-fire, to sit down without conditions and devise a viable *quid pro quo* to be observed in good faith (unlike the Minsk agreements[13]), an appeal to NATO to stop delivering weapons to Ukraine, an appeal to Putin to stop bombarding Ukraine, and an appeal to President Recep Erdogan to renew his mediation.

As everywhere, also in terms of human rights, priorities are important, and peace must also be the HC's priority, since the enjoyment of civil, cultural, economic, political and social rights depends on peace. Everything else is secondary.

In his statement of December 15, 2022, HC Türk also presented a rather unbalanced statement with regard to war crimes taking place during the Ukraine war, focusing on war crimes by Russian forces and ignoring mounting evidence of war crimes by Ukraine. The basic rule of impartiality and objectivity, *audiatur et altera pars*, seems once again to have been replaced by judgmental "naming and shaming" that hitherto has achieved nothing for the victims and has rendered the possibility of compromise with mutual respect ever more remote.

The Deputy High Commissioner made a statement of similar biased matrix,[14] assuming that the overwhelmingly Russian-speaking Crimea and Donbas should be incorporated into Ukraine, notwithstanding the warfare waged by Kiev against Ukraine's Russian-speaking populations since 2014, resulting in some 14,000 deaths, and not giving due consideration to their right of self-determination and their positive vote mandating their desire to return to Russia. This right of self determination is stipulated in Article 1 of the International Covenant on Civil and Political Rights and, as suggested by the 2010 ICJ Advisory Opinion on Kosovo, which everyone in the world other than the U.S., UK, and EU sees as a precedent of general application. Ms Nada Al-Nashif followed the old naming-and-shaming playbook and seemed to ignore the existential danger to all humanity that arises out of the spiral of escalation driven by NATO and the growing threat of a nuclear confrontation between NATO and Russia.[15] What followed in the interactive dialogue was a sad spectacle or charade of Western countries taking the floor and Western NGOs supporting the HC's statement. They all dutifully doubled-down on untenable narratives, presumably believing the world at large would accept the travesty. Such an exercise in reaffirmation of Western prejudices and fantasies, without any effort at balance, or the least element of self-criticism, confirms my gradually growing feeling that the Western powers and Western NGOs have hijacked the Human Rights Council and the OHCHR and politicized it to such a degree that the victims are forgotten. State delegations are only interested in scoring points.

I myself took the floor in order to advocate peace initiatives and try to bring the discussion to the main issue: the urgent need for mediation to avoid a nuclear confrontation.[16] The propaganda enabling the weaponization of human rights has reached such high levels that the participants in the charade do not seem to even realize it, since they are caught up in it and have lost their sense of proportion. To me and others, it is inconceivable that the Human Rights Council would fail to see that the priority in Ukraine must be peace making, not "punishment," which is always *ex post facto*, and does not bring the dead back to life. What the eloquent Western states and Western NGOs should have done is to *prevent* this eminently preventable conflict rather than furthering it. Their moralizing tone rings hollow today. The whole exercise at the Human Rights Council was surrealistic.

The Western pursuit of its narrative seems to be gradually shifting in New York. On February 6, 2023 the UN Secretary-General spoke at the General Assembly,[17] observing:

> I fear the world is not sleepwalking into a wider war. I fear it is doing so with its eyes wide open. But the world needs peace and peace in line with the United Nations Charter and international law.... If every country fulfilled its obligations under the Charter, the right to peace would be guaranteed.... That requires a holistic view of the peace continuum that identifies root causes and prevents the seeds of war from sprouting. One that invests in prevention to avoid conflicts in the first place, focuses on mediation.... These are core elements of the proposed New Agenda for Peace—our plan to revitalize multilateral action for a world in transition and a new era of geostrategic competition.

This is good rhetoric, but Guterres could have said that the Ukraine war was preventable, that the Minsk agreements would have provided for peace and stability if observed by all sides, that the two peace proposals put forward by Moscow in December 2021 were consistent with the UN Charter and should have been the subject of good faith negotiations pursuant to Article 2(3) of the Charter. Guterres should have *expressis verbis* said that one simple word would have spared the world the war in Ukraine: Neutrality. Ukraine must be neutral. Alas, he did not do it in December 2021, not in February 2022, nor in 2023.

Meanwhile High Commissioner Türk has been travelling the world. I commend him for his dynamism, and in particular for his fruitful visit to Venezuela in January 2023. As the first UN rapporteur to visit Venezuela in 21 years, I advocated that the OHCHR establish and maintain a presence in Venezuela, which finally materialized in 2020 under High Commissioner Bachelet. Türk's recognition that advisory services and technical assistance can help the Venezuelan people is a good sign. An understanding that the U.S. sanctions regime has considerably aggravated Venezuela's economic crisis is important. High Commissioner Türk could have gone further in his statement and demanded the immediate lifting of the illegal unilateral coercive measures (UCMs) imposed by the U.S., Canada and some European states. It would have been logical for the High Commissioner to explicitly endorse the reports of the late Dr. Idriss Jazairy and the current rapporteur on UCMs, Professor Alena Douhan. Alas, he did not do so.[18] Some Venezuelan NGOs, including the Red Nacional de Derechos Humanos, also expressed their regret that, although they had asked to be received by the OHCHR team, they were not given that opportunity.

In January 2023 a technical team from the OHCHR visited Peru, where a *coup d'état* against democratically elected President Pedro Castillo had taken place on December 7, 2022. Although Castillo's lawyers implored the team to visit him at the Barbadillo prison, where he is subjected to arbitrary detention, the OHCHR ignored their request.[19]

I have had the privilege of knowing all High Commissioners and interacting at various levels with them. Because they are human like the rest of us, they can and do make mistakes of judgments and sometimes they err on the facts. This is inevitable, but could be curtailed if the HC had wise advisors. Over the decades I have observed numerous dysfunctions and irregularities at OHCHR and, where appropriate, have signalled them to those in a position to fix them. One episode stands out in my mind that may surprise the reader, because it is somehow so unworthy of a human rights institution, violating certain fundamental principles of due process, including the presumption of innocence.

One of the most professional Secretariat members I have had the honour of knowing at OHCHR is Swedish diplomat Anders Kompass, whom I met in 2014–15, when I was Independent Expert on International Order and he was a D-2 at OHCHR in charge of field operations. The then High Commissioner Zeid Ra'ad Al Hussein accused him in 2014 of leaking an internal UN report on sexual abuse by French troops in Central African Republic, and suspended him from his duties at the UN, arguing that he had engaged in misconduct. The confidential report, which Kompass had transmitted through normal channels to the French Mission in Geneva, concerned sexual abuse of minors at a camp for internally displaced persons in Bangui. As the ruling of the United Nations Tribunal of May 6, 2015 in the case *Kompass v. Secretary General of the United Nations Dispute Tribunal*[20] established

In mid-July 2014, the Chief, Rapid Response Unit and Peace Missions Section, OHCHR, provided to the Applicant a copy of a report containing serious allegations of paedophilia allegedly committed in the Central African Republic by French military. 5. According to the Applicant, on or about 23 July 2014, he brought the content of the report to the attention of the Deputy Ambassador of France. 6. The Applicant states that shortly thereafter he informed the Deputy High Commissioner that he had seen the report and had discussed the allegations therein with the Deputy Ambassador of France. 7. The Applicant further states that, in reply to a request from the French Permanent Mission to the United Nations in Geneva, he shared with it a copy of the report. The Applicant alleges that he informed the Deputy High Commissioner about this on 7 August 2014....

The Applicant further maintains that during a meeting on 12 March 2015 with the Deputy High Commissioner, the latter informed him that in light of his handling of the matter, the High Commissioner had requested his resignation, adding that such a request had been made by the Under-Secretary-General for the Department of Peacekeeping Operations. The Respondent did not contest this in his reply. Furthermore, the Applicant refused to resign. 10. As per the Respondent's reply, the High Commissioner requested the Office of Internal Oversight Services ("OIOS") on 9 April 2015 to investigate allegations of misconduct by the Applicant. OIOS subsequently launched an investigation. The High Commissioner sent a note to the Acting Director-General, UNOG, on 10 April 2015, recommending that the Applicant be placed on administrative leave with full pay under staff rule 10.4. 11. The High Commissioner informed the Applicant of the decision to place him on administrative leave with full pay during a meeting held on 17 April 2015.

In vacating the suspension order, the Dispute Tribunal held:

> The Tribunal notes that placing a staff member on administrative leave must be based on serious grounds. Indeed, para. 4 of ST/AI/371 requires that "the conduct in question might pose a danger to other staff members or to the Organization" or a "risk of evidence being destroyed or concealed." As such, placement on administrative leave inevitably has a negative impact on the reputation of a staff member's integrity. Therefore, and since the Applicant is currently being prevented from carrying out his functions as a result of being on administrative leave, which is of public knowledge, the Tribunal finds that if the suspension is not granted, the harm done to the Applicant's reputation will be irreparable and could not be adequately compensated at a later stage.

Instead of apologizing to Kompass, further pressure was brought against him. The High Commissioner proposed to dismantle the field operations unit, so as to administratively removing Kompass' position from OHCHR. This stubbornness demonstrated both intransigence and vindictiveness.

Subsequently, in December 2015, the Office of Internal Oversight completely cleared Kompass of any misconduct. His exoneration followed an independent panel report—set up by the UN secretary general, Ban Ki-Moon, into the child sex scandal in CAR—which ruled Kompass had acted within his mandate and done nothing wrong in passing the internal document, which contained interviews with victims and descriptions of the perpetrators, to the French authorities. In particular, the panel report condemned the "gross institutional failure" of the UN in its inaction over the allegations of child sexual abuse in CAR.[21]

Kompass resigned from the UN on June 8, 2016 citing "the complete impunity for those who have been found to have, in various degrees, abused their authority, together with the unwillingness of the hierarchy to express any regrets for the way they acted towards me."[22] Consistent with his sedate phlegm, Kompass commented "It is important for other staff to see that I was vindicated. That's one of the reasons I had to go through this to give an example to the staff—because otherwise the message was: 'If you try to do something similar to what Anders had done, these will be the consequences.'"

I had seen much in the human rights arena since 1980, including what I would term several instances of *ultra vires* decisions and gross misconduct by another High Commissioner, which I will not describe here. And in those cases, the High Commissioner got away with it. I am saddened by the realization that a long-serving professional can be treated as Anders Kompass and other less combative professionals have been treated—and this for political reasons. Some would call the OHCHR actions in the Kompass case inept, others scurrilous or even sordid. I would prefer describing them as inhuman, contrary to basic human decency, because the integrity and reputation of Anders Kompass were attacked in an inacceptable manner. The good news is that in the United Nations it is possible to appeal to the Office of Internal Oversight and to the Dispute Tribunal, and that at least in this case, both decided correctly.

It is also comforting to know that there is life after the UN, as Anders Kompass became Swedish Ambassador to Guatemala and currently he is the Director of the Swedish National Human Rights Institute in Lund.[23]

At this point it is appropriate to revisit the terms of reference of the High Commissioner, whose mandate is narrowly defined in resolution 48/141 of December 20, 1993. Over the years High Commissioners have gradually expanded the mandate unilaterally and undertaken a variety of studies on specific country situations, even though such reports were not mandated by the General Assembly or by the Human

Rights Council. Among them were two very unbalanced reports, one concerning Venezuela[24] and the other, an "Assessment" concerning China.[25] Alas, it is common practice for many reports to be drafted by OHCHR staff in Geneva without carrying out in situ fact-finding. The credibility of such reports is marred by methodological flaws, since they rely overwhelmingly on submissions by one side only, and on a variety of unverifiable information from the press and activist lobbies. Such OHCHR reports must be taken *cum grano salis*. The reports of two UN rapporteurs who did travel to Venezuela and fact-checked the OHCHR reports do not confirm the OHCHR findings or the narrative, particularly concerning the cause of the economic crisis and the effects of the U.S. sanctions and financial blockade. In fact, both rapporteurs found that the principal cause of the crisis, the scarcity of foods and medicines in Venezuela, was and continues to be directly attributable to the impact of the unilateral coercive measures, secondary sanctions and over-compliance by States and non-state actors.

The China "Assessment," written by anonymous OHCHR staffers, constitutes yet another blunder, as it is incompatible with the findings contained in the comprehensive end-of-mission statement that had been delivered by High Commissioner Michelle Bachelet in Guangzhou on May 28, 2022,[26] after conducting a well-prepared and professional in-situ visit, including Xinjiang.[27] As discussed further in Chapter Three, any observer would realize that whereas Bachelet's end-of-mission statement is professional and constructive, the "Assessment" suffers from serious methodological deficits. The best that can be said is that the subsequent OHCHR China "Assessment" was politically motivated and not properly based on empirical evidence. Indeed, insofar as it was the High Commissioner herself who undertook the mission, it is difficult to understand why or how others who did not participate in the mission would have the temerity to depart from the constructive tone and orientation of the Bachelet statement. At least in this case, such internal manipulations in OHCHR must be discarded as, at minimum, unprofessional.

During my 22 years of working as a lawyer with the Division/ Centre for Human Rights/OHCHR. as Deputy Chief of the Communications Branch, Chief of the Petitions Section and Secretary of the UN Human Rights Committee, I had the opportunity to observe all too many "irregularities" and the growing politicization of the institution. For example, as a frequent speech-writer for two High Commissioners (HC), I witnessed one instance where a D-1 (director of a branch), who was representing the HC in his absence at the opening of an expert meeting hosted by the Sub-Commission Rapporteur on Population Transfers, simply did NOT read out the substantive statement approved by the HC,[28] and offered instead a rambling, politically-correct blah-blah-blah.

As Chief of the Petitions department, I and my successors until this very day have been seriously handicapped by understaffing. When compared with the large secretariats of the European Court of Human Rights (ECHR) or the Inter-American Commission on Human Rights (IACHR), the petitions department of the OHCHR only has about twenty lawyers to deal with all petitions to be examined by the Human Rights Committee, Committee against Torture, Committee on the Elimination of Racial Discrimination, Committee on Economic, Social and Cultural Rights, Committee on the Rights of the Child, etc. And whereas the ECHR is only concerned with Europe and the IACHR only with the Americas, the Petitions department at OHCHR must process petitions from the entire planet. During my years as Deputy Chief of the Communications Branch and subsequently as Chief of the Petitions department, I had only a small team, albeit of very sharp lawyers, to sort out the incoming petitions, prepare them for registration and draft the decisions on admissibility and merits for consideration and adoption by the experts of the various treaty-bodies.

On one occasion I found a petition in the wastepaper basket. The petition was subsequently registered and went on to be considered by the Committee. I had to call in my staff and remind them of our code of deontology and warn them that if I ever caught anyone filtering the communications, disciplinary action would be taken. I frankly wonder how many petitions have landed in the bin since I left my function as Chief of Petitions. I fear many, since I have been approached by numerous petitioners and NGOs who have complained that they never received an acknowledgment of receipt or any information about the registration of their petitions. Some who have called OHCHR and complained were informed that that their petitions were "in the pipeline," but they doubted that, because they never heard anything more after the oral confirmation. As I have learned by discreetly asking, on occasion petitions still do disappear into the bin, an ethically inacceptable practice that has not been properly audited. This should not be confused with the rejection of many petitions for objective reasons, such as lack of jurisdiction or admissibility deficiencies, e.g. failure to exhaust domestic remedies. In such case, however, the petitioner gets a standard letter listing the reason(s) for non-registration. At the same time, as indicated above, we must remember that the Petitions staff remains very small and that there is only so much that the secretariat can process. It is no surprise that sometimes shortcuts are taken. In my function as Independent Expert, I routinely complained in my reports to the Third Committee of the General Assembly about the grave understaffing of Petitions department and the need to properly finance the Secretariat. I even published articles in legal journals outlining this very issue.

During my tenure processing petitions (initially we called them "communications") from victims of human rights violations, I learned from colleagues at the Inter-American Commission on Human Rights, that the practice of making certain politically-sensitive petitions disappear was not entirely unknown there. It was tacitly accepted and discreetly covered up. This explains, *inter alia,* why "politically incorrect" victims have little or no chance of being heard. This kind of "cancel mentality" will continue to flourish until measures are taken to ensure that the code of deontology is embraced by all secretariat members.

The "abuse of power" by some members of the Secretariat goes so far as to deny access to legitimate and credible NGOs that ask to be received by someone in OHCHR in order to personally deliver a petition or report, as I will address below. Several NGOs have brought to my attention the fact that their emails to OHCHR are ignored, that they receive no answer, and that when they succeed in contacting a person by telephone, they are told that the staff is too "busy" and cannot receive them. Of course, this never happens if the NGO is Amnesty International, HRW or ISHR, which get preferential treatment. But what are the criteria, if "too busy" is a legitimate complaint given inadequate staffing, for determining which communications must meet this fate?

As Chief of Petitions, I also had some encounters with non-governmental organizations and law firms who would militantly push some issues and some privileged cases but would refuse to even consider assisting victims of other human rights violations not enjoying comparable levels of public relations potential. I repeatedly asked NGOs and law firms to demonstrate compassion for all victims and represent ALL persons whose rights may have been violated. It became abundantly clear to me, that both NGOs and law firms were more interested in their public image as defenders of victims, and less on the fate of the victims they represented, who were being instrumentalized for PR reasons. Of course, these NGOs and law firms would not publicly admit that they would only defend the West's "consensus" victims and ignore all the millions of voiceless victims, for whom no one ever moves a finger.[29] Among other considerations, there is no financial advantage in representing unpopular victims.

As UN independent expert, I witnessed how several mandate holders and mandates were cold-shouldered by the OHCHR, including my own mandate on the promotion of a democratic and equitable International Order, the mandate on the Right to Development, the mandate on International Solidarity, and on Unilateral Coercive Measures. For entire periods I was deprived of an assistant and in the best of times I only had some support from a half-time assistant. In 2017 I was deprived of any substantive or even logistical support during my high-level mission to the World Bank and IMF—not a single assistant to take notes, reschedule meetings or call a taxi. I went to Washington, DC alone. This contrasts with the enormous assistance generously provided by OHCHR to "trending" or "politically correct" mandates such as the mandate on LGBT issues. This is partly attributable to the fact that trending mandates attract earmarked funds, whereas the non-trending mandates do not.

Worse still, on repeated occasions OHCHR staff members tried to influence my independent choice of subjects to be investigated, and the goals that I should pursue. I experienced a perceptible pushback by some staff members who sought to contradict these, and repeatedly I had to remind them that I was appointed to be an *independent expert* and not to follow instructions from governments, lobbies, NGOs or the OHCHR secretariat. On several occasions assistants clearly "dragged their feet" and failed to expeditiously process requests and petitions sent to them in a timely fashion.

Since I conducted only one fact-finding mission *in situ*, I was forced to have recourse to questionnaires and high-level expert consultations aimed at exploring the root causes of the dysfunctions of the international order. In 2014 I called a consultation in Brussels to discuss military expenditures, their toxic impact on the environment, the necessity of converting military-first into human security–first economies and how to redirect the finances thus released so as to achieve the sustainable development goals. Not only did the OHCHR secretariat fail to invite any of the experts I had requested, instead they actually invited participants who knew nothing about conversion strategies and contributed little to my overall theme: disarmament for development. Notwithstanding the failure to assist in professionally preparing the consultation, the OHCHR, without informing me, unilaterally decided to write a summary of the totally useless "consultation," which essentially would have watered-down the findings and conclusions of my 2014 report to the Human Rights Council.[30] This banal and *ultra vires* summary was actually announced as a forthcoming Add.1 to my report, although I had not asked for any such addendum and had not even been informed of the secretariat initiative. I considered this move by the OHCHR as a deliberate effort to undermine my report and lessen its impact. When I by chance learned of the existence of the proposed "Add.1" to my report, I vigorously protested, accused OHCHR of unprofessionalism, demanded that my assistant be transferred elsewhere. The assistant was transferred (I think it merited disciplinary action), and the addendum was never issued.

Another part-time assistant of mine was visibly ill-at-ease because of the content of my reports. He evidently assumed that being an assistant to a rapporteur who took his mandate seriously and was reporting findings contrary to the West's accepted narrative could have a negative impact on his career development. This apprehension is easy to understand, since the OHCHR Secretariat and States know that an estimated 80% of the reports of the rapporteurs are not written by the experts themselves, but by the OHCHR secretariat, to be approved by the rapporteur afterward. Thus, the presumption would be that it was my assistant who was responsible for the content of my independent reports. At least internally at OHCHR and for purposes of promotion, such a presumption would be toxic for the assistant's career development, since promotion frequently depends on a degree of "popularity" with the senior management. Accordingly, when there is a rapporteur like myself, who writes all of his own reports and all of his media statements and press releases and does not allow the OHCHR to water them down (there are about 20% of us in that category), the unlucky assistant risks being blamed for the reports, especially when they are straight-forward, truthful and contrary to powerful interests.

That said, I always welcomed criticism and constructive exchange with my assistants. I welcomed their input precisely because, for more than two decades, I had been a staff member myself and had had the opportunity of exchanging views with many experts of the former Sub-Commission on Promotion and Protection of Human Rights, members of the Human Rights Committee and Committee Against Torture, with numerous rapporteurs and independent experts, some of whom became enduring friends, including Ben Ferencz,[31] Claire Palley, Marc Bossuyt, Hipólito Solari Yrigoyen, Christian Tomuschat, Rosalyn Higgins, Christine Chanet, Elizabeth Evatt, Virginia Dandan, Virgínia Brás Gomes, Awn Shawkat Al Khasawneh, Peter Burns, Danilo Türk, Olivier de Schutter, Torkel Opsahl, Andrés Aguilar, Andreas Mavrommatis, Miguel Alfonso Martinez, Ben Whitaker, Leandro Despouy, Erica-Irene Daes, John Carey,[32] Felix Ermacora and Louis Joinet.

With Professor Benjamin Ferencz on a panel at the
ILA October 2014 conference in New York

Another example of politicization at OHCHR was the Secretariat's attempt in September 2017 to dissuade me from going on a field mission to Venezuela. First, it was argued that there was no money for the mission, which was false. Next, they warned me that they were overstretched for staff and could not give me the necessary logistical and substantive report (as it turned out, they provided minimal support). Then they tried to persuade me that I should leave such a delicate mission to my successor and not undertake it during my last year on the job. I answered that only thanks to my experience of five full years as rapporteur had I accumulated sufficient skills to manage such a mission and maximize results.

Curiously, OHCHR then appealed to my sense of "justice," arguing that since twelve other rapporteurs had received negative answers from Venezuela to their requests, then out of solidarity with them, I should decline the Venezuelan invitation that I myself had requested and been accorded! I replied that it was a unique opportunity, enabling the UN to break the ice with Venezuela after 21 years. I promised to engage in confidence-building and to establish a working relationship with the Venezuelan government that would help the Venezuelan people and open the doors for the future visits of many more rapporteurs. I even mentioned the possibility of persuading the Venezuelan government to invite the High Commissioner himself to visit Venezuela.

I envisaged a permanent presence of the OHCHR in Caracas, and felt that it deserved a try. But no, the OHCHR Secretariat referred to an earlier report by the High Commissioner on Venezuela, recently released and prepared by the "Venezuela desk," so that my visit was really "unnecessary." I pointed out that the OHCHR report was not based on any kind of monitoring *in situ* and had relied primarily on information provided by opposition NGOs and opposition politicians, and that my visit would complement the report. When I sought a personal meeting with the then High Commissioner, Zeid Ra'ad Al Hussein, hoping to coordinate my actions with his Office so as to maximize results, I was not received by the HC, either before or after my mission, notwithstanding repeated requests.

But why was there an OHCHR report on Venezuela at all, when the Human Rights Council had not asked for it? The 1993 General Assembly resolution 48/141 establishing the mandate of the High Commissioner does not give the HC a blank check to open investigations wherever he/she wants, or wherever the major powers or donors tell him/her to investigate. Indeed, the authority and credibility of OHCHR is at stake when the HC can unilaterally and capriciously decide to target one country but not another. The resolution does not give the HC such a broad mandate. Of course, a politically manipulated Human Rights Council may capriciously decide to request reports on certain countries that oppose the Western unipolar vision, but refuse to request an investigation on torture in Guantanamo, crimes against humanity in Yemen, or concerning the 2019 coup d'état in Bolivia, the 2022 coup d'état in Peru, etc.

During my mission to Venezuela in November/December 2017, I was able to fact-check the OHCHR report and had to recognize that the report was fundamentally flawed—woefully deficient and unbalanced methodologically. I discovered, for instance, that whereas three reputable Venezuelan NGOs—Fundalatin, the Grupo Sures and the Red Nacional de Derechos Humanos—had come to Geneva in 2016 and 2017 and delivered pertinent information to the then High Commissioner and to the "Venezuela Desk," none of this information had been taken into account or incorporated into the report, not even in a footnote. This constituted deliberate suppression of information that would necessarily have changed the assessment of the question whether there existed a "humanitarian crisis" in Venezuela, and whether the crisis was attributable to the conduct of the Venezuelan government or to the devastating impact of U.S. unilateral coercive measures and the comprehensive financial blockade of the country. I incorporated into my own report[33] the information received from these three Venezuelan NGOs and from some 40 other NGOs with whom I personally met in Venezuela. I found the omission of this information in the OHCHR report inexcusable, and attributable to the fact that OHCHR does not or maybe cannot always act independently and professionally, and its Secretariat is often held hostage to ideologies[34]. There is abundant evidence that OHCHR yields to political pressures by governments and donors.

In my assessment, a second report elaborated by OHCHR on Venezuela under the new HC, Michelle Bachelet, also had serious deficiencies.[35] In any event, Bachelet did learn during her four years as HC and partly redeemed OHCHR's honour when, following my September 2018 report and my oral recommendations, she personally conducted a mission to Venezuela[36] and established a "presence" of six OHCHR staff members in Caracas, as I had proposed. Most importantly, the findings and conclusions of my 2018 report to the Human Rights Council were later confirmed by the Special Rapporteur on Unilateral Coercive Measures, Alena Douhan, during her mission to Venezuela in 2021, as reflected in her comprehensive report.[37]

As I learned from some of my colleague rapporteurs in the years 2012–18—and ever since—the OHCHR secretariat remains quite responsive to the *Zeitgeist,* without questioning how it is created or by whom. Their comfort zone lies in their conformity with the mainstream narrative, which they perceive as a virtue. Rapporteurs tasked with politically sensitive mandates have run into similar troubles with the secretariat. One of them, Professor Richard Falk, former rapporteur on Palestine, had to endure defamatory attacks on his honour and reputation by a number of NGOs which, in my opinion, should have been stripped of consultative status for gross misbehaviour years ago. He was called, *inter-alia,* a "terrorist" and an "anti-Semite," although Falk belongs to the Jewish faith. Certain NGOs that have engaged in evidence-free mobbing of rapporteurs still have consultative status and they continue to smear experts with toxic insinuations and absurd allegations—*calumniare audacter, semper aliquid haeret.*[38] Far from defending Professor Falk, some staff in OHCHR actually joined the defamers. I also remember when an assistant of the late Dr. Idriss Jazairy refused to prepare a draft as requested by Dr. Jazairy, because "she disagreed" with the rapporteur. When Dr. Jazairy politely asked her to do so, she reportedly started crying. My only explanation: career panic, because Dr. Jazairy was saying things that everyone else was making a conscious effort to avoid.

Another rapporteur who has been subject to pressures and smears is the Special Rapporteur on violence against women, Ms. Reem Alsalem, who has justly pushed back against the disinformation and insinuations.[39]

Less important, but still significant, is the fact that despite my repeated requests, OHCHR did not inform my colleague rapporteurs of my draft press releases, which frequently also concerned their mandates, or invite them to co-sign the release. Sometimes I called colleague rapporteurs and asked them whether they had been approached by OHCHR to join my press release and their answer was invariably "no." In those cases, I would follow-up by informing the office that so and so wanted to co-sign, and only then were their names added. In other occasions I learned that other rapporteurs had wanted me to join them by signing their press releases, and had so informed the office, but that message had not been conveyed to me, although I reside in Geneva and am easily reachable by telephone and email. There were many press releases by the rapporteurs on international solidarity, on the right to development, on unilateral coercive mea-sures, on freedom of expression, on freedom of peaceful assembly and association, on the independence of judges and lawyers etc. that I would have co-signed if I had been invited. This happened so often, that I wondered whether it was garden-variety incompetence, or more significantly, a desire to limit the impact of certain press releases. I fear that there was "method" in this kind of behaviour because many in the secretariat seem to have an aversion to some mandates and try to reduce their visibility, while proactively propagandizing the press releases of "popular" mandates. In recent conversations with current rapporteurs and independent experts, I have been able to confirm the continuation of this "boycott" of certain mandates by the Secretariat. Although they have signalled this problem to the "leadership," there seems to be no political will to change the situation.

I also experienced a dozen or so of my press releases and info statements being simply not issued by the OHCHR or delayed to the extent that the issuance became ineffective because it was obsolete. I repeatedly had to remind OHCHR that the resolution creating every mandate commits OHCHR to provide all logistical and substantive support required by the mandate holder. The OHCHR senior officer in charge of the rapporteurs either did not answer my concerns or uttered some platitudes. Ultimately, I was able to place my unissued press releases on my personal blog or I transformed them into op-eds. Yet, never did OHCHR help me place an op-ed with *The New York Times, Washington Post* or elsewhere. Whenever I placed an article with *Inter Press Service,*[40] *The Guardian,*[41] or the *Independent,*[42] it was I who made the necessary contacts.

Part of the problem with the OHCHR secretariat is that nearly all senior posts from High Commissioner, down to Deputy High Commissioner, D2, D1 or even some P5s are occupied by political appointees, proposed and parachuted by States into the secretariat.

Despite efforts by the professional staff to protect their right to career development, there is little prospect for them within OHCHR and the new arrivals make it difficult for the "old guard" to continue performing at a high level of professionalism. The influx of high officials who frequently know or care little to nothing of human rights creates an atmosphere of demotivation and sometimes cynicism. Many mid-level P-3s and P-4s, the pillars who do the work and hold the house, are actually mobbed by the newcomers who are afraid of their professionalism and "institutional memory." I experienced several useless and hyper-expensive "restructurings" of OHCHR—none of them based on a legitimate need to rationalize, streamline, or avoid duplication, but rather aimed primarily at accommodating the new "leadership" and marginalizing older staff members.

Judging by the many-faceted overt and covert pressures that the United States and other Western powers exert on the Office of the High Commissioner for Human Rights, there is little doubt that in the hybrid war being waged by the U.S. to maintain a unipolar world, the OHCHR has been assigned a supporting role. In other words, there is a conscious effort at subverting the independence and professionalism of the OHCHR and transforming it into another instrument of Western geopolitics.

Thus, it is our responsibility as human beings and committed defenders of human dignity to push back against the weaponization of OHCHR by many countries and non-governmental organizations and to expose all attempts at blackmail and defamation of its experts and staff. The instrumentalization of human rights for geopolitical purposes is a form of blasphemy, a sacrilege against the sanctity of human life and the equality in dignity of all members of the human family. Admittedly, the non-conventional war that instrumentalizes human rights as if they were Kalashnikovs is not going to abate any time soon. It is our duty to denounce the corrosive effects of this hybrid war and to coordinate our forces, to inform our friends and acquaintances so as to mobilize against the brazen hijacking of the human rights promotion and protection system.

At present I do not see any institutional changes, rules, or procedures which might structurally facilitate such efforts. The ongoing disinformation war and career disincentives militate against reform. For the time being, it seems that OHCHR remains largely in the service of Washington and Brussels. It is time for whistleblowers within the system to further document the dysfunctions that I have endeavoured to briefly describe.

Allow me to end this section by quoting the text of a press release by many of my colleague rapporteurs that exemplifies what Special Procedures is there for—to make concrete recommendations to help victims of violations of the most fundamental human rights, violations that are perpetrated with impunity, and which the mainstream media even supports or condones. This press release was issued on February 10, 2023 following the devastating earthquake in Turkey and Syria.

"Genuine solidarity with earthquake survivors calls for lifting of sanction-induced restrictions: UN experts"[43]

GENEVA (10 February 2023): Extending their heartfelt support to the people of Türkiye and Syria, UN experts* today urged the international community to take prompt action to enable effective emergency response and recovery in the wake of catastrophic earthquakes in the two countries. "This includes the lifting of all economic and financial restrictions caused by unilateral sanctions against Syria, during this time of sorrow and human suffering," the UN experts said. They issue the following joint statement:

"We wish to express our unwavering support and solidarity to the hundreds of thousands affected by the recent devastating earthquakes in Syria and Türkiye, and to all those from inside and abroad who have responded to the call and conducted emergency response operations and provided life-saving assistance in the spirit of human altruism and solidarity.

"For such interventions to be effective, there is a need for an enabling environment for international cooperation and unhindered delivery of humanitarian assistance, including of food, medicines, medical equipment, and construction material, among others, as well as unimpeded financial flows to support such assistance, all of which are constrained by current sanctions regimes against countries, such as Syria.

"We welcome recent decisions to ease Syria sanctions through general licenses. However, we wish to recall that such systems of humanitarian carve-outs may not be sufficient to address the long term negative effects of sanctions, as well as business over-compliance with sanctions and financial de-risking.

"Even during natural disasters, when hundreds of thousands of lives are at stake, it is gravely concerning that humanitarian actors face persisting challenges due to sanctions, including with regard to procurement procedures and bank transfers. It is reported that the Syrian diaspora is unable to provide financial support through remittances or other means of funding.

"It is imperative for the international community and in particular sanctioning states to undertake prompt action by putting an end to unilateral sanctions against Syria, a country deprived of critical infrastructure and in dire need of recovery and reconstruction, following the decade-long war.

"We extend our appeal to businesses and financial institutions and urge them to take appropriate mitigating measures to ensure the protection of human rights, in accordance with international law, including by eliminating practices of over-compliance with sanctions and of de-risking."

The experts: Alena Douhan, Special Rapporteur on the negative impact of the unilateral coercive measures on the enjoyment of human rights; Olivier de Schutter, Special Rapporteur on extreme poverty and human rights; Reem Alsalem, Special Rapporteur on violence against women and girls, its causes and consequences; Saad Alfarargi, Special Rapporteur on the right to development; Pedro Arrojo-Agudo, Special Rapporteur on the human rights to safe drinking water and sanitation; Livingstone Sewanyana, Independent Expert on the promotion of a democratic and equitable international order; Siobhán Mullally, Special Rapporteur on trafficking in persons, especially women and children; Balakrishan Rajagopal, Special Rapporteur on adequate housing as a component of the right to an adequate standard of living, and on the right to non-discrimination in this context; Paula Gaviria Betancur, Special Rapporteur on the human rights of internally displaced persons; Obiora C. Okafor, Independent Expert on human rights and international solidarity.

My questions to the 2023 mandate-holders at Special Procedures are: Why was this press release not unanimous? Did some rapporteurs object or argue that the UCMs should be maintained, that the UCMs were legal or legitimate? Why did the Rapporteurs not state the obvious—that "sanctions kill" and that these UCMs constitute crimes against humanity for purposes of Article 7 of the Statute of Rome?

It bears repeating that notwithstanding frivolous efforts by some states to camouflage UCMs as legitimate "countermeasures," the International Law Commission is clear on the subject. Article 49 of the draft articles on State responsibility clarify the "Object and limits of countermeasures":[44]

1. An injured State may only take countermeasures against a State which is responsible for an internationally wrongful act in order to induce that State to comply with its obligations under part two.

2. Countermeasures are limited to the non-performance for the time being of international obligations of the State taking the measures towards the responsible State.

3. Countermeasures shall, as far as possible, be taken in such a way as to permit the resumption of performance of the obligations in question. Article 50 Obligations not affected by countermeasures.

4. Countermeasures shall not affect: (a) the obligation to refrain from the threat or use of force as embodied in the Charter of the United Nations; (b) obligations for the protection of fundamental human rights.

In this context I dare formulate some recommendations. Acknowledging that OHCHR has a hugely important mandate and that it has achieved much over the past decades, it is nonetheless a matter of conscience to formulate some proposals for possible reforms.

1. In order to safeguard the independence and professionalism of OHCHR, it is indispensable that the Fifth Committee of the UN General Assembly provide adequate funding from the regular budget.

2. OHCHR should henceforth not accept "voluntary" contributions, even if they are not explicitly given with strings attached, and it should never accept "earmarked" contributions, e.g. to support the mandate of a single rapporteur, but not the mandates of the others.

3. The system of selection of High Commissioners should be de-politicized so as to ensure that truly independent and courageous High Commissioners are appointed like in the early days John Humphrey, Theo van Boven, Kurt Herndl, of more recently Navi Pillay.

4. The system of selection of rapporteurs should be de-politicized. It is deplorable that many rapporteurs have been partial to the interests of the donors and major powers.

OTHER HUMAN RIGHTS INSTITUTIONS

The situation is not much better at the European and Inter-American human rights institutions. In particular the European Commission against Racism and Intolerance[45] is developing into a "Ministry of Truth" when it comes to persecuting dissent under the pretext of fighting "hate speech" and disinformation. The harm caused to academic freedom and to the democratic right of access to all information and all points of view is already considerable.

Domestic and international courts and tribunals can and do betray their mandates when they fail to decide based on the facts and legal argument, but instead issue teleological judgments, which blithely ignore contradictory evidence and whose rationale is upside-down. To the trained eye, it is obvious that what is happening is that a court is put under pressure to reach a given conclusion and then works backwards from there to select the evidence that will substantiate the desired ruling.

This is not unlike what some accommodated historians do when they have to buttress a political narrative required by governments, despite such a narrative not being supported by the evidence. As a professor of modern history (I hold a Dr.phil. in medieval and modern history), I have observed this countless times. Thus, a kind of "parallel reality" emerges: On the one side what an independent observer can plainly see, on the other the narrative that political realities impose on historians and the media as necessary for their career maintenance or advancement.

Zeitgeist pressures increasingly affect the daily work and the rulings of the Inter-American Commission on Human Rights (IACHR) in Washington, the European Court of Human Rights (ECHR) in Strasbourg, and the African Court of Human and Peoples Rights in Arusha (ACHPR).

The ample jurisprudence of the ECHR reveals that there are issues of impartiality both at the Court and within the Secretariat servicing it, as already revealed in several studies of the European Center for Law and Justice[46] (ECLJ), the Alliance Defending Freedom[47] (ADF) and other observers. Not only the judges, but also the staff frequently breach their obligation to impartiality. Yet, in spite of their egregious concessions to lobbies, the ECHR and its staff still enjoy a relatively positive image in Europe and the world, attributable to effective public relations, a favourable mainstream media that endorses many controversial and legally questionable rulings, and insufficient pushback by critical thinkers.

In a case which is still pending before the court, *M.L. v. Poland* (No. 40119/21),[48] it has become apparent that pro-abortion lobbies have engaged in disinformation, and that ECHR staff members have manifested a high degree of partiality. This case turns on the fact that the European Convention, as interpreted by the European Court itself, allows States to consider the unborn to be persons and accordingly acts to protect their lives. Poland did make this choice by granting constitutional protection to the life of the unborn child and by recognizing them as a subject of law. Because the Court is bound to apply the European Convention, in respect of Poland, as applying to the unborn child, in accordance with Articles 2 and 35, it follows that the application concerning "abortion rights" should be declared incompatible *ratione materiae* with the Convention, because it entails the possibility of terminating the life of an unborn child, considered in this case as a "person" within the meaning of the Convention. Moreover, since the case before the Court aimed to reduce the protection and rights of unborn children in Poland, it corresponds to the definition of an abuse of rights prohibited by Article 17 of the Convention. Beyond that, it must be remembered that nowhere in the Convention is a "right" to abortion recognized.

In a recent decision, *B.B. v. Poland,* the ECHR avoided having to discuss the merits by declaring the case inadmissible. Among the *amicus curiae,* the ECLJ contributed to the rejection of the arguments of the Center for Reproductive Rights, the Federation for Woman and Family Planning and the Helsinki Foundation for Human Rights, three pro-abortion lobbies that attacked the restrictions on access to abortion in Poland and the right to conscientious objection, where a medical doctor refused in 2014 to perform an abortion after 24 weeks of pregnancy. The level of political argument in the court was regrettable.

This is not unlike the manner in which the ECHR has dealt with numerous Austrian freedom of expression/religion cases, where the Court consistently condemns convictions for insulting Christianity but upholds them with regard to Islam.

When it comes to the authority and credibility of judicial and quasi-judicial institutions, it must be borne in mind that questionable decisions of the ECHR and IACHR have met with pushback in the countries concerned. Thus, for instance, the Polish Constitutional Court rejected a judgment by the ECHR.[49] This has ripples for the entire system of judicial settlement of disputes. International Courts must be aware that when their decisions are perceived as political or *ultra vires*, the countries concerned will refuse to implement them and as a consequence their prestige is diminished. Indeed, the rule of law is not based on force or formality, but ultimately on persuasion.

Far more politicized than the ECHR are the Inter-American Court of Human Rights in San José, Costa Rica, and the Inter-American Commission of Human Rights in Washington D.C. The problem goes back to the origins of the Organization of American States and the enormous influence exerted by the United States in the appointment of its Secretary-General. For instance, although the current Secretary

General Luis Almagro carries considerable responsibility for the false information disseminated about the 2019 elections in Bolivia precipitating the coup d'etat against Evo Morales, he was reelected SG in 2021. This is a disgrace for an organization that does not even respect its own Charter, Articles 3, 19 and 20 of which prohibit the kind of interference in the internal affairs of member States, as we have witnessed with regard to Bolivia, Brazil, Colombia, Cuba, Nicaragua, Peru and Venezuela. It is a disgrace that hitherto the IACHR has not issued interim measures of protection on behalf of the toppled President of Peru, Pedro Castillo,[50] who had been democratically elected in 2021. The Inter-American Democratic Charter[51] should have come into effect. But it didn't.

CHAPTER 3

THE UN HUMAN RIGHTS COUNCIL

*"Mandate-holders ... shall: (a) Act in an independent capacity,
and exercise their functions in accordance with their mandate,
through a professional, impartial assessment of facts based on
internationally recognized human rights standards, and free
from any kind of extraneous influence, incitement, pressure,
threat or interference, either direct or indirect, on the part
of any party, whether stakeholder or not, for any reason
whatsoever, the notion of independence being linked to the
status of mandate-holders, and to their freedom to assess the
human rights questions that they are called upon to examine
under their mandate.... Always seek to establish the facts, based
on objective, reliable information emanating from relevant
credible sources, that they have duly cross-checked to the best
extent possible; Take into account in a comprehensive and
timely manner, in particular information provided by the State
concerned on situations relevant to their mandate; Evaluate all
information in the light of internationally recognized human
rights standards relevant to their mandate, and of international
conventions to which the State concerned is a party...."*

HUMAN RIGHTS COUNCIL RESOLUTION 5/2 OF JUNE 18, 2007[1]

MILLIONS OF HUMAN BEINGS worldwide place their trust
in the United Nations system to deliver a truthful and honest portrayal
of situations and events taking place in the world, and to address same
accordingly. They have a reasonable expectation that concrete measures based on these assessments will be adopted in conformity with
the principles and purposes of the organization, in particular peace,
development and human rights. Millions of human beings are not
interested in the practice of "naming and shaming" so popular with
Western diplomats. What they want is concrete help in the form of
the realization of the right to development, food security, healthcare.
The function of the UN Human Rights Council should be to provide

advisory services and technical assistance to States in order to expedite the realization of a democratic and equitable international order.

The UN Human Rights Council, composed of 47 member states elected for 3-year terms, holds three regular sessions per year at the Palais des Nations in Geneva (in February/March, June/July and September/October), which may have a duration of 3 to 5 weeks. The President of the Council rotates on geographical basis.

At other times of the year, it holds sessions devoted to the Universal Periodic Review[2] of the human rights situation in all 193 member States of the United Nations, on the basis of reports required to be submitted by the States themselves. It also meets for "Special sessions"[3] of which, as of Spring 2023, there have been 35, e.g. concerning "The deteriorating situation of human rights in the Islamic Republic of Iran, especially with respect to women and children," "The deteriorating human rights situation in Ukraine stemming from the Russian aggression," "The grave human rights situation in Ethiopia," the situations in Sudan, the Occupied Palestine Territories, Myanmar, the Syrian Arab Republic, etc.

The Human Rights Council also employs a system of Special Procedures[4] composed of independent experts, special rapporteurs and working groups, all of which are mandated to devote their efforts to the promotion and protection of both individual and collective rights, either in country-related situations or under a general concept such as unilateral coercive measures.

The Council's predecessor, the Commission on Human Rights[5] (1946–2006) elaborated the overall UN framework of human rights protection, which includes the Universal Declaration of Human Rights, nine core human rights treaties and countless declarations, including the United Nations Declaration on the Rights of Indigenous Peoples[6] (2007), and the Declaration on Forced Population Transfers, initially adopted as Annex 1 of the Sub-Commission's Report[7] in 1997, and established monitoring mechanisms and fact-finding missions.

Despite the good will of many States, both the Commission and the Council have not undertaken to work preventively, or to identify the root causes of violations of human rights. Rather, they have routinely ignored constructive initiatives to provide expedient assistance to victims, and instead acquiesced to engaging in confrontational politics, what is known as the practice of "naming and shaming," enabling a propagandistic platform to further the geopolitical ambitions of certain countries.

This is despite the fact that, indeed, the Human Rights Council has enormous potential to do better, if it were reformed and strengthened. Primarily, it must be de-politicized and freed from the binary mentality of the "good" countries and the "bad" countries. Basically, the Human Rights Council should be a universal body, just like the General Assembly. The Council must be inclusive and make an effort to assist those countries that have particular problems in implementing their human rights obligations in full understanding of the context in which this is occurring. Simply excluding or condemning States is counterproductive.

What is crucial is to be willing to engage in dialogue with all countries and formulate constructive proposals, advising them on how to improve their legislation and institutions. It is not a question of giving grades to students. It is a matter of utmost importance to be victim-centered and try to assist states in resolving concrete problems. States and politicians are not evil by nature, but they often face enormous pressures from the military-industrial-financial complex, special interests, whether internal or external, and the corporate media, resulting in the facilitation of grave violations of human rights. These are among the major reasons why bad things happen and why other good things do not happen. These are factors that cannot be ignored.

The function of the Human Rights Council should be to persuade governments that it is in their own interest to promote the enjoyment of human rights by all persons under their jurisdiction. Ultimately, however, there is no escaping the fact that it is the state that bears responsibility for solving the problems on the ground and adopting policies consistent with its own legislation, with the UN Charter and ICCPR/ICESCR. Such policies are frequently frustrated by the illegal unilateral coercive measures and financial blockades imposed by some States, mostly against developing nations—yet another form of 21st century neo-colonialism. Such economic sanctions cause national emergencies in those countries and result in emergency measures by the targeted governments, which far from opening up further retrench and further restrict certain civil and political rights—and then open them to criticism for so doing.[8]

There is a related issue of the privatization of human rights violations, when it is pretended that only States have legal obligations, whereas transnational corporations and other "players" in the international arena can act in total impunity. This is not so, because States have a responsibility to ensure that corporations operating on their territories do not encroach on the human rights of populations in the countries or abroad.[9]

With advisory services and technical assistance offered by the Human Rights Council, with international help and solidarity, States could step by step satisfy more of the needs of the persons living under their jurisdiction and thus promote a contented population in the sense of the pursuit of gross national happiness[10] rather than enhanced gross domestic product (which is increasingly recognized as having little bearing on citizens' wellbeing). The Bhutanese government has made concrete proposals that resulted in the adoption by the General Assembly of "International Day of Happiness,"[11] which is celebrated on March 20 each year. Indeed, happiness is the best guarantee of international peace and security. But again, many states have no freedom of action to undertake domestic policies that benefit their population owing to the pressures from foreign states or the conditionalities imposed by the IMF, as I explained in my 2017 report to the General Assembly[12] and as Naomi Klein elucidated in her book *The Shock Doctrine.*[13]

The confrontational approach pursued by States in the UN General Assembly and Human Rights Council contravenes the letter and spirit of the UN Charter, which aims at facilitating dialogue and international cooperation. What is needed in UN institutions is not invective, but advisory services and technical assistance, enhanced dialogue with governments, fact-finding by rapporteurs, in particular those whose mandates focus on the independence of judges and lawyers, freedom of expression, torture, indigenous peoples, the right to food, health and sanitation, the right to truth, justice and reparation.

Again and again, I have pleaded for the abolition of the confrontational "country mandates," which seldom help the country concerned or the victims in question and mostly serve as a platform for geopolitical grandstanding and a hostile tool of exclusion. Essentially, country mandates are created with the purpose of demonizing a particular country in furtherance of other countries' foreign policies.

Country rapporteurs are seldom in a position to offer concrete help to the victims, other than the dubious pleasure of seeing those countries' governments publicly humiliated. The system of country rapporteurs thus caters to the baser instincts of society, to the desire for critical judgment "from on high" and vengeance rather than reconciliation.

Denouncing violations of human rights has little value unless it is accompanied by a commitment to comprehensively address the grievances in the context of the particular situation and to develop a constructive plan to address the root causes of the problems. The goal is peace and reconciliation, not judgment and punishment. Moreover, "naming and shaming" has no legitimacy whatever, unless such a process can be applied to every country and every person in authority. It seems, however, that some countries and persons are immune from scrutiny and that, despite serious allegations of human rights violations, no country mandates or fact-finding commissions have been established concerning the U.S., Canada, Australia, UK, France, Germany, Japan, Saudi Arabia, etc. Of course, certain thematic rapporteurs have touched upon human rights violations in the above countries, e.g. the reports for the former Commission on Human Rights by Professor Glele Ahanhanzo,[14] Special Rapporteur on racism, xenophobia and intolerance. But there really is very little to show by way of universal standards that apply to and are systematically monitored in the above countries. Here again we are faced with the delegitimizing practice of double-standards.

Special Rapporteurs

Another problem impacting the authority and credibility of Special Procedures is the profound politicization of the selection process as it concerns mandate-holders. Seldom is the candidate chosen on the basis of merit and independence. Again and again, I have witnessed how the selection committee puts forward mediocre candidates and discards those professionals whose expertise and commitment would advance the cause of human rights. As I have learned from conversations with Ambassadors and with members of the secretariat, many of whom I have known personally for decades, the OHCHR secretariat filters the candidates and influences the 5-member committee of Ambassadors, which ultimately establishes the short list and issues its recommendation to the President of the Council, who then makes the final decision, albeit unduly influenced by the OHCHR secretariat. Needless to say, a better process would be to rely on an impartial, professional secretariat.

On numerous occasions I have observed how independent and highly competent candidates have been discarded in favour of "politically correct" candidates who will not rock the boat too much, or worse, who will work to maintain the *status quo*. Not only does the OHCHR secretariat unduly influence the choice of candidates for consideration, but some members actually participate in the defamation of some candidates, as has been reported to me by members of the secretariat whose friendship and candour I cherish.

While I am not at liberty to describe specific examples of OHCHR misconduct in this regard or to identify the culprits, I can say that the procedure is fundamentally flawed and must be revised if we want independent experts to be selected. However, as it concerns my own personal experience, I have precise information from the June 2008 session of the Human Rights Committee, that two members of the secretariat actively campaigned against my candidature for Special Rapporteur on Freedom of Expression and even spoke with the then President of the Council in an attempt to dissuade him from selecting me, despite the fact that three of the five regional groups and numerous NGOs were strongly supporting my candidacy, that at the time I was President of P.E.N. International Centre Suisse Romand[15] and that I had a long track record as an advocate for freedom of opinion and expression with numerous publications on the subject. It was my condemnation of censorship practices by governments and the private sector, my advocacy for access to all information and plurality of views that evidently got me into trouble with those who approve of media manipulation and fear criticism from a UN rapporteur. After long debates, deadlocks and adjournments in the Council, my candidacy proved unsuccessful on the very last day of the session. Several Ambassadors, including the late Algerian Ambassador Dr. Idriss Jazairy, who had been a member of the 5-Ambassador selection committee, told me about the unsavoury practices he had witnessed by the OHCHR secretariat and some NGOs. An Ambassador from a Latin American country actually told me in confidence "las corrientes en la secretaría arrasan" (the fast currents in the secretariat will carry you downstream). Surely more transparency and accountability are necessary in this respect.

Now, how was it that the Council came to appoint me as independent expert on international order in 2012? It was more or less by chance. The case is revealing, bearing in mind that I was only number 3 on the shortlist. The first two candidates on the list, however, were politically inacceptable to certain major powers who pressured the then President of the Council to drop them. Perhaps I was appointed because at that time I was a relatively "clean page" and powerful governments did not fear that I would actually take the mandate seriously and endeavour to make pragmatic, implementable recommendations that would not be compatible with their geopolitical interests—or at least not to the extent that the candidates they had eliminated might have.

There is much in the work of the UN rapporteurs that can be described as brilliant, but there is also much "window-dressing." Rapporteurs—or more precisely, the OHCHR staff that write the reports for the rapporteurs—prefer UN jargon and platitudes to pragmatic, implementable proposals. And even when many reports are solid, there is no follow-up mechanism to ensure that the findings and recommendations find at least minimal implementation, not even to monitor whether the reports have generated any improvement whatever in the states concerned. As an independent expert myself, I saw how the presentation of reports was little more than a ritual, with no one, not even major NGOs, undertaking to give meaning to the reports by operationalizing the reports' findings in their advocacy efforts and demanding changes in the countries concerned. Only a few smaller civil society groups have had the courage give visibility to my 14 reports.

The mainstream media have also failed to give publicity to crucial reports e.g. those submitted by the Rapporteur on the right to development, the Rapporteurs on the adverse human rights impacts of unilateral coercive measures, on foreign debt, and on international solidarity. The only rapporteurs whose reports get any traction in the media are those whose reports advance either special interests or the geopolitical interests of some major powers.

On the other hand, I would NOT suggest that the recommendations of all rapporteurs should be implemented as a matter of course, because in my opinion many recommendations by some rapporteurs are manifestly ill-founded, i.e. not based on a balanced assessment of the evidence, but rather reflect the political biases of the rapporteur or the wishes of the donors who support his/her mandate. Indeed, it is also true that some recommendations are *ultra vires* and go well beyond the mandates of the rapporteurs, or even the feasibility of their implementation within the context of the given situation. Implementation of such recommendations—if ever indeed attempted—would ultimately prove counter-productive. With a better system of selecting and appointing independent experts, this flaw might be overcome.

LACK OF COORDINATION AND OVERLAPPING

Among the many dysfunctions of the system of Special Procedures I would mention the lack of coordination among the rapporteurs, which often leads to contradictions. For instance, following my return to Geneva from my mission to Venezuela in November/December 2017, I called a press conference in which I described what I had seen on the ground, what I had learned from the many personal encounters and interviews that I had conducted with representatives of UN agencies in Caracas, some 40 Venezuelan NGOs, representatives of the churches, academia, chamber of commerce, government ministers, the opposition, the diplomatic corps and even people on the streets, whom I could easily engage since Spanish is my mother tongue. I stated that at that moment in December 2017 there was a serious economic crisis, but not yet a "humanitarian crisis" as such, as confirmed to me by FAO and CEPAL officials in Venezuela and repeated in their contemporary reports. There was, of course, scarcity of certain medicines and food items as a direct result of the U.S. economic sanctions and the financial blockade.

Five weeks later, on February 9, 2018, four rapporteurs then in office, but now retired, who had not been in Venezuela and were essentially basing their views on mainstream media reporting and not on solid evidence, issued a press release stating that there was indeed a "humanitarian crisis" in Venezuela, and that this situation was attributable to the Maduro government. I considered this press release an attempt to sabotage the urgent message of my own report, which was not yet issued and would not become available until August 2018, being then presented to the Human Rights Council in September 2018 by my successor Dr. Livingstone Sewanyana.

What was particularly inappropriate and contrary to professionalism, is that I was never approached by the four rapporteurs in question, or forewarned by the Secretariat that such a contradictory press release was in the pipeline. I was never asked for my opinion, was not informed of their desire to issue a press release ahead of the publication of my own evidence-based report, and accordingly not enabled to interact with them with a view to providing them with information to which they may not have had access, which might have changed their views. Had I been consulted by the Secretariat, I would have transmitted to my colleague Rapporteurs a considerable amount of documentation and statistics that would have persuaded them that their proposed text was untenable.

Furthermore, it is worth noting that the issuance of such a contradictory press release contravened an earlier specific ruling announced by the Coordinating Committee of the Special Procedures mandate holders, which stipulated that when a rapporteur was seized of a particular issue (the mandate of international order on the Venezuela dossier), the other rapporteurs should refrain from making pronouncements about the same issue, so as not to convey the impression that at the UN one hand does not know what the other hand is doing. The contradiction simply manifested a failure of coordination at OHCHR. Even if the initiative to issue the release had come from the rapporteurs themselves (it did not, as I learned from one of the signatories), a professional Secretariat would have advised against issuing it, precisely because of its negative impact on the credibility of OHCHR and the Special Procedures of the Human Rights Council.

On February 12, 2018 I wrote a letter and personally spoke with the then President of the Human Rights Council, Vojislav Suc.

> It is unfortunate that their press release does not go beyond what can be read in the media and does not provide any constructive proposals [and] ... totally ignores the fact that an UN mission had just been conducted on the ground, that the independent expert had convened all UN agencies in Caracas, precisely in order to develop a plan-of-action how to deal with problems of scarcity and distribution. ... I feel

let down by OHCHR in not facilitating a dialogue with my colleagues, since their press release indirectly undermines my own report. Pursuant to Council Resolution 18/6, it was the function of OHCHR to at least inform the four rapporteurs that my report addressed the very issues raised in their press release, analysing the evidence concerning the impact of a non-conventional economic war on Venezuela. . . . At the 2016 meeting of Special Procedures mandate holders held in Geneva, it had been decided, after discussion in the plenary, that when rapporteurs were planning to issue a press release that would overlap with the mandate of another rapporteur, the Office would facilitate coordination. For instance, my colleague Dr. Idriss Jazairy, rapporteur on unilateral coercive measures, who has also been invited to visit Venezuela, would have appreciated being consulted. This was not done, and we were both kept in the dark.

The ruling of the Coordinating Committee on the avoidance of contradictions among the rapporteurs has been violated on a few other occasions. The ruling, however, is not intended to censor the views of independent experts, but rather to coordinate public statements so as to avoid the impression of confusion at the Human Rights Council.

There are, of course, worse instances of professional impropriety that demonstrate the degree of politicization of Special Procedures.

Indeed, it is even more damaging to their credibility and to the credibility of OHCHR as a whole when some rapporteurs go beyond their mandates and publicly criticize a High Commissioner on a mission that was well within the HC's mandate as defined in GA Resolution 48/141. This happened during the annual meeting of Special Procedures in June 2022, a meeting which I attended, when a number of rapporteurs decided to issue a press release more or less disavowing High Commissioner Michelle Bachelet, because they opposed her efforts to establish a working relationship with China and promote advisory services and technical assistance to China. Her extremely well prepared and professional mission to China in May 2022 was not intended as a "naming and shaming" exercise, but evidently that was the only function that these rapporteurs understood as the essence of the High Commissioner's mandate—at least as it concerned contradictions to the dominant narrative established through the mainstream media. The rapporteurs were "outraged" that Bachelet had not immediately and unconditionally condemned China on Xinjiang, Hong Kong, and Tibet. The same mindset was reflected in the statements made by several NGOs.[16] The Statement by Agnes Callamard on behalf of Amnesty International was particularly painful.[17]

On May 28, 2022, Bachelet had issued an end-of-mission statement in Guangzhou,[18] which outlined the purpose of the mission and its preliminary results, namely confidence building, the establishment of a special working group to coordinate China-OHCHR operations, preparations for the visits of UN rapporteurs, etc. Bachelet had had the opportunity to visit Xinjiang and to speak to representatives of the Uyghurs as well as opposition groups and receive petitions and documentation from them. Yet, the High Commissioner's mission was never intended as a "fact-finding commission" aimed *a priori* at investigating criminal activities, but as the beginning of a joint effort to address alleged violations of human rights in China. It is regrettable that some rapporteurs failed to grasp this fact, asserting rather that the High Commissioner's function should simply be to condemn Xi Jinping and support the propaganda war against China. I published two articles concerning this "rebellion" against the High Commissioner and likened it to my experience with my mission to Venezuela.[19] Indeed, the only value that some rapporteurs and the media expected from my mission would have been a blanket condemnation of President Nicolas Maduro and advocacy for regime change as demanded by Washington. These rapporteurs manifested zero interest in concretely helping the people of Xinjiang or the people of Venezuela, zero interest in confidence-building measures, with a view to creating an atmosphere of cooperation and a mechanism for follow-up. By such a vision, the function of the High Commissioner is degraded to that of an attack dog, and the credibility of the office itself is further undermined by such an appearance. The HC's ability to conduct civilized diplomatic discourse is discarded. And yet, Bachelet's mission was meaningful and is already yielding positive results[20] for the people of China.

Similarly, my own mission to Venezuela in November/December 2017 was remarkably successful: I obtained the release of 80 detainees already in December 2017, including Roberto Picón, whose wife and son had petitioned me to advocate his release, which I personally did with Foreign Minister Arreaza. Many more detainees were released in the course of 2018. Beyond that, I had brought all UN agencies in Caracas together so as to draft new cooperation and coordination agreements with the Venezuelan government, so as to better manage the economic, energy, food and medicine crisis. I persuaded the Venezuelan government to invite other rapporteurs, including the rapporteur on the Right to Development and the Rapporteur on unilateral coercive measures. Indeed, the 2021 report of Professor Alena Douhan, who visited Venezuela in February 2021, essentially confirmed my conclusions and recommendations.[21] Most importantly, there is now an OHCHR "presence" in Caracas, which makes it much easier to obtain reliable information from all sources, monitor developments on the ground, visit detention centres, and facilitates the provision of advisory services and technical assistance.

The credibility of the Human Rights Council also suffers when rapporteurs do not act in a manner consistent with their code of conduct, when they go beyond their terms of reference and simply join bandwagons and pursue ancillary matters that are foreign to their mandates, instead producing photo opportunities and public relations activities for what may be termed the "flavour of the month." Both the Council and the rapporteurs frequently pursue non-priority issues that have been artificially blown up by the mainstream media, thereby squandering time and resources on "distractions" rather than on serious but less publicized situations that deserve their attention. Just as we swim in "fake news," we are also distracted by "fake issues."[22]

An example of non-priority, counter-productive and overlapping of missions by Special Procedures mandate holders I could mention the visits to Spain of the Working Group on Disappeared Persons[23] and of the Special Rapporteur on the Right to Truth, Justice and Reparation[24] in the years 2013 and 2014 respectively. The focus of these missions was on war crimes committed during the Spanish Civil War 1936–39. One could and should ask the question whether the members of the WG and the special rapporteur did not have other more immediate and pressing issues concerning recent disappearances in many countries of the world, of recent arbitrary detentions and assassination of human rights defenders, syndicalists, journalists, indigenous peoples in countries like Albania, Argentina, Canada, Chile, China, Colombia, Ecuador, India, Kashmir, Kosovo, Mexico, Russia, Sri Lanka, Ukraine, where there might still be a possibility to reconstruct the facts and discover traces to the disappeared persons? Is it the function of 21st century rapporteurs to engage in historical research with scarce prospects of yielding results?

I have been professor of modern history for many years, ever since I obtained my doctorate at the University of Göttingen in 1977 and have published several essays on the Spanish Civil War, having personally interviewed participants on both sides and consulted the pertinent archives. Yes, there were thousands of disappeared persons and egregious war crimes *on both sides*.[25] Mass graves in Spain contain not only the bodies of victims of the fascist national forces under Francisco Franco, but also the bodies of victims of extra-judicial executions by the Republican forces, including some 10,000 priests, nuns, brothers, seminarians and 13 bishops.[26] Yet, it appears that the members of the Working Group and the rapporteur were only interested in investigating the crimes attributable to the nationalist forces under Franco and neglected the abundant evidence concerning the victims of Republican forces. The lack of balance was spectacular, but consistent with the deliberate manipulation of the perception of history promoted by some officials at OHCHR and generally in the mainstream media.

Yet another wasteful mission was that of the Working Group on Discrimination against Women in Law and Practice, a body that overlaps with the work of the Committee on the Elimination of Discrimination against Women, the Human Rights Committee, and the Special Rapporteur on violence against women. During the working group's visit to Honduras[27] in 2019, the members focused excessively on the country's abortion policies, instead of, for instance, addressing the violation of women's rights by the illegal *coup* regime that had come to power in Honduras and violations occurring as a consequence of the drug wars. The Working Group's focus on abortion failed to take into account the fact that many Catholic and Muslim countries feel that Article 6 of the International Covenant on Civil and Political Rights guarantees the right to life, and that the American Convention on Human Rights defines life as starting with conception. Moreover, Articles 17 and 23 of the ICCPR obliges States parties to promote the family in every way possible, while Article 18 stipulates freedom of religion, conviction and conscience. Abortion does not further the right to a family. What the WG should have done is to call for an increase of governmental subsidies for birth control as well as assistance to women during pregnancy, birth and infancy, further actually enabling women's choice both not to conceive, and to be able to afford wanted children. Similarly, Article 10 of the ICESCR stipulates "The widest possible protection and assistance should be accorded to the family, which is the natural and fundamental group unit of society, particularly for its establishment and while it is responsible for the care and education of dependent children." Therefore, bearing in mind the cultural and religious diversity of the world, a UN Working Group must refrain from interfering with the religious convictions of the populations they visit on official UN mission. On top of that, the Working Group's visit overlapped with the 2014 visit by the Special Rapporteur on violence against women[28] and essentially brought no "added value."

A significant problem with Special Procedures is not so much what the rapporteurs may do wrong from time to time, but what they fail to do most of the time. In all my years as UN staff member and as independent expert, I have waited for the rapporteurs to address the principal goal of the United Nations: the promotion of peace and security. I have waited for Special Procedures to endorse Peace as a human right,[29] as a crucial "enabling right,"[30] essential for the enjoyment of all civil, cultural, economic, political and social rights. I have waited for rapporteurs to establish that existential nexus between peace and the right to life, to take a clear position against the waste of resources in the production and stockpiling of weapons,[31] including weapons of mass destruction. I have waited for the Human Rights Council's Special Procedures to condemn in unison the destruction of life by wars that can always be avoided if States take their obligations under Articles 2(3) and 2(4) of the UN Charter seriously, if they settle their differences by peaceful means, if they are prepared to compromise, to enter a *quid pro quo*, to negotiate if hostilities have broken out, to seek to end a war rather than prolonging it in the expectation of "victory" on the battlefield—indeed, if they are pushed to do so by all institutions and agencies of the United Nations, itself. I still wait for the Council to condemn the obscenity of war mongering as a crime against humanity,

not simply as a violation of Article 20 of the International Covenant on
Civil and Political Rights.

In vain I have waited for the Human Rights Council, the rapporteurs on the indigenous, on food, health, truth and reparation—and
for the human rights system in general, including human rights tribunals—to comprehensively examine the past and ongoing genocide
against indigenous peoples worldwide, to vindicate their right to truth,
justice, and reparation.[32] In vain I have waited for the Rapporteur on
truth, justice and reparation to take up the ongoing decimation of
indigenous peoples worldwide and in particular the genocide committed on the "Indians" of North and South America as documented
by Antonio de Montesinos, Bartolomé de las Casas, David Stannard,
Marcel Grondin, Moema Viezzer, and so many others. With good
reason Martin Luther King Jr. wrote in his book *Why We Can't Wait*,
"Our nation was born in genocide." Historians and lawyers have tried
to turn the page without drawing the lessons or committing to reparations. Human Rights Council Resolution 48/7 on the legacies of
colonialism is a modest beginning. But follow-up is necessary.[33]

I have waited for the many special rapporteurs on freedom of
expression[34] to properly address the issues of academic freedom,
"cancel culture," enforced conformism, "political correctness," career
terror, and the consequent phenomenon of self-censorship, which constitute a significant loss to all of us, because when a scholar is silenced,
the rest of us are deprived of the benefit of his/her research, his/her
insights. When formulating a hypothesis is penalized as spreading
"conspiracy theories" or even criminalized as "hate speech," the whole
philosophy of freedom of research, freedom of opinion and expression
is subverted. In vain I have waited for some working group or rapporteur to denounce the monstrous violation of the U.S. Constitution, the
rule of law, and the right to privacy by the illegal surveillance of private persons, correspondence, emails, and WhatsApp by the National
Security Agency, as we learned from Edward Snowden.[35]

One of the many illustrations of the thorough politicization of
certain mandates and the failure of UN, EU, IACHR, ACHPR, OSCE
mandate holders to resolutely condemn government censorship is their
silence concerning the EU-wide censorship of the Russian media after
the Russian aggression against Ukraine in February 2022. Precisely
in an urgent situation like this, it is necessary for the public to have

access to all pertinent information *a fortiori* to enable and promote the search for peace and possibilities of compromise. It is necessary to understand and address how every belligerent thinks, how they assess the situation, how they respond to allegations of war crimes, and what explanations they bring forward.

Instead of vindicating the right of all peoples to information and condemning the continent-wide blocking of RT, Sputnik and other news services, UN Rapporteur Irene Khan together with other rapporteurs issued an unbalanced statement on May 4, 2022 that negates the very *raison d'être* of these mandate holders, displaying a betrayal of the fundamental principle *audiatur et altera pars* and a breakdown of the deontology of the mandates.[36] Civil society worldwide should protest against this betrayal of the ethics of democratic discourse and the rapid descent to an Orwellian dystopia. Essentially these rapporteurs have joined the ranks of apologists of totalitarianism, *nota bene*, not Russian or Chinese totalitarianism—but European! This joint press release illustrates better than any other that the sickness in the "human rights industry" is widespread, not limited to the United Nations institutions alone, but encompassing regional institutions that have similarly weaponized human rights as well. The damage they do to the credibility of the human rights protection and monitoring mechanisms worldwide cannot be overstated.

Most notably, a Rapporteur on freedom of opinion and expression should, and has the responsibility to, investigate one of the current and perhaps the greatest threat to freedom of opinion and expression—namely the manipulation of public opinion not only by governments but also by the private sector, by massive public relations campaigns, by Google search engines and Wikipedia disinformation,[37] by the algorithms that filter information and give the public a selective, skewed picture of the facts.[38] Most search engines suffer from gross manipulations that exclude essential information necessary for informed decisions in a democratic society.

A rapporteur on freedom of opinion and expression should also take on the European Union's dystopian legislation. Few people know about the EU onslaught on the internet, exemplified by the entry into force of the EU's Digital Services Act on November 16, 2022—notably, shortly after Elon Musk's takeover of Twitter, promising freedom of speech on that platform. Under the DSA, very large online platforms like Twitter, Facebook, and Instagram will have to swiftly remove "illegal content," "hate speech," and so-called disinformation from their platforms under risk of astronomical fines. But who determines what constitutes "hate speech" or "disinformation"? Add to that the problem of "overcompliance" out of fear of crossing any boundaries, as is present with regard to unilateral coercive measures, and a powerful "chilling effect" results. Businesses practice risk minimization, and if there is an enhanced risk from the DSA, internet providers will over-censor. This in turn violates Article 19 of the International Covenant on Civil and Political Rights, which all EU countries are obliged to promote and respect. Hence a paradox. This EU legislation is a frontal attack on the right to access information and the right to freely express one's opinion, including the "right to be wrong," which was vindicated in paragraph 49 of the Human Rights Committee General Comment no. 34 on Article 19. It is a frontal attack on democratic discourse, on the fundamentals of democracy itself. The implications of the DSA are immense, encompassing the regulation of content on the internet and setting a dangerous precedent for the entire world. The EU emerges as a super regulatory agency, an Orwellian Ministry of Truth.[39]

There are countless examples of the politicization of the choice of subjects explored by the rapporteurs. In vain I have waited for the Human Rights Council, the OHCHR, a rapporteur or a working group to focus comprehensively on the crime of "extraordinary renditions" and the complicity of so many countries in this crime, on the "outsourcing" of torture, on the atrocities committed in CIA secret prisons, in Abu Ghraib and Guantánamo. In 2013 the UN Rapporteur on human rights while combatting terrorism, Ben Emmerson,[40] presented a courageous report on these practices, but there was hardly any debate on the issue. The report was more or less shoved aside, because the perpetrators belong to the club of the "good guys." I would have expected several rapporteurs and working groups to examine the many facets of these grotesque human rights violations within their respective mandates—without fear of overlapping, because such activities violate the spectrum of human rights covered by the many mandates. Much too little attention has been devoted to these crimes which constitute a veritable revolt against the most fundamental principles of the UN Charter and the Universal Declaration of Human Rights.

Another huge problem that impacts about a third of the population on the planet is the illegal practice of imposing unilateral coercive
measures. I addressed this scourge in my first reports to the Human
Rights Council and General Assembly in 2012 and 2013. The important mandate of the Special Rapporteur on the human rights impacts
of UCMs was only established in 2014, and although the first two
rapporteurs, Dr. Idriss Jazairy and Prof. Alena Douhan, have submitted outstanding reports, the other rapporteurs have essentially ignored
these reports and cold-shouldered the rapporteurs. The mainstream
media have dealt with their reports as if they simply did not exist. The
practice has been to deny them any visibility, so as to avoid the necessity of discussing their toxic impacts on the enjoyment of human rights
by millions of human beings. It is necessary to discuss these impacts,
implications, responsibilities in townhalls and other forums. This a
huge issue that deserves a book by itself, but I cannot remain silent
about the outrageous measure recently announced by the European
Union—the criminalization of *evading the illegal UCMs*.[41] This is
a purely totalitarian measure that all rapporteurs should condemn in
unison.

There is also the question of the "dark funding" of certain rapporteurs,[42] a pandora's box if we dare to open it. The very independence
of the rapporteurs is at stake if it turns out that the financing of their
mandates comes directly or indirectly from governments that expect
that their geopolitical agendas will be advanced. This deserves yet
another book. This is one of the most problematic issues in the system: earmarked funding. This means that OHCHR is at the mercy of
the donors and expected to sing their tune, otherwise funding will be
withdrawn. This may be a more serious issue than the interference of
the Secretariat with some rapporteurs, and probably one of the root
causes.

A general observation seems appropriate at this juncture. In my
opinion, there are too many rapporteurs who see themselves as prima
donnas and, in a way, exhibitionists. In my experience both as UN
staff member and as rapporteur, I have seen how some rapporteurs
have behaved arrogantly and imperiously vis-à-vis their assistants. I
would go as far as to say that sometimes their behaviour has generated
emotional trauma with some overstretched staff members. At the time
I was a staff member myself, I observed that some colleagues felt

gaslighted by some of the experts, whose behaviour they considered disrespectful, even cruel. This in turn may affect the efficiency of the staff and consequently weaken the system altogether. A bit more modesty and a bit less narcissism would significantly enhance the authority and credibility of Special Procedures. Indeed, when one rapporteur acts insolently vis-à-vis the staff, there is a general blow-back against other rapporteurs and ultimately against the Human Rights Council itself. This is one reason why I, having endured as a staff member the insolence of a few experts, made sure that I treated the secretariat as colleagues, partners in a joint effort to improve the lot of suffering victims out there.

Notwithstanding the above, I do not want to close this section without paying tribute to the dozens of exemplary rapporteurs whom I have met over the decades, rapporteurs of the Commission, Sub-Commission, HR Council, Advisory Committee, who were genuinely committed to the cause and demonstrated independence, professionalism and integrity. Among them I would like to mention Claire Palley, Marc Bossuyt, Felix Ermacora, Leandro Despouy, Katarina Tomasevski, Virginia Dan Dan, Virginia Bras Gomes, John Dugard, Richad Falk, Michael Lynk, Manfred Nowak, Olivier de Schutter, Miloon Kothari, Walter Kälin, Paul Hunt, Hilal Elver, Idriss Jazairy, Alena Douhan, Ben Emmerson, Christof Heyns, Juan Pablo Bohoslavsky, Jean Ziegler, Asma Jahangir, Nils Melzer and Reem Alsalem. It is thanks to the constructive work of these experts that the Council's Special Procedures still enjoys a relatively good reputation—in spite of serious wrinkles here and there.

At the same time, it must be acknowledged that, precisely because of their courage and intellectual honesty, several of these experts have had to endure unfair criticism and even defamation both by some governments and by some non-governmental organizations (see chapter below).[43]

SELECTION OF INVITEES TO OHCHR PANELS

A problem with OHCHR panels concerns the selection of the persons invited to participate. Decades of experience have demonstrated to me that frequently the best experts are deliberately kept out of UN panels for fear that they may upset the comfortable *status quo*, expose real problems, criticize the Secretariat or even the Secretary-General. A kind of internal solidarity seeks to ensure that the panels arrive at certain conclusions and not at others, and the choice of panelists is determined accordingly. This applies particularly to experts in the fields of the right to development, the right to peace, the right of self determination, the right to solidarity, and the promotion of a democratic and equitable international order. OHCHR panels are selected by the secretariat in a superficially "objective" manner, taking account of geographical or gender balance. But never does OHCHR take into account "balance" concerning different legal systems, different perspectives on human rights priorites. The majority of panelists are expected to go along with the Western "consensus."

To give an example: In December 2009 I was invited as an expert to a UN workshop on the human right to peace, during which I reported on the *Declaración de Luarca*[44] on the right to peace (which subsequently became the *Declaración de Santiago*[45]). As I subsequently learned from an Ambassador friend, a person in the Secretariat actually and deliberately tried to exclude me from participating, because it was feared that I would advocate the recognition of peace as a human right and the appointment of a special rapporteur on the right to peace,[46] which OHCHR quite evidently did not want because its major sponsors, the EU and U.S., were against it. Here again, the issue of OHCHR funding—and the fear of losing it—is crucial. Yet, notwithstanding Secretariat opposition, the Ambassadors made sure that I could participate.

Later, when I was already a UN independent expert, it was easier to participate in the various panels concerning unilateral coercive measures, but opposition must have been stronger, because I was never called to participate on panels on human rights, democracy and the rule of law,[47] although I had written extensively on these subjects, nor was I invited to participate in the forum on business and human rights,[48] which I had publicly dubbed the "forum on the business of human rights." As I have learned, other progressive and truly independent experts have been similarly excluded. There is method in the madness.

Civil Society Participation in HRC Procedures

Yet another serious problem is the difficulty that NGOs face to access and participate in the interactive dialogues at Human Rights Council meetings. As has been reported to me by Ambassadors and NGO representatives, the lists of NGO speakers are not established on a first-come first-served basis but are manipulated by the OHCHR secretariat in order to allow only certain privileged NGOs into the first twelve slots, which usually are the only ones that have an opportunity to read out their 90 second statements. Although on several occasions I did manage to speak on behalf of my NGO, the International Human Rights Association of American Minorities, for some reason I was unable to secure a slot in the 50th or 51st sessions of the Council, although we clicked immediately upon the opening of the online registration procedure. As I have learned from other members of progressive NGOs, they have had the same experience, whereas the large NGOs, mostly financed by the United States, United Kingdom, European Union etc. invariably secure an early slot. Another problem is the cumbersome on-line procedures, the INDICO system, the frequent computer glitches and malfunctions, the unreasonable demand that accreditation letters be delivered for each session or the Council or UPR, and not just once a year—all of these obstacles make it very difficult for some NGOs to participate. Bottom line: small NGOs that do not have a permanent presence in Geneva and have little or no staff cannot compete on a level playing field with the corporate-financed NGOs.

Yet another problem is that of simultaneous interpretation. Over the years I have listened to the original NGO statements as spoken, whether in English, French, Spanish or Russian, which I understand, and compared them with the simultaneous translation. Most of the time the interpretation is accurate, sometimes more literary than the original. But on occasion, especially when it is a matter of political sensitivity, the nuances are changed, and sometimes a positive is transformed into a negative or vice-versa. This occurred most recently in a side event concerning Principles of International Order on November 25, 2022.[49]

And yet another problem is that UN Translation services are overstretched. Why are some reports issued promptly and others unreasonably delayed? I cannot abandon the suspicion not just that certain reports are given preferential treatment but that the reports of certain rapporteurs e.g. on international solidarity, unilateral coercive measures, international order are not processed with the same expediency and that their publication is deliberately delayed. Conspiracy theories? Notably, over the years so many narratives decried as "conspiracy theories" have turned out to be accurate. In my personal experience as independent expert, I had opportunity to flag this problem in the years 2012–18, but, of course, my complaints were not duly investigated.

The Universal Periodic Review procedure has the potential for effective participation by NGOs, but it has not yet delivered results. Many observers criticize the UPR as a diplomatic ritual with a lot of window dressing. I have attended many presentations by States and listened to the comments by States, and I still think that the UPR must further mature before it is a useful exercise. Often, it is far from a dispassionate review and is marred by a high level of animosity that pours out—as is perhaps inevitable when those who have had close contact with severe instances of abuse, whether personally or as investigators, confront the representatives of States whom they hold responsible—who in turn hotly contest that responsibility. The Latin slogan *si fecisti, nega!* describes the situation—if you did it, deny it! This tends to nullify efforts to soberly review and ameliorate the situation through coming to a common understanding and mutual cooperation as to what is to be done.

Of course, there are many types of examination, depending on the country concerned and often this depends on the *Zeitgeist*. Sometimes the States completely ignore grave human rights problems in a particular State while applying totally different standards when discussing the same human rights violations when perpetrated by another State. The double standards and politicization of the UPR exercise is becoming painfully evident, and it is getting worse, not better. Some UPR sessions degenerate into mud-slinging exercises in which evidence-free allegations are thrown around.

Objectivity is hardly the hallmark of the UPR procedure, which, however, could be a constructive exercise if it were victim-centered and if it aimed at concretely helping individual human beings or communities and not just engaging in sterile "naming and shaming." Again and again State representatives gloss over the violations of States like the U.S., UK, France, and Turkey, while they are very vocal against

Belarus, China, Iran, Nicaragua, Russia, and Venezuela. Perhaps one day the Council will establish procedures to enable the UPR to become more meaningful so that it transcends being yet another exercise in lip-service to human rights and an opportunity to demonize a geopolitical rival. What the world expects of the Human Rights Council—and this must be underlined—is that it make a genuine good faith effort to formulate concrete, pragmatic, implementable solutions to the ills of developed and developing nations.

Of course, one could consider doing away with the UPR altogether, since a much better examination of reports is conducted by the expert treaty bodies, including the Human Rights Committee, the Committee on Economic, Social and Cultural Rights, the Committee Against Torture, the Committee on the Elimination of Racial Discrimination, etc. Some observers have denounced this "duplication" or "overlapping." But that said, duplication in addressing human rights matters may be a positive thing, when it is seen as giving emphasis to human rights problems that cry out for a solution. Alternative avenues for pursuing such objectives may very well be fruitful. And indeed, is it not likely that NGOs closer to the issues to be addressed may shed new and important light on the issues—and thus contribute to the credibility of the human rights protection system? The sad reality, however, is, that the examination of State reports is anything but uniform and that both the Council and the Committees frequently ignore or overlook the evidence submitted by the UPR civil counterparties in substantiation of allegations of violations of human rights.

COMMISSIONS OF INQUIRY

There are many commissions of inquiry and fact-finding created by the United Nations and other bodies. Personally, I give them the benefit of the doubt, but do not recognize their automatic authority and credibility until and unless their methods of work are shown to be objective and impartial, until the membership of the commission is shown to be professional and truly committed to truth. Experience shows that many commissions of inquiry are but political platforms to demonize a given party, without giving due weight to the context, historical precedents, provocations, causes and effects. Personally, I have more trust in commissions of inquiry established by the International

Committee of the Red Cross,[50] which, as far as I know, has kept clear of producing political pamphlets to serve the propaganda interests of one or more parties.

While constructive dialogue and the provision of advisory services and technical assistance should be the priority of the Human Rights Council, it is sometimes necessary to establish commissions of inquiry that will investigate all sides of an issue and make pragmatic proposals towards solving the problems. Unfortunately, again many of the commissions of inquiry have merely engaged in "naming and shaming" instead of trying to discover the root causes of the problems and devising future-oriented solutions. Among the effective commissions of inquiry I would like to mention the Commission established by the Human Rights Council on May 27, 2021 to "investigate, in the Occupied Palestinian Territory, including East Jerusalem, and in Israel, all alleged violations of international humanitarian law and all alleged violations and abuses of international human rights law leading up and since 13 April 2021." In July 2021, the President of the Human Rights Council announced the appointment of Navanethem Pillay (South Africa), Miloon Kothari (India) and Christopher Sidoti (Australia) to serve as the three members of the Commission. The former UN High Commissioner for Human Rights Navi Pillay serves as its Chair.[51] The HRC further requested the commission of inquiry to "investigate all underlying root causes of recurrent tensions, instability and protraction of conflict, including systematic discrimination and repression based on national, ethnic, racial or religious identity." The Commission of Inquiry was mandated to report to the Human Rights Council and the General Assembly annually from June 2022 and September 2022, respectively.

On December 31, 2022, the UN Commission of Inquiry welcomed General Assembly resolution 77/400 deciding to request an advisory opinion of the International Court of Justice relating to the Israeli occupation of Palestinian territory.[52]

The resolution, in accordance with Article 96 of the Charter of the United Nations, asks the ICJ—pursuant to Article 65 of the Statute of the Court—to render its opinion on the legal consequences arising from Israel's ongoing violation of the right of the Palestinian people to self-determination, its prolonged occupation, settlement and annexation of the Palestinian territory occupied since 1967, including measures aimed at altering the demographic composition, character and status of the Holy City of Jerusalem, and from its adoption of discriminatory legislation and measures.[53] The resolution further asks the Court how Israel's policies and practices referenced affect the legal status of the occupation and what are the legal consequences that arise for all States and the UN.

The OHCHR press release further states:

In its report to the General Assembly, presented on 27 October 2022 the Commission found there are reasonable grounds to conclude that the Israeli occupation of Palestinian territory is now unlawful under international law owing to its permanence and to ongoing actions undertaken by Israel to annex parts of the land de facto and de jure.

The Commission recommended that the General Assembly urgently request an advisory opinion from the International Court of Justice on the legal consequences of the continued refusal on the part of Israel to end its occupation of Palestinian Territory, including East Jerusalem, amounting to de facto annexation, of policies employed to achieve this, and of the refusal on the part of Israel to respect the right of the Palestinian people to self-determination, and on the obligations of third States and the UN to ensure respect for international law.

The Commission found in its first report that the continued occupation by Israel of Palestinian territory and discrimination against Palestinians were the key root causes of the recurrent tensions, instability and protraction of conflict in the region. The Commission's second report to the General Assembly, based on its conclusion about the illegality of such an occupation, made the core recommendation for an advisory opinion from the International Court of Justice.

The Commission considers that a definitive clarification of the legal consequences of Israel's refusal to end the occupation, and what the obligation of third parties to ensure respect for international law are, will be crucial to member States and the UN in considering what further measures should be adopted to ensure full compliance with international law.

This Commission of Inquiry is likely to contribute to impulses for a settlement of the multiple issues associated with the occupation of Palestine since 1967. It is to be hoped that Israel will cooperate both with the Commission and the International Court of Justice.

While this Commission of Inquiry has a constructive human-rights based raison d'être and its purpose is not political but humanitarian, there are numerous other COIs and Fact Finding Commissions[54] whose origins are geopolitical and whose real purpose may be to denigrate and destabilize the targeted government to facilitate undemocratic "regime change" as desired by one or more powerful countries. Such commissions are yet another weapon in the hybrid war arsenal. Such COIs exemplify what I condemned in my 14 reports of the Human Rights Council and General Assembly: the instrumentalization of human rights for purposes contrary to the UDHR and customary international law, the "weaponization" of positive values for ulterior purposes, as a pretext to interfere in the internal affairs of states and demonize its leaders, sometimes with a view to military intervention under the guise of "humanitarian intervention."

This is what happened with the creation of the "Independent International Fact-Finding Commission of Inquiry"[55] on Venezuela, established 2019 by the Human Rights Council, contrary to the recommendations formulated in my 2018 report to the Human Rights Council on my mission to Venezuela,[56] which is anything but independent. If one studies the origin of this COI, it was the now defunct "Grupo de Lima,"[57] which for years had been attempting to topple the Venezuelan Government.[58] They succeeded with the help of the mainstream media to create such a hysterical atmosphere against the government of Venezuela, reversing cause and effect, that the Human Rights Council finally agreed to the creation of what has proven to be a political, biased COI, which hitherto has borne no benefit to the Venezuelan people, in particular to the most vulnerable Venezuelans who suffer deprivations as a direct result of the comprehensive economic war, the financial blockade and illegal unilateral coercive measures imposed by the U.S. and other countries with the declared purpose to induce regime change. I had the opportunity of analysing this COI's biased and methodologically flawed reports.[59] It is always revealing to study when and how a COI is established and by whom.

The Group of Human Rights experts on Nicaragua,[60] established in 2022, is yet another example of a COI set up for the purpose of "naming and shaming" and not for the purpose of objectively investigation all sides of the picture. Of course this "group of experts" is not interested in following up on the work of Katherine Hoyt[61] or studying the legacies of the U.S. intervention in the war of the contras against the government of Nicaragua, or the non-implementation of the letter and spirit of the Judgment of the International Court of Justice on Military and Paramilitary Activities in and against Nicaragua Case.[62] In March 2023 the group presented a report to the Council. I did not think it deserved a comment, since it was a political pamphlet engaging in hyperboles and accusing Nicaragua of "crimes against humanity."[63]

For the interactive dialogue on March 6, 2023, I pre-recorded a statement on behalf of the International Human Rights Association of American Minorities, in which I show the constructive way of helping the Nicaraguan people. Here the short version:

> The International Human Rights Association of American Minorities denounces the negative impact of unilateral coercive measures on the enjoyment of human rights in countries like Cuba, Nicaragua, Syria, Venezuela. IHRAAM endorses the reports of High Commissioner Navi Pillay in 2012, and of Rapporteurs Idriss Jazairy and Alena Douhan. It is demonstrated that UCM's kill tens of thousands worldwide, constituting crimes against humanity under Article 7 of the Rome Statute.
>
> UCM's cause or aggravate humanitarian crises and states of emergency that generate crisis legislation, derogating from certain civil and political rights.
>
> If this Council wants to help the people of Nicaragua, it must advocate the immediate lifting of UCMs.
>
> The less a country feels threatened, the greater incentive to grant more civil and political rights. UCM's are counter-productive, and for this reason they were condemned by the UN General Assembly in resolution 77/214 of December 2022, and Council Resolution 49/6 of March

2022. In the light of these resolutions, it is bizarre to suggest more UCM's on Nicaragua.

IHRAAM denounces UCM's as a weapon to interfere in the internal affairs of states and as a poorly disguised strategy of undemocratic regime change.

Today the Nicaragua people need advisory services and technical assistance from OHCHR and international solidarity. UCM's constitute retrogression in human rights.

REFORMING THE UN HUMAN RIGHTS COUNCIL

There are many areas where the UN Human Rights Council can be reformed. For instance:

1. A redistribution of the membership of the Human Rights Council to take into account not only the geographical regions but also the various legal systems of the world and the size of the populations concerned. The current division into five regions—Western and other 7, Eastern Europe 6, Latin-American and Caribbean 8, Africa 13 and Asia 13[64]—does not reflect the thinking of billions of human beings whose priorities are the right to peace, food, water, sanitation, housing, etc. and not those rights of the Western countries and their allies, which absorb most of the Human Rights Council's attention.

2. A follow-up mechanism to monitor what happens with the findings and recommendations of UN rapporteurs and independent experts is urgently needed. I say follow-up, because it is important to measure the extent of implementation, if any, of the recommendations made, bearing in mind that rapporteur recommendations are advisory only and States are not under an obligation to implement them.

3. The duplication and overlap among rapporteurs must be curtailed. Indeed, there are too many rapporteurs, and their mandates overlap considerably, leading to occasional contradictions and incoherence. It is not uncommon that one rapporteur essentially (but diplomatically) contradicts the reports of a colleague rapporteur. Indeed, while vindicating

the principle of the independence of every rapporteur, an effort must be made—possibly by the OHCHR secretariat—to coordinate among the rapporteurs so as to avoid obvious clashes. This must be done professionally and transparently. On the other hand, provision must be made so that all views are considered. For instance, in the context of fact-finding commissions, it is important that the conclusions of dissenting investigators should not be simply suppressed, thus conveying a false impression of consensus to the public.

4. The sheer proliferation of overlapping mandates must be reduced, because by overloading the system, especially with punitive country mandates, without a corresponding increase in funding, States are able to render the human rights system ineffective *on purpose*, while pretending to strengthen it.

5. The selection method of rapporteurs must be made more transparent and reflect geographical and gender-balance. The current system leads to the appointment of a special cadre of rapporteurs, the majority of whom serve the powerful states and toe the politically correct line. As I have repeatedly observed, rapporteurs who are likely to be innovative and independent are seldom selected. The lack of independence of rapporteurs is manifested in various ways, e.g. by selectively criticizing only certain countries while keeping silent about others, and by the all-too-obvious application of double standards in the evaluation of the evidence.

6. The access of civil society to the Council and the opportunity of NGOs to speak for a mere 90 seconds must be enhanced. The new registration system known as INDICO makes it extremely difficult for smaller NGOs, especially in the developing world, to register for any session or to participate in the interactive dialogues after each item on the agenda.

7. The current registration rules for HR Council sessions must be reformed and streamlined so that all NGOs have equal opportunity to participate in the debates. This might be facilitated, *inter alia*, by increasing the number of agenda items.

8. There should be greater emphasis on preventive strategies, on methods to investigate the root causes of violations of human rights. The HR Council is mostly reactive and relies largely on "naming and shaming," which as been proven to be a counter-productive strategy that generates push-back from governments rather than enhanced cooperation.

9. Notwithstanding point 4, some important human rights concerns are still not being addressed professionally. I have long advocated the creation of the function of a Special Rapporteur on the Human Right to Peace. This new mandate should include an "early warning" faculty and a structured and ongoing relationship with UN agencies, including the Security Council.

10. The creation of the function of a Special Rapporteur on the Self-determination of Peoples would facilitate addressing one of the root causes of armed conflict: the unjust denial of the right of ALL peoples to self-determination, as stipulated in Article 1 ICCPR/ICESCR. It is easy to demonstrate that a great many armed conflicts since 1945 had their origin in the unjust denial of self-determination. Indeed, is it not the denial of the right of self-determination that destabilizes the international community, while the neo-colonial mindset puts territorial integrity and *uti possidetis* ahead of the fundamental collective and individual right of self-determination? For this reason I repeatedly proposed in my reports to the Human Rights Council and in my press releases that the Council, as the Commission before it, should have a permanent item on its agenda devoted to self-determination worldwide. Here again, a special rapporteur on the right of self-determination would advance the conflict-preventive function of self-determination. There are too many potential self-determination disputes that will generate violence, unless the grievances are addressed in a timely fashion.

11. The HRC should urge the United Nations General Assembly to call for, organize and monitor referenda in appropriate cases. Indeed, the violation of the right of self-determination can easily constitute a threat or breach of international peace

and security for purposes of Article 39 of the UN Charter. Perhaps the General Assembly could outsource the responsibility and mandate the Human Rights Council to organize and monitor referenda as a conflict-prevention strategy.[65]

12. The President of the HRC and the Bureau must be alert to attempts by certain NGOs to discredit rapporteurs and independent experts by way of defamatory *ad hominem* attacks, both in the Council room and on their respective websites. Seldom have such attacks been stopped or even criticized by the President of the Council. The OHCHR Secretariat must take disciplinary action against offending NGOs.

13. The HRC should propose a code of conduct for NGOs to ensure that interactive dialogues focus on the merits and do not degenerate into invective. Recidivist NGOs that deliberately disseminate wrong information must be stripped of consultative status.

A CASE STUDY IN DYSFUNCTIONALITY: THE 2022 SUSPENSION OF RUSSIA FROM MEMBERSHIP IN THE HUMAN RIGHTS COUNCIL

The decision of the UN General Assembly to exclude Russia from the Human Rights Council on April 7, 2022 was unwise and counter productive.[66] Why Russia? Indeed, earlier in 2011, why Libya?[67] Why were the U.S. and UK not excluded from the Commission on Human Rights (the Council's predecessor) when in 2003 the "coalition of the willing" illegally invaded and devastated Iraq and proceeded to impose a foreign administration on Iraq and loot its natural resources in gross violation of the 1949 Geneva Red Cross Conventions and 1977 Additional Protocols?

True enough, Secretary General Kofi Annan ultimately admitted that the Iraq war was illegal,[68] but this resulted in his suffering consequences in the form of numerous "unfriendly acts" by the U.S. and UK against the UN and against him personally, with little UN/HRC pushback, to their discredit. Indeed and similarly, it would have been unwise to exclude the U.S. and UK from the Commission on Human Rights, since the Commission should be *inclusive* and aim at persuading rogue States to play by the rules. Exclusion is not the answer—but dialogue. What is shocking is that the Commission did not even make an effort to condemn the illegal Iraq war or appoint a commission of inquiry to investigate the crime of aggression and the ensuing war crimes and crimes against humanity committed by the "coalition" in Iraq and in Afghanistan, to say nothing of the misuse of the R2P "mandate" in Libya.[69] The draft resolutions tabled in the Commission on Human Rights recommending an investigation into torture in Guantánamo were defeated in 2003 and again 2004.

The General Assembly's decision to suspend Russia's member-ship in the Human Rights Council in 2022 embedded this destructive precedent of political exclusion—not only for the future of the Human Rights Council, but for the future of other United Nations institutions.

Here are the consequences of the GA decision: while it consti-tuted a blow to Russia's prestige, and added to the general atmosphere of Russophobia that we have seen over the past three decades, it also added to the world's perception of engineered bias in the UN itself, where the manipulation of States' votes was enabled by a failure to call for a secret ballot, as requested by Russia. We can expect that in the future the GA and the Council will be even more politicized, and efforts may be undertaken to exclude other countries from member-ship, and not only in the Human Rights Council.

If exclusion were undertaken objectively, one would expect the exclusion of other offenders. including but not limited to the following:

- Several NATO countries for the war crimes and crimes against humanity committed by their forces during the wars of aggression against Yugoslavia, Afghanistan, Iraq, Libya, Syria, etc.

- Saudi Arabia, among others, because of its genocidal war against the people of Yemen and because of the gruesome assassination of Saudi journalist Jamal Khashoggi at the Saudi Consulate in Istanbul in 2018.[70]

- India for its systematic war crimes and gross violations of human rights against the people of Kashmir, including wide-spread extra-judicial executions.

- Azerbaijan because of its aggression against the hapless Armenians of Nagorno Karabakh (Artsakh) during the

Blitzkrieg of September–November 2020, where the crime of aggression, war crimes and crimes against humanity were committed, including torture and execution of Armenian prisoners of war.

- Decades of systematic killings of human rights defenders, social leaders, syndicalists and indigenous peoples by successive Colombian governments and lethal para-military forces. The new Colombian government under Gustavo Petro is likely to reverse governmental policies of oppression of the poor and disadvantaged, but the danger posed by the drug cartels and the paramilitary has not been overcome.

But again, why exclude governments from the Human Rights Council? It bears repeating that human rights is an *erga omnes* concern of all of humanity. Might it be better to have a human rights general assembly that would encompass all nations, observer nations, and indigenous peoples of the world? Why not bring them all in and promote constructive dialogue over issues as well as situations? The exclusion or "punishment" of some countries and the tacit consent given to the gross violations of human rights perpetrated by privileged states only demonstrates the politicization of the institution and degrades its legitimacy among the global public.

This could address the present loss of credibility of the Human Rights Council, whose moral authority has become questionable, and whose resolutions are routinely ignored by many countries, including the United States, the United Kingdom and Israel.

Since its creation in 2006 the Human Rights Council has not served human rights well. Rather it has manifestly served the geopolitical and informational interests of the United States and the European Union. The GA decision to refuse secret ballots in the case of Russian suspension from the HRC contributes to the delegitimization of the General Assembly. It starkly manifests how this great world assembly can be and is manipulated by the United States through the bullying, arm-twisting and blackmailing practices of the Department of State.

The decision of the GA sets a dangerous precedent and even further politicizes the Human Rights Council. One would think that precisely because some countries do not like what Russia is doing that they would try to "tame" it by engaging it in the human rights work of the Council. Isolating a country is always counter-productive. What is needed is greater inclusion and greater debate—not exclusion and hatemongering.

The General Assembly vote further demonstrates the success of the "information war" that has been waged against Russia for decades—not just since 2022, not even since 2014 and the Maidan coup—long before there was systematic disinformation about Russia and a consistent negative narrative. This has a simple explanation: NATO has had no *raison d'être* since the Warsaw Pact was dismantled in 1991. In order to continue to exist, NATO must have an "enemy"— and that is the only role that the U.S. and NATO, having rejected many Russian overtures, are willing to assign to Russia. The Russian bogeyman is necessary and guarantees that the maw of the U.S. military-industrial-digital-financial complex can continue to be fed, and its war on the world, contrary to the purposes and principles of the United Nations, can be pursued, even while it pushes its purported "rules-based" international order.

GENERAL ASSEMBLY DOUBLE STANDARDS VIOLATE THE GENERAL PRINCIPLES OF INTERNATIONAL LAW

The principle most violated by UN institutions is *audiatur et altera pars*. The application of double standards is almost systemic while the mainstream media turns a blind eye to obvious violations of *bona fide*. Worse than that, the mainstream media actively participates in the disinformation campaign and the suppression of alternative views.

No doubt, *all* allegations of war crimes should be investigated. And it appears that the new fact-finding commission on war crimes in Ukraine is making an effort to investigate allegations of crimes by Russian and Ukrainian forces.[71] This, however, is not the impression one gets from the mainstream media, which reports and magnifies almost every suspicion of a violation by Russian forces while downplaying or engaging in apologetics when it comes to allegations concerning possible war crimes committed by Ukrainian forces.[72] The perception of reality created by the media is so pervasive that it impacts the thinking of delegates at both the General Assembly and the Human Rights Council, who should be taking care to be more widely informed—but perhaps cannot act on the basis of what they know.

The removal of Russia from membership in the UN Human Rights Council responded to unproved allegations of crimes supposedly committed by Russian forces in Bucha in the vicinity of Kiev. But how much did we know then, and much do we know even today about those events? While Ukraine accused Russia of murdering 400 civilians in Bucha, the Russian government immediately refuted these allegations, pointing out that Russian forces had withdrawn in an orderly fashion on March 30 and that no allegations of extra judicial executions were made until April 2, four days later, when Ukrainian security forces and TV cameras arrived in Bucha. The U.S. and NATO accepted Kiev's claims uncritically and used them to justify imposing further sanctions against Russia. However, serious doubts have arisen about a possible staged event and tampering with the photos and videos.[73]

An international investigation is justified and necessary, but here too, any *ad hoc* commission must investigate allegations of crimes committed not only by Russian soldiers but also by Ukrainian soldiers and paramilitaries, including against the Russian-speaking Ukrainians of Lugansk and Donetsk since 2014, and the pogrom against 50 Russian-speaking Ukrainians in Odessa in May 2014.[74]

Therefore, it can be said without fear of contradiction that the GA vote to exclude Russia from the HRC was premature and violated the most elementary and primary general principles of law concerning due process and the presumption of innocence. According to the principle *"audiatur et altera pars"*—Russia's evidence and arguments should have been heard and given due weight. The absence of due process is yet another disgrace for the General Assembly.

DOUBLE STANDARDS IN THE UN SYSTEM

Double standards are practiced not only in the General Assembly and Human Rights Council but also in and concerning the UN Security Council. The idea of excluding Russia from the Human Rights Council has now gained adepts in relationship to Russia's membership in the Security Council, and Russia's assumption of the rotating Presidency of the Security Council in April 2023. This is being questioned by some countries, including Ukraine and the United States, as expressed by U.S. Ambassador Linda Thomas-Greenfield. Some in the mainstream media have joined the futile call to exclude Russia from the Security Council, which is impossible under the UN Charter without an amendment under Article 108. But why Russia? Why not the U.S., UK, France for all the gross international law violations committed by these powers over the past 78 years, and for their neo-colonial practices, including illegal unilateral coercive measures? This "exclusionary" trend must be resolutely rejected, because the very essence of the UN Charter is inclusion, not exclusion.[75]

   This is not the first and nor will it be the last time that the General Assembly and Human Rights Council apply double standards and adopt flawed resolutions or decisions. It seems apparent not just to this writer but must do so as well to the rest of the non-Western world that the entire United Nations system has been hijacked by the West and that this has the full support of a homologated corporate media that acts as echo chamber of the U.S. State Department.

   Similarly, it is no secret that the UN Human Rights Council essentially serves the interests of the Western developed countries and does not have a holistic approach to human rights. Blackmail and bullying are common practices, and the U.S. has proven that it has sufficient "soft power" to cajole weaker countries. It's amazing to watch how poor countries actually vote against their own interests even though the reasons for it might well be surmised. But it is not necessary to threaten ambassadors or missions in the council chamber or in the corridors; a phone call from the Ambassador or from the Mission's counsellor suffices. Countries are threatened with sanctions—or worse—as I have learned from numerous African diplomats. Of course, if the former colonies abandon the illusion of sovereignty, they are rewarded by being called "democratic." Neo-colonialism is alive and well at the UN Human Rights Council. Only major powers can afford to have their own opinions and to vote accordingly, and indeed one wonders how many of these there actually are.

   Back in 2006 the Commission on Human Rights—which began work in 1946, adopted the Universal Declaration of Human Rights, numerous human rights treaties, and established the system of expert rapporteurs—was abolished. At the time I was surprised by the rationale of the General Assembly; the reason adduced was the "politicization" of the Commission.

The U.S. unsuccessfully lobbied for the creation of a smaller commission composed only of countries that (in its view) observed human rights and could pass judgment over the rest. The GA then established a new body of 47 member States, the Human Rights Council, which, as any observer will confirm, is even more politicized and less objective than its maligned predecessor.

The special session of the HR Council held in Geneva on May 12, 2022 on the Ukraine war was a particularly painful event, marred by xenophobic statements in violation of Article 20 of the International Covenant on Civil and Political Rights (ICCPR) which prohibits incitement to discrimination or hatred. Speakers employed a demeaning tone when demonizing Russia and Putin, while ignoring the war crimes committed by Ukraine since 2014, the Odessa massacre[76], and the eight-year Ukrainian bombardment on the civilian population of Donetsk and Lugansk, etc.

A quick review of OSCE reports from February 2022 is revealing. The February 15 report of the OSCE Special Monitoring Mission to Ukraine recorded some 41 explosions in the ceasefire areas. This increased to 76 explosions on February 16; 316 on February 17; 654 on February 18; 1413 on February 19; a total of 2026 on February 20 and 21; and 1484 on February 22. The OSCE mission reports showed that the great majority of impact explosions of the artillery were on the separatist side of the ceasefire line.[77] We could easily make a comparison of the Ukrainian bombardment of the Donbas with Serbia's bombardment of Bosnia and Sarajevo.[78] But back then NATO's geopolitical agenda favoured Bosnia and there too the world was divided into good guys and bad guys.

Any independent observer would cringe at the lack of balance displayed in the discussions at the Human Rights Council on May 12, 2022. But are there many independent thinkers in the ranks of the "human rights industry" left? The pressure of "groupthink" is enormous.

Precisely the purpose of a commission of inquiry on war crimes during the war in Ukraine should be to collect verifiable evidence on all sides and to hear as many witnesses as possible. Unfortunately, the resolution adopted on May 12 does not augur well for peace and reconciliation, because it is woefully one-sided. For that very reason China departed from its practice of abstaining from such votes and went ahead and voted against the resolution. It is laudable that the top Chinese diplomat at the UN Office in Geneva Chen Xu, spoke about trying to mediate peace and calling for a global security architecture. He deplored the present practice, stating:

> We have noted that in recent years the politicization and confrontation at the [council] has been on the rise, which has severely impacted its credibility, impartiality and international solidarity.

More Irregularities

As every institution administered by human beings, there is good in the bad and bad in the good. It is not surprising that there are many examples of selectivity and incoherence in the work of the HRC. All the more reason to formulate constructive criticism, so that these obstacles to professionalism and objectivity can be removed.

Among the many "irregularities" that I personally observed during my years as Independent Expert was an abstruse video shown in the Council Chamber on November 12, 2015, immediately before the appearance of a Head of State,[79] who was about to make a statement to the HRC in the spirit of international cooperation promoted in the UN Charter and UN human rights instruments. The State expressed its desire to improve and intensify its cooperation with OHCHR in conformity with GA Resolutions 2625 and 48/141. The *dramatis personae* were the then High Commissioner for Human Rights, Zeid Ra'ad Al Hussein, and the President of Venezuela, Nicolas Maduro.[80]

In all my years of working at OHCHR, in all my years of inter-acting with Ambassadors and government officials, I had never witnessed a similar propaganda assault—by video, not even in person—whereby the assembled delegates in the Council had to listen to evidence-free statements about the alleged humanitarian crisis in Venezuela and the responsibility of the government for the scarcity, accompanied by a barrage of insinuations about the Head of State, without that head of state having the opportunity to object to the video or to ask on a point of order to have the video interrupted.[81] This was particularly serious, bearing in mind that Venezuela has cooperated with the UN Treaty bodies and submitted many pertinent reports to the UN Human Rights Committee and the other expert Committees. It was not as if Venezuela had been avoiding scrutiny by the United Nations or rejecting United Nations help to improve the lot of the Venezuelans. To make matters worse, the Human Rights Council was "prepared" for the onslaught on Maduro by a number of preceding inflammatory articles, including by Human Rights Watch.[82] In any event, the High Commissioner's rhetoric was inappropriate, contrary to diplomatic practice, and reflected an arrogant, imperialistic, neo-colonial mindset shared by parts of the mainstream media and some nongovernmental organizations.

There was no outstretched hand from OHCHR, no offer of advisory services and technical assistance. Just arrogant "naming and shaming." I do not think that a similar assault on a head of State had ever occurred in the Chamber, and should never be repeated. Obviously, the purpose was to publicly humiliate a Head of State. It was emblematic in its lack of diplomatic skill and in its counter-productive impact. The video intervention by the High Commissioner aroused fierce criticism in the Council Room, and an open letter to the President of the Human Rights Council, dated November 12, signed by the Ambassadors of Bolivia. Cuba, Ecuador, Nicaragua and Venezuela, all members of the ALBA organization. An official protest was delivered personally to UN Secretary General Ban Ki-moon on November 19, 2015, by the Venezuelan Ambassador to the United Nations Jorge Valero.[83] There has seldom been a more flagrant example of double standards.

While the credibility of the Human Rights Council is not yet totally dead, we must admit that it is seriously wounded *vulneratus non victus*. Alas, the UN Security Council does not earn any laurels in this respect either. Both are gladiator arenas where countries are only trying to score points. Will these two institutions ever develop into civilized fora of constructive debate over matters of war and peace, human rights and the very survival of humanity? Indeed, as the increasing split between the West and the rest of the world deepens, is it conceivable that the latter might decide to abandon these institutions and create their own human rights institutions, as they are already doing in the areas of trade and financial transactions, shipping and insurance?[84]

CHAPTER 4

THE INTERNATIONAL CRIMINAL COURT

"There is a double standard in the ICC's treatment of the situations in Ukraine and Palestine. This is largely due to political coercion by the United States, which isn't even a party to the ICC's Rome Statute."

PROFESSOR MARJORIE COHN, MARCH 25, 2023[1]

THE ADMINISTRATION of justice serves crucial functions in civilized society, both domestically and internationally. Courts are established to preserve the peace among citizens and nations by interpreting laws and regulations in concrete cases, settling disputes, and establishing precedents. They are intended not only to establish justice with regard to the parties to a particular dispute but more broadly to serve as future-oriented guidelines for judges, lawyer, parliamentarians, politicians, police officers, and citizens. Judicial precedents constitute what in the U.S. and UK is called "common law," enjoying significant advantage over codes and statutes in that they do not require further interpretation; their "added value" is precisely their illustrative and concrete application of the law to a specific set of facts and circumstances, which are likely to repeat themselves in future dispute situations. However, precedents are only valuable if and when they are applied uniformly for everyone and if the principle of *stare decisis* is respected.

The authority and credibility of courts necessarily depend on their objectivity and rigorous observance of due process. In other words, courts must be bound by fair and transparent rules of procedure, which must be applied uniformly and not *à la carte*. In any dispute the overarching rule must be *"audiatur et altera pars"*—to listen to all sides, pro-actively search the truth, contextualize and assess facts, evaluate situations on a case-by-case basis without taking "short cuts."

The rule of law must correspond as much as possible to the rule of justice, employing objective tools to arrive at reasonable conclusions that can be accepted by society as valid expressions of the law.[2]

Following the First World War, a Permanent Court of International Justice (PCIJ) was established, which attempted in the period from 1922 to 1946 to settle disputes among nations peacefully. It was replaced by the International Court of Justice (ICJ) after the Second World War, which applies Article 38 of its statute in interpreting treaties, laws and precedents. The ICJ also issues "advisory opinions" on questions of law, which are extremely useful in deciphering the complexities of the law in concrete cases, always aiming at doing justice *ex aequo et bono.*

The function of international criminal courts, however, is more difficult, because the jurisdiction of these courts is not universal, and the courts are not always perceived as being objective in applying norms uniformly in all cases. By their very nature, criminal courts are intended to investigate criminal and asocial behaviour and to condemn those who have harmed domestic society or the international commonweal. The administration of domestic criminal justice is, of course, much easier to supervise than that of international criminal tribunals, which have far greater difficulty in establishing and maintaining their impartiality.

International criminal courts should beware of "playing God" by dividing the world into the bad goats and the good sheep. Needless to say, "Judgement day" must not be equivalent to "winner takes all," whereby the victorious states put the vanquished leaders before a rigged tribunal for the purpose of cementing their victory by imposing a badge of infamy on the vanquished, the badge of being the "bad guy." That said, there is nonetheless no guarantee that, at the end of a military engagement, the "virtuous" side has prevailed, and accordingly no guarantee that it is the "good guys" who are now subjecting the "bad guys" to accountability for their crimes. As has been frequently said, a war does not adjudicate who is right and virtuous, but only determines who is left. The adage has been attributed to Andrew Carnegie, Bertrand Russell and even Winston Churchill.

The credibility of an international penal tribunal will always depend on its impartiality, in its applying the same rules to all those suspected of having breached international law. The Roman "*vae victis*" (woe to the defeated) is irreconcilable with the essential quality of every tribunal—i.e. impartiality. Hence any international penal instance must ensure that its jurisdiction encompasses ALL persons who are suspected of having broken the law, and not merely ousted officials, fallen political leaders or vanquished generals and soldiers.[3]

The U.S. Chief prosecutor at the International Military Tribunal for Nuremberg (IMT), Robert H. Jackson, wisely stated in his opening statement in October 1945 that "while this law is first applied against German aggressors, the law includes, and if it is to serve a useful purpose, it must condemn aggression by any other nations, including those which sit here now in judgment."[4] Similarly, the Tribunal's 1946 judgment concluded that: "to initiate a war of aggression is not only an international crime; it is the supreme international crime, differing only from other war crimes in that it contains within itself the accumulated evil of the whole."[5]

And in the same way as the prohibition of the crime of aggression extends to any aggression committed by any country (e.g. the USSR aggression against Finland in November 1939 and against Poland in September 1939), the prohibition of war crimes and crimes against humanity must provide for the indictment of all suspects, regardless of their country of origin. This does not mean that the "*tu quoque*" (you too have done similarly) principle should result in impunity. On the contrary, "*tu quoque*" must be inclusive and require the prosecution of all subjects, who in turn must enjoy the presumption of innocence and due process as provided for in Article 14 of the International Covenant on Civil and Political Rights. "*Tu quoque*" cannot mean exclusion of one side from just prosecution.

Of course, the London Agreement of August 8, 1945 which laid down the statute of the IMT suffered from a fundamental "birth defect" or "original sin"—it was a classic victor's tribunal. The judges and prosecutors all came from the four victorious powers, none of them came from neutral countries. The only persons indicted and tried were their defeated enemies.

The statute of the IMT did not envisage universal jurisdiction—the capacity to indict all persons who were suspected of violating the Hague and Geneva Conventions on the laws of war and international humanitarian law applicable in 1939, when the war started. It was outside its mandate to prosecute USSR officials for the execution of some

15,000 Polish officers and soldiers at Katyn and elsewhere, impossible to prosecute the Royal Airforce for the carpet-bombing of population centres in Germany[6] causing some 600,000 civilian deaths or for the crimes of the "dam-busters" who destroyed German dams causing horrendous floods and tens of thousands of civilian deaths,[7] for the terror bombing of Tokyo, the atomic bombing of Hiroshima on August 6, 1945 or for the recidivist bombing of Nagasaki on August 9, 1945.

It was not possible to hold the participants of the Potsdam Conference accountable for the decision to "transfer" some 14/15 million ethnic Germans from territories where their ancestors had lived for seven hundred years, for the expulsion and spoliation of the Germans of East Prussia, Pomerania, Silesia, East Brandenburg, Bohemia, Moravia, and for the expulsion of German "minorities" from Slovakia, Hungary, Slovenia, Croatia, Serbia, Romania, Bulgaria etc. Although the far less severe Nazi expulsion of French persons from Alsace and Polish persons from the Warthegau were judged by the Nuremberg Tribunal to constitute war crimes under Article 6b of the Statute and crimes against humanity pursuant to Article 6c of the Statute, none of the Allied powers were indicted, let alone convicted, for the worst "ethnic cleansing" that Europe had ever experienced. These purely racist expulsions were not based on individual guilt determined by a court of law. They were expelled for the one and only reason that they were German and that the victors wanted to take over their lands free of any people on them. Bearing in mind that at least 2 million human beings did not survive their "transfer," this demographic disaster remains one of the greatest crimes of the 20th century.[8] No one was ever held accountable for this crime—not the Soviets, the Poles, the Czechs, the Slovaks, the Hungarians, the Yugoslavs, nor the Anglo-Americans who approved the policy in Article XIII of the Potsdam Communiqué, issued at the conclusion of the Potsdam Conference of July/August 1945. Surely the expulsion of the Germans in 1945–48 was far more serious than the "ethnic cleansing" practised in Yugoslavia during the 1990s, which the international community unanimously condemned.[9]

The requirement that every tribunal be impartial and that all persons suspected of having broken the law be judged by the same tribunal and under the same laws goes back to the most basic principle of equality, enunciated in Article 1 of the Universal Declaration of Human Rights: "All human beings are born free and equal in dignity and rights." Therefore, when it comes to choosing who is to be accused of a crime, discrimination is not acceptable, nor is it legitimate to seek punishment against only some participants in a crime, while others can enjoy impunity.

Besides the IMT at Nuremberg many other tribunals have had their credibility tarnished by the same "original sin," including the 12 U.S. post-Nuremberg Trials, the trials conducted by the British occupation courts, e.g. the *Peleus Trial,*[10] the Tokyo Trials that prosecuted the Japanese but not the British forces for atrocities that are well documented in the *Parliamentary Debates* of the House of Commons in London and in the logbooks of the Royal Navy, or U.S. crimes substantiated in the official history of the U.S. Navy, which describes *inter alia* the systematic killing of Japanese shipwrecked sailors after the battle of the Bismarck Sea.[11] While the Nuremberg and Tokyo tribunals were fundamentally flawed as "victor's tribunals" or "kangaroo courts," there is no doubt that they resulted in considerable "added value," because the trials allowed the systematic collection and evaluation of evidence. The Nuremberg and Tokyo records provide invaluable insights not only for archivists and historians, but also for political scientists, sociologists, psychologists,[12] etc.

FUNCTIONS AND COMPETENCE OF THE INTERNATIONAL CRIMINAL COURT[13]

The idea of establishing an international criminal court (ICC) had been debated since the Nuremberg Trials. Following the dissolution of the Soviet Union and the implosion of Yugoslavia, which engendered the International Criminal Tribunal for the Former Yugoslavia, it seemed like the time was ripe for the creation of an international criminal tribunal with wide competences.

After many drafting exercises, the Statute of Rome was adopted in July 1998 and entered into force in January 2002. The statute gives the ICC jurisdiction to investigate and prosecute under Article 5 (crime of aggression), Art. 6 (genocide), art. 7 (crimes against humanity) and Article 8 (war crimes). The ICC has no jurisdiction over piracy, trafficking in persons, money-laundering, international embezzlement, or drug-trafficking.

Unlike the International Court of Justice, which does possess universal jurisdiction, since all UN member States are automatically parties to the ICJ statute, the new ICC can only exercise jurisdiction *vis à vis* states parties that have signed on and ratified the Statute of Rome. A further "original sin" plaguing the ICC is the fact that major powers like the U.S., Russia and China are not parties to the statute and that the U.S., in gross violation of Article 18 of the Vienna Convention on the Law of Treaties, started subverting the ICC early on by pursuing bilateral treaties with some 80 States parties to the statute, forbidding them from ever delivering an American citizen to the court. Such bilateral treaties institutionalizing impunity are, of course, *contra bonos mores*, and incompatible with the object and purpose of the ICC statute. A future meeting of states parties to the Statute of Rome should address the issue of whether these bilateral treaties are compatible with international law, with the object and purpose of the ICC statute itself, and whether they could ever be honoured by ICC states parties. In principle, states parties must choose between membership in the ICC or withdrawing from the statute altogether if they intend to give effect to the bilateral agreements with the U.S., which should be seen as invalid *ab initio* pursuant to Article 53 of the Vienna Convention on the Law of Treaties.

To add insult to injury, the U.S. government during the administration of Donald Trump imposed sanctions on the ICC Chief Prosecutor Fatou Bensouda (the Gambia) and members of her staff in connection with the planned investigation of war crimes committed by NATO forces in Afghanistan and Iraq. Besides the fact that unilateral coercive measures are illegal in international law, it is important for purposes of the credibility of the ICC to see how issues of principle such as sanctions imposed on an international tribunal were dealt with by the ICC, the international community and the media. Notably, when her term expired, her UK replacement simply discontinued the investigation.

Notwithstanding the above, it is still pertinent to see whether, in its first 20 years of operation, the ICC has lived up to expectations. Such a tribunal would only serve its purpose if there were an apparent commitment by the international community to investigate all war crimes and crimes against humanity, regardless of whom the perpetrator may be. Under the rule of law, there cannot be punishment for some and impunity for others. This runs counter every sense of ethical behaviour and to the very ontology of justice.

The ICC's performance since its establishment in 2002 leaves much to be desired. Indeed, the ICC has demonstrated double standards and selective indignation with respect to the gravest violations of the Statute of Rome. Thus far only Africans have been indicted. Investigations seem to prosper only when the accused are geopolitical rivals of the United States and the European Union. Many observers have even posed the question whether the ICC has developed into a neo-colonial tool of the West, an institution used to intimidate and prosecute enemies of the U.S., UK and EU, in particular former colonies in Africa.

Today we hear politicians demanding a "Nuremberg" Trial against Putin. Well, why not a Tribunal to investigate and condemn the crimes of aggression committed by Bill Clinton in Yugoslavia, by George W. Bush, Tony Blair and Jose Maria Aznar in Iraq and Afghanistan, by Barack Obama in Libya, Syria and Ukraine (after all, Obama was president when the "no fly" zone over Libya was manipulated for "regime change"; we all remember Hillary Clinton's infamous words: "We came, we saw, he died."[14] We also remember Obama's involvement in the Maidan *coup d'état* against the democratically elected president of Ukraine, Victor Yanukovych in February 2014. If the ICC were to become seized of the Ukraine conflict, it would have to investigate the crimes committed by Ukrainian sharp-shooters targeting both sides of the protesters at Maidan,[15] the shelling of civilian targets in the Donbas by Ukraine since 2014, and the refusal of Ukraine to implement the Minsk Agreements of 2014 and 2015.

It should seem obvious to any legally-minded person that the ICC also has a responsibility to investigate and prosecute NATO forces from the U.S., UK, Germany, Australia, who committed atrocities e.g., in Afghanistan and Iraq. There is abundant documentation concerning torture centres in Iraq, Afghanistan and Guantánamo.[16] These deserve ICC attention, which should eventually generate indictments and prosecutions. The use of indiscriminate weapons including depleted uranium weapons, white phosphorus, cluster bombs, and land mines, causing tens of thousands of deaths must be investigated; the "collateral damage" visited upon civilians in Afghanistan, Iraq, Syria, Libya, Yemen.... Where is the accountability for all of these crimes?

It does not seem likely that the ICC will earn any credibility unless and until it decides to apply the Statute of Rome uniformly and to open investigations against George W. Bush, Tony Blair, Barak Obama, Donald Trump, Joe Biden, Benjamin Netanyahu, Mohammed bin Salman, and other powerful figures. Hitherto Western powers have enjoyed impunity, not unlike the impunity enjoyed by the European colonial powers for their atrocities in the colonies of Africa and Asia, or by the United States and Canada with regard to crimes committed against the indigenous nations of the Americas and the sequels thereof,[17] and the crimes committed against the native population of Hawaii, whose kingdom was overthrown by the U.S. in 1893 with its population subsequently reduced to a servile state.[18]

Whereas in 2020 the then chief prosecutor at the International Criminal Court, Fatou Bensouda,[19] had announced that she would investigate allegations of war crimes and crimes against humanity in the Afghan war,[20] including crimes allegedly committed by NATO members, Bensouda's successor Karim Khan[21] (UK) did a U-turn and announced that whereas he would continue investigations concerning war crimes by the Taliban, he would discontinue the investigation against U.S. forces.[22] This refusal to investigate NATO crimes fully delegitimizes the ICC[23] and confirms what many already know, that it is in the service of the Western powers.

Nothing discredits the ICC more than this flagrant absence of objectivity and impartiality.

Following the decision by ICC Chief Prosecutor Karim Khan to discontinue investigations of war crimes by U.S. and NATO forces in Afghanistan, but to resume investigation concerning crimes committed by the Taliban, Patricia Gossman, the associate director for Asia at Human Rights Watch, rightfully told the Associated Press it was a "really disturbing statement by the prosecutor to say the investigation will only prioritize some of the parties to the conflict—and in particular seemingly to ignore entirely the very serious allegations against U.S. forces and CIA."[24]

In an article dated March 25, 2023, Professor Marjorie Cohn reminded us that in March 2020, the ICC had authorized the formal investigation into U.S., Afghan and Taliban officials for war crimes committed in the "war on terror." The ICC prosecutor Fatou Bensouda "had found reasonable grounds to believe that, pursuant to a U.S.

policy, members of the CIA had committed war crimes. They included torture, cruel treatment, outrages upon personal dignity, rape and other types of sexual violence against people held in detention facilities in Afghanistan, Romania, Poland and Lithuania."[25] Cohn believes that when the Biden administration lifted the sanctions that Donald Trump had levied on ICC personnel, "it did so with the tacit understanding that the court's probe on U.S. crimes wouldn't resume."[26] Jennifer Gibson, a lawyer with the human rights group Reprieve said: "This was clearly a political decision—there's really no other way it can be nterpreted." She continued: "It gave the U.S., the UK and their allies a get out of jail free card."

But let us return to the issue of starting an investigation against Vladimir Putin[27] in connection with the Ukraine war. This proposal has been echoed by many Western politicians and the media, which seem to imply that such an investigation would somehow advance justice.

True enough, the Russian invasion of Ukraine on February 24, 2022 entailed the crime of aggression for purposes of Art. 6a of the Nuremberg Statute, UN Resolution 3314, Article 5 of the ICC statute and the 2010 Kampala definition of aggression. This is clear enough, but to begin: the ICC has a serious problem of jurisdiction, since neither Russia nor Ukraine are parties to the Statute of Rome. War crimes have already been committed—on both sides.[28]

Both Russia and Ukraine are states parties to the Four Geneva Red Cross Conventions of 1949 and the 1977 Additional Protocols, which oblige them to investigate and prosecute members of their own armed forces who are suspected of having committed grave breaches of international humanitarian law. To the extent that the State whose soldiers have committed war crimes actually does proceed to investigate and prosecute them, the ICC principle of complementarity excludes the admissibility of those cases. Article 17 of the Rome Statute stipulates in part: "the Court shall determine that a case is inadmissible where: (a) The case is being investigated or prosecuted by a State which has jurisdiction over it, unless the State is unwilling or unable genuinely to carry out the investigation or prosecution...."

Accordingly, to the extent that the Russian and Ukrainian authorities can make a showing that they are carrying out investigations in good faith and are willing to prosecute and do indict those responsible for the alleged crimes, the ICC cannot intervene.

To the surprise and consternation of many international lawyers, ICC prosecutor Karim Kahn announced on March 17, 2023 that the Pre-Trial Chamber had issued an arrest warrant for Russian President Vladimir Putin for the commission of war crimes in Ukraine. The PTC also issued an arrest warrant for Maria Lvova-Belova, commissioner for children's rights in the Office of the President of the Russian Federation, for the same war crimes.[29]

There are those who think that the indictment of Vladimir Putin by the ICC may be the last nail in the coffin burying the ICC's credibility. Bearing in mind that the ICC was established in 2002, in its 20 years of operation it had hitherto only indicted Africans, and for that reason was rightly called neo-colonial. Its present indictment of Putin reveals another flagrant Western bias.

Since the entry into force of the Rome Statute there have been thousands of war crimes that can rightfully laid at the door of NATO governments, for which no one from the West was ever indicted. War crimes have been documented in the NATO wars in Yugoslavia, Afghanistan, Iraq, Libya and Syria. Why has no one ever been indicted there? The ICC can only serve its purpose if it is rigorously independent, objective and professional. The weaponization of the ICC to buttress U.S. imperialism is self-destructive, in view of how it has refrained from indicting Tony Blair, George W. Bush, Barack Obama (the king of the drones), Donald Trump (Soleimani assassination), Boris Johnson, Joe Biden, Benjamin Netanyahu, Mohammed bin Salman. More and more lawyers and journalists in the Global South are asking these questions.[30]

INTERNATIONAL AD HOC TRIBUNALS

Could the United Nations establish an *ad hoc* tribunal similar to the International Criminal Tribunal for the former Yugoslavia or the International Criminal Tribunal for Rwanda? The ICTY was established by UN Security Council Resolution 827 of May 25, 1993; the ICTR by UN Security Council Resolution 955 of November 8, 1994. By contrast, the UN Security Council would not be able to establish an *ad hoc* tribunal to try Putin, or for that matter Zelensky, because

Russia, China the U.S., UK or France would certainly exercise the veto power against it.

It can be concluded that the frequent references to the Nuremberg Trials by journalists and politicians alike serve little more than propaganda purposes, whether by intent or ignorance. The historical conditions that enabled the 1945 International Military Tribunal due to Germany's unconditional surrender, are unlikely in this instance. There is no likelihood of an unconditional surrender by Russia in the Ukraine war, and if NATO were to escalate further, and if Russia were to feel existentially threatened, the world would be risking a nuclear confrontation and the Apocalypse of humanity.

Could this be possible due to the progressive development of international law that has led to the expansion of the concept of universal jurisdiction, which enables any country to detain a person found within its territorial jurisdiction if that person is suspected of having committed war crimes? Some countries like Germany[31] and Sweden[32] have already exercised universal jurisdiction over war crimes. Especially in cases of alleged genocide, a trial under universal jurisdiction would be conceivable if a given country can establish *in personam* jurisdiction against persons who are deemed to be "*hostes humani generis*"—enemies of all mankind. For that, however, the person would have to physically enter the territory of the State exercising universal jurisdiction. And here too, the principle of universal jurisdiction loses legitimacy, unless it is applied uniformly. In other words, if a Saudi official involved in the murder of Jamal Khashoggi were to enter German or Swedish territory, he/she, too, should be arrested and tried. If George W. Bush were to travel to Germany or Sweden, he should be arrested and tried for his responsibility in the commission of the crimes of aggression, war crimes and crimes against humanity.

Yet another possibility to prosecute Putin would be to hold a trial *in absentia,* which would serve the purpose of documenting the crimes, even if the enforcement of the tribunal's judgment would be doubtful, unless Putin were to enter the territory of the country where the judgment was issued.

There remains the possibility of convening a "Peoples' Tribunal" with broad jurisdiction to investigate war crimes committed by all parties to the conflict. Surely the Ukrainians are compiling evidence of Russian crimes, as the Russians are compiling evidence of war crimes by Ukrainians and foreign mercenaries. Admittedly Peoples' Tribunals have no international recognition and their judgments are not enforceable, but they do have the added value of drawing attention to war crimes that the mainstream media has ignored or even white-washed. A Peoples' Tribunal could also collect the evidence, listen to the testimony of hundreds of victims and identify the provisions of the Geneva Conventions that have been violated. The issue is to secure the adequate representation of both sides to the conflict.

I can refer to the Kuala Lumpur War Crimes Tribunal[33] that sat in 2009–2011 and convicted both George W. Bush and Tony Blair of war crimes and crimes against humanity for the invasion of Iraq in 2003, which the then UN Secretary General Kofi Annan correctly described as an "illegal war."[34] The Kuala Lumpur Tribunal sat again in 2013 to examine allegations of genocide perpetrated by Israel against the Palestinians and issued a judgment confirming the commission of the crime of genocide under the 1948 Genocide Convention.[35] Unfortunately, although the Kuala Lumpur Tribunal was a very serious court and not a PR exercise, the mainstream media has given it no visibility, precisely because the convicted criminals are still being whitewashed in the U.S. and UK, and the apologetics for Western crimes has become an epidemic. It is pure negationism.

The *Fondazione Lelio Basso* established the famous Permanent Peoples Tribunal.[36] which has held 49 sessions and heard many cases since 1979, starting with the crimes committed by Morocco against the people of Western Sahara.[37]

Maybe a trial of Vladimir Putin, Volodymyr Zelensky, Joe Biden, Jens Stoltenberg and others would clarify many outstanding legal and moral issues surrounding the war in Ukraine, but the ICC would certainly not be the right venue.

USEFUL INVESTIGATION THAT THE ICC COULD BUT WILL NOT UNDERTAKE

In connection with the crime of aggression, comparable with the crime against peace stipulated in Article 6a of the Nuremberg statute, the ICC could consider the question whether the crime of "provocation" does not in itself constitute a violation of Article 2(4) of the UN Charter as a "threat or use of force" within the meaning of

Article 39 of the Charter. Is not the eastern expansion of NATO to the very borders of Russia a threat of the use of force, i.e. a provocation, despite the barrage of Western media narratives constantly referring to it as "unprovoked"? Does this expansion, contrary to promises made to Gorbachev 1989–91, constitute an existential menace to Russia's national security justifying some kind of self-defence? The ICC could also consider whether the refusal to negotiate in good faith under Article 2(3) of the UN Charter or the refusal to even consider peace negotiations after hostilities have started in itself does not constitute a crime against humanity for purposes of Article 7 of the Statute of Rome.

In order to vindicate its *raison d'être*, the ICC must serve humanity by advancing its sense of justice and security; it must use the Statute of Rome constructively so as to identify the root causes of the four crimes under its jurisdiction. Only thus can it contribute to prevention of future crimes.

Punishment cannot be the ICC's primary concern because punishment is always *ex post facto* and practically never delivers on its claims to provide deterrence of future crime. Punishment essentially only satisfies the basest instincts of the human being: revenge. Moreover, punishment, when it is not perceived as just but only as a continuation of the war by judicial means and an additional form of character assassination and humiliation, does not serve either peace or justice. Such punishment merely keeps the animosities and resentments between peoples simmering and may ultimately contribute to inflame future passions for countermeasures to avenge the humiliation. In a very real sense punishment can prove counter-productive and engender further crimes. Instead, what is most necessary is to break the vicious circle of crime and revenge.

What else can the ICC do to vindicate its mission? For one, the ICC should investigate the corrosive impact of unilateralism and exceptionalism on the commitment of world leaders to prevent the crime of aggression, which is then invariably followed by war crimes and crimes against humanity. It should investigate the role of fake news and propaganda in creating negative caricatures of geopolitical rivals and constituting incitement to racial hatred. Such incitement and war propaganda are prohibited by Article 20 of the International Covenant on Civil and Political Rights. While many of these issues could be considered outside the mandate of the ICC, nothing prevents the judges from addressing them in their rationale. Indeed, some important progress in international jurisprudence has had its origins in "*obiter dicta*" contained in prior judgments.

Opening of an investigation into the crimes committed in connection with the "extraordinary rendition"[38] program, the systematic torture[39] practiced in Abu Ghraib, Guantanamo and secret CIA-prisons would all be within the ICC's mandate, both *ratione materiae* and *ratione temporis*.[40] The ICC could also consider whether the existence of military alliances like NATO, with its history of illegal interventions in many countries, is compatible with the Statute of Rome and with the UN Charter itself, which confers on the Security Council the exclusive authority to use force pursuant to Chapter VII. The ICC should consider whether, in the light of the wars of aggression conducted by NATO countries and the gross violations of human rights and international humanitarian law perpetrated by NATO forces, particularly in Afghanistan and Iraq, NATO can be placed in the category of a "criminal organization" for purposes of Articles 9 and 10 of the Statute of the Nuremberg Tribunal.[41]

The crimes committed by the Sri Lankan government against the Tamil population during the unsuccessful 30-year war for Eelam Tamil self-determination would certainly fall within its competence pursuant to Articles 7 and 8 of the Rome Statute.[42] Here, an investigation is overdue.

The 2014 Ayotzinapa disappearance, massacre and subsequent cover-up of the murder of 43 students with the involvement by Mexican state actors could not be properly investigated prior to the election of Mexican President Andrés Manuel Lopez Obrador in December 2018, who has promised to get to the bottom of the scandal.[43] Because of the complementarity rule, the ICC would have had no jurisdiction to investigate, but should the Mexican investigation falter, perhaps the ICC could lend a helping hand.

More generally, the ICC should investigate whether a new phenomenon—the proliferation of unilateral coercive measures as a principal U.S. weapon in the hybrid war to maintain its unipolar hegemony—should be recognized as a significant threat to the peace and security of mankind for purposes of Article 39 of the UN Charter. It must be remembered that Art. 2(4) of the UN Charter, which prohibits both the threat and the use of force, does *not* limit the concept of force to military force. Indeed, states use many kinds of force against other states, and economic coercion in the form of sanctions and financial blockades must be understood in the reality of 21st century nonconventional warfare as constituting "force" for purposes of Article 2(4). It must be acknowledged that sanctions kill,[44] that sanctions trigger famine and disease that may cause the death of hundreds of thousands of human beings, just as much as the siege of Leningrad by the Nazis 1941–44 killed between 700,000 and a million human beings.[45]

It is important for the ICC to understand and address the non-conventional wars that are being waged to asphyxiate the economies of targeted countries, without the perpetrator(s) ever bothering to issue a formal declaration of war, without firing a single drone or missile against the perceived "enemy." Financial and naval blockades deliberately create humanitarian crises as is the case in Gaza[46] and Yemen,[47] where famine and scarcity of medicines have resulted in many thousands of deaths. Such blockades certainly constitute the "use of force" and are a form of aggression that must be investigated by the ICC as falling within the scope of Articles 5 and 7 of the Rome Statute. Indeed, UCM's demonstrably have resulted in tens of thousands of deaths in Cuba, Nicaragua, Syria, Venezuela.[48]

For more than two decades, UCM's have been examined by numerous UN bodies and repeatedly condemned,[49] e.g., by the Sub-Commission on the Promotion and Protection of Human Rights in a comprehensive report written by Belgian Professor Marc Bossuyt,[50] by the Committee on Economic Social and Cultural Rights in its 1997 general comment Nr. 8,[51] by UN High Commissioner for Human Rights Navi Pillay in her thematic report A/19/33 issued in January 2012,[52] and by two special rapporteurs of the UN Human Rights Council, Dr. Idriss Jazairy and Professor Alena Douhan,[53] in several reports since the establishment of the mandate in 2015.

Another issue which the ICC should investigate is whether the persecution of whistleblowers like Julian Assange[54] facilitate the commission of war crimes and crimes against humanity and thus fall within the scope of Articles 7 and 8 of the Statute, as part of a conspiracy to enable impunity for war crimes and crimes against humanity by legitimizing coverups and state secrecy. The ICC should interpret the Statute of Rome broadly, so as to give concrete meaning to the object and purpose of the ICC, which must also focus on the *prevention* of future crimes.

As indicated above, war crimes have undoubtedly been committed, both on the Russian and the Ukrainian sides, also by the thousands of mercenaries and international brigades that have not observed the applicable Geneva Conventions, who have tortured and killed prisoners of war without mercy. For greater effectiveness, such investigations and trials should be conducted only by the countries concerned. The Ukrainians have an interest in maintaining discipline in their armies. Ditto the Russians. Were either to do so, would it not positively impact global opinion? All States parties to the 1949 Geneva Red Cross Conventions are already obliged to try their own criminals. Here is where emphasis must be placed.

AMNESTIES AND TRUTH COMMISSIONS

On the other hand, there are valid historical precedents for ending major wars with amnesties[55]—too many to count. Let us start with the Thirty Years' War (1618–48) that wiped out some 8 million Europeans. Notwithstanding the monstrous atrocities committed, no war crimes trials were ever held or even envisaged, no retribution was stipulated in the 1648 Treaties of Münster and Osnabrück but rather, Article 2 of both peace treaties provided for a general amnesty. Too much blood had been spilt. Europe needed a rest, and "punishment" was left to God: "There shall be on the one side and the other a perpetual Oblivion, Amnesty, or Pardon of all that has been committed...in such a manner, that no body . . . shall practice any Acts of Hostility, entertain any Enmity, or cause any Trouble to each other."[56] The Peace of Westphalia of 1648 has gone down in history as a milestone of international law and a reasonable effort at establishing a European security architecture.[57]

We can also refer to Article 3 of the Treaty of Rijswijk (1697), which ordained amnesty for the soldiers of the French and British monarchies. Article XI of the Final Act of the Congress of Vienna (1815) stipulated amnesties, notwithstanding the atrocities of the Napoleonic wars. In the Brest-Litovsk treaty of March 3, 1918, a treaty imposed by the Central powers on Russia, the parties renounced any claims for their costs of warfare as well as any compensation for war damages. No war crimes trials were envisioned. Germany was forced to abrogate the Treaty of Brest-Litovsk pursuant to Art. 116 of the Treaty of Versailles of 1919, which introduced the idea of trying the Kaiser and some 1000 German officers.[58] More recently, Chapter II of the Evian Accords of 1962, which ended the ferocious Algerian war of independence, ordained an amnesty for both sides.

The idea of reconciliation is also endorsed in Article 6 of the 1977 Second Additional Protocol to the Geneva Conventions of 1949, which stipulates in part: "At the end of hostilities, the authorities in power shall endeavour to grant the broadest possible amnesty to persons who have participated in the armed conflict." This does not intend to ensure overall "impunity." Rather, it is intended to further peace and reconciliation. Peace is indeed a higher good. *Pax optima rerum.*

Admittedly, the Western media and many Western academics reject the concept of "amnesty" and seem to be hooked on vengeance. In a very real sense, the establishment of the International Criminal Court and its dismal 20-year record document the proposition that in human rights terms, this kind of "international criminal justice" actually constitutes a retrogression.

Far from advancing toward a universalist system of justice under the rule of law, a system that would promote equity and reconciliation, we are falling back to archaic times of *vae victis* and *lex talionis*, where punishment and revenge were equated with justice. Yet, should enlightened society not endeavour instead to break the vicious circle of injustice and counter-injustice, pursue an honest search to identify the sources of grievances and remove the root causes of conflict? Civilization entails acknowledging the wisdom of forgiveness in the name of reconciliation.

The atmosphere surrounding the ICC and its self-serving propaganda serves peace badly, and is a disservice to the enlightened thinking reflected in the UN Charter and the UDHR. The ICC means the continuation of war by lawfare and by the attempt to perpetuate the dominance of the victors by relentless propaganda and the falsification of the historical record into a caricature of events, a black and white narrative. Ultimately this means civilizational retrogression, a rejection of the fundamental truths of all world religions from Hinduism to Christianity, of humanistic philosophy from Confucius to Buddha, from Socrates to Noam Chomsky.

In my earlier publications I had advocated the establishment of an international criminal court.[59] In my year as visiting professor of international law at DePaul University, I collaborated with the late Professor Cherif Bassiouni in the drafting of a possible statute. We also jointly published a book titled *Human Rights in the Administration of Criminal Justice*.[60] Developments have taught me otherwise. I am profoundly disappointed.

While the present ICC deserves to be abolished, can the possibility of such an international legal project be saved?

CHAPTER 5

The Organization for the Prohibition of Chemical Weapons (OPCW)

"The manner in which this serious controversy has been handled by OPCW management. . . . has sought to cover up any serious questioning of the OPCW through stonewalling and unacceptable smear tactics. . . . The Security Council cannot be surprised that there is increasing public pressure for UN leadership to find an unbiased resolution of this troubling controversy."[1]

HANS VON SPONECK, FORMER ASSISTANT SECRETARY GENERAL AND HUMANITARIAN COORDINATOR FOR IRAQ, BEFORE THE SECURITY COUNCIL, APRIL 16, 2021

WAR IS THE MOTHER of lies.[2] Since time immemorial Trojan horses,[3] perfidy, and false flags have accompanied armed conflict. Today's propaganda is far more proficient than in prior centuries and the dissemination of fake news and fake narratives not only by governments and its intelligence services, but also by private lobbies, internet bots, and paid operatives has multiple purposes, among them to buttress the myths that engendered a given conflict, justify illegal aggression and coercive actions, and manufacture consent and dissent. The penetration of the mainstream media by intelligence services has been frequently documented[4]—but this reality is essentially ignored by the general public.[5] Why is this? Is it, as Julius Caesar wrote in *De bello civile*, because humans just believe what they want to believe? (*quae volumus, ea credimus libernter*), or as St. Augustine termed it, *mundus vult decipi*—the world wants to be deceived? I suspect that all humans have a psychological need to believe in something, and we are taught to believe in authority. We want to believe that our authorities are good and virtuous, and setting affairs on the right course. It takes temerity to question conventional truths. It took me decades to gradually realize and accept that the political game is played differently, that we are deceived on a daily basis, and that there are consequences if we challenge those conventional truths, which are there to buttress the power structures that govern us. Thus, it is hardly surprising that so many of us place our faith in our governments and in turn, in certain international institutions that are sold to us as honourable and truthful.

When allegations of war crimes are made, a modicum of prudence and a healthy level of scepticism should tell us not to jump to conclusions before the facts can be reliably established. There is plenty of time to ponder on the consequences. What is not wise is to let ourselves be swept by the propaganda. Independent minds should never rush to conclusions, much less rush to violent "reprisals," when no one is certain of what exactly has occurred. A reprisal without factual basis is not only unwise; it constitutes a war crime.

The first question that an intelligent person should pose is the old Ciceronian question, *"cui bono?"*[6]—who benefits from a particular event, fact, omission, or interpretation thereof?

Civilized society depends on a network of institutions and organizations under the rule of law that are tasked with investigating allegations and suspicions, verifying compliance with treaty obligations, separating fact from fiction. One of those treaties is the Non-Proliferation Treaty[7] of 1968 (in force 1970), with 191 states parties to date. The NPT is intended to pave the way to nuclear disarmament, as stipulated in Article 6. Alas, the nuclear powers have failed in 53 years to engage in good faith negotiations aimed at nuclear disarmament and the destruction of nuclear stockpiles. The world missed a unique opportunity in 1989–91 when Mikhail Gorbachev offered just that to the Western powers, but NATO would have none of it, because NATO is a self-perpetuating institution that needs an enemy to justify its very existence. Thus, Gorbachev's peace overtures[8] and humanity's chance to be freed from the menace posed by nuclear weapons and to postpone Apocalypse was lost, deliberately wasted, to the benefit of the military-industrial complex, the merchants of death and other war profiteers.

Another treaty that makes a lot of sense—if taken seriously and applied in good faith—is the Treaty on the Prohibition of Chemical Weapons[9] under which auspices the international Organisation on the Prohibition of Chemical Weapons with 193 states parties was established.[10] This organization has been entrusted with a hugely important task—to ensure that countries stop producing chemical weapons and destroy existing stockpiles. Of course, the use of chemical weapons constitutes an internationally wrongful act that must be denounced, investigated, and prosecuted. As we have seen in the previous chapter on international criminal justice, the record of prosecution for the use of prohibited weapons, including chemical weapons, is dismal.

Transparency and accountability are hallmarks of every institution under the rule of law. Here too, the authority, credibility and ultimately the effectiveness of institutions depend on the professional and impartial performance of their mandates. *Ultra vires* activities and unethical tampering with evidence constitute a form of fraud perpetrated against society and destroy the trust placed in the institutions.

This unsatisfactory situation can lead to cynicism, because when unethical conduct has been exposed, when evidence has been tampered with and when reports are based on incorrect facts or incorrect narratives, the very *raison d'être* of the institution is put into question. Many who realize that they have been lied to will no longer respect the institution and will reject its exercise of authority, considering it illegitimate or a manifestation of *magna latrocinia* (kingdoms of theft).[11] This may induce the further tearing of the social contract that holds society together.

There are abundant examples of organizations being so subjected to political pressures, intimidation and blackmail that they can no longer function professionally, and their reports must be put into question. All too often teleological reports are issued by governments, pseudo-investigations that seek *à priori* to arrive at politically desirable conclusions or to justify *à posteriori* the illegal use of force in "retaliation" for a non-existent fact (e.g., the invasion of Iraq in 2003 based on false accusations of weapons of mass destruction, the bombardment of Syria in 2017 based on false accusations of a chemical attack). "Assessments," "investigations" and reports that are not conducted under a strict code of deontology are *contra bonos mores,* because they are methodologically corrupted and distort reality.

All states parties to the Chemical Weapons Convention have the right and duty to demand transparent investigations of flawed methodologies and the withdrawal of politically-tainted reports. The situation becomes aggravated when an institution fails to conduct timely internal investigations and refuses to address pertinent questions raised by its own inspectors. There is an *erga omnes* obligation on all States parties to the Chemical Weapons Convention to ensure that its monitoring body, the OPCW, rigidly observes its own terms of reference and refrains from partisan activities. A coverup makes matters even worse. This is why whistleblowers play such an important role in exposing coverups, why whistleblowers are indispensable to democratic societies. Alas, there is a high level of complacency in democratic societies and very little courage on the part of the average citizen to react to institutional misdeeds by demanding accountability from those who have manipulated reality. In such situations whistleblowers must be relieved of the obligation to observe "professional secrecy," because such secrecy would actually facilitate the commission of crimes.

Nevertheless, for any investigation and pushback against coverups to be successful, a free and independent press is necessary. Alas, our experience of the past thirty years is that the mainstream media increasingly disinform the public, uncritically disseminate political narratives and suppress crucial information that the public has a right to know pursuant to Article 19 of the International Covenant on Civil and Political Rights. Again and again, the media has failed to expose what constitutes fraud on the public and on the world.

When international institutions are hijacked and instrumentalized for geopolitical and other ulterior purposes, not only that single hijacking, but the credibility of the entire system of oversight is impacted. *Quis custodiet ipsos custodes?*[12] Who will guard over the guardians? Indeed, when the guardians are no longer trustworthy, when the guardians themselves are corrupted, we can only rely on ourselves, our own judgment, our conscience, our faculties of reason and logic. *Sapere aude!*[13] We are the guardians.

When we deal with the OPCW, we are dealing with a highly politicized body with a pre-history of serious partiality and institutional misconduct. The OPCW's first Director-General Jose Bustani (1997–2003) had ordered an investigation into the question whether Saddam Hussein of Iraq had chemical weapons, something fully within OPCW's remit. The United States, which had been intent on bombing Iraq since 2001, vigorously opposed any such investigation. Bustani was threatened and bullied out of the office, although he had been re-elected for a second term of four years as Director-General.[14] As has been reported in many press organs, if Bustani had conducted the investigation, this would have placed the U.S. in a difficult situation, because the Bush Administration was set on regime change in Iraq,[15] and the investigation would show that there were no such weapons. Later we learned that the UN inspectors appointed by the Security Council, Hans Blix and Mohammed ElBaradei,[16] were not finding any weapons of mass destruction, thus removing the ostensible pretext for a U.S. bombardment of Iraq. It is reported that U.S. Ambassador John Bolton threatened the OPCW first with withdrawal of U.S. support for the organization, so as to cajole member states to support the U.S. initiative to oust Bustani. When Bustani refused to resign, he was bullied by Bolton, who allegedly told him "You have 24 hours to leave the organization, and if you do not comply with this decision by Washington, we have ways to retaliate against you.... We know where your kids live. You have two sons in New York."[17] This should alert every reader to the credibility issue. Can anyone trust an organization that is subjected by government officials to this kind of mobbing and blackmail? Indeed, what is the impact on the credibility of the government that is so doing?

Let us now review the history of the alleged use of chemical weapons by the government of Syrian President Bashar al Assad during the civil war that started in 2011 and quickly developed into an international proxy war. As indicated above, the first question to be asked is "*cui bono?*" Would Assad draw any advantage by using chemical weapons against his own people—and at the risk international condemnation and sanctions weapons? The answer is clearly no.

In the headlong rush to impose regime-change in Syria, NATO's principal talking point was the evidence-free accusation that Assad was using chemical weapons on his own people; this became a widely circulated propaganda meme in 2013, after an alleged sarin attack in Ghouta. Although Bashar Al Assad vigorously denied every allegation, it became necessary for him to destroy his existing stockpile of chemical weapons in 2014 under the supervision of the OPCW[18] so that he would never again be accused of using them, even as he affirmed never to have used them. What other state has done that? Not the U.S., which claims it will meet its 2023 deadline, ten years after Syria.[19]

But did indeed Assad use chemical weapons, when there was no military advantage in doing so but significant public relations disadvantages? False accusations and calumny die hard. Despite the subsequent revelations of the false accusations levelled against Saddam Hussein in 1990 in preparation of the first Gulf War of 1991, and in 2003 in preparation of "Shock and Awe," against Slobodan Milosevich of Serbia with regard to both Bosnia and Kosovo, the calumnies against Muhammar Ghaddafi in 2010–11—what remains embedded in the public's mind?

Why does the public continue to believe government reports that are evidence-free and lack confirmation by a methodologically proper international investigation? Why does the mainstream media act as the echo chamber of the Pentagon and U.S. State Department?

Responsible people do not jump to conclusions, no matter what propaganda is being disseminated. When in May 2013 the Swiss judge, Carla del Ponte, suggested that the Syrian "rebels" and "terrorists" were using sarin,[20] she was promptly silenced by a barrage of criticism and *ad hominem* attacks that eventually led to her resignation from the UN Commission of Inquiry on Syria.

The continuing accusations that the Assad government has used chemical weapons in Syria—even after the public destruction of its stockpiles verified by the OPCW and undertaken by the U.S. itself[21]—is worrisome. It is as if NATO understands that it can rely on public inattention to admitted facts, enabling it to further embed bogus allegations by repeating them at will. If all you have is a hammer, everything looks like a nail.

A particularly outrageous example of misconduct by OPCW officials in connection with the investigation into the alleged use of chemical weapons by the Syrian government concerns the alleged Douma incident in 2018, years after the destruction of Assad's weapons in 2014, leading to the illegal bombing of Syria by the U.S. and UK with extensive "collateral damage." Such an illegal bombardment entailed a violation of Article 2(4) of the UN Charter, the *jus cogens* prohibition of the use of force without approval by the UN Security Council. This brings to mind the internationally wrongful acts by the 49 governments of the "coalition of the willing," which participated in the assault against the Iraqi people in 2003 under the false pretext that Saddam Hussein's possessed weapons of mass destruction and would use them against the West, although he had not threatened anyone and had shown his readiness to cooperate with the United Nations and the Security Council in any investigation. No one was ever punished for the crime against the Iraqi people. There was no reparation paid for the destruction of the country, the looting of its resources, and the death of some one million Iraqis.

Similarly, the use of chemical weapons in Douma was widely attributed by the U.S., UK and Western media to have been perpetrated by the Syrian government. Thus, for these parties, it was imperative that the OPCW confirm the existence of a chemical attack and then pin the blame on the Syrian government and not on the insurgents. The OPCW report had to be drafted in a way that would legitimize the bombardment of Syria by the U.S. and UK, justifying their "retaliation" for the alleged use of chemical weapons—despite the fact that, even if that had been proven beyond the shadow of a doubt, it would not have legitimized the illegal bombardment by the U.S. and UK, which was an egregious violation of Article 2(4) of the UN Charter.

The initial OPCW draft report—which could not establish the responsibility of the Syrian government—was not issued, and a new report had to be elaborated, confirming the U.S.-ordered narrative that there was indeed a chemical attack in Douma in April 2018 and that the Syrian government was responsible.[22] Then long-serving inspectors who were on the ground protested internally against the manipulation of the report. When their internal objections were first ignored and then covered-up, they went public and ever since have endured mobbing, defamation and threats.[23]

A "Statement of Concern" by a group of prominent lawyers and scientists, including the first President of OPCW José Bustani, UN Assistant Secretary General Denis Halliday and UN Assistant Secretary General Hans von Sponeck was issued in 2021:

> We wish to express our deep concern over the protracted controversy and political fall-out surrounding the OPCW and its investigation of the alleged chemical weapons attack in Douma, Syria, on April 7, 2018.
>
> Since the publication by the OPCW of its final report in March 2019, a series of worrying developments has raised serious and substantial concerns with respect to the conduct of that investigation. These developments include instances in which OPCW inspectors involved with the investigation have identified major procedural and scientific

irregularities, the leaking of a significant quantity of cor-
roborating documents, and damning statements provided to
UN Security Council meetings. It is now well established
that some senior inspectors involved with the investigation,
one of whom played a central role, reject how the investigation derived its conclusions, and OPCW management now
stands accused of accepting unsubstantiated or possibly
manipulated findings with the most serious geo-political
and security implications. Calls by some members of the
Executive Council of the OPCW to allow all inspectors to
be heard were blocked.

The inspectors' concerns are shared by the first Director
General of the OPCW, José Bustani, and a significant number of eminent individuals have called for transparency and
accountability at the OPCW. Bustani himself was recently
prevented by key members of the Security Council from participating in a hearing on the Syrian dossier. As Ambassador
Bustani stated in a personal appeal to the Director General,
if the Organization is confident in the conduct of its Douma
investigation then it should have no difficulty addressing the
inspectors' concerns.

To date, unfortunately, the OPCW senior management
has failed to respond to the allegations against it and, despite
making statements to the contrary, we understand has never
properly allowed the views or concerns of the members of
the investigation team to be heard or even met with most of
them. It has, instead, side-stepped the issue by launching an
investigation into a leaked document related to the Douma
case and by publicly condemning its most experienced
inspectors for speaking out.

In a worrying recent development, a draft letter falsely
alleged to have been sent by the Director General to one of
the dissenting inspectors was leaked to an "open source"
investigation website in an apparent attempt to smear the
former senior OPCW scientist. The "open source" website
then published the draft letter together with the identity of
the inspector in question. Even more alarmingly, in a BBC4
radio series aired recently, an anonymous source, reportedly

connected with the OPCW Douma investigation, gave an interview with the BBC in which he contributes to an attempt to discredit not only the two dissenting inspectors, but even Ambassador Bustani himself. Importantly, recent leaks in December 2020 have evidenced that a number of senior OPCW officials were supportive of one OPCW inspector who had spoken out with respect to malpractice.

The issue at hand threatens to severely damage the reputation and credibility of the OPCW and undermine its vital role in the pursuit of international peace and security. It is simply not tenable for a scientific organization such as the OPCW to refuse to respond openly to the criticisms and concerns of its own scientists whilst being associated with attempts to discredit and smear those scientists. Moreover, the on-going controversy regarding the Douma report also raises concerns with respect to the reliability of previous FFM reports, including the investigation of the alleged attack at Khan Shaykhun in 2017.

We believe that the interests of the OPCW are best served by the Director General providing a transparent and neutral forum in which the concerns of all the investigators can be heard as well as ensuring that a fully objective and scientific investigation is completed.

To that end, we call on the Director General of the OPCW to find the courage to address the problems within his organization relating to this investigation and ensure States Parties and the United Nations are informed accordingly. In this way we hope and believe that the credibility and integrity of the OPCW can be restored.[24]

The Berlin Group has asked for a professional investigation of the facts and the interpretation thereof. They demanded what should have been evident in the original report: transparency and accountability. Will the Berlin Group be discredited and silenced as the whistle-blowers and the first Director General of OPCW have been?

In this context it is worth remembering that the UN Human Rights Council has created the mandate of a special rapporteur on the right to truth,[25] and that all people—in this instance the relatives of the victims of Douma—are entitled to truth-seeking investigations of and reliable reports on internationally wrongful acts. This requires not only holding the perpetrators of the alleged use of chemical weapons to account, but also those responsible for the deliberate tampering with the evidence and the obvious politicization of what should be a technical investigation carried out by impartial professionals. And here again, measures must also be taken to protect the honour and reputation of whistleblowers, who have been subjected to defamation and intimidation both by the OPCW, by the media and even by governments.

The fall-out of the OPCW scandal is far-reaching, because there is reason to believe that many UN "fact-finding-missions" are similarly politicized and do not deserve to be considered authoritative.

What is one to make of the instrumentalization of international institutions with regard to the savage sanctions regime imposed by the Security Council against the Iraqi people, resulting in more than a million deaths, a crime against humanity which Assistant Secretary General Denis Halliday termed "a form of genocide"[26] when in 1998 he resigned his post as humanitarian coordinator in Iraq. His successor, Assistant Secretary General Hans-Christof von Sponeck resigned for the same reasons in 2000 and wrote a book about it, *A Different Kind of War*.[27]

As a further instance, what are we to make of the half-hearted investigation by the International Atomic Energy Agency into the origins of the shelling of the nuclear power plant in Zaporizhzhia? It tests our gullibility if we actually believe that the Russians would be so irrational as to bomb a facility over which they, themselves, were in control. *Cui bono?*, as Cicero would ask. It takes simple logic to realize that Putin would derive no benefit from shelling a nuclear power plant that Russia has held since the beginning of the war.

International civil society must demand from the institutions created to maintain peace and promote our human rights that they exercise more transparency, accountability, due process, and rule of law. If these institutions fail to observe their own statues and constitutions that require their impartiality, the highly regrettable and increasingly widespread view that the United Nations, the Office of the High Commissioner for Human Rights, the Human Rights Council, the International Criminal Court, and the OPCW are more or less in the service of the United States, United Kingdom and the European Union could lead to their demise.

CHAPTER 6

THE ROLE OF CIVIL SOCIETY IN THE PROMOTION OF HUMAN RIGHTS

"NGOs are an important sector of society because changing the attitude of the community and community development are not just the task of the government. It is the task of the entire society. If the country is going to progress, an idea must not just be held by the government; it must be held by all the key decisionmakers in society."

NELSON MANDELA[1]

I HAVE BEEN a human rights activist since my high school days in Chicago, followed by years at the Jesuit university in New York, Fordham College Rose Hill, where I participated in many religious-linked humanitarian initiatives and demonstrations. Later at Harvard Law School and at the Graduate School of Arts and Sciences, I was immersed in international law and human rights issues, mostly concerned with world peace and the Vietnam war.

I was keenly aware of the danger posed to the survival of humanity by the huge stockpiles of nuclear weapons and strongly believed, even then, that nuclear disarmament and general conventional disarmament were humanity's only rational priority, peace the most important human right, because without peace the enjoyment of civil, cultural, economic, political, and social rights is next to impossible. We protesters felt that we needed peace as we needed the very air we breathe. I rejected the idea that the only valid human rights were individual, encompassing only civil and political rights. That just did not click with me. I also believed in human duties, especially responsibilities to our communities and to the world at large as stipulated in Article 29 of the Universal Declaration of Human Rights.[2]

As a practicing Catholic I wanted to see elements of the Sermon on the Mount[3] implemented in daily politics, and in particular the right to peace. I believed that our country, the United States of America, was so rich that we could well afford better education, food and housing for all Americans. I looked for like-minded colleagues, and when I was a young lawyer at Simpson, Thacher and Bartlett, I was allowed by the firm (under our senior partner Cyrus Vance) to do a certain amount of pro-bono work per week, primarily in Spanish Harlem, where most of the Puerto Ricans lived.

My enthusiasm for the nongovernmental organizations involved in human rights work was initially high. I participated in church groups assisting racial minorities and in community organizations working for social justice. Gradually I came to understand that some non-governmental organizations were not entirely committed to human rights, even if they used the label, for they depended on donors, who had other agendas. These NGOs had allowed themselves to be drawn into the world of mercenaries, what we could term "human rights condottieri," who did not engage in human rights activities out of conviction, but *pecuniae causa*, because someone else was paying them to do so.

I was certainly not the first to make this discovery. Many independent observers and academics have been aware of the problem and written about it long for decades. Already in 2012 Nikolas Barry-Shaw, Yves Engler, and Dru Oja Jay, published a challenging book titled *Paved With Good Intentions: Canada's Development NGOs from Idealism to Imperialism.*[4] In a review by Sangeeta Kamat, Associate Professor, University of Massachusetts Amherst, and author of *Development Hegemony: NGOs and the State in India,* she observed:

> If you want to know the real story of how even "progressive" NGOs undermine democracy and people's struggles for justice in the Third World, read *Paved with Good Intentions.* The authors offer an intimate and historically comprehensive portrayal of how the best of international NGOs survive only by mortgaging their ideals to powerful vested interests.

Indeed, as Brigette DePape wrote, "It is not through development NGOs—which are not so 'non-governmental' but often vehicles for neoliberal government agendas—but rather through working in solidarity with grassroots movements that we can address issues like global poverty."

The average citizen must be cautious about the pronouncements of many NGOs, which often can be relegated to the category of fake news and biased narratives. There are few fields that are as penetrated and corrupted by intelligence services as the human rights NGOs. I would dare venture a guess that 30 per cent of the human rights NGOs pursue policies that are actually contrary to peace and understanding among peoples and nations, engage in evidence-free allegations and participate in the information war against countries and even against genuine NGOs and those truly independent UN rapporteurs who dare challenge the mainstream narratives and insist on the implementation of human rights norms uniformly—not selectively.

In my opinion, many of the NGOs financed by the National Endowment for Democracy[5] or by the Soros Foundation belong in this group of hijacked NGOs. I advise readers to investigate the sources of financing of NGOs and to consider whether dependence on such donors does not immediately compromise their assessments of human rights situations, especially in countries that are targeted by the United States and threated with U.S.-imposed "regime change."

Another 30% of the NGOs is partly in the service of governments and use the mask of "civil society" to spread their political propaganda. Some of them can be referred to as "mixed bags" because they do produce some valid reports, which serve as a useful cover for carrying out other activities that are contrary to the universal principles and purposes of the United Nations. These NGOs sacrifice their independence and lend their services to corporations and governments in a manner unbecoming of true civil society organizations. I have my own list of organizations in this category, but with a bit of observation, every reader can establish his/her own list of "mixed bags."

There remain an approximate 40% of NGOs that are genuine and perform a service to humanity. These are the struggling, least endowed NGOs. This chapter will attempt to name some of the genuine civil society organizations whose reports are reliable and who are not serving Washington, Brussels, Beijing or Moscow. Again, I would warn readers to be careful to whom they make contributions. Often enough contributions to Amnesty International, Human Rights Watch, the International Service for Human Rights, enable disproportionally high salaries of the senior and middle staff and huge "golden handshakes"[6] when the leadership departs. A significant credibility problem arises due to the fact that there is a "revolving door" at many of these NGOs, who draw their senior personnel from the U.S. government, State Department, FBI or CIA.

Established NGOs are keen on keeping their corporate and governmental sponsors and for that very reason compromise their work. In a real sense, they are in the service of the status quo and use "human rights" as a convenient bait to attract donations.

As a strong believer in the crucial role of civil society in identifying problems, formulating constructive solutions, facilitating the step-by-step reform of institutions and breathing life into the sometimes sclerotic system, I definitely want to see the NGOs pro-actively engage as both initiators and catalysts of change. The world's NGOs are indispensable and should be given more quality space and visibility.

There are literally thousands of NGOs in the field of human rights, some small and working on modest budgets, others equipped with large secretariats and generous financing. If we were to judge by the perception we gain from the mainstream media, we would mistakenly regard the NGO component of civil society as basically limited to Amnesty International (AI) and Human Rights Watch (HRW), both of which enjoy good reputations and have produced important studies for the use of governments, inter-governmental organizations, and, of course, the Human Rights Council (HRC). One could say that they enjoy more visibility than the Office of the UN High Commissioner for Human Rights or even the HRC. However, these two major players do not hold a monopoly over human rights ideas and ideals.

It must be stressed that NGOs are very necessary in the modern world, especially when they demand transparency and accountability from government and elected officials. It is important to have a spectrum of NGOs that cover all areas of human endeavour, especially those NGOs that give voice to the voiceless and neglected. This chapter will reflect some of the criticism of NGO practices that has been formulated by responsible observers. Moreover, it is not so much what NGOs might do wrong, but what they fail to do. As an instance, sometimes one wonders why AI and HRW keep silent with regard to some egregious violations of human rights, why they have the priorities that they have. Why do they apply double standards?

In any event, we must acknowledge that NGOs have done much to raise awareness and contribute to the emergence of a "culture of human rights." NGOs also perform important functions domestically, drive punctual change and new legislation, and can also accelerate human rights progress internationally. Looking back on years of active membership in civil society initiatives—as a simple member of NGOs with and without UN consultative status (and eventually as member of the board or president of several of them), member of academic institutions and think tanks, fundraiser for human rights organizations—I can confirm that the consciousness-raising campaigns by grass roots activists worldwide have significantly advanced the enjoyment of human rights by millions of people, contributed to public awareness and even to a change in the *Zeitgeist*.

Civil society and nongovernmental organizations have concretized our perception of human rights; their potential for making ongoing advances in the enjoyment of human rights by all human beings continues to be enormous. Among the results already achieved is the improvement in the situation of half of the world's population: women. Considerable advances in implementing not just women's rights, but also in the reduction of gender, racial and linguistic discrimination and in the progressive abolition of capital punishment worldwide have been achieved over these fifty years.

The noble promise of the UN's 17 Sustainable Development Goals is yet to be achieved, and we only have seven more years before 2030. Meanwhile we witness the eloquent but empty lip service given by most politicians to the SDGs, while wasting tax revenue in wars and military interventions. Therefore, it is for civil society and non-governmental organizations on the local, regional, and international levels to demand that governments recast their priorities away from military adventures and their attendant exorbitant expenditures and gradually supplant national-security economies with human-security ones. Disarmament for development should be our mantra, bearing in mind that governments will fight us tooth and nail to stick to their agendas.

Hence, NGOs should double down on their demands for a change of priorities, for the eradication of extreme poverty, famine, and pandemics. They should demand institutions and programs promoting education for peace and empathy, conflict-prevention mechanisms, the justiciability of human rights in local courts and tribunals, and a level playing field for all.

It is good that human rights have become—at least superficial-ly—a political priority in many countries. Unfortunately, there is a growing problem of the corruption of human rights language, of the instrumentalization of its values for geopolitical purposes. We have observed how "human rights" have been weaponized by some countries in order to advance imperialistic and neo-colonial agen-das. The growing influence of corporate donors and special interest groups is nefarious when they seek to set the priorities of the NGOs and consequently detract from their impartiality and objectivity. We have observed how human rights institutions and NGOs have been penetrated by intelligence services and used in many countries as trojan horses to destabilize those countries in the name of "human rights." One should acknowledge that this kind of weaponization of values constitutes a form of secular sacrilege, a kind of blasphemy. We must push back against the attempt by politicians and some NGOs to transform the noble ideals of the *dignitas humana* into instruments for neo-liberal regime change in foreign countries.

In chapters 2–4 we explored the question of whether we can trust the institutions whose constitutions charge them with protecting our rights, asking: can we trust the human rights institutions that have been established to monitor compliance with the ICCPR and ICESCR, with the climate change agenda, with the prohibition of chemical weapons? But now: can we trust the NGOs? Can we trust the media? Once again, we must pose the question: Who will be guarding the guardians? *Quis custodiet ipsos custodes?*[7] And indeed, who can we trust to choose those who guard the guardians? Can we trust nongovernmental orga-nizations to advance human rights impartially, without discriminating among victims, without applying double standards?

Many challenges remain for our present and future generations, particularly in learning how to live with each other. Peace is yet to be recognized as a human right. Notwithstanding the excellent civil society initiatives of the International Peace Bureau,[8] the Women's International League for Peace and Freedom,[9] the *Asociación Española para el Derecho Internacional de los Derechos Humanos,*[10] the global association of writers P.E.N. international,[11] the Austrian think tank International Progress Organization,[12] the San Francisco movement Eleanor Lives[13]—to name only a few—we are still very far away from implementing the human right to peace.

In spite of the clear language of Article 20 of the International Covenant on Civil and Political Rights, many governments engage in blatant war propaganda, often with the support of major intergovernmental organizations (IGOs) and NGOs that encourage military "humanitarian interventionism" and killer sanctions. These are made more plausible because they are synchronized with the managed narratives of governmental institutions like the National Endowment for Democracy, by certain "charitable foundations," by national human rights institutions, and then further buttressed by the corporate media which controls the human rights narrative and provides echo chambers for governments.

Whereas there is a need for greater space for individuals and civil society in general, the binary approach to political engagement whereby the players are neatly divided into the "good guys" meaning the NGOs, and the "bad guys" meaning governments is an absurd simplification. Nonetheless, there prevails a certain "perception" which *a priori* and uncritically accepts NGO reports and demands as legitimate. Often enough it is the mainstream media that promotes this misleading perception, at least for their favored NGOs.

Obviously not all NGOs act in good faith, and many of them are in the service of certain "elites," powerful foundations and special interests which essentially promote inequality and demand privileges—not rights. Ideally, NGOs should work together with national human rights institutions and with local and federal governments in order to implement policies arrived at through dialogue and cooperation. However, many of these NGOs are busy "manufacturing consent" for certain neo-liberal "rights," agitating for certain causes that benefit only a few and are seldom in the best interests of a peaceful society, busy in their obsession to "manufacture dissent" against political rivals and subvert or ridicule moral and religious beliefs, deliberately contributing to generalized social malaise, loss of a moral compass and ultimately the destabilization of governments. Some NGOs actually engage in "manufacturing hate" against geopolitical rivals in such a manner as to create a negative image of a politician or government, so as to make foreign-imposed "regime change" appear virtuous. I do not wish to dwell on this unappetizing subject of NGO propaganda, character assassination, use of hateful phrases as "axis of evil" or seemingly

THE ROLE OF CIVIL SOCIETY IN THE PROMOTION OF HUMAN RIGHTS 113

harmless subliminal postings. All I wish at this stage is to flag this endemic ill of the NGO world.

Needless to say, I strongly support the idea of genuine "people power," i.e., greater participation in the conduct of public affairs, including legislative initiative and referenda on issues of ethical importance, to advance public health, to protect the environment, oppose the waste of resources in military adventures and redirect tax revenue toward education, healthcare, maintenance of infrastructures, and the eradication of poverty. But many NGOs go to foreign countries primarily to create confusion, interfere in the internal affairs of those states, and pave the way for "colour revolutions" and undemocratic regime change. It is unpopular to say this, but it must be acknowledged as verifiable fact.

As William Engdahl wrote in *Manifest Destiny: Democracy as Cognitive Dissonance*:

> In 1983 amid many scandals regarding failed CIA regime change operations around the world, the Reagan Administration CIA director, Bill Casey, initiated a new "private" non-governmental organization to "do what the CIA did 25 years ago" according to the man who drafted the legislation for the National Endowment for Democracy. Since its founding in 1983, that agency and allied "democracy" NGOs like Soros' Open Society Foundation have succeeded in toppling countless regimes deemed "hostile" to U.S. foreign policy aims around the world.[14]

"People power" is precisely what Article 25 ICCPR aims to establish, but the mainstream view of "democracy" in the West is limited to periodic elections, which are easy to manipulate and seldom offer genuine democratic choices or produce action on pre-election promises.

We observe that all too often NGOs deflect attention from the overall needs of society by focusing on certain groups which leads to the prioritization of "victims." Consensus victims get all the attention. Other victims, e.g. the massacred and exploited indigenous peoples of North and South America, the exploited migrant workers and Kafala workers who live in a situation of modern day slavery, the peoples struggling for self-determination, including the Bubi people of the Island of Bioko,[15] The South Cameroonians,[16] the Kashmiris,[17] the Sahraouis,[18] the Kurds,[19] the Yemenis, the Ogonis of Nigeria,[20] the Tamils of Sri Lanka,[21] the Ryukyuans of Okinawa,[22] the West Papuans,[23] the Catalans of Spain,[24] are systematically ignored by the major NGOs and the mainstream media.

Civil society and NGOs have not only a right but a duty to articulate their support for human-rights-oriented legislation and practices and to oppose governmental and private sector abuses. We depend especially on courageous whistleblowers to uncover governmental and private sector scams, to identify those responsible for the perpetration of geopolitical crimes, ecocide, the perpetuation of economic and social injustices. Whistleblowers are entitled to a Charter that will protect their rights, otherwise the price for uncovering misconduct and disseminating the truth becomes too onerous, even for courageous persons.[25]

This chapter will not focus on the complicity of the media and major news agencies like Reuters and AP in disseminating fake news and suppressing dissent. Chapter 7 of this book analyses those issues. Yet, in examining the dysfunctions of governmental and private human rights institutions, it is important to keep in mind that information is power. Indeed, when the media does not fulfil its vocation to inform accurately and comprehensively, when the media is not pluralistic, it betrays democratic societies, and all of us, including the NGOs, are the losers. A functioning democracy requires people participation, and this means that the citizens must have access to the information they need in order to formulate their own opinions.

The dysfunctions and arbitrariness of many human rights institutions, their misplaced priorities, and their ineffectiveness are partly the result of the disinformation and indoctrination that they too receive from the homologated corporate media. Civil society does not live in a vacuum; it, too, is influenced by the information that is disseminated—or suppressed.

My personal human rights activism spans collaboration with United Nations agencies, regional human rights institutions, inter-governmental organizations such as South Centre, academic institutions including the *Max Planck Institut für ausländisches öffentliches Recht und Völkerrecht* (Heidelberg), the *Académie Internationale du droit constitutionnel* (Tunis), the Spanish Society for International Human Rights Law (AEDIDH, Luarca, Spain),[26] as well as many nongovernmental organizations, notably P.E.N. International, the Geneva International Peace Research Institute (GIPRI),[27] the International Human Rights Association of American Minorities (IHRAAM),[28] the *Internationale Gesellschaft für Menschenrechte,*[29] the Association Suisses et Internationaux de Genève (ASIG), the association *Millennium Solidarity* (Geneva), and the United Nations Christian Association.

My activism predates the founding of Human Rights Watch (Helsinki Watch) in 1978, and coincides with the early days of Amnesty International, especially during its years under Sean MacBride and Martin Ennals. Initially I strongly supported the work of AI and HRW.[30] Today I am more circumspect. It is with regret that I must acknowledge that as these and other human rights NGOs grew, their political independence diminished, and their agendas were increasingly influenced by their donors—especially when sufficient funding for operations is so hard to achieve from simple solicitation of support from the public at large.

As with everything human, even religious and philanthropic institutions can be easily hijacked and instrumentalized for geopolitical and other purposes. It has become increasingly difficult to explain why AI and HRW frequently apply double standards, why they condemn human rights violations by certain countries while keeping silent about others—if, indeed, they are actually silent in these issues, as opposed to being ignored in some instances by the media. Of course, both organizations still make important contributions and produce solid reports on a variety of issues. But who sets their priorities? To what extent do donors dictate their agenda? What is the extent of penetration by intelligence services? It is difficult to obtain much information on these crucial issues that inevitably impact their credibility and reduce their effectiveness in influencing governmental policy and concretely helping victims.

No one reading this chapter should think that I am against the non-governmental movement. On the contrary. I want to strengthen the role of civil society while ensuring that NGOs are not instrumentalized by corporate interests and do not become the "benign" tools of governments to advance geopolitical agendas. NGOs have a crucial role in democratic society, and for that very reason it is imperative that they guard their independence and objectivity.

The codification of human rights was undertaken in a spirit of human solidarity, not with the binary intent to divide the world into "good countries" and "bad countries." Such a division is tantamount to a kind of neo-colonialism and contrary to the letter and spirit of the UN Charter. The whole idea remains how best to reaffirm our common human dignity and constructively help others to improve their lives.

It is important to be alert to the dangers of "groupthink" and "stampedes" by some NGOs to legitimize certain governmental actions camouflaged as human rights actions, e.g. endorsing the imposition of sanctions regimes that constitute "collective punishment" and result in the deaths of tens of thousands of innocent persons in the targeted states as a kind of "collateral damage," which are somehow camouflaged as promotion of human rights, accepting the "collateral damage" because, after all, doesn't the end justify the means? Many NGOs display uncritical groupthink and actually applaud xenophobia, Russophobia or Sinophobia against entire peoples at large—e.g. excluding Russian sportspeople from international competition, or Russian disabled persons from the Paralympics in Beijing and elsewhere. This is profoundly wrong and contrary to human dignity because these sportspeople have no role whatsoever in the policies of their governments.

NGOs must reconsider their priorities in human rights terms. They must focus on genuine problems, examine the root causes of those problems, and endeavour to formulate constructive solutions. It is disconcerting to note, at the Human Rights Council, the extent to which some issues crucial to the survival of millions of human beings, like access to clean water and sanitation, are largely ignored by NGOs, while a disproportionate amount of time is devoted to discussion of issues related to "LGBT rights" and the "human right to abortion," which impact significantly fewer numbers of people. What has happened to addressing the reality of extreme poverty, famine, torture, slavery, genocide against indigenous populations, the cruel denial of self-determination of the Kashmiris, Kurds, Biafrans, Sahraouis, Tamils, Catalans, Corsicans, Southern Tyrolians?

One would expect major NGOs like Amnesty International and Human Rights to unconditionally condemn both warmongering and war, to condemn the squandering of national budgets in the arms race, in propaganda for war, in financing the bombardment of civilians in Yemen. Like everywhere else—it is a matter of priorities, and neither AI nor HRW have their priorities right. If these two NGOs put their emphasis on peace, peace-making, mediating cease-fires, then the enjoyment of other rights becomes possible. If they document and condemn tax havens, currency and commodity speculation, then governments will be able to recoup tax revenue to finance education, healthcare and the SDGs. It is regrettable that the priorities of AI and HRW—or at least those most publicized by the mainstream media— seem to be aligned to those of Washington and Brussels. Thus, some observers have legitimately asked whether there exists a sense for priorities and a sense for proportions left in the "human rights industry."

How many mercenaries from government and corporations are employed in the industry? How does the "revolving door" function between government offices and "independent" NGOs? Undoubtedly, many human rights *condottieri* fill the ranks of national human rights institutions, non-governmental organizations, universities, think tanks, ministries, United Nations, European, American, and African human rights commissions and committees.

A vast human rights industry has emerged and expanded, attracting not only those persons genuinely committed to the promotion of human dignity, equity, justice, social peace, solidarity—but also some who are interested in well-paying jobs and the non-monetary remuneration of club membership in a synergy of operatives who nurture the illusion of belonging to the *avant-garde*, the club of "progressives," the "enlightened," the "good guys."

REPORTERS WITHOUT BORDERS (RWB)
REPORTERS SANS FRONTIÈRES (RSF)

This non-governmental organization has a rather mixed track record. On the positive side RSF has condemned the destruction of videos concerning war crimes by the U.S. in connection with the war on terror. It has advocated the release of Julian Assange[31] and of C.I.A. whistleblower Jeffrey Sterling,[32] and suffered cyberattacks because of it. On the other hand, as far as I know, RSB/RSF has not vindicated the

rights of Russian journalists killed or arrested in Ukraine long before
the Russian invasion of February 2022 and ever since, and has not
unambiguously condemned the censorship by the European Union
and UK against numerous Russian news services, including RT and
Sputnik.

There have been numerous articles in the press suggesting that
RSF has collaborated with the CIA and that intelligence services have
penetrated it, but there has never been a satisfactory clarification of the
issue.[33] In 2017 Brandon Turbeville wrote:

> Reporters Without Borders is a fully funded organiza-
> tion receiving money from the National Endowment for
> Democracy, USAID, International Republican Institute and
> George Soros' Open Society Foundation. As F. William
> Engdahl wrote in his article "Reporters Without Borders
> seems to have a geopolitical agenda," "After years of trying
> to hide it, Robert Menard, Paris-based Secretary-General of
> Reporters Sans Frontières or RWB, confessed that the RWB
> budget was primarily funded by "U.S. organizations strictly
> linked to U.S. foreign policy."[34]

RWB is also reported to have accepted funding from a lobby of
exile Cubans, the Center for a Free Cuba.[35]

While RWB has been very vocal in criticizing the Russian
crackdown on foreign media and foreign-financed NGOs, which
Russia considers as "foreign agents" interfering in the internal affairs
of Russia with the intent to destabilize Russian institutions and the
Russian constitutional order,[36] it has been conspicuously lukewarm
in its criticism of the European Union and UK's blanket rejection of
Russian news outlets and the imposition of sanctions on journalists,
although in a democratic society, all persons have a right to know
and the necessity to access all sources of information, as stipulated in
Article 19 ICCPR. This is even more important today, in the midst of
a war in Ukraine, when it becomes indispensable to know what the
other side is thinking and saying. It is unhelpful and unacceptable to
claim that the other side only disseminates "fake news" and phoney
narratives. This kind of argument is totally incompatible with the
obligations of the UK and EU states under Article 19 ICCPR. This EU

"cancel culture" campaign, which has been advocated and supported by YouTube, Twitter, Facebook, has not encountered any meaningful opposition from RWB.

RWB activities during the Syrian war have also thrown light on its independence, or lack thereof. For instance, in 2017 RWB put pressure on the Swiss Press Club because of the Club's decision to host a debate on the alleged corruption and manipulation of facts by the "White Helmets." The question is whether the Western media ideologically refused to accept that it has been grossly mistaken or indeed has been deliberately misleading the public in promoting a heroic portrayal of the White Helmets.

Guy Mettan, President of the Swiss Press Club and former President of the Grand Conseil de Genève[37] stated in 2017: "It was very surprising and very disappointing to see a journalists' association asking for a kind of censorship," commenting that Reporters Without Borders (RSF) are "supposed to protect the freedom of speech and the freedom of the media ... and they just wrote to me and to all the committee members of the Swiss Press Club to ask for cancelling the press conference about the White Helmets, which is completely in contradiction with their charter; with their goal."

The Swiss Press Club head said that he replied to RSF, specifying that their demands were in violation of Geneva's legislation. "We're here in Switzerland, a country, which is democratic, which believes in the freedom of the press. It's written in our Constitution." According to Mettan, the Swiss Press Club is "accustomed to get pressures from everywhere in the world and mainly from dictatorial countries—like Saudi Arabia, Bahrain and others—because they don't accept that we give the floor to political opponents or to human rights' defenders."

The conference/debate at the Swiss Press Club featured independent journalist Vanessa Beeley, who has done extensive reporting from inside Syria, alongside French journalist Richard Labévière, an expert on the Middle East and international terrorism, and Marcello Ferrada de Noli, chair of Swedish Doctors for Human Rights (SWEDHR).

Mettan also said that he received "dozens of messages from all around the world—from Sweden, the U.S., UK, Australia, Canada," supporting the Swiss Press Club for "staying firm" to the ideals of free speech and hosting the press conference about the White Helmets, regardless of the pressure.

Witnesses have meanwhile accused the White Helmets—and substantiated their claims—of collaborating with terrorist groups, filming staged reports about their rescue work, engaging in looting and other misdeeds. Members of the group have been caught on camera several times performing dubious acts, including assisting with an apparent execution of a prisoner. In 2021 evidence of widespread corruption with the financing of the White Helmets came to light.[38] But the damage to the Syrian people—and to the perception of the war by millions of people has been done and continues to be done without any meaningful push-back from RSF. Some observers have therefore expressed the suspicion that RWB is somehow in the service of Washington and Brussels.

HUMAN RIGHTS WATCH[39]

While HRW has done many positive things for human rights and has submitted valuable reports to the UN Human Rights Council, some of its activities are incomprehensible in human rights terms. It is only when you "follow the money," and observe where donations come from, that you realize HRW draws its finances from George Soros and other hawkish interventionists. This explains why it is so often on the side of U.S. geopolitical interests.

On the positive side, we note that Human Rights Watch was a founding member of the International Campaign to Ban Landmines, which was awarded the Nobel Peace Prize in 1997.[40] It also played a significant advocacy role in the 2008 treaty banning cluster munitions.[41]

Among the constructive aspects of HRW's work, we can acknowledge its careful criticism of Israel's policies of Apartheid in the occupied Palestine territories and Gaza and the violation of the right of self-determination of the Palestinian people.[42] To HRW's credit, it endorsed the report of Judge Richard Goldstone[43] on Gaza and the work of Professor Michael Lynk, the UN Special Rapporteur on Palestine.[44] For this audacity, HRW's ex-chief Kenneth Roth was initially "punished" by the Harvard Kennedy School in 2023 and excluded from its fellowship program.[45] On January 10, 2023, HRW wrote to the Harvard president that it was concerned about the "lasting impact on scholars and activists, particularly Palestinians, who should not have to fear professional repercussions from Harvard University of another institution if they write or speak critically about the Israeli government."[46] After protests by the American Civil Liberties Union and PEN America, Harvard reversed its decision on banning Kenneth Roth.[47]

Another honorable contribution, though less surprising, is HRW's criticism of U.S. complicity in the war crimes being committed by Saudi Arabia in Yemen.[48] Moreover, in many of HRW's useful reports, it highlighted, for instance, the abuse of migrant rights in Singapore.[49] In 2020, HRW called out Lebanon[50] demanding the abolition of the Kafala system, which has been termed a modern form of slavery, practised in many countries in the Middle East, reducing migrant workers to serfdom.[51]

Unfortunately, in areas of geopolitical interest to the United States, HRW's treatment of the human rights situation in China, Nicaragua and Venezuela seems to follow the State Department line; this may be due to its so-called "revolving door" practice, a genuine problem that needs to be addressed and not just dismissed as propaganda or conspiracy theory. It is an elephant in the room.

Since its founding days, HRW has functioned as a revolving door between the NGO sector and the U.S. government.[52] It has repeatedly refused to oppose American wars and military interventions, and displayed double standards toward Washington's allies like Colombia, while fixating obsessively on the supposed misdeeds of independent nations targeted by the U.S. As has been written by others, HRW was founded during the height of the Cold War as Helsinki Watch, an anti-Soviet lobby group closely linked to the U.S. government, funded by the Ford Foundation, allegedly serving as a CIA passthrough.

Kenneth Roth directed HRW since its inception and until his retirement in 2022.[53] Having begun his career as a federal prosecutor in the U.S. Attorney Southern District of New York Office, Roth has not deviated much from Washington's foreign-policy agenda. The following letter was sent on May 8, 2014 to him on behalf of Nobel Peace Prize Laureates Adolfo Pérez Esquivel and Mairead Maguire, former UN Assistant Secretary General Hans von Sponeck, the then UN Special Rapporteur on Human Rights in the Palestinian Territories Richard Falk, and over 130 scholars:

Dear Kenneth Roth,

Human Rights Watch characterizes itself as "one of the world's leading independent organizations dedicated to defending and protecting human rights." However, HRW's close ties to the U.S. government call into question its independence.

For example, HRW's Washington advocacy director, Tom Malinowski, previously served as a special assistant to President Bill Clinton and as a speechwriter to Secretary of State Madeleine Albright. In 2013, he left HRW after being nominated as Assistant Secretary of State for Democracy, Human Rights & Labor under John Kerry.

In her HRW.org biography, Board of Directors' Vice Chair Susan Manilow describes herself as "a longtime friend to Bill Clinton" who is "highly involved" in his political party, and "has hosted dozens of events" for the Democratic National Committee.

Currently, HRW Americas' advisory committee includes Myles Frechette, a former U.S. ambassador to Colombia, and Michael Shifter, one-time Latin American director for the U.S. government-financed National Endowment for Democracy. Miguel Díaz, a Central Intelligence Agency analyst in the 1990s, sat on HRW Americas' advisory committee from 2003–11. Now at the State Department, Díaz serves as "an interlocutor between the intelligence community and non-government experts."

In his capacity as an HRW advocacy director, Malinowski contended in 2009 that "under limited circumstances" there was "a legitimate place" for CIA renditions—the illegal practice of kidnapping and transferring terrorism suspects around the planet. Malinowski was quoted paraphrasing the U.S. government's argument that designing an alternative to sending suspects to "foreign dungeons to be tortured" was "going to take some time."

HRW has not extended similar consideration to Venezuela. In a 2012 letter to President Chávez, HRW criticized the country's candidacy for the UN Human Rights

Council, alleging that Venezuela had fallen "far short of acceptable standards" and questioning its "ability to serve as a credible voice on human rights." At no point has U.S. membership in the same council merited censure from HRW, despite Washington's secret global assassination program, its preservation of renditions, and its illegal detention of individuals in Guantánamo Bay

Likewise, in February 2013, HRW correctly described as "unlawful" Syria's use of missiles in its civil war. However, HRW remained silent on the clear violation of international law constituted by the U.S. threat of missile strikes on Syria in August.

The few examples above, limited to only recent history, might be forgiven as inconsistencies or oversights that could naturally occur in any large, busy organization. But HRW's close relationships with the U.S. government suffuse such instances with the appearance of a conflict of interest.

We therefore encourage you to institute immediate, concrete measures to strongly assert HRW's independence. Closing what seems to be a revolving door would be a reasonable first step: Bar those who have crafted or executed U.S. foreign policy from serving as HRW staff, advisors or board members. At a bare minimum, mandate lengthy "cooling-off" periods before and after any associate moves between HRW and that arm of the government.

Your largest donor, investor George Soros, argued in 2010 that "to be more effective, I think the organization has to be seen as more international, less an American organization." We concur. We urge you to implement the aforementioned proposal to ensure a reputation for genuine independence.

Sincerely,

Adolfo Pérez Esquivel, Nobel Peace Prize laureate

Mairead Maguire, Nobel Peace Prize laureate

and 130 other signatures follow

The concerns expressed in the above 2014 open letter have been confirmed again and again. Personally, I do not see how HRW can reform itself. It survives because it does what the donors tell it to do, and the donors have enormous economic power. Thus, HRW will presumably continue doing some good things, and many bad things as well.

There are many critics of HRW, and their criticism may or may not be justified. What is needed is an open discussion on these issues, which are real, and are not about to go away. On March 23, 2003 independent journalist Garry Leech[54] published an indictment of HRW under the title "The Bias of HRW,"[55] stating:

> despite its claims to be an advocate of international human rights law, the reports issued by Human Rights Watch over the past decade have increasingly exhibited a bias towards certain rights over others. More precisely, Human Rights Watch repeatedly focuses on political and civil rights while ignoring social and economic rights. As a result, it routinely judges nations throughout the world in a manner that furthers capitalist values and discredits governments seeking socialist alternatives. It is this bias that lies at the root of Human Rights Watch's scathing attacks on the government of Venezuela and its recently deceased president Hugo Chávez. This bias was also evident in comments made in 2012 by Ken Roth, executive director of Human Rights Watch, when he declared that Venezuela is "the most abusive" nation in Latin America.

In the context of HRW's report on Venezuela, Leech writes:

> Human Rights Watch wilfully ignored the international context in which the U.S. government has a long history of funding only those sectors of civil society opposed to governments it does not like. In recent years, such funding was provided by the U.S. Agency for International Development (USAID) and the National Endowment for Democracy (NED) to NGOs in Haiti that opposed President Jean Bertrand Aristide, whose democratically-elected

government was eventually overthrown by the U.S. military in 2004. The United States has a similar history of funding Venezuelan NGOs, such as *Súmate*, whose primary objective was to remove Chávez from office. The aforementioned declassified State Department documents revealed that Washington provided $40 million in funding to Venezuelan opposition groups between 2007 and 2009. Such actions constitute blatant interference in the internal politics of a sovereign nation; an interference that is possible only because of the unequal distribution of global political power that provides wealthy nations with sufficient wealth and power to intervene in the internal affairs of poor nations under the guise of providing "aid."

HRW AND WAR

With regard to the 2003 Iraq invasion by the "coalition of the willing" HRW failed to take a position clearly condemning the aggression, as Secretary General Kofi Annan had done, first calling it a war contrary to the UN Charter and then clearly an "illegal war."[56] Every human rights NGO was under obligation to immediately condemn the massive violation of Article 2(4) of the UN Charter and subsequently to call for accountability for the crimes of aggression, for the war crimes and crimes against humanity that followed. HRW's initial silence and its downplaying and whitewashing of the crimes disqualifies HRW from consideration as an independent NGO, not in the service of Washington. HRW wrote:

> To preserve its neutrality in assessing adherence to the laws of war in the Iraq conflict, Human Rights Watch did not take a position on whether the war itself was justified or legal.[57]

HRW tried to save face by inserting a mild criticism of the coalition's toxic behavior:

> Coalition forces generally tried to avoid killing Iraqis who weren't taking part in combat.[58]

and

> Air attacks on leadership targets, like those launched in
> Iraq, should not be carried out until the intelligence and
> targeting failures have been corrected. Leadership strikes
> should not be carried out without an adequate collateral
> damage estimate....

To establish HRW's own neutrality, HRW starts off by finding
fault with its own side, deploring the death of a (greatly underestimated) number of civilian victims. Then, it relativizes the crimes,
whitewashing them by comparing them with other genocides and
wars, and asserting that neutrality regarding the war permits killing the
leaders of the opposite side, just so long as the intelligence is correct
and that the collateral damages are adequately evaluated—by whom?
How? On what basis?

The HRW report "Off Target. The Conduct of the War and
Civilian Casualties in Iraq,"[59] constitutes a culpable downplaying of
that monstrous criminality. It played the same type of epistemological
games during the 2006 Lebanon war.[60] The record of HRW concerning
the world war in Syria has been similarly deplorable.[61]

HRW AND THE UN RESPONSIBILITY TO PROTECT "DOCTRINE"

Since the General Assembly adopted the omnibus Resolution
60/1 on October 24, 2005, HRW has been an enthusiastic supporter
of the so-called "responsibility to protect" doctrine, which is not a
doctrine, but a scam to attempt circumventing the *jus cogens* prohibition of the use of force stipulated in Article 2(4) of the UN Charter.
The "doctrine" is formulated in paragraph 138 of the omnibus resolution and has already been misused by the U.S. to justify military
interventions abroad on the pretext of "humanitarian" assistance, most
disastrously in Libya. Many observers have already denounced R2P
as imperialistic and neo-colonial propaganda that uses human rights
and humanitarian values as a pretext for hard geopolitical aggression.
No human rights NGO should lend itself to that deceit, but many do.

Paragraph 138 of General Assembly Resolution 60/1 must be read in context. In fact, three paragraphs before the General Assembly seems to be saying something entirely different—namely that all countries have a right to find their own way and that there is no single model for democracy. Paragraph 135 of GA Resolution 60/1 stipulates:

> We reaffirm that democracy is a universal value based on the freely expressed will of people to determine their own political, economic, social and cultural systems and their full participation in all aspects of their lives. We also reaffirm that while democracies share common features, there is no single model of democracy, that it does not belong to any country or region, and reaffirm the necessity of due respect for sovereignty and the right of self-determination. We stress that democracy, development and respect for all human rights and fundamental freedoms are interdependent and mutually reinforcing.

Moreover, the General Assembly held a general debate on R2P in July 2009 in which many countries expressed concern about the potential for abuse, deemed by the Global South as a form of "neo-colonialism."[62] Two years later, in 2011, NATO invoked R2P to justify its military intervention in Libya, which transformed the previously prosperous country into a failed state and home to open-air slave markets.

HRW has also helped justify the Trump administration's extrajudicial execution of top Iranian general Qassem Soleimani, a brazen act of war that nearly plunged the region into a catastrophic conflict. In recent months, HRW has taken its longstanding resentment of China's government to unhinged levels, likening Beijing to Nazi Germany and spreading a fake video of a special effects training which, it implied, depicted Chinese "killer robots."

All the while, HRW has marketed itself as a noble and absolutely impartial defender of human rights. Its disingenuous global branding campaign has been possible thanks to a $100 million grant from George Soros, a key financier of the regime-change industry and a zealous cold warrior who worked closely with the United States and Western Europe to help overthrow socialist-oriented governments in

Eastern Europe through a series of "colour revolutions," privatize their economies, and integrate the newly capitalist states into the European Union and NATO.

HRW's stand on Unilateral Coercive Measures

It is incomprehensible that an NGO ostensibly devoted to the promotion and protection of human rights would endorse illegal unilateral coercive measures, economic war, financial blockades etc., which affect the most vulnerable in some 30 countries worldwide.[63] As I wrote in my 2018 report to the Human Rights Council, "Sanctions Kill."[64] The UN General Assembly and the Human Rights Council have repeatedly condemned UCMs as illegal and contrary to human rights, as already discussed in this book.

Far from publicly condemning UCMs, HRW endorses the U.S. policy of imposing economic sanctions.[65] By so doing, HRW becomes complicit in the crime. One would have expected that every single human rights NGO would acknowledge that UCMs constitute a form of illegal "use of force" prohibited in Article 2(4) of the UN Charter, an illegal interference in the internal affairs of States, and that they have resulted in the deaths of tens of thousands of human beings, being as deadly as any military intervention.[66] Precisely because of the magnitude of the crime, it can be safely concluded that UCMs constitute "crimes against humanity" within the meaning of Article 7 of the Statute of Rome. It is particularly obscene to try to justify UCMs with reference to human rights violations committed by the targeted state, when the UCMs themselves are illegal and cause even greater human rights violations and greater suffering among totally innocent people. As has been frequently admitted by a variety of U.S. officials, the sanctions are intended to induce "regime change."

Yet HRW refuses to acknowledge that unilateral coercive measures have anything to do with human rights and thereby, purportedly, outside its mandate. Why doesn't HRW join the vast majority in the General Assembly and Human Rights Council in condemning UCMs, most recently in December 2022 in General Assembly Resolution 77/214 and in Human Rights Council resolution 49/6 of March 2022? One would think that the staff of HRW should be familiar with the pertinent general comments of the Committee on Economic, Social and

Cultural Rights, with the report of the UN Sub-Commission on the Promotion and Protection of Human Rights in 2000, which analysed all the human rights norms that UCMs violate and demanded that they be lifted. The Thematic report of UN High Commissioner for Human Rights Navi Pillay similarly condemned UCMs.[67] One would expect that a true human rights organization would challenge UCM's instead of endorsing them.

It is incomprehensible, a *contradictio in adjecto*, when human rights organizations criticize the European Union for lifting sanctions against Burundi for what the EU said was progress on human rights, good governance, and the rule of law. The EU action follows the U.S. lifting sanctions in November. Some human right groups contended that Burundi authorities continue to commit abuses, including against political dissidents. Mausi Segun, the executive director of HRW's Africa Division stated: "It's unfortunately premature. Nothing on the ground in Burundi gives any foundation or basis for lifting the sanctions.... The EU and others like that institution are too much in haste to give credit to the government of Burundi when the victims of abuses and vicious crimes in Burundi deserve a lot more from the international community."[68]

While HRW is right in calling on those responsible for human rights violations and abuses in Burundi and elsewhere to be held accountable, it has failed to answer the objections from those who have demonstrated that economic sanctions impact the most vulnerable and kill vast numbers of innocent people. Furthermore, and notably, there is no empirical evidence that sanctions have ever influenced countries to ameliorate their human rights performance. On the contrary, the evidence is clear that UCMs are counterproductive and that targeted states consider them a form of hybrid warfare endangering the survival of the nation and therefore adopt legislation in defence of the constitutional order. UCM's lead to retrogression in the enjoyment of all human rights.

It is a matter of public record that HRW has supported U.S. sanctions against Cuba, Nicaragua and Venezuela, even as the Covid-19 pandemic was raging. This entails responsibility for the untimely deaths of thousands of people since economic sanctions significantly diminish the capacities of governments to combat the pandemic. For this reason, Max Blumenthal of *The Grayzone* describes HRW as "the human rights arm of the U.S. empire."

And worse, HRW has actively lobbied Washington to impose asphyxiating sanctions on leftist governments in Latin America, applauding Donald Trump for ramping up U.S. unilateral coercive measures. For persons not familiar with the world of human rights institutions, it may come as a surprise that NGOs like HRW try to "sell" sanctions as a more palatable alternative to military action, despite the fact that these measures are widely recognized by international legal experts to be barbaric economic weapons that result in the deaths of thousands of human beings,[69] destroy livelihoods, devastate national economies, and cause uncontrollable migratory flows.

As the coronavirus pandemic spread across the globe, HRW operatives took credit for new sanctions the Trump administration had imposed on Nicaragua's democratically elected leftist government. Among those cheering on the escalation of economic warfare was HRW Australia development and outreach manager Stephanie McLennan, who gloated that the fresh round of sanctions was "great news!"

HRW's staunch support for U.S. sanctions illustrates how the group has been instrumentalized as an arm of U.S. pressure against independent states in the Global South. NGOs like HRW provide cover for economic warfare, preventing nations like Nicaragua from rebuilding and healing the social divisions that have been exacerbated through successive U.S.-backed destabilization campaigns.

HRW REPORTS ON LATIN AMERICA

HRW's track record on Latin America is particularly dismal, having aligned itself with the interventionist policies of USAID and the National Endowment for Democracy. Locally, HRW operatives traditionally associate with industrialists over syndicalists, with rich landowners over land workers. The neo-liberal mindset of many HRW staff quite naturally draws them to powerful economic forces that continue abusing the rights of the poor and indigenous populations; continue destroying the environment, polluting rivers and lakes; and supporting violent opposition groups, mostly financed by the United States, in an attempt to facilitate "regime change." HRW's support of the 2019 *coup d'état* in Bolivia against President Evo Morales, and the subsequent downplaying of the junta's massacre of indigenous protesters is a particularly painful chapter.[70]

Venezuela

In 2008, following a wave of sabotage and violence perpetrated by the U.S.-backed opposition, HRW published a report uncritically reproducing the unsubstantiated claims of right-wing activists as facts, while systematically whitewashing their violence and ignoring all of the contrary evidence provided by legitimate Venezuelan NGOs (not financed by either the Venezuelan government or by NED) including Fundalatin and the Grupo Sures.

The HRW report prompted more than 100 scholars to pen an open letter accusing HRW of failing to meet "minimal standards of scholarship, impartiality, accuracy or credibility."

In 2008 the Washington-based NGO Council on Hemispheric Affairs (COHA)[71] took HRW to task. I can confirm their charge of HRW inaccuracy, because before my November/December 2017 mission to Venezuela, the first by a UN rapporteur in 21 years, I studied all the pertinent HRW reports on Venezuela and found them flawed in methodology, biased and counterproductive. I later fact-checked them on the ground and therefore consider them not only misleading, but culpably so, drafted *mala animo*, in order to assist the U.S. government in its drive to impose regime change on the Venezuelan people. Alas, HRW has a long history of falsely reporting on Venezuela and supporting U.S. interventionism. As COHA reports:

> The following letter was sent to the Board of Directors of Human Rights Watch, carrying the signatures of over 100 U.S. and foreign Latin American scholars. The letter raises serious concerns over that organization's recently issued highly critical report on the human rights situation in Venezuela and the conduct of its president, Hugo Chavez. It is now being distributed by the Council on Hemispheric Affairs to its mailing list at the request of a number of signatories of that document. COHA's staff is taking this step (with considerable reluctance) because it feels that it is

obliged for any organization committed to social justice and democratic values, to speak out regarding the dispute now raging over HRW's recent and very controversial report on Hugo Chavez's human rights performance.

Any reservation COHA may have had over taking issue with a sister organization was voided by the egregiously inappropriate behavior exhibited by HRW. Most specifically it was the issuance of this report and the needlessly venomous tone resorted to by HRW's head for Latin America, Jose Miguel Vivanco. In his charges, HRW's lead researcher and writer of the report used intemperate language and patently disingenuous tactics to field a series of anti-Chavez allegations that are excessive and inappropriate. It is not a matter that President Chavez and the Venezuelan government are above reproach—far from it. The problem is the presence of a mean-spirited tone and a lack of balance and fair play that characterizes Vivanco's reportage and his tendentious interpretation of the alleged misdeeds of the Chavez revolution are demonstrably bereft of scale and accuracy.

The full text of the letter follows:

We write to call your attention to a report published by Human Rights Watch that does not meet even the most minimal standards of scholarship, impartiality, accuracy, or credibility. The document, A Decade Under Chávez: Political Intolerance and Lost Opportunities for Advancing Human Rights in Venezuela, appears to be a politically motivated essay rather than a human rights report. Indeed, the lead author of the report, Jose Miguel Vivanco, stated as much when he told the press just a few days after its publication, "We did the report because we wanted to demonstrate to the world that Venezuela is not a model for anyone...."

Clearly Mr. Vivanco is entitled to his views about Venezuela, but such statements run counter to the mission of Human Rights Watch and indeed any organization dedicated to the defense of human rights. By publishing such a grossly flawed report, and acknowledging a political motivation in doing so, Mr. Vivanco has undermined the credibility of an important human rights organization.

We do not make these charges lightly and we hope you will understand the seriousness of such grave errors in judgment. As scholars who specialize in Latin America, we rely on what are supposed to be independent, non-partisan organizations such as Human Rights Watch for factual information about human right abuses committed by governments and sometimes non-governmental actors. So do many other constituencies, including the press, government officials, and the public. It is a great loss to civil society when we can no longer trust a source such as Human Rights Watch to conduct an impartial investigation and draw conclusions based on verifiable facts.

The report makes sweeping allegations that are not backed up by supporting facts or in some cases even logical arguments. For example, the report's most important and prominent allegation is that "discrimination on political grounds has been a defining feature of the Chávez presidency." (p. 1) Yet the report does not show, or even attempt to show, that political discrimination either increased under the current government (as compared to past governments), or is more of a problem in Venezuela than in any other country in the world.

What is the evidence offered for such a broad generalization?

In most cases, it was not possible to prove political discrimination—with rare exceptions, citizens were given no grounds at all for the actions taken—yet many were told informally that they were losing their jobs, contracts, or services for having signed the referendum petition [to recall President Chávez]. For example, in one case reported to Human Rights Watch, a 98-year-old woman was denied medicines that she had long received from a state development agency because, as her family was told by the program secretary, she had signed the referendum petition."

Taking services first, the above paragraph refers to an allegation that one Venezuelan citizen was denied medicines for political reasons. Amazingly, this is the only alleged instance of discrimination in government services cited in the entire 230-page report. In other words, the Barrio Adentro program has provided health services to millions of poor Venezuelans each year since 2003, and the authors found one allegation (as reported to the authors in a phone conversation with the nephew of the alleged victim) of discrimination involving one person. On this basis the authors make the sweeping generalization that "Citizens who exercised their right to call for the referendum—invoking one of the new participatory mechanisms championed by Chávez during the drafting of the 1999 Constitution—were threatened with retaliation and blacklisted from some government jobs and services."

This is outrageous and completely indefensible. We do not expect a report of this nature to adhere to rigorous academic standards, but there have to be some standards.

With regard to employment, there is no doubt that there were cases where individual government officials discriminated on the grounds of employees' political beliefs. (There were also cases of discrimination and firing of pro-government employees in the private sector, which the report mentions in a parenthesis (p.10) and does not investigate). However, the report does not show that there was any organized or systematic effort to purge the government of anti-government employees. Indeed, as anyone who is familiar with the government of Venezuela knows, after nearly ten years since the election of President Hugo Chávez, the civil service is still loaded with employees who are against the government.

The report does not demonstrate whether the firings that occurred, in both the public and private sector, were simply the result of individual actions in a highly polarized society in which the opposition spent at least four years (according to opposition leader Teodoro Petkoff) trying to dislodge the government though a military overthrow. Indeed, it is not hard to imagine that many government officials would, in such a climate, be apprehensive about employing people who are against the government. The report does not consider this possible cause of observed discrimination. Of course, this would not justify such discrimination, but neither would it support the sweeping allegations of this report, which attempts to argue that the government is using its control over employment in the public sector in order to repress political opposition.

Indeed, the report's most serious allegation of discrimination in employment concerns a case where discrimination was not based on political partisanship, but in regard to unlawful subversion that no government would, nor should tolerate: "In the aftermath of the oil strike, PDVSA purged its ranks of thousands of workers who participated in the strike." But as anyone who was in Venezuela at the time can attest, this was quite openly a strike to topple the government, which the opposition had succeeded in doing less than eight months earlier. The oil strike devastated the economy—which lost 24 percent of GDP in the resulting recession—and came close to achieving its goal a second time.

The report implies that public employees, in this case oil workers should have the right to strike for the overthrow of an elected government; we do not support that view. It is especially dubious when that group of employees makes up less than one percent of the labour force, and is using its control over a strategic resource—oil revenues made up nearly half of government revenues and 80 percent of export earnings—to cripple the economy and thereby reverse the result of democratic elections. The view that such a strike is "a legitimate strike" is not, to our knowledge, held by any democratic government in the world.

But most importantly with regard to the credibility of the HRW report, it is profoundly misleading for the authors to argue that "political discrimination is a defining feature" of a government that is not willing to risk the continuing employment of people who have carried out such a strike.

The report's overwhelming reliance for factual material on opposition sources of dubious reliability also undermines its credibility and makes it difficult for most readers to know which parts of the report are true and which aren't. The most cited source with regard to political discrimination is the newspaper El Universal. This is not only a stridently opposition newspaper, it has also, for the years during which it is cited, repeatedly fabricated news stories. For example, in a typical fabrication of the type deployed to libel government officials, El Universal reported that then Interior Minister Jesse Chacón had purchased a painting for $140,000. This turned out to be completely false. There are many examples of fabrications in El Universal, as well as other opposition sources cited by the report.

We find it troubling that a report on Human Rights depends heavily on unreliable sources. Would a report on human rights in the United States be taken seriously if it relied so heavily on Fox News, or even worse *The National Enquirer*? Indeed, this report ventures even further into the zone of unreliable sources and cites a mentally unstable opposition blogger as a source. (p. 20, footnote 30). This is a person who indulges not only in routine fabrications and advocates the violent overthrow of the government, but also has publicly fantasized about killing his political enemies and dumping the bodies from helicopters into the slums, and torturing others by "pour[ing] melted silver into their eyes."

A disturbing thing about the report's reliance on these sources is that it indicates a lack of familiarity with the subject matter, or perhaps worse, a deep political prejudice that allows the authors to see most of these sources as unproblematic. Indeed, there is only one passing indication that the newspapers *El Universal* and *El Nacional*, are opposition newspapers, and it is a reference to the past, which the reader might therefore reasonably judge to be irrelevant. On the other hand, the report refers to the newspaper Últimas

Noticias as "largely sympathetic to Chávez and his government" and "a generally pro-government tabloid." (p.70, p.89) This is a newspaper that prints articles that are harshly critical of the government on a daily basis, and according to polling data in Venezuela is seen as vastly more independent than any other major newspapers. The authors' view of the Venezuelan media seems to mirror the view of the right-wing Venezuelan opposition, or the U.S. Right's view of the "liberal media" in the United States.

Such profound prejudice, in which events are interpreted overwhelmingly through the lens of Venezuela's right-wing opposition, is apparent throughout the document: for example when the authors describe groups that helped organize and supported the April 2002 coup as "new organizations dedicated to the defense of democracy and the rule of law." (p. 203).

But the worst thing about the report's reliance on opposition sources like *El Universal, El Nacional, or Súmate*, is that these sources have engaged in enough fabrications as to make them unreliable sources for factual material.

In its discussion of the media, the report also paints a grossly exaggerated picture of reality, while presenting some valid criticisms of existing law and practice. It is acknowledged in footnotes buried deep within the text that the opposition still dominates both broadcast and print media (footnote 184, p.74; footnote 181, p.73). Yet the government is reproached for "having significantly shifted the balance of the media in the government's favour" by creating pro-government TV stations since the 2002 coup, when "Chávez faced an almost entirely hostile private media." This is an odd position for a human rights organization to take. While it would be nice if the government could create TV stations that had no bias whatsoever, isn't it better to have some competition in the media—from left-leaning, pro-government stations—than to have a right-wing, anti-democratic, private monopoly? Especially when that right-wing monopoly had, as never before in world history, organized a military coup against a democratically elected government and led a devastating oil strike that nearly toppled the government a second time? Do the authors consider this type of media monopoly to be more protective of human rights than a media that is still dominated by the opposition but also presents some other sources of information?

The report refers repeatedly to the danger of "self-censorship," but does not provide any examples of this actually happening. This is a major weakness in its argument, since it is not that difficult to find examples of self-censorship in response to government pressure in, for example, the U.S. media.

In the 2004 U.S. Presidential election, the Sinclair Broadcast Group of Maryland, owner of the largest chain of television stations in the U.S., planned to show a documentary that accused candidate John Kerry of betraying American prisoners during the Vietnam War. The company ordered its 62 stations to show the film during prime-time hours just two weeks before the election. Nineteen Democratic senators sent a letter to the U.S. F.C.C. calling for an investigation into this proposed intervention by Sinclair in the campaign, and some made public statements that Sinclair's broadcast license could be in jeopardy if it carried through with its plans. As a result of this pressure, Sinclair backed down and did not broadcast the film.

This example is directly relevant to the HRW report on Venezuela, because it shows that, in order to have a broadcast license in the United States and other democratic countries, the licensee is expected to follow certain rules and not to become a major political actor, e.g. by intervening in elections. As Vivanco himself has noted, "lack of renewal of the contract [broadcast license], per se, is not a free speech issue." Yet this report cites the denial of RCTV's broadcast license renewal as a simple, and indeed its primary, example of the Venezuelan government's alleged attack on free speech. It does not seem to matter to the authors that the station had participated in a military coup and other attempts to topple the government and would not receive a broadcast license in any democratic country.

The report even uses innuendo to imply that the government is to blame for attacks on journalists, which have occurred against both opposition and pro-government journalists. The authors state that the opposition TV station Globovisión "has received warning letters from CONATEL because of the political tone of its reporting, it has been frequently refused entry to government press conferences, and its reporters and cameramen have been physically attacked and threatened by Chávez supporters" (p. 117). The authors provide no evidence that the government in any way condoned or supported such alleged attacks.

The major media in Venezuela to this day are practically unmatched in this hemisphere, and indeed most of the world, for their vehement, unfettered, and even vicious, libellous, and violence inciting attacks on the government. While the HRW report presents a number of valid criticisms of existing law and a few cases of unwarranted intervention by government officials, it serves no legitimate purpose to hide or distort the actual state of Venezuela's media.

The same can be said for the rest of the report, including its treatment of the judiciary. HRW has an obligation to criticize any laws or practices of the Venezuelan government that it sees as endangering human rights, and we welcome the valid criticisms that it raises in its report. But Mr. Vivanco has gravely undermined the credibility of Human Rights Watch by producing a report that, by his own admission, is politically motivated, as well as grossly exaggerated, based on unreliable sources, and advertises broad and sweeping allegations that are unsupported by the evidence.

We therefore request that HRW retract and revise its report so as to produce a credible document. Mr. Vivanco should also retract his remarks as to the political motivation for the report.

We would be glad to meet with you to discuss this issue further, and would welcome a debate with Mr. Vivanco in any public forum of his choosing, should he be willing to defend his report in public.

We hope you will consider these requests with the seriousness they deserve. Our letter is not meant as a justification for the Venezuelan government's decision to expel the authors of the HRW report from the country. Human rights are too important to be used as a political football, as has so often been the case when Washington singles out another government as an enemy state. This is why we depend on civil society organizations for independent, non-partisan, non-political reporting and investigation.

Sincerely,

1. Rodolfo Acuña, Professor, Chicano/a Studies, California State University, Northridge

2. Federico Álvarez, Professor, Universidad Nacional Autónoma de México

3. Tim Anderson, Senior Lecturer in Political Economy, University of Sydney, Australia

4. Miguel Angel Herrera, Historia, Universidad de Costa Rica

5. Robert Austin, Ph.D, Honorary Fellow, School of Historical Studies, University of Melbourne

6. Márgara Averbach, Professor of Literatura, Universidad de Buenos Aires, Argentina...."

108 additional signatures follow

My personal experience during my UN mission to Venezuela, conducting interviews with civil society, government officials, religious institutions, evaluating documents from the government and opposition, leads me to confirm the malaise expressed in the above letter.

When I fact-checked HRW's reports, I concluded that they were political, biased and unprofessional—that they contained too many inaccuracies, insinuations, too many hyperboles, that there was "method in the madness." My experience during my mission revealed a completely different picture from that painted by HRW and most of the mainstream media.

Following the publication of my report[72] in September 2018 there was mitigated discussion of my findings, which were subsequently confirmed by a new mission to Venezuela[73] conducted by UN Special Rapporteur Alena Douhan in 2021.[74]

In my opinion HRW did not use good judgment in entrusting Mr. Vivanco with such politically-charged reports, precisely because he has been accused of being too close a friend of the Venezuelan opposition, notorious for advancing their maximalist positions under the guise of human rights. This stance frustrates any effort at negotiations with leftist governments that comprise the "Troika of Tyranny"[75] and arrogantly claims that sanctions are "the only language they understand."

Nicaragua

HRW reporting on Nicaragua has been similarly marred by bias.[76] Some sources have documented the role of numerous "human rights" organizations in the attempted coup in Nicaragua in 2018 and in related attacks on the Sandinista government.[77] At the time, the Trump administration backed the bloody *coup* in which opposition extremists shot, tortured and killed state security forces and Sandinista activists, burning down buildings and setting people on fire, with the intent to destabilize the government. When the attempted *coup* fizzled out, the "democratic" opposition groups funded by the U.S. government turned to sanctions as the strategy of choice in their regime-change arsenal.

The violence in Nicaragua in 2018 and related incidents showed how some human rights organisations actually play an integral part in the political process. At the local level, foreign-funded NGOs built up a completely distorted picture of what was happening, in which all violence was blamed on the government (or, if it was too obviously opposition violence, left uninvestigated). At the international level, numerous institutions relied on unverified reports to advance a caricature of a despotic regime that kills its citizens, white-washing opposition violence. Then the Organization of American States, the Inter-American Commission on Human Rights and even the United Nations echoed the same biased narratives, subsequently magnified by foreign governments and the international media.

China

HRW's billionaire sponsor George Soros has taken a hardline position against China, calling it a "mortal danger" to neoliberal capitalist democracies, pouring money into groups to try to weaken and destabilize Beijing and remove the Communist Party from power.

A.B. Abrams' book *Atrocity Fabrication and its Consequences* pointed out that the Network of Chinese Human Rights Defenders (CHRD), a major source of Xinjiang genocide allegations, was heavily funded by the U.S. Congress through the National Endowment for Democracy. Having spent years campaigning against Beijing and in support of extreme opposition figures, the CHRD report was widely cited in the Western media as a credible and impartial source on Xinjiang.[78] CHRD listed its address as the Washington D.C. office of Human Rights Watch on its tax forms, which also, Abrams noted, had longstanding ties to Western intelligence agencies and which had played a central role in promoting many of the fabricated atrocities against targets such as Iraq and North Korea.

AMNESTY INTERNATIONAL

Like HRW, Amnesty International does many good things and produces some remarkable reports. Its condemnation of the persecution of journalists, including Julian Assange,[79] is commendable. In my experience, most of Amnesty's reports to the Human Rights Council are well researched and very helpful for the experts.

Amnesty's worldwide activities impact many countries and promote economic, social and cultural rights more than HRW. For instance, in 2011, in its submission to the Human Rights Council in the context of the Universal Periodic Review of Singapore, Amnesty International called out Singapore for numerous breaches on human rights[80]—not only freedom of expression, association, and assembly, but also migrant workers' rights to legal funding when pursuing claims of unpaid salaries from their employers, and the exclusion of migrant domestic workers in the Employment of Foreign Workers Act [81]

Amnesty International's statement of October 5, 2021 to the outrageous decision by the ICC Chief Prosecutor Karim Khan to discontinue investigations into war crimes and crimes against humanity by NATO forces in Afghanistan is exemplary.

AFGHANISTAN: ICC PROSECUTOR'S STATEMENT ON AFGHANISTAN JEOPARDISES HIS OFFICE'S LEGITIMACY AND FUTURE

Amnesty International urges International Criminal Court (ICC) Prosecutor Karim Khan to conduct a full investigation in Afghanistan into all parties to the conflict and to urgently reconsider his decision to "deprioritise" investigations into Article 5 crimes allegedly committed by Afghan National Security Forces (ANSF) and the armed forces of the United States of America and its Central Intelligence Agency (CIA). Failure to do so would present grave questions on the ICC-OTP's future legitimacy and purpose. On September 27, 2021, Prosecutor Karim Khan announced that he had filed an application seeking authorisation for the Office of the Prosecutor (OTP) to resume its investigation in the Situation in Afghanistan. The statement provided that he had "decided to focus my Office's investigations in Afghanistan on crimes allegedly committed by the Taliban and the Islamic State—Khorasan Province (IS-K) and to deprioritise other aspects of this investigation." Amnesty International is gravely concerned by the Prosecutor's approach and urges the OTP to proceed with a full investigation in Afghanistan, a situation which has been subject to OTP preliminary examination and investigation for 14 years, during which victims of crimes committed by all parties to the conflict have ceaselessly demanded justice from the ICC. In his stated approach, Prosecutor Khan appears willing to bow to political as well as resource pressure, applied by powerful states, whose actions would restrict the activities of a "universal" ICC which may investigate situations where their nationals and interests are affected. We recall that, until April this year, U.S. government sanctions were applied on Former Prosecutor Fatou Bensouda and other OTP staff with the overt intention of halting investigations into U.S. nationals—despite the Court having clear territorial jurisdiction to do so. Having faced-down the U.S. government's egregious attacks, that the Prosecutor would take a decision which aligns with the objectives of those who had sought to infringe his Office's hard-fought independence, is almost unfathomable. Of course, the Prosecutor's announcement that—if authorisation is granted—he will seek to resume investigations into crimes allegedly committed by the Taliban and the Islamic State—Khorasan Province ("IS-K") is welcome. However, the Prosecutor's decision to deprioritise certain investigations fails to respect the rights of victims and has the discriminatory effect of denying justice to certain victims of crimes that fall under the Court's jurisdiction. In recalling the limited resources available to his Office, the Prosecutor appears to fatally accept arbitrary financial restrictions which have, for many years, been imposed by states parties based on political considerations rather than the requirements of the OTP to conduct its work. The Prosecutor could have used the opportunity of the statement or authorisation request to demonstrate why a significant increase of resources is required to pursue a comprehensive justice strategy for Afghanistan. Instead, the Prosecutor has adopted weak resource justifications to pursue one-sided investigations. Similarly, the Prosecutor's statement that "there is no longer the prospect of genuine and effective domestic investigations into Article 5 crimes within Afghanistan" does not logically lead to the conclusion that only investigations into the Taliban or IS-K should be pursued by the OTP at the present time. The implication that, at present, there may be a more likely prospect of successful cooperation and investigations of the Taliban outside of Afghanistan than into the ANSF or U.S. nationals is unconvincing. At present, the Court will likely face significant cooperation challenges in

Afghanistan, as well as from non-states parties, which may require creative solutions, including investigative activities outside of Afghanistan. This is not a new development, and the OTP has already been creative in situations where cooperation is not readily forthcoming from a State, or if it cannot access a State's territory. It should be recalled that all states parties to the Rome Statute have an obligation to cooperate with the Court in relation to the Afghanistan investigation. Therefore, while securing cooperation in Afghanistan may be challenging, the OTP could actively (and perhaps in a less resource intensive manner) pursue investigations in relation to certain parties and allegations, including those concerning well-documented cases of torture in CIA "black sites," on the territory of states parties other than Afghanistan. In this instance, cases concerning a number of men apprehended in the aftermath of the 9/11 attacks, who were held by the U.S. in a secret prison in Afghanistan and subsequently transferred to secret detention sites in Lithuania, Poland and Romania. Indeed, as the OTP has provided, "with regard to States Parties, in addition to Afghanistan, the available information suggests that the cooperation of Lithuania, Poland, and Romania may also be desirable in some respects." While the OTP may be called to prioritise its activities and cases, the Prosecutor's decision to exclude certain conflict actors from a situation before it has commenced a thorough active investigation seems—at best—premature. As Amnesty International has reported, thousands of Afghan civilians have been killed in the conflict by international forces, and thousands more have been injured. The Prosecutor's approach would continue to leave victims "in the dark" and compound failures of accountability for civilian casualties caused by international military operations in Afghanistan. Crucially, of course, prioritisation should never be based, or appear to be, on whether certain perpetrators are more powerful, or whether investigating them would be more challenging or resource intensive to the Court. The OTP must also be acutely aware when its prioritisation decisions will lead to almost certain impunity for perpetrators who have not been genuinely investigated or prosecuted, and who—without the ICC's intervention—are likely to enjoy perpetual impunity. The CIA's use of "black sites" for its rendition program of enforced disappearance, arbitrary detention and torture was designed to evade scrutiny and accountability, and it is particularly galling that the Prosecutor's decision appears to reward such illegality and helps entrench impunity. In its own words, the OTP's information (at the preliminary examination phase) related to CIA black-sites was limited by "the clandestine nature of the detention and interrogation programme; efforts to conceal the number and identity of victims [and]; the denial of access to national and international reporting mechanisms mandated to monitor and report on the conditions of detention." That the Prosecutor is not willing to prioritise the active investigation of these "clandestine" sites of torture, despite finding "the treatment of CIA detainees appears to have been particularly grave on a qualitative assessment," calls into serious question the ICC's credibility as a "universal" court and its purpose to end impunity for all persons without any distinction. Ultimately, and we do not say this lightly, the Prosecutor appears willing to pursue a selective justice strategy in Afghanistan couched in the language of prioritisation, and justifying what amount to "double standards" as "pragmatism." The dangerous message this is sending is that the most powerful human rights abusers are able to avoid ICC investigation and prosecution, and that their victims cannot even look to "the Court of last resort" for truth, justice, and reparations. Amnesty International strongly urges Prosecutor Karim Khan to urgently reconsider his decision."[82]

Concerning the sanctions imposed by the United Sates on the former ICC Prosecutor Fatou Bensouda and her staff, Amnesty reacted clearly and correctly on September 20, 2020:

U.S. SANCTIONS AGAINST ICC STAFF CREATE CHILLING EFFECT FOR INTERNATIONAL JUSTICE

Responding to today's announcement of U.S. sanctions against the International Criminal Court (ICC), Daniel Balson, advocacy director at Amnesty International USA, said:

"The Trump administration's decision to enact sanctions against senior ICC staff is another brazen attack against international justice. The court is made up of legal professionals who have dedicated their professional lives in pursuit of justice for victims and survivors of some of the most horrific crimes, including crimes against humanity. They should be commended for their commitment, not subjected to a punitive campaign of intimidation. Grotesquely, the White House's actions may dissuade survivors of human rights abuses from demanding justice, and create a chilling effect on those who would support their efforts.

"Today's announcement is designed to do what this administration does best- bully and intimidate. It penalizes not only the ICC, but civil society actors working for justice alongside the court worldwide.

"Today's reckless actions constitute a demand that the U.S. government be granted a political carve out of impunity for nationals accused of having committed crimes under international law in Afghanistan. No one responsible for the most serious crimes under international law should be able to hide from accountability, under a cloak of impunity.

"Amnesty International USA is calling on Congress to stand up for international justice and object to this transparent abuse of the executive's congressionally mandated sanctions power by speaking out forcefully against this decision and modifying the powers it grants to the executive so that they can no longer be abused in pursuit of impunity."

Amnesty International's Latin American Reporting

On the other hand, Amnesty International's position on Latin America, its focus on alleged violations of civil and political rights in countries that are struggling to shake off the yoke of U.S. domination, is unfortunate. It would be better if Amnesty would accept the reality that it was U.S. hostility toward Cuba and its attempt to topple the Castro government by force actually drove Castro into the arms of the Soviet Union, because that was the only way to preserve the sovereignty of Cuba. Amnesty still suffers from a mindset that gives priority to "first generation" rights while forgetting the so-called "second" and "third" generation rights advocated by leaders of Argentina, Bolivia, Brazil, Mexico, Honduras, Nicaragua, and Venezuela. When Fidel Castro passed away in 2016, Amnesty published a commentary[83] and evaluation. I agree only with part of it, because it fails to understand cause and effect, the history, the context, the adverse impact of illegal U.S. unilateral coercive measures.

Very briefly, Amnesty's reporting on Venezuela and China, two areas about which I do know something from personal experience, is just plain biased—and wrong.

Venezuela

When in January 2023 UN High Commissioner for Human Rights, Volker Türk, undertook a mission to Venezuela, Amnesty wrote an open letter which seems to align itself with the "Washington consensus" and does not seem to follow the constructive proposals of my own report on Venezuela[84] and the subsequent reports of UN rapporteur Alena Douhan.[85]

Amnesty's open letter sounds like the song of the State Department—and it fails to recognize cause and effect, the history of Hugo Chavez, the necessary struggle against U.S. imperialism in Latin America and the absurdity of the Monroe Doctrine. The open letter does not address the illegal unilateral coercive measures imposed by the United States on Venezuela or the devastating impact of these "sanctions" not only on economic, social, and cultural rights, but also on civil and political rights, because UCMs cause a state of emergency which in turn leads governments to take emergency measures which restrict rather than expand civil and political rights. Indeed, sanctions kill and are invariably counter-productive.[86] This does not seem to be understood by the AI leadership. The AI communication to Volker Türk below is illustrative of this orientation.

MAIN CONCERNS AND RECOMMENDATIONS REGARDING THE HUMAN RIGHTS SITUATION IN VENEZUELA

Dear Mr. Volker Türk,

In recent years, Amnesty International has been part of the collective effort by Venezuelan and international civil society organizations seeking to ensure that mechanisms of scrutiny and international justice relating to the serious human rights violations committed against the Venezuelan people remain in place and continue to operate. Some of these violations may amount to crimes against humanity, as established by the Office of the Prosecutor of the International Criminal Court, the UN International and Independent Fact-Finding Mission on Venezuela (the Fact-Finding Mission), as well as in our own research. Although your Office has had a presence in the country since 2019, with a dual mandate of reporting on the human rights situation and providing technical cooperation, at Amnesty International, we remain concerned by Venezuelan authorities' ongoing implementation of a policy of repression against any form of dissent or criticism against the government, the rampant impunity for human rights violations and crimes under international law, as well as the continued deterioration in access to economic and social rights. Based on the above, we take this opportunity to suggest you take the following issues into consideration during your visit to the country:

The closure of civic space and stigmatization of human rights defence. Venezuelan civil society, human rights defenders, activists, personnel providing humanitarian assistance and all those working to improve access to human rights in Venezuela in general, are carrying out their roles in an environment of constant threats, intimidation and attacks aimed at silencing them and quashing their criticisms. For years, Venezuelan authorities have used various administrative, judicial and propaganda mechanisms to impede their work, eroding civic space, access to justice and the independence of public institutions. Recently, the possibility of the approval of a law to regulate and oversee international cooperation to non-governmental organizations has resurfaced, which for years has served as a threat against human rights defenders and humanitarian workers, the purpose of which is to arbitrarily control, supervise, intimidate and impede the work of non-governmental organizations in the country. We believe it is of the utmost priority that your Office intervenes to put a stop to this initiative because of the serious risk it would pose to human rights organizations, humanitarian organizations and victims and survivors of human rights violations whose work is essential for the defence and protection of fundamental rights in Venezuela.

The release of politically motivated arbitrary detainees. Human rights organizations and your own Office have documented the use of arbitrary detention to silence criticism of the government of Nicolás Maduro. Reference: AMR 53/6371/2023 Volker Türk UN High Commissioner for Human Rights, January 26, 2023. www.amnesty.org

According to a number of organizations in the country providing them with legal defence, there are currently around 300 people still arbitrarily detained for political reasons, and hundreds of people who have been detained in the past still face severe restrictions on their freedom, as they are subject to arbitrary criminal proceedings which lack judicial guarantees. The Government of Venezuela must end its policy of repression and systematic arbitrary detentions. Of particular concern is the use of arbitrary detention against journalists, such as Roland Carreño, and human rights defenders, such as Javier Tarazona, coordinator of the non-governmental organization FUNDAREDES, who has been arbitrarily detained since July 2, 2021, in retaliation for his work defending human rights. Amnesty International reiterates its call for an immediate and unconditional end to their detentions and for their health and physical integrity to be protected while they remain in detention. Such detentions are a serious violation of human rights, but they also send a message designed to discourage and intimidate other human rights defenders in Venezuela. Therefore, any attempt to move towards an improvement in the situation in Venezuela must encompass the release of politically motivated arbitrary detainees and, especially, human rights defenders.

The strengthening of the presence of the Office of the High Commissioner for Human Rights and other international scrutiny mechanisms Amnesty International has supported the Venezuelan human rights movement in seeking mechanisms for international scrutiny over the dire human rights situation in the country. It has supported calls for the establishment of specific mandates regarding your Office and the establishment of the Fact-Finding Mission, with a view to ensuring that both bodies can have a complementary impact on preventing human rights violations and increase the likelihood of accountability processes. Amnesty International considers it essential that the presence of your Office in the field be strengthened, not only in regard to financial and human resources, but also with institutional support so that its reporting on the country has a real deterrent effect in preventing serious human rights violations and acts as protection for human rights defenders in the country. Likewise, it is essential that the valuable work of technical assistance, monitoring and reporting that your Office has carried out for years, also maintains rigorous and public scrutiny over the Venezuelan state's progress or regression regarding the recommendations made in previous years; without this, the lack of follow-up on their implementation risks eroding the importance and credibility of its mandate. To increase scrutiny and monitoring of Venezuela, it is also of utmost importance that relevant steps be taken to enable United Nations special procedures and rapporteurs to visit the country. As agreed with your predecessor, Michelle Bachelet, Venezuela had made a commitment of 10 in-situ

visits in the coming years. However, it should be noted that
not only have only three visits been made, but also none of
the mechanisms that have obtained official invitations from
Venezuela have mandates to monitor civil and political
rights. We therefore consider it a priority that your Office
reiterates a call to authorities to allow the Working Group
on Arbitrary Detention, the Special Rapporteur on Torture,
the Special Rapporteur on the Situation of Human Rights
Defenders, and other mandates related to civil and political
rights to visit the country in the near future. Moreover,
Amnesty International views the work carried out by the
Fact-Finding Mission, established by the Human Rights
Council in 2019 and whose mandate has been renewed until
2024, as a milestone. The organization urges your Office
to ensure its efforts to document human rights violations
are carried out in a complementary and coordinated manner
with the Mission. The mandate of the Mission is to ensure
accountability for serious human rights violations and it has
established that there are reasonable grounds to believe that
crimes against humanity have been committed in Venezuela,
so the efforts of your Office to document the situation and
provide technical cooperation to the Venezuelan government
must—at least and in order to ensure consistency between
both mandates—consider the systematic and widespread
nature of human rights violations and how they reflect a
policy emanating from the highest levels of government.
In conclusion, Venezuelan authorities continue implementing a severe policy of repression that threatens to silence
those people who are considered critical of the government
of Nicolás Maduro, while, at the same time, the situation
regarding access to economic and social rights is becoming
more precarious by the day, forcing the Venezuelan people to
demand their rights. The coexistence of these realities puts
at risk and threatens those at the mercy of the authorities'
arbitrariness. As a consequence of the severe human rights
crisis and complex humanitarian emergency, by the end of
2022, the InterAgency Coordination Platform for Refugees
and Migrants from Venezuela estimated that 7.13 million

Venezuelans have left the country, 84% seeking protection in 17 countries in Latin America and the Caribbean. Most of these people have faced various obstacles in accessing their right to seek asylum or receive international protection, often experiencing human rights violations, ranging from gender-based violence, lack of access to basic health and education services, to death and enforced disappearance. The Office you head has a privileged role compared to other international bodies and, in our view, this must be used to advance the protection of victims and survivors seeking truth, justice, reparation and guarantees of non-repetition both in Venezuela and outside, as well to those who defend human rights in Venezuela. Finally, Amnesty International calls on you and your Office to intervene to ensure that civic space is maintained; that human rights defenders are protected; that politically motivated arbitrary detainees and human rights defenders, such as prisoner of conscience Javier Tarazona, are released; and that trade union and workers' rights activists, as well as other social activists, who strongly demand their right to a decent salary and living conditions, are protected. It also urges you to advocate for the strengthening and opening up to international scrutiny through your Office's presence in the country; the effective invitation of special procedures and treaty bodies relevant to reports from civil society; and establish dialogue and feedback with the mandate of the Fact-Finding Mission. Yours sincerely, Erika Guevara Rosas Americas Regional Director Amnesty International, International Secretariat.[87]

ALLEGED PENETRATION OF AMNESTY INTERNATIONAL BY INTELLIGENCE SERVICES[88]

Many who criticize Amnesty International complain that it applies double standards, that it has a neo-liberal agenda, that it is in the service of Washington and Brussels. Some observers have tried to establish that AI and other NGOs have been penetrated by intelligence services. I wish I had the time to investigate these allegations.

In any event, I do think that they are worth earnest consideration. Unsurprisingly, the corporate media ignores these critics as if they did not exist, dismissing them as purveyors of "fake news" and "conspiracy theories." Amnesty International enjoys such prestige and such a powerful position in the establishment and media that its critics are seldom heard, never taken seriously, never get a platform, other than in the "alternative media" and the social media.

In 2012 former U.S. Marine Brian Berletic[89] pointed out:

> Mistakenly considered by many as the final word on human rights worldwide, it might surprise people to know that Amnesty International is in fact one of the greatest obstacles to real human rights advocacy on Earth. In its most recent 2012 annual report (page 4, .pdf), Amnesty reiterates one of the biggest lies it routinely tells:
>
> > Amnesty International is funded mainly by its membership and public donations. No funds are sought or accepted from governments for investigating and campaigning against human rights abuses. Amnesty International is independent of any government, political ideology, economic interest or religion.
>
> This is categorically false. Amnesty international is indeed funded and run by not only governments, but also immense corporate-financier interests, and is not only absolutely entwined with political ideology and economic interests, it is an essential tool used for perpetuating just such interests.

Amnesty International's Funding

Finding financial information on Amnesty International's website is made purposefully difficult—specifically to protect the myth that the organization is "independent." Like any organized criminal operation, Amnesty separates compromising financial ties through a series of legal manoeuvres and shell organizations. Upon Amnesty's website it states:

The work carried out through Amnesty International's International Secretariat is organised into two legal entities, in compliance with United Kingdom law. These are Amnesty International Limited ("AIL") and Amnesty International Charity Limited ("AICL"). Amnesty International Limited undertakes charitable activities on behalf of Amnesty International Charity Limited, a registered charity.

And it is there, at Amnesty International Limited, where ties to both governments and corporate-financier interests are kept. On page 11 of Amnesty International Limited's 2011 Report and Financial Statement it states (emphasis added):

The Directors are pleased to acknowledge the support of the John D. and Catherine T. MacArthur Foundation, the Oak Foundation, Open Society Georgia Foundation, the Vanguard Charitable Endowment Programme, Mauro Tunes and American Jewish World Service. The UK Department for International Development (Governance and Transparency Fund) continued to fund a four-year human rights education project in Africa. The European Commission (EuropeAid) generously awarded a multi-year grant towards Amnesty International's human rights education work in Europe.

Clearly then, Amnesty does take money from both governments and corporate-financier interests....

Amnesty's leadership is also telling of its true agenda. Suzanne Nossel, Executive Director of Amnesty International USA, for instance was drawn directly from the U.S. State Department—again, utterly contradicting Amnesty's claims of being "independent" of governments and corporate interests. Nossel continued promoting U.S. foreign policy, but simply behind a podium with a new logo, Amnesty International's logo, attached to it. Amnesty

International's website specifically mentions Nossel's role behind U.S. State Department-backed UN resolutions regarding Iran, Syria, Libya, and Cote d'Ivoire.

It has been documented at great length how these issues revolve around a decades long plan devised by corporate-financier interests to divide, destroy and despoil these nations who are seen as obstacles to U.S. global hegemony. In the case of Syria specifically, it was revealed that the current "human rights" catastrophe stems back to a malicious 2007 conspiracy documented by *New Yorker* journalist Seymour Hersh, between the U.S., Israel, and Saudi Arabia which sought to purposefully fund, arm, and deploy sectarian extremists to undermine and overthrow the Syrian government—this knowing full well the human tragedy that would unfold.

Nossel's "contributions" then are simply to dress up naked military aggression and the pursuit of global corporate-financier hegemony with the pretense of "human rights" advocacy.

A glance at AmnestyUSA.org reveals that each and every front the U.S. State Department is currently working on and has prioritized is also coincidentally prioritized by Amnesty International. This includes rallies and campaigns to support U.S. State Department-funded Russian opposition groups (currently fixated on "Pussy Riot"), undermining the Syrian government, toppling the government of Belarus, and supporting the Wall Street-London created Aung San Suu Kyi of Myanmar (still called by its British Imperial nomenclature of "Burma" by Suu Kyi herself).

In some areas Amnesty International Betrays Real Human Rights Advocacy

Amnesty does indeed cover issues that are critical of U.S. foreign policy, toward the bottom of their websites and at the back of their reports. Likewise, the corporate media selectively reports issues that coincide with their interests while other issues are either under-reported or not reported at all. And it is precisely because Amnesty covers all issues, but selectively emphasizes those that are conducive to the interests of immense corporate-financiers that makes Amnesty one of the greatest impediments to genuine human rights advocacy on Earth....

Ordinary people are given the false impression that "someone is watching out" for human rights abuses, when in reality, all Amnesty and other organizations like it are doing, is managing public perception selectively of global human rights abuses, fabricating and/or manipulating many cases specifically to suit the agenda of large corporate-financier interests. This can be seen when entire reports out of Amnesty or Human Rights Watch consist solely of "witness reports" compiled from accounts of U.S.-backed opposition groups....

When people erroneously believe that credible organizations are handling "rights advocacy" they will not only become complacent, they will become negligent of their own responsibilities to objectively examine potential abuses and speak out against them. Wall Street and London's corporate-financier interests have filled a void—that should be occupied by their greatest opponents—instead with a large advocacy racket of their own creation. Not only are they given a free pass to abuse human rights globally, they've actually used their controlled opposition to attack their opponents. [90]

A recent commentary by Berletic on Amnesty International and the Ukraine war is worth listening to.[91] Indeed, war crimes are not committed by only one side, and it is important for institutions and NGOs to remain impartial when it comes to the crimes of aggression, war crimes and crimes against humanity.

Although I am not in a position to verify the above allegations, I am surprised that no open discussion has taken place concerning the issues that it raises. The issues are important, and they do deserve our attention.

At this point it may be useful to turn to AI's genealogy. In October 2020, an article published by Vanessa Beeley addressed "the secret history of how British intelligence created Amnesty International"[92]:

Amnesty International projects itself as the watchdog on human rights worldwide with the stated mission to campaign for "a world in which every person enjoys all of the human rights enshrined in the Universal Declaration of Human Rights and other international human rights instruments." However, lesser known is the fact that Amnesty International was created by British Intelligence for intelligence gathering to carry out social engineering of targeted nations critical of the British Empire. Amnesty International was involved in not only the cover-up of torture and regime change by British agents but also in sparking a war. Amnesty's stellar image as a global defender of human rights runs counter to its early days when the British Foreign Office was censoring reports critical of the British Empire. During the 1960s the U.K. was withdrawing from its colonies and the Foreign Office and Colonial Office were hungry for information from human-rights activists about the situations on the ground. In 1963, the Foreign Office instructed its operatives abroad to provide 'discreet support' for Amnesty's campaigns.

... *The relationship between Amnesty and Whitehall was placed on a more solid footing in 1963, when the Foreign Office wrote to overseas missions urging "discreet support" for Amnesty: discreet, because its public endorsement would have seriously undermined the campaign's credibility.*

Peter Benenson, the co-founder of Amnesty International, had deep ties to the British Foreign Office and Colonial Office. During the war, he worked in military intelligence at the Bletchley Park code-breaking center. Benenson worked as an undercover spy gathering intelligence under the cover of Amnesty International, directly sponsored by The Crown....

In 1966, Amnesty International was rocked by a major scandal when its founder, Peter Benenson, claimed that the organisation was infiltrated by British intelligence agents and called for its headquarters to be moved to another country.

This is followed by claims from the U.S. that the Central Intelligence Agency (CIA) was also involved in Amnesty. Benenson himself was then exposed for accepting funds from the British Government. Unclassified documents also reveal how Israeli intelligence operated the local branch of Amnesty International. The Israeli government funded the establishment and activity of the Amnesty International branch in Israel in the 1960s and 70s. Official documents reveal that the chairman of the organization was in constant contact with the Foreign Ministry and received instructions from it.

It is difficult to judge HRW and Amnesty International except on a case-by-case basis. There does not seem to be an over-arching coherence about their work. Some reports and initiatives are fully in conformity with the UN's most noble human rights principles and aspirations, while other activities seem to be contrary to accepted norms stipulated in the UN Charter, key principles of international law and international solidarity. Unfortunately, both depend on donations and seem to be too close to Western neo-liberal power centers and think tanks, too close to the Washington and Brussels establishment. That diminishes their authority and credibility.

The penetration by intelligence services of HRW, Amnesty International, the Office of the High Commissioner for Human Rights, the International Criminal Court, the Organization for the Prohibition of Chemical Weapons, etc. all deserve proper investigation, whether that penetration come from the U.S., UK, France, Israel, Qatar, Saudi Arabia, China, Russia—or anywhere else. Such an investigation exceeds the scope of this book. The reader, however, should be aware that some big questions concerning the authority and credibility of human rights institutions have been posed and that hitherto no one has provided a satisfactory answer.

The Allegation that NGOs are Foreign Agents

Effective nongovernmental organizations are those that stay within their terms of reference and try to persuade rather than cajole, try to inform and educate rather than lecture and disseminate unsubstantiated allegations. When NGOs go beyond the boundaries of common sense, there is pushback from governments and also from parts of civil society that reject *ultra vires* activities and interference in internal affairs. Hence, NGOs are well advised to be patient and persevere, to do solid work in building bridges between society and their respective governments, in persuading governments that it is in their own interest to promote the human rights of the population, so as to achieve a happier social climate. Especially when NGOs establish offices in foreign countries, they should never forget that they are guests, and should therefore behave as guests. They can have a lot of "added value"—or they can spoil it for themselves and for the peoples they are supposed to help. They can definitely offer their assistance to governments on how to improve their human rights performance. But this obviously requires certain diplomatic skills that not all NGOs possess. Moreover, NGOs must observe a code of deontology and refrain from meddling in politics in States where they operate.

"Foreign agent" laws were pioneered by the U.S. in 1938 when it passed the Foreign Agents Registration Act (FARA), imposing strict controls on NGOs. McCarthyism in the 1950s exacerbated matters. FARA is still active against Russian and Chinese NGOs. Should it be a surprise that the Russians and Chinese copied us? While I agree with the rationale of the Foreign Agents Registration Act, I reject the hypocrisy of the U.S. government and the media that then criticize other countries for enacting similar legislation in the name of social stability and national security. When Nicaragua passed legislation comparable to FARA, when they started enforcing the law and some U.S. allies and funding recipients (like Violeta Chamorro) were punished, the U.S. media sent out howls of outrage.[93] I think it is reasonable to let the courts of each country decide whether foreign-funded NGOs are engaging in subversive political activism or not. In any event, it has become evident that the level of NGO interference in the internal affairs of states and their destabilizing impact on the constitutional order has become so prevalent that more and more countries have adopted or are considering the adoption of legislation to control this "invasion" of foreign interests, or simply to ban them.[94] And even so, it may be the case that such penetration has proceeded to the point where banning foreign NGOs as foreign agents becomes nearly impossible in certain countries. When the Georgian government attempted to simply request foreign agents to register as such under the Georgian replication of the U.S.'s FARA, widespread protests ensued, which did not cease once the government withdrew the legislation.[95]

Lavish Compensation and Generous Golden Handshakes

It would certainly surprise many poor and middle-class folks who donate to HRW and Amnesty International that they have fifteen staff making over $200K, with Ken Roth at HRW making $560K plus $60K in benefits. In February 2011, newspaper stories in the UK revealed that the Secretary-general of Amnesty International, Irene Khan, had received a payment of £533,103 following her resignation from the organization on December 31, 2009, a fact from Amnesty's records for the 2009–2010 financial year. Her payout was in excess of four times her annual salary of £132,490.[96] Khan's deputy secretary general, Kate Gilmore, who also resigned in December 2009, received an *ex-gratia* payment of £320,000. The amount paid out to Khan and her deputy (who was also removed by AI's International Executive Committee [IEC]) amounted to 4% of Amnesty International's budget that year.[97]

Peter Pack, the chairman of IEC, initially stated on February 19, 2011: "The payments to outgoing secretary general Irene Khan shown in the accounts of AI (Amnesty International) Ltd for the year ending March 31, 2010 include payments made as part of a confidential agreement between AI Ltd and Irene Khan" and that "It is a term of this agreement that no further comment on it will be made by either party."[98]

The payment and AI's initial response to its leakage to the press led to considerable outcry. Philip Davies, Conservative MP for Shipley, decried the payment: "I am sure people making donations to Amnesty, in the belief they are alleviating poverty, never dreamed they were subsidising a fat cat payout. This will disillusion many benefactors. An Amnesty donor said last night: 'I won't be giving any more money. How can this woman lecture the world about abuses and then walk off with this staggering amount of cash?'" [99]

WORTHY INDEPENDENT NGOS ADDRESSING HUMAN RIGHTS

What follows is a brief overview of my personal experience with NGOs and my thoughts about how civil society can contribute to advancing human rights without falling into the trap of advancing the geopolitical interests of Washington and Brussels.

Women's International League for Peace and Freedom (WILPF)[100]

Founded in 1915, this NGO has over 100 years of genuine human rights and peace activism. It is the first women's peace organization and has achieved much in promoting the rights of women worldwide. WILPF's activism has not been marred by the betrayal of values, cheap politicization and that "bandwagon" mentality that characterizes other NGOs that are seeking donations and trying to make themselves "attractive" by sounding "progressive" while echoing the narratives of Washington and Brussels.

In 2015 in my capacity as Professor and UN Independent expert, I nominated WILPF for the Nobel Peace Prize,[101] and persuaded 20 of my fellow rapporteurs to join me in the nomination. Alas, they did not get it—indeed; it is no secret that the Nobel Peace Prize Committee has morphed into a political body that no longer follows the clear intent of Alfred Nobel as expressed in his last will and testament.[102] Nonetheless, as was reported to me, WILPF made the 2015 "short list."

WILPF is a proactive non-governmental organization whose key work has been to challenge militarism, invest in peace and strengthen multilateralism. In order to achieve its aims, WILPF has four key programs: human rights, disarmament, gender-peace-security and crisis response. WILPF has national sections in 30 countries.

International Peace Bureau (IPB)

Founded in 1890, the International Peace Bureau has remained true to its vision of a World Without War. It has Consultative Status with the Economic and Social Council since 1977 and is active in the work of the Human Rights Council. Back in 2014 I had the opportunity of participating in several of their panels and side events and gained insights for my 2014 report to the Human Rights Council[103] on the issue of Disarmament for Development. IPB plays a crucial role in the Geneva-based NGO Committee for Disarmament.

In 1910 IPB was awarded the Nobel Peace prize and it would certainly deserve a second NPP in recognition of its excellent initiatives in the field of disarmament and its contributions to the Geneva-based NGO Committee for Disarmament, where it plays a crucial role.

Its current focus is on persuading countries to convert military-first economies into human security economies and advancing its programs on Disarmament for Sustainable Development, confident that the 17 Sustainable Development Goals can be achieved by 2030—but only if states radically reduce military expenditures and reallocate the budget to achieve human rights and human development goals so as to fulfil real human needs and the protection of the environment. IPB supports a range of disarmament campaigns and furnishes data on the economic dimensions of weapons and conflicts. Its campaign for nuclear disarmament began back in the 1980s and continues because of the increased dangers of nuclear confrontation following the Russian invasion of Ukraine.

IPB rightly criticizes the arms race and the increase in military expenditures, particularly by NATO countries. IPB is interested in addressing the root causes of conflict and reducing tensions. Unfortunately, this does not seem to be on the agenda of Western countries.

IPB's 300 member organisations in 70 countries, together with individual members, form a global network that brings together knowledge and campaigning experience with synergies with experts and advocates active in civil society movements.

In my many years of cooperating with the IPB Geneva office (which had to closed in 2017 for lack of funds), I learned to appreciate their genuine commitment to human rights and international solidarity unlike other well-funded Geneva based NGOs that essentially serve the interests of Washington and Brussels.

In the spirit of a true human rights NGO, the International Peace Bureau launched an appeal in November 2022 for a truce in the Ukraine war. Unfortunately, without success, proclaiming:

Let us call for a ceasefire in Ukraine for Christmas 2022/2023, from [December 25] to [January 7], as a sign of our shared humanity, reconciliation, and peace.

The Christmas Truce of 1914 in the midst of World War I was a symbol of hope and courage, when the people of warring countries organized an armistice on their own authority and joined in spontaneous reconciliation and fraternization. This was proof that even during the most violent conflicts, in the words of Pope Benedict XV, "the guns may fall silent at least upon the night the angels sang."

We turn to the leaders of the warring parties: let the weapons be silent. Give people a moment of peace and, through this moment, open the way to negotiations.

We call on the international community to strongly support and advocate for a Christmas ceasefire and to push for a new start to negotiations between the two sides.

Our vision and goal is a new peace architecture for Europe which includes security for all European countries on the basis of common security.

Peace, reconciliation, a shared sense of humanity can triumph over the hatred, violence and guilt that currently dominate the war. Let us be reminded that we are all humans and that war and destruction against one another is senseless.

A Christmas truce is a much-needed opportunity to again recognize our compassion for one another. Together— we are convinced—the cycle of destruction, suffering and death can be overcome.

I am reminded of the song by the Irish group "Celtic Thunder,"[104] and the statement attributed to Bertrand Russell: "War does not determine who is right, but who is left." While there is no source proving that Russell ever said it, similar thoughts were expressed before and after Russell.[105]

The International Progress Organization (IPO)[106]

Another outstanding NGO promoting peace is the International Progress Organization (IPO), an Austrian think tank founded in Innsbruck in 1972. IPO has done remarkable work in awareness building, conducted international conferences and consultations with a view to building bridges and promoting peaceful coexistence among nations and peoples, an equitable international order, the right to development, global respect for human rights and the rule of law in the spirit of the UN Charter. It has consultative status with the UN Economic and Social Council and members in more than 70 countries. Its expert meetings have focused *inter alia* on conflict resolution, civilizational dialogue,[107] multilateralism, the uniform application of international law, and UN reform.[108]

The IPO has published *Studies in International Relations* since 1978, as well as studies on international relations theory, under the guidance of Professor Hans Köchler, former Dean of the Philosophy Faculty at the University of Innsbruck. Among their recent activities has been the publication of a blueprint for peace in the Ukraine war.[109]

International Human Rights Association of American Minorities[110]

IHRAAM was founded in 1985 at The Hague Academy of International Law in the Netherlands by African American law students Dr. Y. N. Kly, Dr. Yvonne King and Dr. Charles Knox. It serves as an umbrella organization to facilitate and coordinate the efforts of national minorities, indigenous peoples, and unrepresented and occupied nations to gain access to international law and its enforcement mechanisms concerning human rights. IHRAAM was awarded Consultative Status with the Economic and Social Council of the United Nations in 1993.

As member of the Board of IHRAAM, I have had the opportunity to speak at the Human Rights Council on IHRAAM's behalf on a variety of issues, mostly during the interactive dialogue that follows the presentation of reports by UN Special Rapporteurs, and during the general debate. I have also participated in numerous side-events held at the Palais des Nations when the HRC is in session.

IHRAAM actively assists individuals, minorities, unrepresented peoples and nations to gain access to the many human rights monitoring, petition and enforcement mechanisms, deepening awareness by peoples and governments of the array of institutional options for the exercise of the right to self-determination as a means of conflict prevention and conflict resolution, with a view to ensuring social harmony while promoting cultural preservation and equal-status development. [111]

To that end, it has submitted written and oral interventions to the Human Rights Council, the Expert Mechanism on Indigenous Peoples, the UN Forum on Minority Issues, the Committee on the Elimination of All Forms of Racial Discrimination, the Permanent Forum on Indigenous Issues, the UN Working Group on Peoples of African Descent, the UN Special Committee on Decolonization, and the Human Rights Council's Universal Periodic Review.

IHRAAM has submitted petitions to and been engaged in subsequent cases with the Inter-American Commission on Human Rights (IACHR) and has drafted important legal documents concerning Indian occupied Kashmir. It has undertaken educational events in furtherance of its mission, by means of sponsoring conferences, seminars and side events at the United Nations in New York and Geneva. Most notably, it held two international conferences on the right of self-determination in Geneva in 2000 and 2004, which engaged the participation of UN Special Rapporteurs, government ministers, and a broad range of experts and spokespersons for related national groups, and other international NGOs. A follow-up conference on self-determination is currently being planned for October 2023.

Geneva International Peace Research Institute[112]

As a member of the GIPRI board I have had the opportunity to participate in numerous conferences on issues such as disarmament for development, the adverse human rights impacts of unilateral coercive measures, the UN sustainable development goals, and the sorry state of the media, especially when it comes to the promotion of peace and reconciliation.[113]

Notwithstanding the important work performed by this NGO, the corporate media largely ignores its initiatives and its conferences. Whoever wants to learn about GIPRI should go to its website and consult the reports on our many conferences as well as the interviews and essays by our members.[114] Numerous of our press releases and op-eds have been censored by the corporate media and by tech giants like Google, Twitter, Facebook and YouTube—one of the major problems facing NGOs that work for peace and condemn war propaganda, imperialism, neo-colonialism, the abuses of the military-industrial complex, etc. It has become increasingly evident that there is a high price to pay for independence and intellectual honesty, for having the temerity to criticize certain powerful countries instead of meekly following the "prescribed narrative" as expected.

GIPRI has been in consultative status with the United Nations since 1996 and accordingly can speak at the Human Rights Council. Alas, NGOs are only given 90 seconds to make their contributions to the interactive dialogues. GIPRI has a rich history[115] and many luminaries who have spoken at its conferences and endorsed its initiatives, including Professor Alexandre Berenstein of the University of Geneva, and Guy Mettan, long-time President of the Geneva Press Club and current member of the Grand Conseil de Genève.

P.E.N. International: Poets-Essayists-Novelists, the international association of writers[116]

P.E.N. International (Poets Essayists Novelists) is the foremost global association of writers, with 144 centres in more than 100 countries. Its principal goals are to promote understanding and intellectual co-operation among writers everywhere, anticipating the Constitution of UNESCO. It was founded in London on October 5, 1921 by the British novelist Catherine Amy Dawson Scott, with John Galsworthy as its first president, and has included many illustrious members like Joseph Conrad, Elizabeth Craig, George Bernard Shaw, H.W. Wells, Arthur Miller, and many others.

The text of the Charter of P.E.N. shares a great deal with the UN Charter:

Literature knows no frontiers and must remain common currency among people in spite of political or international upheavals.

In all circumstances, and particularly in time of war, works of art, the patrimony of humanity at large, should be left untouched by national or political passion.

Members of PEN should at all times use what influence they have in favour of good understanding and mutual respect between nations and people; they pledge themselves to do their utmost to dispel all hatreds and to champion the ideal of one humanity living in peace and equality in one world.

PEN stands for the principle of unhampered transmission of thought within each nation and between all nations, and members pledge themselves to oppose any form of suppression of freedom of expression in the country and community to which they belong, as well as throughout the world wherever this is possible. PEN declares for a free press and opposes arbitrary censorship in time of peace. It believes that the necessary advance of the world towards a more highly organised political and economic order renders a free criticism of governments, administrations and institutions imperative. And since freedom implies voluntary restraint, members pledge themselves to oppose such evils of a free press as mendacious publication, deliberate falsehood and distortion of facts for political and personal ends."

In 2013 PEN's Writers for Peace Committee issued the Bled Manifesto[117] which stated, *inter alia*:

"1. All individuals and peoples have a right to peace and this right should be recognised by the United Nations as a universal human right....

...

4. PEN considers one of the world's greatest challenges to be the transition from violence to debate, discussion and dialogue. We aim to be active participants in this process

promoting where necessary the principles of international law....

. . .

7. In order to achieve sustainable conditions for peace, PEN calls for the respect of the environment in conformity with the Rio Declaration on Environment and Development (1992). We condemn the excesses of technology and financial speculation that contribute to the impoverishment of a large part of the world's population.

The above declarations and the actual work of P.E.N. International render it an indispensable human rights NGO. I have been a member of P.E.N. Centre Suisse Romand since 1989. I was Secretary-General for two years and then President of our chapter in 2006 to 2009 and again 2013 to 2017. In this capacity I represented P.E.N. before the UN Human Rights Council, together with our former President Professor Fawzia Assaad and with Nguyen Hoang Bao Viet, a Vietnamese poet and member of our Board. I proactively participated in advancing the two principal goals in our Charter—Peace and freedom of expression. I collaborated with our Writers for Peace Committee and our Writers in Prison Committee. We all endorsed PEN International's support of Julian Assange.

On December 10, 2021 Ma Thida, Chair of PEN International's Writers in Prison Committee, wrote: "PEN International strongly condemns the UK High Court's ruling to allow the extradition of Julian Assange to the U.S. That the verdict came on Human Rights Day is a shocking blow to press freedom around the world and sets a dangerous precedent that could affect the legitimate work of journalists and publishers everywhere. Once again, we call for the charges against Assange to be dropped and urge the UK authorities to release him immediately and to block his extradition to the U.S."[118]

It is worth to reprint here the special Appeal of PEN International dated April 22, 2022 with regard to Julian Assange:

PEN International joins Reporters Without Borders and 17 organisations—including English PEN, German PEN, PEN Melbourne, PEN Norway, PEN Sydney, Scottish PEN, Slovene PEN and Swedish PEN—in calling on UK Home

Secretary Priti Patel to reject Julian Assange's extradition to the U.S. and to release him from prison.

Dear Home Secretary,

We, the undersigned press freedom, free expression and journalists' organisations are writing to express our serious concern regarding the possibility of extradition of WikiLeaks publisher Julian Assange to the United States and to ask you to reject the U.S. government's extradition request. We also request a meeting with you to discuss these points further.

In March, the Supreme Court refused to consider Mr Assange's appeal against the High Court decision, which overturned the District Court ruling barring extradition on mental health grounds. We are deeply disappointed with this decision given the high public interest in this case, which deserved review by the highest court in the land.

However, it is now in your hands to decide whether to approve or reject Mr Assange's extradition to the U.S. The undersigned organisations urge you to act in the interest of press freedom and journalism by refusing extradition and immediately releasing Mr Assange from prison, where he has remained on remand for three years despite the great risks posed to his mental and physical health.

In the U.S., Mr Assange would face trial on 17 counts under the Espionage Act and one count under the Computer Fraud and Abuse Act, which combined could see him imprisoned for up to 175 years. He is highly likely to be detained there in conditions of isolation or solitary confinement despite the U.S. government's assurances, which would severely exacerbate his risk of suicide.

Further, Mr Assange would be unable to adequately defend himself in the U.S. courts, as the Espionage Act lacks a public interest defence. His prosecution would set a dangerous precedent that could be applied to any media outlet that published stories based on leaked information, or indeed any journalist, publisher or source anywhere in the world.

We ask you, Home Secretary, to honour the UK government's commitment to protecting and promoting media
freedom and reject the U.S. extradition request. We ask you
to release Mr. Assange from Belmarsh prison and allow him
to return to his young family after many years of isolation.
Finally, we ask you to publicly commit to ensuring that no
publisher, journalist or source ever again faces detention in
the UK for publishing information in the public interest."

The above demonstrates that P.E.N. and many other organizations do see human rights in context, concretely and pragmatically.
Amnesty International has separately made some statements in favour
of Assange[119] and started a petition campaign for his release,[120] and
Human Rights Watch has written to the U.S. Attorney General asking
him to drop the prosecution of Assange.[121]

Peace and freedom of expression are the pillars of PEN's Charter.
Accordingly, the 144 PEN centres have taken strong positions against
war and in particular with regard to the issue of freedom of expression
in Turkey, Russia, China, Vietnam and many other countries—all of
which, however, might be regarded as countries targeted by the West.
It has not sufficiently criticised the Western phenomenon of "woke-
ness" and "political correctness," which has led to "cancel culture,"
self-censorship. intimidation and physical violence against non-con-
formist thinkers and writers.

In the year 2006, when I was President of PEN Suisse romand, we
invited the late Hrant Dink (1954–2007),[122] a noted Turkish-Armenian
author and editor, who was subsequently assassinated in Istanbul in
connection with his advocacy of Turkey's recognition of the Armenian
"massacres" of 1915–23 as genocide.[123]

Notwithstanding the above, P.E.N. is far from being a perfect
organization, bearing in mind that many poets, essayists, and novelists
are notorious for hubris and idiosyncrasies. Like every organization
made up of human beings, PEN International does many good things,
but also fails to undertake action when it is needed, e.g. it has not
found the necessary consensus to tackle the growing problem of the
instrumentalization of history for political purposes, the enactment
of "memory laws" and legislation that tries to crystalize history and
criminalize dissenting views. Notwithstanding my own initiatives,

PEN International never endorsed the clear language of the Human Rights Committee's General Comment Nr. 34 on Freedom of expression, paragraph 49 of which reads:

> Laws that penalize the expression of opinions about historical facts are incompatible with the obligations that the Covenant imposes on States parties in relation to the respect for freedom of opinion and expression. The Covenant does not permit general prohibition of expressions of an erroneous opinion or an incorrect interpretation of past events. Restrictions on the right of freedom of opinion should never be imposed and, with regard to freedom of expression, they should not go beyond what is permitted in paragraph 3 or required under Article 20.[124]

Nor did PEN endorse the crucial "Appel de Blois" of the French academic group "*Liberté pour l'histoire*," which plainly states:

> Concerned about the retrospective moralization of history and intellectual censure, we call for the mobilization of European historians and for the wisdom of politicians. History must not be a slave to contemporary politics nor can it be written on the command of competing memories. In a free state, no political authority has the right to define historical truth and to restrain the freedom of the historian with the threat of penal sanctions. We call on historians to marshal their forces within each of their countries and to create structures similar to our own, and, for the time being, to individually sign the present appeal, to put a stop to this movement toward laws aimed at controlling history memory. We ask government authorities to recognize that, while they are responsible for the maintenance of the collective memory, they must not establish, by law and for the past, an official truth whose legal application can carry serious consequences for the profession of history and for intellectual liberty in general. In a democracy, liberty for history is liberty for all."[125]

PEN International and the national PEN Centres continue to work in the spirit of UNESCO to build bridges among peoples and nations and to promote local, regional and global peace.

P.E.N. Conference in Geneva, from left to right P.E.N. President Alix Parodi, former PEN presidents Alexis Koutchoumow, Alfred de Zayas, Claude Krul, Fawzia Assaad and Committee members Glorice Weinstein and Hoang Nguyen

The San Francisco NGO, Eleanor Lives[126]

San Francisco lawyer and human rights lecturer Dr. Kirk Boyd has been an active NGO person for decades and in 2009 organized at Berkeley Law School a major human rights conference attended by Berkeley and UCLA students and many luminaries, among them the first UN High Commissioner for Human Rights, Jose Ayala Lasso, the former Acting High Commissioner, Professor Bertrand Ramcharan, the UN Special Rapporteur on Torture Professor Manfred Nowak, Justice Theodore Meron, and Professor David Caron.

On March 8, 2019, International Women's Day, Dr. Boyd formulated a mission statement for his new NGO dedicated to reviving the legacy of Eleanor Roosevelt and plan for humanity. On the organization's website, Dr. Boyd writes:

After 50 million people were killed in WWII, many of them in gas chambers and other horrific ways, there was agreement that steps had to be taken to prevent authoritarian tyrants from violating the rights of citizens and waging war on their neighbours. The creation of the United Nations was the first step in this direction, but it was understood that it was not enough to make rules to stop countries from waging war on one another, there needed to be a set of rights for people in all countries and courts to enforce them. To this end, at the War Memorial building in San Francisco, President Truman told the closing ceremony for the U.N. Charter in San Francisco: *"The first thing we will do is prepare an International Bill of Rights.*[127]

Dr. Boyd remainds us that Rene Cassin, who worked with Eleanor on the UDHR and was one of the first judges on the European Court, won the Nobel Peace prize.[128] With respect to the European Court, he told the Nobel Committee two simple words "It works." Indeed, regional courts do work and their decisions are enforceable. The Inter-American Court on Human Rights has been slowly advancing, as has the African Court on Human and Peoples' Rights.[129]

One of the major projects of Eleanorlives.org is to draft a new International Bill of Rights that can be used by lawyers, judges, and courts throughout the world. UN human rights standard-setting and the codification of human rights in regional treaties should be condensed and streamlined into a unitary document, like the Universal Declaration of Human Rights, where there is no artificial distinction between civil and political rights, as separate from economic, social, and cultural rights, insofar as all human rights must be seen as universal, interrelated and interdependent.

Articles 27 to 34 of the proposed new International Bill of Rights are devoted to the establishment and functioning of an International Court of Human Rights, whose judgments should be enforceable by domestic courts. I have been writing about the need for such a court since the 1990s and submitted my proposal to the 1993 World Conference on Human Rights in Vienna.[130] Meanwhile we have drafted a possible statute for the Court.

*Some of the participants at the San Francisco conference on
"What Human Rights in 2048" (100 years after the adoption of the
UDHR), held at Berkeley Law School, November 9–11, 2009.
Left to right: the former Acting High Commissioner for Human
Rights Professor Bertrand Ramcharan and his wife, the former UN
Rapporteur on torture Professor Manfred Nowak, the first UN High
Commissioner José Ayala Lasso, Professor Theodor Meron, Bruna
Molina, Dr. Kirk Boyd, Dr. Mishana Hossenioun, Professor David
Carron, Alfred de Zayas, and UCLA Professor Cesare Romano*

Asociación Española para el Derecho Internacional de los Derechos Humanos (AEDIDH)[131]

The Spanish Society for international Human Rights Law (in consultative status with the UN Human Rights Council) spearheaded the civil society initiative to adopt a declaration recognizing Peace as a human right and envisaging the establishment of an Observatory for the implementation of this right. Over the years it has issued a large number of scholarly publications and reports that have covered disarmament for development, education for peace, the right to truth and reparation, the right of self-determination of peoples and other topics[132]. A member of AEDIDH since 2004, I participated in the drafting of the 2006 *Declaración de Luarca,*[133] was rapporteur for the 2008 *Declaración de Bilbao*[134] and endorsed the *Declaración de Santiago de Compostela*[135] of December 10, 2010. I have participated in several of its side-events at the UN Human Rights Council and contributed to several of its publications. Some of my interviews on the right to peace can be consulted on the AEDIDH website.[136]

Panel at the United Nations Human Rights Council with Professor Carlos Villan Duran (speaking), President of the Asociación Española para el Derecho Internacional de los Derechos Humanos At far left is Mexican Ambassador Luis de Alba, Human Rights Council President 2006–2007

International Commission of Jurists

Among the preeminent associations of lawyers, I must mention the International Commission of Jurists, with its seat in Geneva, whose website (icj.org) is often confused with that of the International Court of Justice (icj-cij.org). Throughout its history it has been at the vanguard of promoting the rule of law worldwide.

On February 9, 2023 it issued this press release entitled "Israel/Palestine must end collective punishment of Palestinians":

On 26 January 2023, Israeli forces conducted a military raid into the Jenin refugee camp in the northern occupied West Bank, killing ten Palestinians, including a 61-year-old woman and two children, and injuring at least 20 people. Since the beginning of 2023, at least 41 Palestinians, including five children have been killed, either by Israeli military and security forces or Israeli settlers in the occupied West Bank. Israeli forces have frequently used unlawful lethal force against Palestinians in the Palestinian Occupied Territory (OPT).

A day after the military raid, a Palestinian gunman shot dead seven Israeli civilian settlers, including a child, and injured three others, in an Israeli settlement in occupied East Jerusalem. The ICJ deplores this act of unlawful killing.

The Israeli authorities responded to the attack with a series of collective punishment measures, including sealing the home of the shooter's family, in a preliminary step ahead of the expected demolition of the building, and detained a number of his family members and acquaintances.

House and property demolitions are part of a long-standing Israeli policy that imposes measures of collective punishment against the families of Palestinians—dead or alive—suspected or convicted of serious crimes. Collective punishment measures have also included the arbitrary revocation of residency and citizenship rights, arbitrary detention, and forcible transfer and deportation of Palestinians from the Occupied Palestinian Territory (OPT).

"Collective punishment and forcible transfer of protected persons from an occupied territory are war crimes that should be investigated and prosecuted by Israeli authorities, not condoned and supported at the highest levels of the government." said Said Bernarbia, the ICJ's MENA Programme Director.

Under international human rights law, the principle of personal culpability, according to which punishment is personal and cannot be extended to any person other than the defender, prohibits non-individual punishment.

Similarly, measures of collective punishment against protected persons for offences they did not personally commit are absolutely prohibited under international humanitarian law, including under Article 33(1) of the

Fourth Geneva Convention, which provides: "[c]ollective penalties and likewise all measures of intimidation or of terrorism are prohibited." The imposition of a collective punishment is a war crime under international criminal law. International humanitarian law also absolutely prohibits the forcible deportation and transfer of protected persons within or outside the occupied territory, regardless of their purpose, which is listed as a grave breach of the Geneva Convention and a war crime in international criminal law instruments

Israel, as the Occupying Power, has an obligation to respect and ensure the human rights of all inhabitants of the OPT. The United Nations High Commissioner for Human Rights, Mr Volker Türk, has urged Israel to ensure that "all operations of its security forces in the occupied West Bank, including East Jerusalem, are carried out with full respect for international human rights law."

Other UN human rights experts have previously called on Israel to stop all actions amounting to collective punishment of the Palestinian people.

The ICJ calls on Israel to immediately end its policies of collective punishment and unlawful and excessive use of force, and abide by its obligations under international humanitarian law and human rights law.

"States must act, individually and collectively, to ensure that the lives of those living in the occupied territory are protected and their rights are preserved," Benarbia said. "Impunity is only widening the cycle of violence and suffering in the OPT and Israel."

Among the many constructive press releases issued by the ICJ, I would like to mention one dated February 8, 2021 concerning the ICC decision on accountability for crimes under international law:

The ICJ welcomes the International Criminal Court's (ICC) decision establishing that the Court can assert its jurisdiction over serious crimes alleged to have occurred in the State of Palestine since 13 June 2014.

On 5 February 2021, the ICC Pre-Trial Chamber I held by majority that: (i) Palestine has correctly acceded to the Rome Statute and has thus become a State party to it; and (ii) the ICC's territorial jurisdiction extends to "the territories occupied by Israel since 1967, namely Gaza and the West Bank, including East Jerusalem."

"The ruling is a first step towards breaking the cycle of impunity for crimes under international law committed by all parties to the conflict in Palestine," said Said Benarbia, the ICJ's MENA Programme Director. "The Prosecutor should immediately open an investigation with a view to establishing the facts about such crimes, and identifying and prosecuting those most responsible."

The decision was prompted by a request of the ICC Office of the Prosecutor seeking confirmation of the Court's territorial jurisdiction.

The Prosecutor had previously concluded that there is a reasonable basis to believe that "war crimes have been or are being committed in the West Bank, including East Jerusalem, and the Gaza Strip."

On 16 March 2020, the ICJ submitted *amicus curiae* observations in support of the Court's jurisdiction, arguing that:

- Palestine has successfully acceded, and is a State Party, to the Rome Statute. The Court should accordingly exercise its jurisdiction over Palestine as it does in respect of any other State Party;
- The Palestinian Territory over which the Court should exercise jurisdiction comprises the West Bank, including East Jerusalem, and Gaza; and
- Palestine is a State under international law, satisfying recognized international law criteria for statehood, displaying State activity and engaging in diplomatic relations with other sovereign States. The decades-long belligerent occupation of Palestine by itself has no decisive legal effect on the validity of its claim to sovereignty and statehood.

The Pre-Trial Chamber decision confirmed the first two
of these observations, without considering the status of
Palestine's statehood under general international law.

I have good personal memories of the ICJ thanks to my cooperation with them since the 1980s, my friendship with Dr. Adama Dieng,
its Secretary-General 19902000, my publications in the ICJ review,[137],
and the lovely preface that Dr. Federico Andreu Guzmán wrote for my
book *The Genocide against the Armenians and the Relevance of the
1948 Convention.*[138] Among the distinguished Commissioners whom I
met over the years, I especially admired the Australian Elizabeth Evatt
and the late Sir Nigel Rodley, paragons of integrity with intellect, both
of them former members of the UN Human Rights Committee, which
I served as Secretary.

LET US NOT FORGET THE LOCAL NGOS THAT DO SO MUCH GOOD AND DO NOT GET ANY PUBLICITY

The good news is that we do not have to put all of our trust in the
mega-NGOs and donate to them, even though many people think it is
politically correct to do so. We do not have to join their bandwagons
and embrace their priorities, which, as we have seen, are sometimes
influenced by governmental and corporate priorities. We don't have to
absorb their newspeak and reinterpretation of human rights. We don't
have to participate in their campaigns that are so frequently driven by
less noble aims, such as facilitating "regime change" in countries that
Western powers want to overthrow. We do not have to become complicit in their opportunism, double-standards, corruption of values,
militant advocacy of genderism, and denigration of religious values.

The good news is that there are hundreds of smaller, authentic
NGOs that reflect the democratic spirit of civil society. There are
plenty of opportunities for civil society to become active in vibrant
organizations that have no consultative status with the United Nations
and ECOSOC, but which do perform important functions for society
locally and regionally, which with patience and perseverance reaffirm
human dignity and the right to access to information, the right to dissent, the right to peaceful manifestation in our municipalities, in our
towns and big cities. There are many like-minded people who work

incessantly in these vibrant NGOs devoted to community service and in a broader sense for world peace and international solidarity.

Association Suisses et Internationaux de Genève

Together with the late Jacqueline Berenstein-Wavre,[139] her husband, the late Professor Alexandre Berenstein,[140] and a number of UN colleagues I founded Association Suisses et Internationaux de Genève (ASIG), becoming co-president, representing the internationals, while Jacqueline was co-President representing the Swiss community. In the years 1995–2005, we organized conferences and colloquia at the United Nations and at the *Institut Universitaire des Hautes Etudes Internationales* in Geneva, focussing primarily on human rights issues of concern both to the Swiss and to the large community of internationals residing in Switzerland, working for the United Nations and its agencies, or working for the many non-governmental organization and foreign business enterprises.

Because I was a senior lawyer with the Office of the High Commissioner for Human Rights, I was able to shape our priorities so as to focus our activities on matters such as peace and human dignity, women's rights, and sustainable development. Alexandre and Jacqueline Berenstein became important supports of the Geneva International Peace Research Institute. We also focused on and in particular freedom of opinion and expression, the integration of migrants and refugees, the right to development. We advocated Swiss entry into the United Nations and a human rights-centered approach to the Swiss economy and, in particular, the banking sector.

Millennium Solidarity

My PEN colleague Professor Zeki Ergas[141] is not only a good poet and essayist, he is also a human rights activist with numerous publications on Africa, Israel/Palestine, Gaza and the Millennium Development Goals. It was he who founded *Millennium Solidarity* in the late 1990s and I fondly look back at dozens of activities that we undertook then and in the early 2000s, including demonstrations at the Place des Nations, before the UN seat in Geneva, before the ILO, WHO, WTO, WIPO and the World Council of Churches. Here a photo of what was a true "people power" organization. We also hosted a number of conferences with economists and demographers who spoke at our side-events. Our problem—like the problem of so many NGOs—is that we could not attract sufficient funds to permit sustained action.

Zeki and I also organized literary events under the banner of the United Nations Society of Writers.

With Zeki outside the World Council of Chu

*Demonstrating in front of the Palais des Nations,
the seat of the UN in Geneva*

CHAPTER 7
THE MEDIA AND HUMAN RIGHTS

"The Ministry of Peace concerns itself with war, the Ministry of Truth with lies, the Ministry of Love with torture and the Ministry of Plenty with starvation. These contradictions are not accidental, nor do they result from ordinary hypocrisy: they are deliberate exercises in doublethink."

GEORGE ORWELL, *1984*

THE MAINSTREAM media's facilitating role is key to understanding the hostile takeover of many human rights institutions and programs by governments, intelligence services, corporate interests, and lobbyists. Indeed, the media is one of the principal purveyors of fake news and false narratives about alleged human rights violations by some countries and not others. The binary world of good and bad states relies heavily on the weaponization of human rights by mainstream media supporting narratives in the service of powerful countries and economic interests.

We all depend on our newspapers, television news, and the internet to access information and formulate an opinion about persons and issues. For a democratic society to actually function as such, the media must be truthful, objective and make an effort to separate facts from opinion. Bearing in mind that the media has enormous influence on the way we think, it should endeavour to be as balanced and complete as possible. The media has a direct impact on the enjoyment of human rights, in particular the right to know, the right to truth, the right to plurality in the marketplace of ideas. Out of ethical respect for its function as a "fourth power"[1] of governance, sometimes referred to as the "fourth estate,"[2] the media itself should be democratized[3] and serve the entire population and not just certain "elites." It can and should be a pillar of democracy. But is it? Does it exercise its enormous influence to promote peace and human rights?

Unfortunately, in the view of many astute observers, the media abandoned its role as a "watch dog" of democracy and morphed into an attack dog of powerful interests, an echo chamber of governments and corporations. Moreover, we regularly witness a distortion of language by the media and public relations agencies that have been phenomenally successful in devising a new epistemology that imposes a skewed morality on everything and is able to elicit positive or negative knee-jerk reactions from the public.

"Sanctions," a term that implies legitimate exercise of authority and just punishment for wrongful action, is used to describe unilateral coercive measures, which are nothing but illegal use of force contrary to Article 2(4) of the UN Charter. A "terrorist" is a member of a national liberation movement trying to overthrow oppression and exploitation. A "patriot" is a warmonger who believes in "my country right or wrong." "Traitors" are those who open our eyes to governmental crime, whistleblowers who alert us to the crimes that are being committed in our name. "Conspiracy theorists" are those analysts who postulate politically incorrect hypotheses, in an effort to clarify situations that the government is deliberately trying to cover up. A "revisionist" is someone who challenges the mainstream narrative. An "Antisemite" is anyone who questions the policies of the Israeli government or who sympathize with the Palestinian people. A "Putin puppet" is a person who tries to understand Putin's policies, who uses rational methods to assess Putin rather than just shouting *anathema sit*. The "free media" encompasses only mainstream corporate media. "Fake news" means what a political rival says. The "Rules-based international order" means the rules that the West concocts as it goes along. "The Nobel Peace Prize" is an award that can be given to militarists and warmongers.[4] "Reproductive rights" do not entail governmental support of women during pregnancy and after childbirth but rather the facilitation of abortion, the very opposite of reproduction. Gender "equality" often means special privileges. This abstruse political and propagandistic lexicon delivers ready-made labels to be stamped on scores of persons for the purpose of creating automatic and immediate positive or negative perception by the public. In this manner the media is slowly easing us into a massive acceptance of cognitive dissonance, an attack on our very ability to think, as reflected in Orwell's Ministry of Truth's slogan, "War is Peace. Freedom is Slavery. Ignorance is Strength."[5]

Yes, freedom of the press and media is crucial for democratic society. But what happens when it is not the government but the private sector that becomes the principal purveyor of "fake news" and biased narratives, when it manipulates reality, censors, and distorts? Or indeed, on the other hand, when the government coerces the private sector to do so, as has been revealed in the cases of Twitter and Facebook? How can we fix this, when today the media is "homologated," when conglomerates control the news agencies like AP and Reuters, when the "quality press," the major newspapers and television networks advance only one point of view, while suppressing other possible narratives and engaging in character assassination of dissenters? Indeed, dissenting in the modern world can spell career-death, job loss, tenure denial, the loss of friends, and being "cancelled" and socially ostracized.

Today the media creates a parallel reality in which certain issues are given disproportionate attention, while others are kept out of the public's eye. The media indoctrinates us into liking some politicians and disliking others, divides the world into good and bad, moralizes about everything—in the service of those very special interests that finance the media, notably the military-industrial-complex, the oil and gas enterprises, and the pharmaceutical industry. The media instil fear in us against real or imagined enemies, makes us hate the Russians and Russian culture, the Chinese and Chinese culture. Every aggression against another country, whether Vietnam, Cuba, Chile, Honduras, Nicaragua, Yugoslavia, Afghanistan, Iraq, Libya, Syria, Venezuela has been accompanied by a demonization of the leaders of those countries, a veritable barrage of disinformation and skewed narratives aimed at making us fear and hate the putative enemy that we, the virtuous ones, are about to invade, bombard or overthrow through a *coup d'état*.

In a quasi-democratic or pseudo-democratic society, it is important to "persuade" a majority of the population of the legality and legitimacy of governmental whatever action, of egregious abuses by pharmaceutical giants, racketeering strategies of the oil and gas industry, looting practices by transnational corporations *inter alia* through the Investor-State-Dispute Settlement[6] mechanism, the economic blackmail by the loan-sharks at the IMF.[7] We are taught to believe in our leaders, to love "Big Brother." Indeed, many well-paid "narrative managers" are at work to make the epistemological control of public opinion a success. And a success it has been. The formidable propaganda machine can make or break politicians and academics, prepare the ground for war, and justify war crimes and crimes against humanity in the name of peace and human rights.

This chapter will touch upon the mainstream media's biased reporting on human rights, on hyperbole about some countries' violations and coverups of the violations by other countries, the artificial creation of issues, "humanitarian crises," atrocity stories, evidence-free allegations—but only concerning certain countries, while others can do anything in total impunity.

However, let us not think that this manipulation of public opinion is a 21st century phenomenon. It was already practiced in the early 20th century. As we can read in Walter Lippmann's book, *Public Opinion,* "The hypothesis, which seems to me the most fertile, is that news and truth are not the same thing, and must be clearly distinguished."[8]

And we learn in *The Edward Bernays Reader: From Propaganda to the Engineering of Consent,*[9] the Viennese journalist openly embraced propaganda, because he believed that it worked well and was beneficial to society. He believed in war and propaganda campaigns that served the interests of the ruling power classes against the unreliable, undisciplined, but malleable masses.

In principle, most people would agree that a free and pluralistic media is absolutely necessary to sustain democratic governance. Most people would support the abstract idea that the media should advance human rights by educating society not only on individual, but also on collective rights, by proposing peaceful solutions to global problems, by endeavouring to justify why the unjust economic and social order should be changed. But does the media serve these purposes? A careful observer will conclude that the mainstream media manipulates public opinion to the detriment of all of us.

SELECTIVE HUMAN RIGHTS, SELECTIVE HUMANITARIANISM, SELECTIVE INDIGNATION

When I was a teenager in Chicago, I read a great deal without any system, just to satisfy my curiosity. I came across a quote by Malcolm X "If you're not careful, the newspapers will have you hating the people who are being oppressed, and loving the people who are doing the oppressing."[10]

I did not understand it, because I wanted to believe in the objectivity of the "quality press," and I considered myself quite progressive by reading the *New York Times* and the *Chicago Tribune*. Yet, the Malcolm X quote was intriguing and stayed with me. Sure enough, I could not take it very seriously, precisely because the mainstream media shaped my perceptions, told me whom to admire and whom to fear, impressing on me a negative image of Malcolm X. As a young, aspiring voter, I would not want to be associated with radical ideas. At that time, like most young people, I had many role models like John F. Kennedy,[11] his brother Robert,[12] and Dwight Eisenhower.[13] (I particularly liked Eisenhower's 1947 address at the Graduation Exercises at the United States Military Academy at West Point: "War is mankind's most tragic and stupid folly; to seek or advise its deliberate provocation is a black crime against all men."[14])

I wanted to believe in heroism and devotion to duty. I needed to believe in my teachers, my school, my coach, the editors of the *Chicago Tribune*. . . . I honestly believed that the U.S. was by far and away the best country in the world, surely the best democracy, the one "indispensable country," as Madeleine Albright would formulate it some forty years later.[15] Young people must believe in something. Only gradually does life teach us to discern, that not all of our heroes are or were knights in shining armour.

I also read Martin Luther King, Jr., including his book *Why We Can't Wait*.[16] Somewhere I came across this—for me, totally incomprehensible—statement by Dr. King: "The greatest purveyor of violence in the world: My own Government, I cannot be Silent." (April 4, 1967). What did he mean by that? Why would he say such a thing? I was led to believe in my school that he was a religious man, a well-meaning person, not a fire-eater like Malcolm X. But I still thought that it was pretty crazy to say something like that, which I duly discarded as a rhetorical hyperbole.

It took me many decades to realize that the U.S. was not the kindest and most humanitarian country in the world. I took distance from the notion that the U.S. was an indispensable country and started to understand that pretending to be the "indispensable country" entailed a veiled menace against all other countries and could be understood as constituting a threat to the peace and security of mankind, for purposes of Article 39 of the UN Chater.

The management of public narratives in the press, comic books, and by Hollywood was and continues to be effective, and "patriots" like to double-down on certain truths. Once when I challenged some "accepted truths" in college, I nearly got beaten up. I understood that people who considered themselves "patriots" are convinced that they own the truth and therefore have zero tolerance for dissenters. The consequence of this brainwashing of the population is devastating, because it handicaps our own thinking processes,[17] and paralyzes us when we must stand up and protest against crimes committed in our name. We lose our capacity to imagine other scenarios, our faculty of discernment.

Many years later I read Noam Chomsky's indictment of the neo-liberal establishment as criminal and his description of the U.S. and the worst terrorist state in the world.[18] Even President Carter described the U.S. as "the most warlike nation in world history."[19] But there is no follow-up, addressing why that is. It is remarkable that while such honourable people have uttered these thoughts and that the media has reported thereon, there has been no further investigation of why such a statement could be made, let alone raising the issue that something should therefore be done—because these statements belong in that category of moral judgments that the mainstream media tacitly leave without consequences. Of course, the media could pick them up and demand a general debate, but economic and political reasons militate against any action.

The practice of selective indignation is embedded in the mainstream media. Only certain crimes are denounced, others are either downplayed or white-washed. Sometimes the government engages think tanks to draft spurious justifications in perfect legalese. That is how the game is being played. The myth that the U.S. is the exceptional country has become a matter of faith (or rather, indoctrination)—not reason—even in Europe, and this myth is perpetuated by Hollywood movies, television features, townhall celebrations and even cartoons. Challenging this foundational myth of the United States constitutes a form of apostasy, heresy, something to be punished by ostracism, banishment or worse.

When one realizes that the mainstream media is anything but "quality" press, that it is political and manipulative, the first reaction may be one of disbelief. One resists. Gradually the disbelief gives way to anger, because it pains one to realize that one has been intellectually aggressed, that one has been taken for a ride. Gradually one matures and accepts this reality as a factum, prepared to face the future of fake news and phoney narratives with greater circumspection. My epiphany is not unlike the famous "5 stages of grief": denial, anger, bargaining, depression, and acceptance.[20] I would not go as far as saying "acceptance," but refer to say resignation and equanimity. I wish other Americans would go through this epiphany faster than I did. I was a slow learner.

The best defence is to try to read as many different sources as possible, to pro-actively search the internet for alternative explanations of the facts that have been reported.[21] Since I read and write in six languages, I have the opportunity to see the perspectives of six linguistic groups. But for those who only speak English, at least there is the "alternative media," which includes serious journalists at *Consortium News, CounterPunch, Truthout, Democracy Now*, the *Intercept*, the *Grayzone, Pushback*, the *Real News Network* and many others. Thus, a citizen who wants to know what is going on can be well served by accessing as many news services as possible, always keeping a healthy scepticism about all sources and not surrendering to the illusion that any one news service has a monopoly of the truth. Because I read news reports in several languages, I can formulate this opinion: The Western mainstream media in most of the world is largely toxic and manipulative—including the *New York Times, Washington Post, CNN, Fox,* the *BBC,* the *Times, El Pais, El Mundo, La Razon, France Info, Le Figaro, Le Monde, De Telegraaf, Volkskrant, Der Spiegel, Die Zeit, Die Welt, Bild, Frankfurter Allgemeine Zeitung, Neue Zürcher Zeitung, Blick,* etc.

The mainstream media has also been guilty of disseminating and magnifying palpably wrong information and conspiracy theories against political opponents. As surrealistic as this may sound, the *Washington Post* and the *New York Times* were awarded the 2018 Pulitzer Prize for their national reporting of President Donald Trump's alleged collusion with Russia.[22]

With time one develops a "nose" for fake news and for the weaponization of human rights, which is particularly obscene when we see a country that egregiously violates human rights accusing another country of the same. A review of the media deserves an entire book.

This chapter is intended only to signal some glaring problems and obvious failures of the mainstream media that can and should be corrected. The cases dealt with below are only illustrative of the larger problem. Readers will have their own experiences and their own examples.

A RESPONSIBLE MEDIA PROMOTES PEACE, NOT WAR

Article 20 (1) of the International Covenant on Civil and Political Rights stipulates: "Any propaganda for war shall be prohibited by law."[23] Some States parties to the ICCPR, mostly Western states like the U.S. and UK, have introduced legal reservations to their adherence to this article, by that very fact indicating that they do not want to limit their options—as U.S. presidents have repeatedly reminded the world, "all options are on the table," meaning even including the nuclear option. This is a disgrace.

The media is not directly bound by the ICCPR, but nothing prevents the media from following an ethical code of deontology and striving to be responsible instead of sensationalist. History demonstrates that many wars were preceded by uncontrolled fake news, exaggerations, and warmongering in the media, with such fearmongering inciting racial and religious hatred.

Article 29 of the Universal Declaration of Human Rights should be a guideline—and that does apply to the media, because journalists and editors are also humans who enjoy the protection and also the obligations set out in the Universal Declaration of Human Rights: "Everyone has duties to the community in which alone the free and full development of his personality is possible."

In other words, media moguls, editors-in-chief of newspapers, journalists, TV anchors and commentators, bloggers and vloggers all have a duty of truth to the community and to the world. The absolute priority must be to promote and keep local, regional, and international peace. It is absolutely criminal to see how major news agencies, major newspapers, and television stations actually incite to hatred and violence.

Alas the mainstream media in the United States, Canada, United Kingdom, and other European countries were hyperactive in pushing for war against Yugoslavia, Afghanistan, and Iraq. The media censored criticism and actually justified the aggression by the "coalition of the willing" against the people of Iraq.[24] The media bears considerable responsibility for the millions of deaths in the wars in Vietnam, Yugoslavia, Afghanistan, Iraq, Libya, Syria and Yemen.

According to Julian Assange, "nearly every war has been the result of media lies."[25] According to Media Lens, the mainstream media not only lied about the Iraq war, but continued lying and giving a platform to warmongers, whereas peace activists were hardly given any visibility.[26] The Ukraine war is a case in point, and here the disinformation campaigns carried by the mainstream media were also supported on the internet by paid bloggers and special operators. Indeed, social media warfare has been one of the many practices of intelligence services of the U.S., UK, Israel, Russia and China. A Canadian-Ukrainian academic at the University of Ottawa, Ivan Katchanovski, observed, "Before the invasion, U.S. Special Operations troops were running two irregular warfare surrogate programs in Ukraine. In one, 'We had people taking apart Russian propaganda and telling the true story on blogs.'"[27] So are we to believe that the U.S. Special Operations troops' surrogate programs were indeed telling the true story of the war on Ukrainian blogs? Perhaps it would have been possible to prevent the Ukraine war—or at least its prolongation to disastrous effect for Ukraine—if the mainstream media had objectively reported on the arguments of all parties concerned, if there had not been a consistent pattern of Russophobia in the Western press.[28]

DISINFORMATION BY THE MAINSTREAM MEDIA

The case of Julian Assange

Professor Nils Melzer of the University of Geneva and ICRC legal chief investigated the Julian Assange case in his capacity as UN rapporteur on torture and visited Assange at Belmarsh prison in London. In his book *The Trial of Julian Assange*[29] he documents the breakdown of the rule of law in the U.S., UK, Sweden and Ecuador, the multiple violations of due process and the role of the media in demonizing Julian Assange so that the peoples of the U.S., UK, Sweden and Ecuador would accept the monstrosities that were being done against Assange in order to punish and make an example of a journalist for doing his work. If this were happening in Russia or China the Western press would not stop writing about it, would denounce the violations of international law and human rights law by Russia and China and demand an international commission of inquiry.

Melzer's revelations about the disgraceful framing of Julian Assange by the lawyers and judges of the U.S., UK, Sweden and Ecuador by far exceed the irregularities that accompanied the infamous Dreyfus affair[30] of 1894–99, when Alfred Dreyfus became the victim of judicial framing in France, a matter that was denounced by Emile Zola and became a *cause célèbre,* leading to the liberation of Alfred Dreyfus. Nothing of the kind happened in the Assange case. The mainstream media essentially ignored Professor Melzer's book and there was no "outcry" about the egregious violations of the rights of Julian Assange. Let us not forget that the media bears a degree of responsibility, because it actually joined in the defamation against Assange since 2010 and essentially covered up all the violations of the rule of law in the U.S., UK, Sweden, and Ecuador. The case is emblematic for the contempt of the mainstream media for international law and human rights law.

The persecution and prosecution of Julian Assange has one purpose, to intimidate journalists and whistleblowers so that they never again dare to disclose war crimes and crimes against humanity committed by the U.S. and its allies. It constitutes a frontal attack on journalism and on the right of all people to know, the right to truth. This illustrates the serious retrogression that the world is experiencing in the field of human rights, in particular the field of freedom of expression and freedom of journalism. Fifty years ago at the time of the Daniel Ellsberg disclosures, which were far less serious than those disclosed by Julian Assange, Daniel Ellsberg was not treated in the barbarous and inhumane manner that Assange was treated, although Ellsberg had committed a "crime" of *lese majesté* against President Richard Nixon.[31]

The civil war in Syria

The Syrian civil war started in 2011 and was internationally stoked and financed by those who, for geopolitical reasons, wanted to overthrow President Bashar Al Assad and impose "regime change" on the Syrian people. Without massive foreign intervention and massive disinformation in the media, the civil war would have ended in 2011 and not dragged on for twelve years.

One of the best books on the subject is A. B. Abrams *World War in Syria,*[32] a comprehensive analysis of the first ten years of the Syrian War, which ably provides background into the history of Syria's long-standing conflict with the West and its regional strategic partners such as Turkey and Israel. It correctly refers to the war as a "world war," because it is the foreign powers who drove the conflict, which the Syrians could have solved by themselves without foreign intervention. It was another classical proxy war, accompanied by media cheerleading of the "democratic opposition," including fanatical Islamists and mercenaries. The Syrian war manifests an unusually high level of false flags and disinformation. Abrams further provides information vital to understanding the conflict's implications for international security and the motivations and interests of all major parties involved.

In an earlier chapter of this book we saw how the Organization for the Prohibition of Chemical Weapons was put under massive pressure by the U.S. to accuse Assad of using chemical weapons, although these had been verifiably destroyed in 2013. We saw how international public opinion was and continues to be manipulated against Assad and how even the OPCW lent itself to the fraudulent Western charges against Assad.

The mainstream media has incessantly reported on anything that could look bad for Assad, suppressing any official denials and verifiable rebuttals. It has relied on dubious sources of information, including from the self-proclaimed "Syrian Observatory for Human Rights,"[33] essentially a one-man show with questionable financing. While the media, including the BBC,[34] the Guardian,[35] and Netflix[36] bent over backwards to make the corrupt organization "White Helmets"[37] (otherwise known as the Syrian Civil Defence) and its founder James Le Mesurier appear heroic, it failed to question its evidence-free allegations of war crimes levelled against Assad, or the multiple cases of false flag and staged interviews attributed to it.[38]

In a perceptive article published 2018 in *CounterPunch,* Rick Sterling wrote:

> Besides promoting themselves as a humanitarian group, the
> White Helmets have become essential to the propaganda

war by gaining—along with similar pro-rebel "activists"—a virtual monopoly on information from rebel-controlled areas, supplying a steady stream of heart-rending stories and images about suffering children to a credulous Western media wanting to believe everything bad about the Syrian government.

One of the reasons why the "White Helmets" have been so successful in inserting their propaganda into Western media is that most of the rebel zones of Syria, especially east Aleppo, have been off limits to Western journalists and other outside observers for years. Two of the last Western reporters to venture into rebel territory, James Foley and Stephen Sotloff, were subsequently beheaded by the Islamic State.

So, as the Syrian government and its allies finally try to expel Al Qaeda terrorists and their cohorts from east Aleppo, the White Helmets have become a major source for the Western news media which treats these "relief workers" as credible providers of on-the-ground information.

Thus, the positive image of the White Helmets and the group's skilful use of social media deflect attention from the sectarian, violent and unpopular nature of Al Qaeda's Nusra Front (recently renamed the Syria Conquest Front) and other armed opposition groups while hyping accusations that Syrian and Russian attacks are primarily hitting civilians.

In other words, the White Helmets have gone from being talked about to being the ones doing the talking. News stories increasingly use White Helmet witnesses as their sources, often in ways that promote the self-serving myth of White Helmet heroism. One day, CNN announced that a White Helmet aid center had been hit. Another day, *TIME* magazine claimed that White Helmet workers were being "hunted."

Reports from the White Helmets also have served as "eyewitness" accounts about the Syrian military using "barrel bombs," including in an attack to destroy a Syrian Arab Red Crescent humanitarian convoy and warehouse on

September 19 in Orem al Kubra. But there were reasons to be suspicious of this claim since this town is controlled by the infamous Nour al Din al Zinki terrorist group, which recently filmed itself beheading a Palestinian Syrian boy.

It was also illogical that Syrian or Russian planes would attack a SARC convoy, which they could have stopped when it was in government held territory. Plus, the Syrian government works with SARC. And, the ones to "benefit" from the attack were the rebels and their Western backers who cited this atrocity as another reason for "regime change" and to condemn the Russians for assisting the Syrian government. The attack also took attention away from the U.S. airstrike that killed some 70 Syrian soldiers on September 17.[39]

Needless to say, neither Rick Sterling's article nor the *Grayzone* revelations ever got very much traction in the mainstream media. In fact, both Rick Sterling and Max Blumenthal are either ignored or defamed in the mass media.

The civil war in Syria provides multiple examples of the media's suppression of "inconvenient facts." A glaring example is the defamation and very near blacklisting of independent Canadian journalist Eva Bartlett who has been repeatedly in Syria for prolonged periods of time.[40] She has also spoken at UN Press conferences in New York,[41] but again the media largely ignored her. Similarly ignored was Carmelite nun Agnes Mariam of the Cross,[42] whom I met in Geneva when I was still UN Independent Expert. I participated on a panel on war crimes in Syria together with Mother Agnes, and after the session I took the opportunity to ask her about her views on the war crimes committed by all sides, the allegations against Al Assad of using chemical weapons, about the general mood of the population, etc. The conversation was very revealing and her counternarrative presented at the side event of the Human Rights Council was brilliant. But I did not see any mention in the Geneva or Swiss press. When you do a search for Mother Agnes, you are likely to find some spurious attacks questioning her credibility, since she does not sing the U.S. or EU anti-Assad song.[43]

One of the worst chapters in mainstream media disinformation is how they treated the OPCW scandal and cover-up concerning the OPCW report on Douma, dealt with extensively in chapter 5 *supra*.

Most in the mainstream press failed to explain to the reader the implications of tampering with the evidence by an organization with a very
important mandate and an obligation to observe rigorous impartiality
like the OPCW. The media became complicit in the scandal, because
it largely endorsed and participated in the failed effort to discredit[44]
the professional OPCW inspectors and whistleblowers including Ian
Henderson.[45]

One of the most manipulative and toxic news services is the
Netherlands-based group that goes by the name "Bellingcat," founded
in 2014 by Eliot Higgins, a British former senior fellow at the Atlantic
Council, NATO's quasi-official think tank.[46] Among its "donors" are
the Open Society Foundation and the U.S. National Endowment for
Democracy. It is reported to have close links to the U.S. intelligence
community and since 2021 has been classed as a "foreign agent" by
Russia. Attempts by Bellingcat to discredit the OPCW whistleblower
Ian Henderson are not only unconvincing, in my view they constitute
a serious breach of journalistic ethics.[47] As someone who has worked
with petitions for decades, with experts, with journalists, with victims,
I am familiar with false flag operations and biased reporting. I regret the
disrespect with which Bellingcat attacks those inspectors who have a
conscience and who refuse to bend to political pressure. We have dealt
with the role of the White Helmets in providing false and misleading
information[48] and with the disgraceful threats by Washington against
OPCW officials, including its first Director General José Bustani.[49]

Again, American journalist Rick Sterling warned us about the
role of biased reporting on Syria as a factor in the prolongation of the
War.[50] Sterling wrote,

> It has been confirmed that TV journalist Richard Engel's
> kidnapping/rescue in norther Syria in late 2012 was
> a hoax. NBC management knew the story was probably
> false but proceeded to broadcast it anyway. There are
> at least two good things about "Engelgate": 1. It is clear
> evidence of mainstream media bias in their reporting and
> characterization of the conflict in Syria. The kidnapping
> was meant to show that "bad" Assad supporters had kid-
> napped Richard Engel only to be rescued by the Western/
> Turkey/Gulf supported "good" rebels. NBC management

knew the scenario was dubious but promoted it anyway. 2. Engelgate is also proof that Syrian anti-government rebels consciously manipulated western media for political gain. An elaborate ruse was performed to demonize the Syrian government & supporters and to encourage more support for the anti-government rebels.

Sterling goes on to examine the implications of the fake news. He asks "Will this confirmation of deception lead to any more scepticism about reports from and about Syria? Will there be any more critical or sceptical look at stories that demonize the Syrian government and favor the western narrative? We have a test case right now."

The alleged chlorine gas attacks report by Human Rights Watch gives us food for thought. According to HRW: "Evidence strongly suggests that Syrian government forces used toxic chemicals in several barrel bomb attacks in Idlib." HRW Deputy Director Nadim Houry accused the Syrian government of "thumbing its nose at the (UN) Security Council and international law yet again." However, is the allegation evidence based? The use of chlorine gas was never established, but the propagandistic goal had been reached. *Calumniare audacter, semper aliquid haeret*. Always something sticks.

In 2021 Dr. Alan MacLeod,[51] a member of the Glasgow University Media Group, published a highly informative article about the outrageous bias of Bellingcat's "investigations"[52] since 2014:

> Bellingcat is far from independent and neutral, as it is funded by Western governments, staffed with former military and state intelligence officers, repeats official narratives against enemy states and serves as a key part in what could be called a "spook to Bellingcat to corporate media propaganda pipeline" presenting Western government narratives as independent research. An alarming number of Bellingcat's staff and contributors come from highly suspect backgrounds. Senior investigator Nick Wabers, for example, spent three years as an officer in in the British Army, including a tour in Afghanistan, where he furthered the British state's objectives. . . . Former contributor Cameron Colquhoun's past is even more suspect. Colquhoun spent a decade in a senior

position in GCHQ (Britain's version of the NSA), where he ran cyber and Middle Eastern terror operations.... There are plenty of former American spooks on Bellingcat's roster as well. Former contributor Chris Biggers, who penned more than 60 articles for the site ... previously worked for the National Geospatial-Intelligence Agency—a combat support unit that works under the Department of Defense.... Biggers is now the director of an intelligence company headquartered in Virginia ... that boasts of having retired Army and Air Force generals on its board. Again, none of this is disclosed by Bellingcat, where Biggers's bio states only that he is a "public and private sector consultant based in Washington D.C." For six years Don Kaszeta was a U.S. Secret Service agent specializing in chemical, biological and nuclear weapons and for six more he worked as a program manager for the White House Military Office.... Imagine ... the opposite scenario: an "independent" Russian investigative website staffed partially with ex-KGB officials, funded by the Kremlin, with most of their research focused on the nefarious deeds of the U.S., UK. And NATO. Would anyone take it seriously? And yet Bellingcat is consistently presented in corporate media as a liberatory organization, the Information Age's gift to the people.

With regard to Bellingcat's reporting on the Syrian war, Dr. Macleod comments:

What we are uncovering here is a network of military, state, think-tank and media units all working together, of which Bellingcat is a central fixture.... This would be bad enough, but much of its own research is extremely poor. It strongly pushed the now increasingly discredited idea of a chemical weapons attack in Douma, Syria, attacking the members of the OPCW who came forward to expose the cover-up and making some bizarre claims along the way. For years Higgins and other members of the Bellingcat team also signal-boosted a Twitter account purporting to be an ISIS official, only for an investigation to expose the account as belonging to a young Indian troll in Bangalore. A leaked U.K. Foreign Office document lamented that: "Bellingcat was somewhat discredited, both by spreading disinformation itself, and by being willing to produce reports for anyone willing to pay."

Professor Oliver Boyd-Barrett, emeritus at Bowling Green State University and an expert in the connections between the deep state and the fourth estate, further attested that "the role of Bellingcat is to provide spurious legitimacy to U.S./NATO pretexts for war and conflict.[53]

The question that this chapter tries to explore is why the mainstream media deliberately disseminates the wrong impression that Bellincat is reliable and credible, when we know who pays the Piper. I am not sure that it is still possible to reverse the trend, but I fear that the information/psychological war will get worse before it gets better. There are still journalists with conscience and competence—but they are mostly in the alternative media. What I observe is that the once "quality press" has been hijacked to participate in disseminating the obscene instrumentalization of human rights and humanitarian values by the U.S., UK and NATO, whitewash its crimes and legitimize its aggressions.

The War in Ukraine

Here again, if the media had performed its function and informed the public on all aspects of the Ukraine conflict, the war may not have occurred. But instead, the media prepared the ground for the Ukraine war by consistently supporting the hawks in Washington, London, and Brussels, and silencing the peace movement.

The psychological justifications for the confrontation between NATO and Russia were laid down decades ago, and the media contributed to constructing the Russian archfiend, bogeyman, evil spirit, menacing bear, ogre—the scapegoat for the ills of Western society, a distraction away from domestic problems and dysfunctions.

Putin has been slandered and demonized in the West from the very beginning, along with bigoted and racist depictions of Russian history. There has been biased reporting and outright wrong information on all sorts of events in Russia, on the 2008 war in Georgia, evidence-free allegations and conspiracy theories concerning the poisoning of Alexei Navalny,[54] the Skripal scandal,[55] etc.—to say nothing of the years-long and ultimately discredited fraud of Russian interference in American elections—anything to create and nurture a negative image of Russia, that would subsequently make it palatable to the American and European public to justify a war against the monster Putin. The same kind of incitement to hatred was practised against geopolitical foes of the United States—Saddam Hussein, Muammar Gadaffi, and Bashar al-Assad.

This is not to imply that Putin, Hussein, Gadaffi and al-Assad are innocent of war crimes and gross violations of human rights. What is at stake is how governments and the media have weaponized facts and events, magnified them, focused on them while neglecting the war crimes and crimes against humanity committed by NATO countries in Yugoslavia, Afghanistan, Iraq, Libya and Syria, by Saudi Arabia in Yemen, by Israel in Gaza and the Occupied Palestinian territories. What is at stake is the abhorrence of war crimes and the universal need to suppress them and the deliberate use of allegations of war crimes as an additional weapon of war, frequently evidence-free and intended only to smear and discredit the opponent. The issue here is the failure of the mainstream media to report fairly and professionally on all war crimes committed by all sides and not to convey the false impression that war crimes are committed only by one party, whereas the other party is virtuous. It is this kind of unbalanced reporting that constitutes incitement to hatred and violence. It reminds us of the exercise known as "hate week"[56] in Orwell's dystopian novel, *1984*.

The behavior described above is contrary to the letter and spirit of the UN Charter and the UNESCO Constitution, contrary to the mindset necessary to ensure international peace and understanding, and contrary to Article 20 of the ICCPR, which stipulates: "Any advocacy of national, racial or religious hatred that constitutes incitement to discrimination, hostility or violence shall be prohibited by law." Since at least the year 2000 the mainstream media engaged in this kind of incitement against Russia, in the creation of an artificial "enemy," although Russia did not want to be the enemy of the West, on the contrary, post-Cold-War Russia has wanted to have best relations with the West and the rest of the world.

It would have been the role of the media to inform the public thoroughly and without bias about all aspects of the Ukraine conflict, to present the conflict rationally, in the light of a necessary balancing of Western and Russian interests. After all, a confrontation between nuclear powers is not *peccata minuta,* it is a very big deal.

Independent Canadian journalist Eva Bartlett has also reported on alleged Ukrainian war crimes in the Donbas, but these reports have been largely ignored.[57] In fact, the Western mainstream media seldom mentions anything in this direction and rejects all Russian claims and those of independent Western journalists as "disinformation." In August 2022 Bartlett reported on banned butterfly mines allegedly used by Ukraine against civilians in Donetsk.[58] None of such information ever makes it into the Western media. If one wants to get a more complete picture of what is happening, it is necessary to pro-actively search for it on the internet—which is not always successful, because videos are frequently removed by YouTube and the algorithms of search engines filter many reports out. When one types into a search engine "war crimes in Ukraine," only war crimes by Russians against Ukrainians are documented, not otherwise, even though there has been a war crimes tribunal in Moscow[59] which reviewed the evidence as of the summer of 2022.

Another journalist/witness who is totally ignored by the mainstream media is Sonja van den Ende, who visited the republics of Donetsk and Luhansk as an embedded reporter with the Russian army. According to Van den Ende, "Ministries have reported the high number of children killed [by the Ukrainian military] to various organizations, such as UNICEF, Human Rights Watch and Amnesty. But to this day, it hasn't been publicized. These human rights organizations only report if it is in their own interest, that is, if their Western donors instruct them to report on it.[60]

The Blowing Up of the Nordstream Pipelines[61]

Reporting by the mainstream media over the blowing up of the Nordstream Pipelines in September 2022 was accompanied by the usual disinformation and vulgar Russophobia that has been the hallmark of the Western media since the August 2008 war in Georgia. It was as if they were taking their news directly from the Pentagon or the State Department. The reluctance of the Western media to properly report on the sabotage of civilian infrastructures, the violations of international law and customary international law on the safety of pipelines, the gravity of State terrorism—and instead coming up with the preposterous notion that Russia blew up its own pipelines, when it could easily have simply shut off their flow, if so desired—is disgraceful. A responsible media would not only report but also call for transparency and accountability, denounce the terroristic acts and demand a full international investigation. Can they use the excuse of wartime reporting? But the U.S. and NATO, so they claim, are not at war with Russia. Of course, the media in the non-Western world has taken a different approach and many justly believe that all the evidence point at U.S. responsibility.[62]

Persons who dared utter the possibility that the United States could be behind the terrorist action were immediately smeared. Even the distinguished economist, Professor Jeffrey Sachs of Columbia University, was abruptly taken off the air during an interview with Bloomberg for so doing.[63]

The revelations contained Seymour Hersh's analysis of the evidence pointing to U.S. authorship of the September 26, 2022 sabotage of the Nordstream pipelines,[64] published on February 8, 2023, is compelling. In countries claiming to stand for freedom of the press, this should have caused a broad-based media uproar, a call for an internal investigation into illegal activities by the CIA and Pentagon, for a condemnation by Congress, and an international investigation under UN auspices, and even a call for the Biden Administration to step down in the light of the magnitude of the gross violation of the UN Charter and international treaties.

It is mind-boggling: The country that claims to be a defender of international law engages in a brazen terror operation which, if the American people knew, they certainly would oppose—that and the U.S. government involvement in false flag operations and outright State terrorism. But instead, due to media complicity, these very events are addressed—if at all—in such a way as to galvanize public support for government policy.

Of course, the White House and the Pentagon immediately denied responsibility and tried to smear Seymour Hersh, following the Romans injunction: If you did it, deny it, stonewall! *Si fecisti, nega!*

Hersh, a former reporter for the *Associated Press* and the *New York Times*, as well as a long-time contributor to *The New Yorker*, quoted White House spokesperson Adrienne Watson as calling his report "false and complete fiction." CIA spokesperson Tammy Thorp wrote: "This claim is completely and utterly false." This reminded me of my childhood. I recall my teachers referring to the expression *"tira la piedra y esconde la mano"*—throw the stone and hide your hand—and impressing on me that such behaviour was unethical.

Long before the Hersh revelations. all the evidence pointed at the United States and its NATO allies. After all, the United States had done everything possible to prevent the completion of the Nordstream pipeline, imposed illegal sanctions on enterprises engaged in its construction, threatened, blackmailed, bullied. Moreover, on February 7, 2022, prior to the invasion of Ukraine by Russia, Biden had stated: "If Russia invades.... there will be no longer a Nord Stream 2.... We will bring an end to it." All of this would have been confirmed if the Swedish investigation had been forthcoming,[65] if the European and Russian owners of Nordstream had been allowed to see the evidence. But Sweden stonewalled. And the mainstream media lets all of this happen without drawing the necessary conclusions and demanding transparency and accountability. Yet another egregious failure of our "watchdog."

Interviewed after the publication of his study on the Nordstream sabotage, Hersh stated that the major news outlets are failing to report a lot of things about the ongoing conflict between Moscow and Kiev. *"The war I know about is not the war you're reading about,"* Hersh observed. *"It's amazing to me how they fall in line, my colleagues,"* he added, lamenting that many outlets such as the *New York Times, Washington Post,* CNN and more generally the mainstream media have become a front for the White House and the Biden administration.

Not surprisingly, the mainstream media mention the revelations, but no one wants to draw the consequences, because these would demolish the Western narrative. None dare analyse and explain the implications. Professor Dr. Jan Oberg,[66] a Danish-Swedish peace activist and chair of the Transnational Foundation for Peace and Future Research,[67] commented:

The present situation is extremely dangerous: We live in times fundamentally characterized by intellectual and ethical disarmament coupled with immense military armament, with militarism as the only one answer to the problems. . . . The West chooses to use weapons, threats, secret operations and media manipulation instead of using talks, mediating, engaging the UN or OSCE (the Organization for Security and Cooperation in Europe), and it abandons diplomacy and plays tough on others. . . . Militarism has become the religion that keeps the declining West together, with NATO (as) its church. That's why also the Western mainstream media won't give Hersh's sensational analysis the attention it deserves.[68]

It does, however, receive attention in China,[69] which is concerned about being the next NATO target.

The Nordstream saga is yet another example of how the mainstream media works. When Seymour Hersh published his well documented and convincing report, the *New York Times* ignored it. Compare that to the orgy of media atterntion given to a thoroughly implausible scenario alleging that a nongovernmental group of five pro-Ukrainian operatives leased a yacht in Rostock and carried out the sabotage. The tsunami of publications and commentary on this preposterous theory, contrasts with the overwhelming silence and blanket denials concerning the Hersh report.

As Dr. Jan Oberg wrote a critical piece on March 8, 2023: "How stupid do they think we are? A small pro-Ukrainian group in a yacht did whaaaat? Western 'intelligence' and the *New York Times* in deeper waters than usual, offering us a devious spin and fake story—sadly swallowed by the same media that omitted Hersh's analysis."[70] And to show that there is method in the madness, Reuters added its two cents' worth by reporting that this "amounts to the first significant lead about who was responsible." This is too pathetic for words, and reminds us how the media disseminated all the official lies put out by the Pentagon to justify the illegal invasion of Iraq in 2003.

Asked what he thought of the new "report" on the blowing up of Nordstream, Hersh wryly replied "You should decide for yourself. It's up to you."[71] On March 9, *Asia Times* published a commentary:

"Assemble a whole from the two versions and you might come up with this: On U.S. President Joe Biden's orders, U.S. government covert types put together and with Norwegian help carried out the operation (that's Hersh's story); to avoid detection, they left some clues pointing elsewhere, to Ukrainians or "pro-Ukrainians"—the main clue mentioned so far being that the yacht from which the divers worked could be traced back to a yacht-rental company in Poland, a company owned by Ukrainians." Another false flag in the long tradition of NATO false flags.

PENETRATION OF THE MEDIA AND SOCIAL MEDIA BY INTELLIGENCE SERVICES

On February 25, 2014 journalist Glenn Greenwald published an article that should have raised some eyebrows:[72]

HOW COVERT AGENTS INFILTRATE THE INTERNET TO MANIPULATE, DECEIVE, AND DESTROY REPUTATIONS

One of the many pressing stories that remains to be told from the Snowden archive is how western intelligence agencies are attempting to manipulate and control online discourse with extreme tactics of deception and reputation-destruction. It's time to tell a chunk of that story, complete with the relevant documents.

Over the last several weeks, I worked with *NBC News* to publish a series of articles about "dirty trick" tactics by GCHQ's previously secret unit, JTRIG (Joint Threat Research Intelligence Group). These were based on four classified CGHQ documents presented to the NSA and the other three partners in the English-speaking "Five Eyes" alliance. Today, we at the *Intercept* are publishing another new JTRIG document, in full, entitled "The Art of Deception: Training for Online Covert Operations."

By publishing these stories one by one, our NBC reporting highlighted some of the key, discrete revelations: the monitoring of YouTube and Blogger, the targeting of Anonymous with the very same DDoS attacks they accuse "hacktivists" of using, the use of "honey traps" (luring people into compromising situations using sex) and destructive viruses. But, here, I want to focus and elaborate on the overarching point revealed by all of these documents: namely, that these agencies are attempting to control, infiltrate, manipulate, and warp online discourse, and in doing so, are compromising the integrity of the internet itself.

Among the core self-identified purposes of JTRIG are two tactics: (1) to inject all sorts of false material onto the internet in order to destroy the reputation of its targets; and (2) to use social sciences and other techniques to manipulate online discourse and activism to generate outcomes it considers desirable. To see how extremist these programs are, just consider the tactics they boast of using to achieve those ends: "false flag operations" (posting material to the internet and falsely attributing it to someone else), fake victim blog posts (pretending to be a victim of the individual whose reputation they want to destroy), and posting "negative information" on various forums. Here is one illustrative list of tactics from the latest GCHQ document we're publishing today:

SECRET//SI//REL TO USA, FVEY

DISRUPTION
Operational Playbook

• Infiltration Operation
• Ruse Operation
• Set Piece Operation
• False Flag Operation
• False Rescue Operation
• Disruption Operation
• Sting Operation

SECRET//SI//REL TO USA, FVEY

Other tactics aimed at individuals are listed here, under the revealing title "discredit a target." The article and the documentation is shocking, but there was no significant reaction to it.

In November 2022 the *Intercept* published another cache of documents revealing the degree of penetration of the media by intelligence services and the "revolving door" between government and media.

Caitlin Johnstone's analysis

On November 1, 2022, Caitlin Johnstone, an Australian journalist from Melbourne, commented in her essay entitled "Destroying Western Values to Defend Western Values."[73]

> So it turns out the U.S. intelligence cartel has been working intimately with online platforms to regulate the "cognitive infrastructure" of the population. This is according to a new investigative report by the Intercept, based on documents obtained through leaks and an ongoing lawsuit, on the "retooling" of the Department of Homeland Security from an agency focused on counterterrorism to one increasingly focused on fighting "misinformation, disinformation, and malinformation" online....
>
> "The report reveals pervasive efforts on the part of the DHS and its Cybersecurity and Infrastructure Security Agency (CISA), along with the FBI, to push massive online platforms like Facebook, Instagram and Twitter to censor content in order to suppress "threats" as broad as fomenting distrust in the U.S. government and U.S. financial institutions.
>
> "There is also a formalized process for government officials to directly flag content on Facebook or Instagram and request that it be throttled or suppressed through a special Facebook portal that requires a government or law enforcement email to use," the Intercept reports.
>
> "Emails between DHS officials, Twitter, and the Center for Internet Security outline the process for such takedown requests during the period leading up to November 2020,"

says the Intercept. "Meeting notes show that the tech platforms would be called upon to 'process reports and provide
timely responses, to include the removal of reported misinformation from the platform where possible.'"

While these government agencies contend that they
are not technically forcing these tech platforms to remove
content, the Intercept argues that its investigation shows
"CISA's goal is to make platforms more responsive to their
suggestions," while critics argue that "suggestions" from
immensely powerful institutions will never be taken as
mere suggestions.

"When the government suggests things, it's not too
hard to pull off the velvet glove, and you get the mail
fist," Michigan State University's Adam Candeub tells the
Intercept. "And I would consider such actions, especially
when it's bureaucratized, as essentially state action and
government collusion with the platforms."

. . . The current CISA chief is seen justifying this
aggressive government thought policing by creepily referring to the means people use to gather information and form
thoughts about the world as "our cognitive infrastructure":

> Jen Easterly, Biden's appointed director of CISA,
> swiftly made it clear that she would continue to shift
> resources in the agency to combat the spread of dan-
> gerous forms of information on social media. "One
> could argue we're in the business of critical infra-
> structure, and the most critical infrastructure is our
> cognitive infrastructure, so building that resilience to
> misinformation and disinformation, I think, is incredi-
> bly important," said Easterly, speaking at a conference
> in November 2021.

Another CISA official is seen suggesting the agency
launder its manipulations through third party non-profits "to
avoid the appearance of government propaganda."

To accomplish these broad goals, the report said, CISA
should invest in external research to evaluate the "efficacy

of interventions," specifically with research looking at how alleged disinformation can be countered and how quickly messages spread. Geoff Hale, the director of the Election Security Initiative at CISA, recommended the use of third-party information-sharing nonprofits as a "clearing house for trust information to avoid the appearance of government propaganda."

But as a former ACLU president tells the Intercept, if this were happening in any government the U.S. doesn't like, there'd be no qualms about calling it what it is:

> "If a foreign authoritarian government sent these messages," noted Nadine Strossen, the former president of the American Civil Liberties Union, "there is no doubt we would call it censorship."

Indeed, this report is just another example of the way western powers are behaving more and more like the autocracies they claim to despise, all in the name of preserving the values the west purports to uphold. As the Intercept reminds us, this business of the U.S. government assigning itself the responsibility of regulating America's "cognitive infrastructure" originated with the "allegation that Russian agents had seeded disinformation on Facebook that tipped the 2016 election toward Donald Trump." To this day that agenda continues to expand into things like plots to censor speech about the war in Ukraine.

Other examples of this trend coming out at the same time include Alan MacLeod's new report with Mintpress News that hundreds of former agents from the notorious Israeli spying organization Unit 8200 are now working in positions of influence at major tech companies like Google, Facebook, Microsoft and Amazon (just the latest in MacLeod's ongoing documentation of the way intelligence insiders have been increasingly populating the ranks of Silicon Valley platforms), and the revelation that The Grayzone's Max Blumenthal and Aaron Maté were barred from participating in a Web Summit conference due to pressure from the Ukrainian government.

We're destroying western values to defend western values. To win its much-touted struggle of "democracies vs autocracies," western civilization is becoming more and more autocratic. Censoring more. Trolling more. Propagandizing more. Jailing journalists. Becoming less and less transparent. Manipulating information and people's understanding of truth.

Much has been written—and little understood—about the growing penetration of the media by intelligence services. This penetration goes back to the 1960s and the controversial "Operation Mockingbird," which to this day some in the media want to erase.[74]

DISMISSAL OF JOURNALISTS FOR PRACTICING JOURNALISM

In today's world it is no longer possible for a journalist to do his/her work without fear of being punished if he dares to criticize the United States or its allies. A case in point is the firing by CNN of Mark Lamont Hill, a professor of media studies at Temple University in Philadelphia, after a speech he delivered at the United Nations concerning human rights violations by Israel in the Palestinean occupied territories. The move came as a result of protests by the Anti-Defamation League and other pro-Israel groups.

In justifying his speech Professor Hill said "I support Palestinian freedom. I support Palestinian self-determination," and added "I do not support anti-Semitism, killing Jewish people, or any of the other things attributed to my speech. I have spent my life fighting these things."[75] This is but one of so many cases of media terror against dissenters, that one wonders why the UN Special Rapporteurs on Freedom of Expression have not taken up the matter, investigated it thoroughly, quantified it, and reported on the extent of mobbing that today characterizes the media landscape in the United States, Canada, United Kingdom, etc.

MEDIA MOBBING OF ACADEMICS

> *"Rights have become what the political sovereign or ephemeral*
> *master decides to dispense and whatever gratifies the*
> *undisciplined cravings and desires of the individual."*
>
> RUSSELL KIRK, *ACADEMIC FREEDOM: AN ESSAY IN DEFINITION*

> *"The most important aspect of freedom of speech is freedom to*
> *learn. All education is a continuous dialogue—questions and*
> *answers that pursue every problem on the horizon. that is the*
> *essence of academic freedom."*
>
> JUSTICE WILLIAM ORVILLE DOUGLAS

> **"By** *academic freedom I understand the right to search for*
> *truth and to publish and teach what one holds to be true. This*
> *right implies also a duty: one must not conceal any part of what*
> *one has recognized to be true. It is evident that any restriction*
> *on academic freedom acts in such a way as to hamper the*
> *dissemination of knowledge among the people and thereby*
> *impedes rational judgment and action."*
>
> ALBERT EINSTEIN

For decades the Western media has been disseminating disinformation about Russia, engaged in vulgar Russophobia and smeared many academics who dared question the official NATO narrative on Russia. As shown in this book, the information war against Russia has been waged for decades, in the United States, Canada, United Kingdom, France, Germany, Spain, Netherlands, Lithuania, Estonia, Latvia, Poland, Norway and Sweden.

In 2021, long before the Russian invasion of Ukraine, Norwegian Professor Glenn Diesen[76] of the University of South Eastern Norway, an expert in Russia and Eastern Europe, endured unfair media attacks because of his dissenting views on Russian history and politics and his occasional op-eds in the Russian news channel, *RT.* Norway's TV2 published a "hit piece"[77] on Diesen's work with RT, accusing him of assisting what it called a "Russian propaganda platform" and calling his tenure at the University of South Eastern Norway problematic. "An academic who participates on RT . . . has lost his credibility. He must be regarded as part of the Russian propaganda machinery and has thereby lost his scientific relevance in a democracy," Swedish journalist and editor Patrik Oksanen, associated with the Stockholm-based think tank Free World, told TV2. "There is freedom of expression in Norway and people can think what they want. But this is a sauce of erroneous allegations that is very close to the main lines of what we associate with Russian propaganda," adviser to the Norwegian Helsinki Committee Aage Borchgrevink told TV2. Some of the Norwegian channel's invited experts who went so far to question Diesen's tenure as professor.

"Has Diesen himself and the academic environment he belongs to thought about the situation and are they comfortable with one of their professors acting as a propagandist?" Sven Holtsmark, a professor at the Institute of Defence Studies, said, calling Diesen's articles "problematic," "unjustifiable," and "conspiratorial."

Addressing the criticism, Diesen himself called the Western media's coverage of Russia detached from reality, denouncing the intimidation and censorship, and making it very clear that attacks on academic freedom constitutes a threat to democracy in Norway. "Rejecting counter-arguments as Russian propaganda is a form of censorship that demonises the other party and polarises the debate," he told TV2.

Already in 2019 Diesen[78] published a review of Stephen Cohen's book *War with Russia*,[79] and then an article titled "The EU in its current form is a tragic mistake in European History"[80] had raised eyebrows because of his analysis, published together with former Czech President Vaclav Klaus.

Klaus has also been the butt of criticism in the mainstream media. At the Crans Montana Forum in Geneva on November 17, 2022, he delivered a brilliant speech highlighting the betrayal of European values by the European Commission. After the conference I had the opportunity of discussing with Klaus the implications of the war with Russia and the necessity of an immediate cease-fire and the mediation[81] of former Presidents and Prime Ministers like himself.

Vaclav Klaus and Alfred de Zayas at the
Crans Montana Forum in Geneva in November 2022

Another example of media-mobbing is that of Professor Norman Finkelstein, born in Brooklyn, New York, son of Holocaust survivors,[82] a keen observer of history, and a man with a strong sense for justice and historical truth. His books have been highly praised, but also maligned,[83] misquoted, distorted, quoted out of context. He has been accused of being a "self-hating Jew," an anti-Semite, an intellectual pariah, a terrorist.

Because of a vicious media campaign against him, he was denied tenure at DePaul University[84] in Chicago in 2007, where I myself had been visiting Professor of Law in 1993–94. Finkelstein, the author of some 20 books, including *The Holocaust Industry*[85] and *Gaza,* has been subjected to mobbing and defamation by the media, with considerable success, since DePaul University felt its pocketbook so threatened, so intimidated that it preferred to sacrifice academic freedom on the altar of expediency.

I have a copy of the disgraceful letter dated June 8, 2007 addressed to Dr. Finkelstein by the then President of DePaul University, Rev. Dennis Holtschneider, caving in to pressures from the media and lobby groups that had threatened to make sure that donations to the University would dry up if Finkelstein were to be granted tenure.

Professor emeritus Raul Hilberg, the preeminent expert on the history of the Holocaust, protested in a letter to the university.

... Finkelstein was the first to publish what was happening in his book, *The Holocaust Industry*. And when I was asked to endorse the book, I did so with specific reference to these claims. I felt that within the Jewish community over the centuries, nothing like it had ever happened. And even though these days a couple of billion dollars are sometimes referred to as an accounting error and not worthy of discussion, there is a psychological dimension here which must not be underestimated.

I was also struck by the fact that Finkelstein was being attacked over and over. And granted, his style is a little different from mine, but I was saying the same thing, and I had published my results in that three-volume work, published in 2003 by Yale University Press, and I did not hear from anybody a critical word about what I said, even though it was the same substantive conclusion that Finkelstein had offered. So that's the gist of the matter right then and there.

...

And then, again, I gave a lecture a year and a half ago in Chicago, which is the place where Finkelstein had been employed at DePaul University, and my lecture was about Auschwitz, and it was based on the records, which we've now recovered from Moscow, about the history of this camp. Not exactly a simple topic. But there was a question period, and I awaited pertinent questions, when someone rose from his chair and asked, "Should Finkelstein be tenured?" Now, for heaven's sake, I said to myself, what is going on here?

And whether he's being intimidated, whether he is in a situation where, whatever else may be happening, the employers are being intimidated, it's hard for me to say, but there is very clearly a campaign, which was made very obvious in *The Wall Street Journal*, when Professor Dershowitz wrote in a style which is highly uncharacteristic of the editorial page of this newspaper, which incidentally I read religiously. So I, myself, cannot fully explain this outburst, but it clearly emanates from the same anger, from the same revolt, that prompted the whole action against the Swiss to begin with.

. . . [L]et me say at the outset, I would not, unasked, offer advice to the university in which he now serves. Having been in a university for 35 years myself and engaged in its politics, I know that outside interferences are most unwelcome. I will say, however, that I am impressed by the analytical abilities of Finkelstein. He is, when all is said and done, a highly trained political scientist who was given a Ph.D. degree by a highly prestigious university. This should not be overlooked....

It takes an enormous amount of academic courage to speak the truth when no one else is out there to support him. ... So I would say that his place in the whole history of writing history is assured, and that those who in the end are proven right triumph, and he will be among those who will have triumphed, albeit, it so seems, at great cost."

As a former visiting professor of international law at DePaul 1993–94 (on leave of absence from the Office of the UN High Commissioner for Human Rights), I myself addressed a letter of protest to Rev. Holtschneider, to which I did not receive any response. Among other things I emphasized that "Academic freedom is indispensable for any kind of scientific advance—whether in law, history, economics—and Universities must never capitulate to outside pressure and blackmail by lobbies. I have seen the kind of unethical activities deployed against DePaul also practised against other universities. This is a worrisome development—not only for academia, but for the survival of pluralism and democracy itself . . . I salute Finkelstein's courage. He is the Sisyphus who will yet carry the boulder to the crest."

In this context, I would like to quote my friend and colleague Norman Finkelstein:

To step into a classroom today is to walk into a nuclear minefield. It's become a terror-ridden, humourless barracks. The problem, however, is not just the codified restrictions on speech and the phalanx of smug, dour thought-police, the holier-than-thou nonentities, employed by the university to enforce them. It's even more the suffocating and intimidatory atmosphere of cancel culture that permeates the campus.

This is so partly because the mainstream media actively participates in the mobbing of academics who do not toe the prescribed line. The media is responsible for nurturing an atmosphere of terror among academics, and university presidents. There is ever less opportunity to carry out research and to publish ideas that do not conform with the mainstream "narrative."

Alfred de Zayas and Dr. Finkelstein in New York, 2017

In 2018, a well-known academic journal from a leading university invited me to write an article on my mission to Venezuela, what I saw there, whether there was a humanitarian crisis, and who was responsible for it. As I was in the process of writing my report for the Human Rights Council, I found it relatively easy to describe the

situation on the ground and substantiate it with the plethora of documents that I had collected from government and opposition, from civil
society and the churches. I submitted my article within the time and
space limit provided. Some six weeks later I received an email that it
was not being published "because of its content." At least my report to
the Council did see the light of day.

WIKIPEDIA

Although Wikipedia[86] is not "media" as such, it influences journalists and politicians and constitutes a dangerous source of unreliable
information. Because of its flawed methodology, it is thoroughly
unreliable as a source of information. It has been established that intelligence services, governments, corporations, and special interests have
massively influenced the contents of Wiki articles, that bots are paid to
add misleading information and delete corrections, that defamation is
allowed against certain personalities but criticism is promptly removed
when it is directed against mainstream figures. Many users who in good
faith try to improve the content of the Wikipedia find their IPs blocked
by the senior "editors" at the Wikipedia. Moreover, Wikipedia declares
entirely reliable sources to be unreliable and any user who attempts to
make reference to the arbitrary blacklist finds his correction removed
and if they insist, they are banned from the Wikipedia.

For several years I was on the editorial Committee of the
Encyclopaedia of Public International Law, published by the Max
Planck Institute for International Law in Heidelberg, Germany. I have
also been co-editor of several books and have learned the ethics of
editing. The lack of professionalism in Wikipedia and the manner in
which fake news enters Wikipedia and corrections are removed is an
absolute disgrace. I have told my students, they will be penalized if they
cite Wikipedia as a source, because it does not qualify as an academic
source. Moreover, I have warned them about the subtle and not so subtle
manipulation of historical and political articles. Personally, I have many
negative experiences with it, having attempted to correct objective
errors in it, and seeing my corrections removed within a few hours.

The danger of Wikipedia is such that not only students, but many
journalists and politicians rely on it—even judges have been misin-
formed by it.[87] This is truly Orwellian.

Conclusion

One of the greatest dangers to democracy and human rights is the corruption of the media by conglomerates and the instrumentalization of the media for purposes of indoctrination of the population. As we have seen in earlier chapters of this book, democracy is not coterminous with periodic elections, because elections are only meaningful when the population has real choices and when they have not been brainwashed into supporting one candidate over another. Elections have no democratic validity when the electorate has been deliberately disinformed and when there is no limit to the amount of money that political parties can receive from billionaire donors like George Soros.[88]

One of the most frightful and totalitarian decisions of the U.S. Supreme Court, the *Citizens United* v *Federal Elections Commission* judgment of 2010,[89] essentially subverts the democratic process, since corporations and super rich individuals can actually "buy" elections by flooding the electorate with partisan information and disinformation. The *raison d'être* of the right to freedom of speech was to facilitate all points of view to get a hearing and not to enable the superrich to control the media. It was a black day for democracy when the judges decided that donations to political parties and candidates constituted a protected exercise of the right of freedom of expression guaranteed in Article 1 of the U.S. Bill of Rights.

Bearing in mind that democracy depends on public awareness based on comprehensive and accurate information, the first democratic right that must be fought for is the right to access truthful information, to know what the government is doing in our name, to reduce State secrecy to a minimum because secrecy facilitates crime and corruption, the right to demand transparency from public officials and the private sector. Indeed, large corporations are exercising quasi-governmental powers because some governments have "outsourced" or privatized functions that are essentially state functions. This privatization does not exclude the private sector from its social responsibilities, including an obligation of transparency. That is yet another reason why every democracy needs whistleblowers who will give the electorate the information they need to responsibly exercise their right to vote.

We need a charter of rights of whistleblowers, so that governmental and private sector scams are exposed.

For those who follow the press and the media, it is obvious that many journalists approach human rights based on their potential for sensationalism, where a particular violation of human rights can be magnified into an international scandal. Sometimes one even gets the impression that the media see human rights stories as a kind of human interest entertainment, and manufacture heroes and villains as required.

The same applies to the coverage given to the reports of certain UN independent experts and special rapporteurs. Among those experts who are essentially ignored are the Special Rapporteur on the Adverse Consequences of Unilateral Coercive Measures, the Special Rapporteur on the Right to Development, the Independent Expert on International Solidarity, the Independent Expert on the Promotion of a Democratic and Equitable International Order. Other rapporteurs like the LGBT rapporteur receive disproportionally more attention and abundant earmarked funds to support that one mandate.

And yet, notwithstanding everything stated and documented in this book, there continues to exist a "perception" of the credibility of certain members of the "quality press," which effectively allows them to continue to manipulate public opinion. For the average citizen it is difficult to reject the "quality press" based on their limited knowledge of or access to alternative views. The public at large is not perverse or radical; it wants and psychologically needs to believe in something. Moreover, the average citizen does not have the time or inclination to read all news providers and compare the narratives and digest them. The priorities for a normal person include the family, sending the kids to school, getting food on the table, making ends meet. The great stories of international politics and human rights violations in China or Russia do not occupy a very high place on their agenda.

Another worrisome problem is that almost all newspapers rely on the same "news agencies."

Precisely because the media is so crucial to democracy, we must be aware of the manipulations by special interests and lobbies. One of them is George Soros and his network of NGOs. In an article published in mrcNewsbusters[90] in January 2023 we read:

At least 253 organizations across the world that focus on news and activist media were funded by Soros' organizations. A number of these groups wield massive power over the flow of information in international politics. The Soros-funded, liberal outlet Project Syndicate claimed its commentaries were published 20,393 times in 156 countries in 2021. Project Syndicate boasted its articles also have appeared in 66 different languages. Soros gave $1,532,105 to Project Syndicate between 2016 and 2020. Another leftist U.K.-based outlet funded by Soros, openDemocracy, claimed it "attracts more than 11 million visits per year" and has projects published "in Russian, Spanish and Portuguese as well as English." Soros gave openDemocracy $1,633,457 between 2016 and 2020. The Poynter Institute's Soros-funded International Fact-Checking Network controls global fact-checking for 100 organizations and influences much of Big Tech content and social media with that power. Soros gave the IFCN $492,000 between 2016 and 2020.[91]

This kind of influence over the media is hyper-dangerous and undermines the necessity of independence, balance and plurality in the media.

But it is not just billionaires who do this out of their Wall Street fortunes obtained through clever speculation. The manipulation of public opinion is very widespread when one considers how many anti-China and Uyghur[92] organizations and media outlets are co-financed by the U.S. National Endowment for Democracy. Most people do not know that the most vocal anti-China newspapers and NGOs are actually financed by Washington. And when Wikileaks reveals that the allegations are false, the rest of the mainstream media ignores the evidence. As I have written before, there are "facts without consequences," "books without follow-up," and "news items that one should forget."

Take, for instance, the 2011 bombshell disclosures by Wikileaks.[93] According to the *Telegraph,* in an article by Malcolm Moore, dated June 4, 2011, we read "Secret cables from the United States embassy in Beijing have shown there was no bloodshed inside Tiananmen Square when China put down student pro-democracy demonstrations

22 years ago." Can this be true? I was not there. You were not there. But if secret U.S. cables substantiate that, then a general discussion should have been undertaken and efforts to corroborate or refute the cables would be in order.[94] What happened? Silence. What should not be, is not. At least one would have expected a modification of the mainstream narrative and a commitment not to repeat errors, if indeed they were errors.

What society needs is the *democratization* of the media and a close examination of the finances of media outlets, because every exercise of power requires some democratic oversight, requires transparency and accountability.

As I wrote in a press release[95] on the occasion of International Day of Democracy, September 15, 2017:

> Democracy is essential to achieving a more just world order. Only by genuinely reflecting the interests of the people can governments stem the tide of disillusionment, exploitation and conflict that plague today's world. True democracy requires education, access to multiple, reliable sources of information and opinion, consultation in good faith with all those affected by decisions, and open debate free of intimidation, ostracism and the constraints of 'political correctness'. It means combining majority rule with respect for minority opinions and the human dignity of all.

CHAPTER 8

THE BOTTOM LINE:
THE VOTING RECORD OF STATES

"Remota iustitia quid sunt regna nisi magna latrocinia?
Far away from justice, what are great kingdoms
but grand larceny?"

AUGUSTINE OF HIPPO, *DE CIVITATE DEI* 4,4

"Fools and fanatics are always so certain of themselves,
and wiser people so full of doubts."[1]

BERTRAND RUSSELL

"The best lack all conviction, while the worst are full of
passionate intensity."[2]

WILLIAM BUTLER YEATS, "THE SECOND COMING"

LIP SERVICE to "values" such as democracy, freedom, rule of law, due process, and human dignity is widespread. These values continue to be valid and merit our commitment. But states' representatives and the media have degraded these values and made them into propagandistic weapons to destabilize rivals, demonize geopolitical competitors, justify wars and military interventions.

The issues discussed in previous chapters have focused on the dysfunctions of what we have termed "the human rights industry" and have explored some of the problems that plague the international mechanisms and institutions established to promote and protect human rights. At the end of the day, the success or failure of the monitoring and protection mechanisms largely depends on the orientation of states and the policies they actually pursue, their lip service aside.

This in turn requires a degree of objectivity and the faculty of self-criticism, which is largely absent among the Western power elites and media. Notwithstanding empirical evidence to the contrary, many among those in the West steadfastly hold on to the myth that they are the "good guys," that they can teach others and impose sanctions when they fail to persuade their targets that they are right and the targeted are wrong.

Over the years I have observed in Ambassadors, Ministers and counsellors of powerful countries a combination of self-righteousness, hubris and solipsism, which only psychologists can adequately explain. I have come to understand that although hawks, bullies and exploiters are objectively bad and a danger for the peace and security of humankind, subjectively they see themselves as crusaders fighting for the good cause. Of course there is a degree of hypocrisy on all sides, but ultimately it is more a phenomenon of conviction and stubbornness. Call it a terminal case of national narcissism.

As a historian who decades ago interviewed dozens of Nazis,[3] I was struck by the fact that most of them did not have any remorse and certainly did not see themselves as the "bad guys." While recognizing excesses and crimes committed by the Reich, my interviewees saw themselves as ordinary German citizens engaged in the revision of the injustices of the Treaty of Versailles. This attitude is not surprising in light of the all-too-human faculty of self-deception and the psychological defence mechanisms we all share. Hence, it does not help to think of Fidel Castro, Daniel Ortega, Nicolas Maduro, Vladimir Putin, Xi Jinping etc. as "bad people" per se. By the same token it is unhelpful to moralize about Bill Clinton, George W. Bush or Barack Obama. Governments and military tend to act in a manner they consider rational at the particular time and in the concrete circumstances. Accordingly, if we want to keep clear of harm's way, it is prudent to study the rationale of governmental action. This explains not only lofty geopolitical moves, but also the more mundane way delegations vote in the General Assembly and Human Rights Council. Leaving utilitarianism and Machiavellianism aside, we should endeavour to understand the psychology of voting.

Elementary and secondary education, television, Hollywood movies as well as well-orchestrated public relations campaigns influence our perception of the world we live in, including how we feel about other peoples, how we evaluate their cultures, including a particular country's human rights performance. We are led to believe that certain countries are "models," whereas other countries are deficient. This binary approach of good states vs. bad states, democracies vs. autocracies adversely impacts the work of the United Nations at many levels. Efforts at multilateralism as required by the UN Charter and the UNESCO constitution are hampered by this mindset as reflected in the voluble assertions of some states against their rivals.

There are certain benchmarks and litmus tests that can assist us to assess the real situation. Indeed, the voting record of States in international organizations is a reasonably objective indicator of where the state really stands, its rhetoric aside. This chapter will explore a very limited number of examples drawn from UN practice, notably the UN General Assembly and Human Rights Council. The statements made by delegations during the negotiation of resolutions and the "explanations of vote" given by certain states to soften the incoherence of the vote or to whitewash what otherwise would be seen as evidence of a serious disregard of human dignity are particularly revealing of a country's real relationship to the philosophy and practice of human rights, that is, of its political and economic priorities. As we all know, lawyers and diplomats are trained to defend the indefensible, to use legalese to justify the unjustifiable, to dress aggression in the garbs of humanitarianism.

As a reasonably objective measuring stick for commitment to human dignity and equality in concrete situations, the voting record tells us who is really committed to human rights, and who is engaging in public relations exercises. It is easy to commit to human rights *in abstracto*, but the "proof of the pudding is in the eating."

Other human security indicators include states' ratification and implementation in domestic law of human rights treaties, including the ICCPR, ICESCR, ICERD, CAT, CEDAW, CMW, and notably, the reservations and declarations made to human rights treaties, derogations from their provisions, adherence to petitions procedures. Major powers like China, U.S. and UK do not adhere to petitions procedures. France, Germany, Russia and Belarus do, but then they frequently do not implement the decisions of the quasi-judicial expert committees.

Other significant indicators are a state's declaration under Article 36 of the ICJ Statute accepting the jurisdiction of the ICJ.[4] According to the UN Office of Legal Affairs, 73 states have given the declaration under Article 36 of the ICJ statute. China, France, Russia, U.S., have not given the declaration. As for their ratification of the Statute of Rome accepting the jurisdiction of the ICC,[5] 123 States have ratified the Statute of Rome, but not the United States, which has signed bilateral agreements with more than 80 States parties to the ICC to exclude the possibility of ever delivering an American to ICC jurisdiction. It is to be hoped that a future Assembly of States Parties to the ICC Statute will one day declare these bi-lateral agreements invalid as *contra bonos mores* and contrary to the object and purpose of the ICC statute. Of the P5 countries, only France and UK have ratified the Statute of Rome. Adherence to International humanitarian law conventions, implementation in good faith of rulings by UN bodies, respect for resolutions of international judicial and quasi-judicial organs, compliance with a philosophy of uniform application of rules without exceptionalism or looking for loopholes, and promotion of a level playing field nationally and internationally are useful tests in evaluating a country's human rights profile.[6]

Beyond that we should always take into account the budgetary priorities of states, how they actually distribute national wealth, and their efforts to bridge the gap between the super-rich and the abject poor, to reduce extreme poverty domestically and worldwide, improve housing, healthcare, education, effective rehabilitation of victims of violations of human rights and the furtherance of each person's right to his/her identity. This approaches Bhutan's ideal of "gross national happiness."[7]

This chapter is only intended as a "teaser." The reader is invited to explore his/her favourite resolutions and see how their states of concern voted on them.[8] Obviously we cannot review the voting record of all states at the General Assembly and Human Rights Council. But it is worthwhile to look at a few emblematic resolutions, a few easy choices between peace and war, between social justice and privilege. Some recent resolutions of the General Assembly, Security Council and Human Rights Council are revealing.

Peace is certainly the central issue of the UN Charter; the mission of the entire organization is foregrounds peace and peace-making. The Preamble of the UN Charter is still our guide: "We the Peoples of the United Nations determined to save succeeding generations from the scourge of war . . . to reaffirm faith in fundamental human rights . . . to promote social progress and better standards of life in larger freedom. . . ." Such beautiful language requires concrete action. Indeed, the realization that peace is a human right that enables the exercise of all other rights is absolutely central to the work of the United Nations and the Office of the UN High Commissioner for Human Rights. Let us revisit how the leading States have behaved in the debate on the human right to peace.

Already in the 1980s the Soviet Union was promoting the idea of the right of all peoples to peace, as reflected in resolution 39/11 of November 12, 1984.[9] This short resolution states:

> The General Assembly,
>
> Reaffirming that the principal aim of the United Nations is the maintenance of international peace and security,
>
> Bearing in mind the fundamental principles of international law set forth in the Charter of the United Nations,
>
> Expressing the will and the aspirations of all peoples to eradicate war from the life of mankind and, above all, to avert a world-wide nuclear catastrophe,
>
> Convinced that life without war serves as the primary international prerequisite for the material well-being, development and progress of countries, and for the full implementation of the rights and fundamental human freedoms proclaimed by the United Nations,
>
> Aware that in the nuclear age the establishment of a lasting peace on Earth represents the primary condition for the preservation of human civilization and the survival of mankind,
>
> Recognizing that the maintenance of a peaceful life for peoples is the sacred duty of each State,
>
> Solemnly proclaims that the peoples of our planet have a sacred right to peace;
>
> Solemnly declares that the preservation of the right of peoples to peace and the promotion of its implementation constitute a fundamental obligation of each State;
>
> Emphasizes that ensuring the exercise of the right of peoples to peace demands that the policies of States be directed towards the elimination of the threat of war, particularly nuclear war, the renunciation of the use of force in international relations and the settlement of international disputes by peaceful means on the basis of the Charter of the United Nations;

Appeals to all States and international organizations to do their utmost to assist in implementing the right of peoples to peace through the adoption of appropriate measures at both the national and the international level.

One could call it bizarre that countries bound by the UN Charter would fail to endorse this resolution, but some did.

But this is not really all that surprising, because Western states have huge military-industrial-financial complexes that commit them to war and military interventions. There are too many vested interests at stake; too many corporations are making billions of dollars of profit in the arms industry, which are dependent on wars, provocations and an atmosphere of hostility to keep the machines turning—to say nothing of the number of jobs and, it could be argued in the case of the United States, the overall health of the economy.[10] This is the reason why Western states refused to adhere to the prohibition of war propaganda contained in Article 20 of the International Covenant on Civil and Political Rights. Australia, Belgium, Denmark, Finland, France, Iceland, Ireland, Luxembourg, Malta, Netherlands, New Zealand, Norway, Sweden, Switzerland, United Kingdom, and the United States all have reservations and declarations against the prohibition of war propaganda. No Latin American or African State made such reservations, which mean opting out of the commitment to peace contained in the UN Charter. Of course, many countries that did not formulate reservations or declarations against a prohibition of war propaganda do engage in such propaganda and incitement to hatred of other peoples and governments. It only becomes painfully evident when a country openly admits that it is unwilling to curtail one of the principal causes of armed conflict.

It is illustrative to observe how the Western States behaved in the course of the debates in the Human Rights Council when the new resolution on the right to peace was being discussed in the years 2012–16.[11] At the time I was the UN Independent Expert on International Order and participated in all of the meetings of the open-ended intergovernmental working group on the right to peace[12] and later also followed the discussion in the plenary of the Human Rights Council, where I also took the floor.[13] Western delegations literally eviscerated the excellent draft that had been prepared and adopted by the experts of the Advisory Committee to the Council.[14]. Most shocking were the statements by the U.S. delegation, a complete distortion of international law, which even a first-year law student would see through as frivolous, contrived, and invalid. A distinguished NGO representative, Professor Curtis Doebbler, commented on August 1, 2016 at 15:11 hours at the Human Rights Council:

> While the Cuban delegation deserves congratulations for succeeding where Costa Rica failed in getting the declaration adopted (and Costa Rica deserves recognition for the effort it made during the previous year), the adopted declaration is an insult to human rights defenders and anyone who puts their faith in the UN to promote peace in the world. Most strikingly the declaration does not reconfirm the right to peace that was recognized for all peoples in a UN General Assembly declaration adopted in 1984. To adopt a declaration on the right to peace that does not clearly and unambiguously state the right to peace sends the message to all of us that our diplomatic representatives are not acting in our best interests. Either the diplomats need to be changed or the government officials who appoint them.[15]

What was even more embarrassing is how the Western delegations at the Council eventually voted and what arguments they made. First the Western delegations did everything to water down the declaration. When they succeeded in weakening it to the point of being less that GA Resolution 39/11, adding insult to injury, they even then went on to vote against what was left of it.[16]

Human Rights Council Resolution 32/28 was adopted with 34 votes in favour, 4 abstentions and 9 against. In favour: Algeria, Bangladesh, Bolivia (Plurinational State of), Botswana, Burundi, China, Congo, Côte d'Ivoire, Cuba, Ecuador, El Salvador, Ethiopia, Ghana, India, Indonesia, Kenya, Kyrgyzstan, Maldives, Mexico, Mongolia, Morocco, Namibia, Nigeria, Panama, Paraguay, Philippines, Qatar, Russian Federation, Saudi Arabia, South Africa, Togo, United Arab Emirates, Venezuela (Bolivarian Republic of), Viet Nam. Against: Belgium, France, Germany, Latvia, Netherlands, Republic of Korea, Slovenia, the former Yugoslav Republic of Macedonia, United

Kingdom of Great Britain and Northern Ireland. Abstaining: Albania, Georgia, Portugal, Switzerland.

For me personally, as a long-time peace activist and human rights defender, this seemed like the pinnacle of cynicism and bad faith. The less-than-nothing declaration was then adopted by the General Assembly on December 19, 1976 as Resolution 71/189.[17] As recently as December 15, 2022, the General Assembly adopted Resolution 77/216 entitled "Promotion of peace as a vital requirement for the full enjoyment of all human rights by all" by a vote of 131 in favour, 53 against and one abstention. Who could possibly disagree? Who could vote against it? Well, think again—the Western militaristic economies.

Another important issue that has been debated for many years both in the General Assembly and in the Human Rights Council is that of the adverse human rights impacts of unilateral coercive measures.[18] As UN Independent Expert on International Order I issued several press releases on the subject.[19] Elsewhere in this book I have explained why in modern hybrid warfare, the imposition of unilateral coercive measures must be considered "use of force" for purposes of Article 2(4) of the UN Charter, and that such force that may constitute a threat to international peace and security for purposes of Article 39 of the UN Charter (see chapter 4 above). GA Resolution 77/214, was adopted on December 15, 2022 by a vote of 130 in favour, 50 against and one abstention.

After this outrageous vote, tantamount to a rejection of the letter and spirit of the UN Charter by those states that voted against it, I wrote the following op-ed:

> The scourge of unilateral coercive measures on the enjoyment of human rights by billions of human beings worldwide has been the subject of examination and condemnation by numerous United Nations bodies for decades, notably by the General Assembly, the Commission on Human Rights, the Sub-Commission on the Promotion and Protection of Human Rights, the Human Rights Council and its Advisory Committee, the UN Committee on Economic, Social and Cultural Rights and the Working Group on the Right to Development.

The Office of the UN High Commissioner for Human Rights has repeatedly organised panel discussions to document the adverse impacts of unilateral coercive measures on the right to life, the right to health, the right to food, the right to clean water and sanitation, the right to housing, the right to work, the right to education etc. In my capacity as UN Independent Expert on International Order, I have participated in these panels.

UCMs have been condemned as contrary to the UN Charter and customary international law, particularly because of the illegal extra-territorial application of domestic legislation, their assault on the sovereignty of States, the violation of the norm of non-intervention and non-interference in the internal affairs of States, freedom of commerce and navigation—principles which are enshrined in several international legal instruments. Moreover, it has been noted that the destabilising impact of UCMs on international order can amount to a threat to international peace and security within the meaning of Article 39 of the UN Charter.

In 2014 the function of the Special Rapporteur on Unilateral Coercive Measures was created and the first two Rapporteurs, the late Dr. Idriss Jazairy and Professor Alena Douhan have submitted to the HR Council and General Assembly detailed thematic and country reports demanding the lifting of sanctions, in view of their detrimental impacts on nearly all human rights.

In his 2018 report to the Human Rights Council the Independent Expert on International Order analysed the adverse impacts of UCMs and financial blockades on the Venezuelan population, which demonstrably have caused and continue to cause many deaths as a result of scarcity of foods, medicines, medical equipment and parts. The report succinctly states: "Sanctions kill." UCMs have also caused bankruptcies and unemployment, leading to mass emigration. Although these economic migrants are not refugees, their plight has been examined by the United Nations High Commissioner for Refugees....

Resolution 77/214 recalls inter alia that, according to the Declaration on Principles of International Law concerning Friendly Relations and Cooperation among States in accordance with the Charter of the United Nations, resolution 2625 (XXV) of October 24, 1970, and the relevant principles and provisions contained in the Charter of Economic Rights and Duties of States, proclaimed by the Assembly in its resolution 3281 (XXIX), in particular Article 32 thereof, no State may use or encourage the use of economic, political or any other type of measures to coerce another State in order to obtain from it the subordination of the exercise of its sovereign rights and to secure from it advantages of any kind,

Resolution 77/214 further acknowledges that unilateral coercive measures are one of the major obstacles to the implementation of the Declaration on the Right to Development and the 2030 Agenda for Sustainable Development.

In the specific case of U.S. sanctions against Cuba, it bears repeating that the General Assembly has adopted 30 Resolutions condemning the U.S. embargo against Cuba, the last one, Resolution 77/7 on November 3, 2022, with nearly universal approval. Only the U.S. and Israel voted against it.

The last relevant Resolution by the Human Rights Council was Resolution 49/6 of March 31, 2022, reaffirming all prior resolutions including 46/5,[20] recalling that the International Covenant on Civil and Political Rights and the International Covenant on Economic, Social and Cultural Rights stipulate that in no case may a people be deprived of its own means of subsistence, which frequently is precisely the purpose of unilateral coercive measures.

Res 49/6 urges all States to stop adopting, maintaining or implementing unilateral coercive measures because they are contrary to international law, international humanitarian law, the Charter of the United Nations and the norms and principles governing peaceful relations among States, in particular those of a coercive nature with extraterritorial effects, which create obstacles to trade relations among States, thus impeding the full realisation of the rights set forth in the Universal Declaration of Human Rights and other international human rights instruments, in particular the right of individuals and peoples to development. The Resolution calls upon States and relevant United Nations agencies to take concrete measures to mitigate the negative impact of unilateral coercive measures on humanitarian assistance, which should be delivered in accordance with General Assembly resolution 46/182 of December 19, 1991.

Unlike the near unanimity of the General Assembly in condemning the U.S. embargo against Cuba,[21] 14 states members of the Human Rights Council voted against the HRC resolution—among them the U.S. and European Union states. This is a scandal, a disgrace for all of those states, who give lip service to human rights but bear responsibility for the deaths of the most vulnerable in Cuba, Nicaragua, Syria, Venezuela, Zimbabwe and other countries targeted by the U.S.

We must conclude that notwithstanding the obvious illegality of unilateral coercive measures and their proven incompatibility with the ICCPR and ICESCR, powerful states still impose unilateral coercive measures in total impunity. This is a matter that should be addressed by the General Assembly under Article 96 of the UN Charter, requesting the International Court of Justice to issue an advisory opinion on the subject, in particular on the legal consequences of the continued violation of international law by those states that impose or comply with UCM's and their obligation to make reparation to the victims. The ICJ should also examine the question whether UCMs constitute the "use of force" within the meaning of Article 2(4) of the UN Charter. Indeed, modern wars are hybrid wars and encompass many forms of force and coercion, which are surely against the letter and spirit of the UN Charter.

Those states who impose UCMs may try to escape responsibility by arguing that international law has changed, because so many States including the U.S., Canada, UK and EU have hitherto imposed sanctions and gotten away with it, thereby "legitimising" the practice. This argument, however, contains a serious logical fallacy. Violating international law with impunity does not and cannot change international law. It simply illustrates the fact that at present there is no effective international mechanism to enforce international law. The general principle of law (Article 38 of the ICJ statute) *ex injuria non oritur jus* makes it clear that no right emerges from a wrong.

Moreover, besides the responsibility of states for international wrongful acts, the international criminal aspect of unilateral coercive measures should be examined by the International Criminal Court. To the extent that tens of thousands of persons have demonstrably lost their lives as a direct or indirect result of sanctions regimes, it is provable that certain unilateral coercive measures constitute crimes against humanity for purposes of Article 7 of the Rome Statute.

It is the duty of the international community to demand accountability from States imposing sanctions and to ensure that redress is provided for the victims of U.S. imperialism and neo-colonialism."[22]

Another remarkable Resolution adopted by the General Assembly concerned "Combating glorification of Nazism, neo-Nazism and other practices that contribute to fueling contemporary forms of racism, racial discrimination, xenophobia and related intolerance." Resolution 77/204 was adopted on December 15, 2022 by a vote of 120 in favour, 50 against and 10 abstentions. Among the states that voted against it were the United States and Ukraine. An earlier GA resolution in 2021 had met the same fate.[23]

On December 8, 2022, the General Assembly adopted a resolution asking Israel to give up its nuclear Arsenal. The vote was adopted by 149 in favour, 26 abstentions and six against—the United States, the United Kingdom, Canada, Israel, Micronesia and Palau. Evidently the cause of nuclear disarmament still has its enemies.

An older General Assembly resolution that appears to be totally forgotten and thoroughly ignored by Israel and the international community is the Resolution of the Emergency Session of the General Assembly of July 20, 2004,[24] asking the Israeli government to implement the Advisory Opinion of the International Court of Justice on the Wall being built in Palestine.[25] Who could possibly be against a resolution asking a country to implement an ICJ advisory opinion ? The vote of 150 States in favour, six against and ten abstentions certainly expressed the feeling of the vast majority of the world. But there were these six voting against; Australia, Federated States of Micronesia, Israel, Marshall Islands, Palau, and the United States of America.

Towards a New International Economic Order

On December 14, 2022, 123 countries voted in favor of the General Assembly Resolution "Towards a New International Economic Order"[26]—64% of the UN's 193 member states. (The number would have been even higher, but several nations that have been illegally sanctioned by the U.S., such as Venezuela and Zimbabwe, had their UN voting rights temporarily suspended, because they have been unable to pay their membership fees in dollars, precisely on account of the UCMs.) 50 nations voted against the resolution.

For many readers who are not familiar with the style of General Assembly resolutions, it may be instructive to reproduce here extensive parts of the preambular and operative paragraphs of Res. 77/174.[27] Might the reader—as an exercise—try to formulate objections to it, to imagine why any country bound by the UN Charter and ostensibly committed to the UN's Sustainable Development Goals would vote against it. What game are these States playing and why?

> The General Assembly,
>
> ...
>
> Recalling the principles of the Declaration on the Establishment of a New International Economic Order and the Programme of Action on the Establishment of a New International Economic Order, as set out in resolutions 3201 (S-VI) and 3202 (S-VI), respectively, adopted by the General Assembly at its sixth special session, on 1 May 1974,

...Reaffirming the United Nations Millennium Declaration,[1]

Recalling the high-level plenary meeting of the General Assembly on the Millennium Development Goals and its outcome document,[2]

Recalling also the outcome document of the United Nations Conference on Sustainable Development, entitled "The future we want,"[3]

... Reaffirming also its resolution 69/313 of July 27, 2015 on the Addis Ababa Action Agenda of the Third International Conference on Financing for Development, which is an integral part of the 2030 Agenda for Sustainable Development, supports and complements it, helps to contextualize its means of implementation targets with concrete policies and actions, and reaffirms the strong political commitment to address the challenge of financing and creating an enabling environment at all levels for sustainable development in the spirit of global partnership and solidarity,

... Noting that there have been systemic challenges to the global economic architecture, demanding a review of global economic governance, calling for the reform of the international financial system and the relevant institutions and the broadening and strengthening of the voice and participation of developing countries in international economic decision-making and norm-setting and in global economic governance, in order to address the unique needs and capacities of developing countries when designing macroeconomic policies, recognizing that it is important that the International Monetary Fund continue to be adequately resourced, and supporting and reiterating its commitment to further governance reform at both the Fund and the World Bank to adapt to changes in the global economy,

Noting with great concern the severe negative impact on human health, safety and well-being caused by the coronavirus disease (COVID-19) pandemic, as well as the severe disruption to societies and economies and the devastating impact on lives and livelihoods, and that the poorest and most vulnerable are the hardest hit by the pandemic, reaffirming the ambition to get back on track to achieve the

Sustainable Development Goals by designing and implementing sustainable and inclusive recovery strategies to accelerate progress towards the full implementation of the 2030 Agenda for Sustainable Development and to help to reduce the risk of and build resilience to future shocks, crises and pandemics, including by strengthening health systems and achieving universal health coverage, and recognizing that equitable and timely access for all to safe, quality, effective and affordable COVID-19 vaccines, therapeutics and diagnostics are an essential part of a global response based on unity, solidarity, renewed multilateral cooperation and the principle of leaving no one behind,

. . . Noting with concern that the total external debt of developing countries increased from 6.5 trillion United States dollars in 2011 to 11.9 trillion dollars by 2021, and deeply concerned about the impact of high debt levels on countries' abilities to withstand the impact of the COVID-19 shock and to invest in the implementation of the 2030 Agenda,

. . . Concerned further about recent economic developments in the context of the continued challenges to achieving sustained economic growth, in which persistently high levels of inequality pose a challenge to robust growth and sustainable development, declining private investment in infrastructure highlights the obstacles to bridging the infrastructure financing gap and advancing the long-term financing of sustainable development, emerging debt challenges and vulnerabilities have intensified across developing countries, global exchange rate volatility has intensified and global inflationary trends have diverged, and that the weak prospects for the global economy put at risk vital public investment in education, health and action on climate change, as well as progress in poverty eradication, especially in developing countries,

Concerned that billions of the world's citizens continue to live in poverty and are denied a life of dignity and that there are rising inequalities within and among countries and enormous disparities of opportunity, wealth and power, Stressing the lack of strong coordinated international response in dealing with the challenges referred to above, illustrating that the calls made in the Declaration and the Programme of Action on the Establishment of a New International Economic Order are still highly relevant,

...

Recognizing that widespread financial deregulation has contributed to larger net capital outflows from developing countries to developed countries, Noting with deep concern the impact of illicit financial flows on the economic, social and political stability and development of developing countries, resulting in the urgent need to adopt measures to combat them, which could enhance fiscal space for Governments to finance the achievement of the 2030 Agenda, Towards a New International Economic Order A/RES/77/174 22-28792 5/7

Stressing the need for policy space to allow for the formulation of national development strategies by developing countries, aimed at bringing prosperity for all, Concerned with the increasing protectionist measures and adoption of inward-looking policies that undermine the multilateral trading system and increase the vulnerabilities of developing countries, and emphasizing the importance of promoting an open world economy and generating greater positive effects of globalization,

Emphasizing that multilateralism, including a universal, rules-based, open, transparent, predictable, inclusive, non-discriminatory and equitable multilateral trading system, is the most appropriate platform of international cooperation for addressing the challenges facing humanity,

... [operative paragraphs]

4. Reiterates that States are strongly urged to refrain from promulgating and applying any unilateral economic, financial or trade measures not in accordance with international law and the Charter of the United Nations that impede the full achievement of economic and social development, particularly in developing countries;

5. Reaffirms that national development efforts need to be supported by an enabling international economic environment, including coherent and mutually supporting world trade, monetary and financial systems and strengthened and enhanced global economic governance, as well as by respect for each country's policy space;

6. Also reaffirms the need to step up coordination of macroeconomic policies among countries to avoid negative spill over effects, especially in developing countries;

. . .

9. Also reaffirms the necessity to respect the territorial integrity, national sovereignty and political independence of States;

. . .

11. Reaffirms that international trade is an engine for development and sustained economic growth, as well as the eradication of poverty in all its forms and dimensions, and also reaffirms the critical role that a universal, rules-based, open, non-discriminatory and equitable multilateral trading system can play in stimulating economic growth and development worldwide, thereby benefiting all countries at all stages of development;

12. Expresses concern over the increasing debt vulnerabilities of developing countries, the net negative capital flows from developing countries, the fluctuation of exchange rates and the tightening of global financial conditions, and in this regard stresses the need to explore the means and instruments needed to achieve debt sustainability and the measures necessary to reduce the indebtedness of developing countries;

13. Takes note with appreciation of the Sustainable Development Goals stimulus proposed by the Secretary-General and his calls for action for a new allocation of special drawing rights, which should be handled according to developing countries' needs, taking into account that special drawing rights play an important role in enabling developing countries to invest in recovery and the Goals, on the need for an increase in concessional funding from

multilateral development banks and to reform the global financial system, which must include lending criteria that go beyond gross domestic product and provide a true view of the vulnerabilities faced by developing countries;

14. Calls upon Member States and international financial institutions to provide more liquidity in the financial system, especially in all developing countries, in order to make available necessary fiscal space and liquidity and help them to manage the unfolding crisis caused by the COVID-19 pandemic while achieving sustainable development, emphasizes the need to strengthen development cooperation and to increase access to concessional finance, and calls upon donors that have not done so to fulfil their respective official development assistance commitments, particularly to least developed countries;

15. Reiterates the significance of addressing the constraints on technology transfer to developing countries, including the transfer of sound technology from developed countries to developing countries on favourable terms, including on concessional and preferential terms;

16. Decides to continue considering the international economic situation and its impact on development at its seventy-ninth session, and in that regard requests the Secretary-General to include in his report to the General Assembly, under the item entitled "Globalization and interdependence," an updated overview of the major international economic and policy challenges for equitable and inclusive sustained economic growth and sustainable development and of the role of the United Nations in addressing those issues, as well as possible ways and means to overcome those challenges, bearing in mind the outcomes of the major United Nations conferences Towards a New International Economic Order A/RES/77/174 22-28792 7/7 and summits in the economic, social and related fields and the principles contained therein, and the 2030 Agenda, in the light of the relevant principles contained in the Declaration and the Programme of Action on the Establishment of a New International Economic Order."

As seen above, vast majority of the General Assembly emphasized in this resolution its concern over key vectors, including the increasing debt vulnerabilities of developing countries, the net negative capital flows from those countries, the fluctuation of exchange rates and the tightening of global financial conditions, and in this regard proposed to explore the means and instruments needed to achieve debt sustainability and the measures necessary to reduce the indebtedness of developing States.

For those who approve of the practice of "naming and shaming," maybe they would consider shaming those countries that voted against Resolution 77/174 that is fully consistent with the letter and spirit of the UN Charter.

It bears repeating the question: Why did most Western countries vote against this resolution "Towards a New International Economic Order"?[28] Was it because these states only give lip service to human rights, because these states are intent on continuing their hegemonic neo-colonial and imperialistic policies? Is it because these states are squandering their resources in wars that they themselves have provoked and that they refuse to negotiate any peace agreement because they want to prolong the conflict on behalf of their respective military-industrial-financial complexes that have vested interests in war?

Another General Assembly Resolution that is close to my heart is Resolution 77/215 of December 15, 2022 concerning the mandate of my successor Dr. Livingstone Sewanyana, whose reports have continued the patient and persevering struggle to build a just world order, notwithstanding all the roadblocks in his way.[29]

In its operative paragraphs, the resolution

> 5. Reaffirms that democracy includes respect for all human rights and fundamental freedoms for all and is a universal value based on the freely expressed will of people to determine their own political, economic, social and cultural systems and their full participation in all aspects of their lives, and re-emphasizes the need for universal adherence to and implementation of the rule of law at both the national and international levels;
> 6. Affirms that a democratic and equitable international order requires, inter alia, the realization of the following: (a)

The right of all peoples to self-determination, by virtue of which they can freely determine their political status and freely pursue their economic, social and cultural development; (b) The right of peoples and nations to permanent sovereignty over their natural wealth and resources; (c) The right of every human person and all peoples to development; (d) The right of all peoples to peace; (e) The right to an international economic order based on equal participation in the decision-making process, interdependence, mutual interest, solidarity and cooperation among all States; (f) International solidarity, as a right of peoples and individuals....

But who could justifiably vote against the above? What is wrong with them? What are they doing in the General Assembly? Resolution 77/215 was adopted by a vote of 122 in favour, 54 against and ten abstentions. There again, only the Western countries and their allies voted against. Indeed, as I have been able to confirm again and again, notwithstanding empty rhetoric, many countries really do not want a democratic and equitable international order. They prefer continued exploitation and neo-colonialism.

The voting record on the latest resolution on the mandate of the Working Group on the use of mercenaries as a means of violating human rights and impeding the exercise of the right of peoples to self-determination, Res. 51/13 of October 6, 2022, was adopted by a vote of 28 in favour, 15 against and 4 abstentions. The objectors were: Czechia, Finland, France, Germany, Japan, Lithuania, Luxembourg, Marshall Islands, Montenegro, Netherlands, Poland, Republic of Korea, Ukraine, United Kingdom of Great Britain and Northern Ireland, and United States of America.

With regard to international solidarity, the Council's Resolution 50/8 of July 7, 2022 was similarly opposed by the Western block: Czechia, Finland, France, Germany, Japan, Lithuania, Luxembourg, Marshall Islands, Montenegro, Netherlands, Poland, Republic of Korea, Ukraine, United Kingdom of Great Britain and Northern Ireland, and United States of America.

The most recent Human Rights Council resolution on foreign debt, Res. 49/15, was adopted on March 31, 2022 by a vote of 29 in favour 14 against and 4 abstentions. Here again the objectors:

Brazil, Finland, France, Germany, Japan, Lithuania, Luxembourg, Montenegro, Netherlands, Poland, Republic of Korea, Ukraine, United Kingdom of Great Britain and Northern Ireland, and United States of America.

The United Nations Declaration on the Rights of Peasants was adopted by Human Rights Council Resolution 39/12 of September 28, 2018 by a vote of 33 in favour, 3 against and 11 abstentions.

Against: Australia, Hungary, United Kingdom of Great Britain and Northern Ireland. Abstaining: Belgium, Brazil, Croatia, Georgia, Germany, Iceland, Japan, Republic of Korea, Slovakia, Slovenia, Spain].

The voting record of the West on the Right to Development is consistent and deplorable, notwithstanding the fact that the right to development is enshrined in the UN Charter and is the only right specifically mentioned in the Resolution establishing the Office of the UN High Commissioner for Human Rights GA Resolution 48/141. The most recent Human Rights Council resolution on the Right to Development, Resolution 51/7 of October 6, 2022, was accepted by 29 votes in favour, 13 against and 5 abstentions. The nay-sayers: Czechia, Finland, France, Germany, Japan, Lithuania, Luxembourg, Montenegro, Netherlands, Poland, Ukraine, United Kingdom of Great Britain and Northern Ireland, and United States of America.

We could go on citing urgently necessary resolutions which have met with fierce opposition from Western states. Among them Resolution 26/9 of June 26, 2014, titled "Elaboration of an international legally binding instrument on transnational corporations and other business enterprises with respect to human rights." Who voted against it: Austria, Czech Republic, Estonia, France, Germany, Ireland, Italy, Japan, Montenegro, Republic of Korea, Romania, the former Yugoslav Republic of Macedonia, United Kingdom of Great Britain and Northern Ireland, United States of America.

Bottom line, the West wants their corporations and transnational corporation to continue exploiting society and the most vulnerable countries in total impunity, relying on a kind of "self-supervision," which, of course, is a farce. I participated in some of the sessions of the open-ended intergovernmental working group and denounced the hypocrisy in my 2016 report to the Human Rights Council, A/ HRC/33/40, paras 77–84.

A PROMISING RESOLUTION

On the positive side, a recent Human Rights Council Resolution deserves our particular attention. Res 48/7, concerning the sequels of colonialism, was adopted on October 8, 2021. It is worthwhile revisiting the discussions and looking at the voting record, again posing the question, why would any self-respecting State object to its text or abstain from voting? This resolution has already had follow-up in subsequent sessions of the Human Rights Council and several side-events have been held at the Palais des Nations[30]in which I have had the honour to participate. It is important to study the full text of the resolution:

NEGATIVE IMPACT OF THE LEGACIES OF COLONIALISM ON THE ENJOYMENT OF HUMAN RIGHTS

The Human Rights Council,

Guided by the purposes and principles of the Charter of the United Nations, Recalling the Universal Declaration of Human Rights, which states that all human beings are born free and equal in dignity and rights,

Recalling also all relevant international human rights treaties, including the International Covenant on Civil and Political Rights and the International Covenant on Economic, Social and Cultural Rights,

Recalling further the Declaration on the Granting of Independence to Colonial Countries and Peoples and the Durban Declaration and Programme of Action, Acknowledging the crucial role of the General Assembly and its Special Committee on the Situation with regard to the implementation of the Declaration on the Granting of Independence to Colonial Countries and Peoples on the matters of decolonization,

Reaffirming that the existence of colonialism in any form or manifestation, including economic exploitation, is incompatible with the Charter, the Declaration on the Granting of Independence to Colonial Countries and Peoples and the Universal Declaration of Human Rights, and regretting that measures to eliminate colonialism by 2020, as called for by the General Assembly in its resolution 65/119 of December 10, 2010 have not been successful,

Acknowledging that the period 2021–2030 is the Fourth International Decade for the Eradication of Colonialism designated by the General Assembly, and that all Member States, the specialized agencies and other organizations of the United Nations system, and other governmental and non-governmental organizations are invited to actively support and participate in the implementation of the plan of action for the Decade,

Stressing the role of the Human Rights Council in promoting universal respect for human rights and fundamental freedoms for all, without distinction of any kind and in a fair and equal manner, on the same footing and with the same emphasis,

Recognizing with concern that the legacies of colonialism, in all their manifestations, such as economic exploitation, inequality within and among States, systemic racism, violations of indigenous peoples' rights, contemporary forms of slavery and damage to cultural heritage, have a negative impact on the effective enjoyment of all human rights,

Recognizing that colonialism has led to racism, racial discrimination, xenophobia and related intolerance, and that Africans and people of African descent, Asians and people of Asian descent and indigenous peoples were victims of colonialism and continue to be victims of its consequences,

Expressing deep concern at the violations of human rights of indigenous peoples committed in colonial contexts, and stressing the need for States to take all measures necessary to protect rights and ensure the safety of indigenous peoples, especially indigenous women and children, to restore truth and justice and to hold perpetrators accountable,

1. Stresses the utmost importance of eradicating colonialism and addressing the negative impact of the legacies of colonialism on the enjoyment of human rights;

2. Calls for Member States, relevant United Nations bodies, agencies and other relevant stakeholders to take concrete steps to address the negative impact of the legacies of colonialism on the enjoyment of human rights;

3. Reaffirms that persecution of members of any identifiable group, collective or community on racial, national, ethnic or other grounds that are universally recognized as impermissible under international law, and the crime of apartheid, constitute serious violations of human rights and, in some cases, qualify as crimes against humanity;

4. Urges States to refrain from the forced assimilation of persons belonging to minorities, including indigenous populations, and to work to ensure that educational curricula and other materials do not stereotype minorities and indigenous populations on the basis of their ethnicity;

5. Invites United Nations human rights mechanisms and procedures, in fulfilling their mandates, to continue to pay attention to the negative impact of the legacies of colonialism on the enjoyment of human rights;

6. Decides to convene a panel discussion at its fifty-first session and to make the discussion fully accessible to persons with disabilities, and invites Member States, relevant United Nations bodies and agencies, international organizations, national human rights institutions, non-governmental organizations and other stakeholders to participate in the panel discussion, to identify challenges in addressing the negative impact of the legacies of colonialism on human rights, and to discuss ways forward, and requests the Office of United Nations High Commissioner for Human Rights to prepare a summary report on the panel discussion, including in an accessible format, and to submit it to the Human Rights Council at its fifty-fourth session;

7. Requests the United Nations High Commissioner for Human Rights to provide all resources necessary for

the services and facilities for the above-mentioned panel discussion;

8. Decides to remain seized of the matter.

I consider this a landmark resolution of the Human Rights Council, which should have been adopted by consensus. At least no member of the Human Rights Council dared to vote against it, although there was plenty of bullying and arm-twisting to "persuade" some countries to abstain.it. The debate and subsequent vote speak volumes about the real state of human dignity in the Human Rights Council. Here is the vote: 27 in favour with 20 abstentions. What are the implications of the twenty abstentions? Who is who, here?

In favour: Argentina, Armenia, Bahamas, Bangladesh, Bolivia (Plurinational State of), Brazil, Burkina Faso, Cameroon, China, Côte d'Ivoire, Cuba, Eritrea, Fiji, Gabon, India, Indonesia, Malawi, Mexico, Namibia, Nepal, Pakistan, Philippines, Russian Federation, Somalia, Sudan, Uruguay and Venezuela (Bolivarian Republic of)

Abstaining: Austria, Bahrain, Bulgaria, Czechia, Denmark, France, Germany, Italy, Japan, Libya, Marshall Islands, Mauritania, Netherlands, Poland, Republic of Korea, Senegal, Togo, Ukraine, United Kingdom

Res ipsa loquitur (Cicero, *Pro Milone*)—*the facts speak for themselves*

While most resolutions of the Human Rights Council are adopted without a vote, consensus is obtained at the expense of reducing the resolution to the least common denominators. For this reason, many resolutions are empty rhetoric and many are cut-and-paste jobs, merely reproducing a resolution from a prior session. What is significant is that many of the most important and urgent decisions do end up in wrangling and voting. These give us a better view of what is really going on in the Council.

Anyone who wants to know which countries are in favour of a holistic approach to human rights, which countries support the right to peace, the right to development, the right to food, water, sanitation, housing, the right to international solidarity should study the voting record of all countries before the General Assembly and Human Rights Council.

Who supports the promotion of a democratic and equitable international order, corporate social responsibility, the prohibition of interference in the internal affairs of states? Who opposes the arms race, the imposition of unilateral coercive measures, the use of mercenaries to frustrate the exercise of self-determination?

As a U.S. and Swiss dual citizen, I have difficulty accepting the fact that our ostensibly democratic governments frequently vote in a manner that would be contrary to the wishes of the vast majority of American and Swiss constituencies. Surely, if these questions were directly posed to the electorate by referendum, most Americans and all Swiss would vote for peace, most Americans and all Swiss would vote for mediation and reconciliation in Ukraine. I am convinced that the people of the United States, United Kingdom, France, Germany, the Netherlands, Switzerland would vote differently than their representatives with regard to a great many resolutions. Alas, the system has its own illogic and irrationality. Representative democracy can only be called democratic when politicians, diplomats and delegates regularly consult and effectively represent the will of the majorities in their constituencies.

In his *Tractatus Politicus* (1677), Baruch Spinoza[31] has a sentence that should apply to all scholars and all researchers:

Sedulo curavi, humanas actiones non ridere, non lugere, neque detestari, sed intelligere

I have labored carefully, not to mock, lament, or execrate human actions, but to understand them.

Understanding requires open-mindedness, access to all relevant information, pro-actively looking for facts that are not readily available in the mainstream media, listening to all points of view, evaluating all perspectives, applying uniform standards, making an effort to "feel" what the rival feels. Understanding means freeing ourselves from ideological chains, prejudices and contradictions. It also requires a modicum of humility, a faculty of self-criticism, a commitment to truth.

Throughout my career my approach to human relations has been enlivened by the spirit of Baruch Spinoza and by his commitment to peace[32]and rationality. This book is an expression of an honest effort to understand, of a genuine desire to assist those who are in a better position to improve our world.

CONCLUSIONS AND RECOMMENDATIONS

"Where, after all, do universal human rights begin? In small places, close to home - so close and so small that they cannot be seen on any maps of the world. Yet they are the world of the individual person; the neighborhood he lives in; the school or college he attends; the factory, farm, or office where he works. Such are the places where every man, woman, and child seeks equal justice, equal opportunity, equal dignity without discrimination. Unless these rights have meaning there, they have little meaning anywhere. Without concerted citizen action to uphold them close to home, we shall look in vain for progress in the larger world."

ELEANOR ROOSEVELT, SPEECH AT THE UNITED NATIONS
"THE GREAT QUESTION," 1958

THE FOREGOING chapters have outlined the extent of misappropriation and duplicity with which the finest notions of our collective endeavour—the universality of human rights and the urgent need to protect them—have been countered on all levels by powerful states, global institutions, universities, and what is most worrisome, by nongovernmental organizations ostensibly devoted to human rights and a just world order, all of which have to a greater or lesser degree denatured human rights and weaponized them to advance their interests. There has been much to criticize and indeed, much to reveal that may have disheartened many.

This is not an idle issue. It concerns the core of humanity's ability to withstand a descent into barbarism and chaos, to preserve our most noble attributes—compassion, mutual aid, and solidarity. This is indeed imperative if we are to survive not just physically, but morally and spiritually. For this we have a lofty precedent in the spirituality of the Universal Declaration of Human Rights.

In the nuclear age human survival strategy rests on our capacity for dialogue and readiness to compromise, on our recognition that our commonalities by far outweigh our differences and that it is necessary to build a viable *modus vivendi.* The paramount need is peace, and the only rational policy to move towards it is verifiable nuclear disarmament—and more generally, general de-militarization, turning that enormous waste of resources and expense for missiles and drones towards human security through development and social justice. The alternative to coexistence is Apocalypse.

There are many obstacles, among them the intensity of the information war, which disseminates fake news, fake history and fake law, misleading millions of people into an intransigent mindset which will not allow genuine dialogue and compromise. The brainwashing conducted by governments and the mainstream media through selectivity and deliberate disinformation have resulted in an almost religious belief among the general population at least—if not even the leadership, which may be conscious of the extent to which such skewed notions have been engineered—that we in the West are by definition "the good guys" and that we have a "mission" to bring democracy and human rights to the rest of the world.

Our faculty of self-criticism is woefully underdeveloped. Indeed, we are taught that dissent is unpatriotic, even treasonous—notions driven home by an awareness that this is dangerous to our personal prospects. Even our presidential debates have lacked rational qualities, filled instead with *ad hominem* attacks. For the general public, independent journalists and free thinkers, the situation may be worse, and include "cancellation," mobbing, a sudden stop to career advancement and even death threats.

Notwithstanding the above concerns, we cannot afford to abandon cautious optimism that we can weather the present Ukraine and Taiwan crises and the other future world crises, which undoubtedly lie ahead flowing from the deliberate exacerbating of world tensions and the pursuit of hegemony. I still believe that there are plenty of politicians and journalists in the world who have a sincere desire to resolve the current crises and vindicate our faith in humanity, among them Mexican President Andrés Manuel López Obrador and Brazilian President Luiz Inácio Lula. Of course, humanity has the intellectual capacity to do this—if we really want to. But we must expose and denounce the messages of the Orwellian media that poisons the minds of millions of honest people on a daily basis. We must silence the drums of war and the organs of propaganda by piercing them with thousands of beams of truthful light.

It is not impossible that in the Western democracies, in the "developed world," the paradigm will shift, that a change of mind-set will liberate us from self-righteous provincial intransigence and facilitate transition to a culture of dialogue and cooperation, a kind of survivalist universalism.

While we recognize that there are multiple problems, obstacles and equivocations, the human rights values proclaimed in the UDHR remain valid as ever, even when certain facets of the system of promotion and protection of human rights have been hijacked and weaponized, even when the agenda of the UN Human Rights Council has been instrumentalized to pursue the geopolitical agendas of a few powerful countries.

The tools to correct the situation and redirect our energy toward international cooperation and solidarity are in our hands. We shall now sow with the conviction that we will also reap peace and development. Of course, the first step toward correcting dysfunctional institutions is to accept that there are multiple dysfunctions, the second step entails identifying the sources of the malfunctions, the third is to formulate a plan of action and then to persevere in taking measures to repair the problems. This entails more than making cosmetic changes here and there or applying bandaids on the wounds of billions of human beings subjected to exploitation, odious debt, and unfair financial manipulations. Instead, it is up to us to patiently review the situation, identify the root causes of problems, so as to implement effective reforms, step by step.

In order to take those first steps, we need correct, reliable information, not rhetoric or political narratives. We need access to a pluralistic press. We need good faith on the part of all players, a commitment to respect general principles of law, to observe treaties, *pacta sunt servanda*, as stipulated in Article 26 of the Vienna Convention on the Law of Treaties. We must be prepared to listen to all sides, *audiatur et altera pars*, and determined to depart from a "culture of cheating."[1] As Horatius put it in his First Book of Letters: "*Dimidium facti, qui coepit, habet; sapera aude, incipe!*"—meaning he who has begun is half done. Accordingly: Dare to know, dare to start!" Immanuel Kant took this "*sapere aude*" imperative as the motto for the Enlightenment period and encouraged all to have the courage to use his or her own judgment. Alas, as the past two centuries have shown, politicians still do what they want and the masses tend to follow them. "Groupthink" is not a 21st century ailment. Many who practice *sapere aude* pay a high price for their temerity.

We can also take inspiration from a thought attributed to Socrates: "Falling down is not failure. Failure comes when you stay where you have fallen." Thus if the human rights system has "fallen," or if some parts of it have been corrupted, it is for us to fix it. Hence, this book aims at healing the human rights system from the gradual erosion of values attributable to rampant politicization, materialism and greed. Our initial diagnosis must then be followed by a regimen of exposure to truth.

However, it seems like some States and NGOs have not taken to heart the *raison d'être* of the OHCHR and Human Rights Council—and perceive them only as tools to advance geopolitical agendas. These vandals of human rights do not see the faces of the victims that their policies create. These saboteurs of human values only want to engage in the "blaming game," in accusing others without ever applying the same standards to themselves.

The early heroes of human rights delivered, and institutions were established, notably the United Nations. Indeed, as many have pointed out, if the UN did not exist, we would have to invent it, because the UN is needed more than ever as a negotiating and coordinating forum—however much it may require the kind of changes I recommend in my earlier book, *Building a Just World Order*, to do just that.

The UN Charter, our world constitution, entered into force on October 24, 1945, and it committed all nations to the achievement of three principal goals—peace, development and human rights. Soon a Commission on Human Rights was established and on 9 December 1948 the General Assembly adopted the Convention against Genocide, and on December 10, 1948 the Universal Declaration of Human Rights. Since then ten core human rights treaties have been adopted and monitoring mechanisms have been established, most notably the two principal International Covenants—on Civil and Political Rights and on Economic, Social and Cultural Rights, proclaimed in 1966, and brought into force ten years later, in 1976.

Today we have norms, monitoring and implementation mechanisms—but now we must address the significant enforcement gap. That is where the Office of the UN High Commissioner for Human Rights (OHCHR) and the UN Human Rights Council come in. These bodies must be strengthened and streamlined so that they can advance the human rights agenda through advisory services and technical assistance, fact-finding, monitoring and direct assistance to victims. This must be done while respecting the sovereign equality of states and the right of self-determination of all peoples, that fundamental human right to shape one's present and that of future generations.

What are some of the major obstacles on the way to the strengthening and streamlining of the human rights system? Let us list the most notable:

- the absence of political will on the part of the major powers,
- the tendency to apply norms selectively,
- double standards in the evaluation of similar cases,
- growing politicization in the work of the OHCHR and Human Rights Council,
- insufficient transparency and accountability,
- the penetration of institutions by intelligence services, corporate interests, lobbies,
- peer pressure on the UN secretariat and UN rapporteurs to conform to "politically correct" views,
- the information war and domination of the information space,
- the control of the media by certain conglomerates,
- the Orwellian destruction of language resulting in endemic epistemological problems,
- the persecution and defamation of whistleblowers,
- inadequate financing of OHCHR and the ten core treaty-based bodies,
- understaffing of ILO, OHCHR, UNCTAD, UNDP, UNEP, UNESCO, UNHCR, WHO, etc.

Changing the *Zeitgeist*—the *a prioris* embedded in us with our formal and informal education, thereby establishing our comfort zones, or to use another expression, changing the paradigm—is an urgent mission and a long-term enterprise. But, because we believe in human dignity and feel a commitment to make human rights a reality for all human beings on the planet, we must revive the spirituality of the Universal Declaration of Human Rights in order to promote its actuality. There is no nobler task.

My decades-long involvement in the activities of human rights institutions and NGOs enables me to formulate some recommendations at that level aimed at illustrating certain implementable reforms in the medium and short term.

ESTABLISHING PRIORITIES APPLICABLE TO ALL SECTORS OF SOCIETY

1. The first priority of humanity must be to strengthen our commitment to maintain world peace. This entails respect for the UN Charter, notably both Article 2(3) that requires peaceful negotiations and Article 2(4) which prohibits not only the use of force but also the threat thereof.

2. In the nuclear age, our priority must be to avoid provocations and escalation of tensions. President John F. Kennedy was right when saying in 1963, "Above all, while defending our own vital interests, nuclear powers must avert those confrontations which bring an adversary to a choice of either a humiliating retreat or a nuclear war. To adopt that kind of course in the nuclear age would be evidence only of the bankruptcy of our policy—or of a collective death-wish for the world."[2]

3. Education for peace and empathy. A Global Compact on Education should be adopted and implemented worldwide, along with Peace Studies departments in universities. Wars can be avoided if there is a psychological readiness to settle differences through dialogue and diplomacy, and an understanding that this can and has been done, as demonstrated by case histories and best practices. Intransigence and inflexibility must come to be perceived as antisocial and vulgar.

4. The prevailing paradigm based on political dominance and economic and trade considerations must transition to a human-security paradigm based on the concept of human dignity and the commonalities of all members of the human family.

5. International cooperation and solidarity must be the rule, not the exception.

6. Global problems require global solutions, e.g. the arms race, armed conflict, energy crises, pollution, climate change, deforestation, and pandemics. Multilateralism and multipolarism must replace unilateralism.

7. Military-first economies must evolve into human security economies focused on defense rather than aggression, which will ensure the right to life in dignity and security—this means first and foremost the human right to peace. This includes a sharp reduction in military expenditures and the practical implementation of the right to food, clean water, sanitation, housing, medical care, etc.

8. The human rights paradigm is currently oriented toward individual rights and neglects collective rights. This must be replaced by a holistic approach to all rights, civil, cultural, economic, political and social. The artificial division of rights into those of the first, second and third generation must be abandoned, because it clouds our vision of what human dignity actually means, and what must be done to vindicate it.

9. Governments must refrain from interfering directly or indirectly in the internal affairs of other states.

10. Unilateral coercive measures (UCMs) are illegal and must be immediately lifted. They are incompatible with the UN Charter and the customary international law prohibition of interference in the internal affairs of other states.

11. UCMs are frequently justified by false human rights arguments. Experience shows that UCMs are imposed with a view to inducing undemocratic "regime change" in targeted countries.

12. UCMs are a form of hybrid war and kill as any armed conflict. To the extent that UCMs demonstrably kill tens of thousands of persons, the most vulnerable, they constitute crimes against humanity

for purposes of Article 7 of the Statute of the International Criminal Tribunal. UCMs kill through the dislocation of the economies of countries, resulting in scarcity of foods and medicines, bankruptcies, and mass emigration.

13. Governments must promote the realization of the right of self-determination of peoples as a conflict-prevention strategy. Hundreds of wars since 1945 found their origin in the unjust denial of self-determination.

14. States must not instrumentalize the right of self-determination of peoples as a pretext to foment conflicts within states.

15. Governments must recognize that while "territorial integrity" is a factor in ensuring peace and stability in the international community, it is not an absolute principle, but must be made compatible with the right of self-determination, which can be exercised internally in the form of autonomy within federal states, or externally through secession. To wage war against the right of self-determination of peoples is the *ultima irratio*.

16. Governments must ensure that people have access to information and to a plurality of views. Freedom of opinion and expression constitutes a pillar of democracy, as recognized in Article 19 of the International Covenant on Civil and Political Rights, and means far more than just the right to echo whatever narratives we hear in the news.

17. All countries, intergovernmental organizations, nongovernmental organizations, and civil society must be committed to achieving the Sustainable Development Goals. This entails disarmament for development and a radical reduction of military budgets.

18. Global science and technology must be harnessed for preparedness to address emergencies such as global warming, pandemics, volcanic eruptions, earthquakes, tsunamis, even potential asteroid impacts.

THIS BOOK HAS ENDEAVOURED TO REMIND US OF SOME "LESSONS LEARNED"

1. Human rights are dynamic, not static. They must be lived on a daily basis. They are work-in-progress, to be increasingly implemented and better defined.

2. As President John F. Kennedy once said, "ask not what your government can do for you, but ask what you can do for your country." In universal terms, all levels of society should be asking how they can serve world peace and development.

3. There are many threats to peace and security. We must address them in a timely fashion and in a multitude of ways, both established and creative new ones.

4. Aggression and war crimes have root causes that are not lessened by any putative fear of being punished sometime in the future. What is essential is to develop preventive strategies to address grievances before they degenerate into violence due to injustice. Punishment and *lex talionis* are not effective medicines to suppress violations of human rights or even military aggression. Prevention is paramount.

5. There is a high level of disinformation and "fake news," of politicization of human rights, of weaponization of values. Our silence makes us complicit. We must speak up by all possible avenues.

6. There is a fake discussion between legality and legitimacy. "Legitimacy" cannot replace legality. It is a subsidiary or supportive factor. First the legality of an action must be determined, then test whether in the specific situation it would be just or *ex aeque et bono*. This phoney debate is only intended to undermine and facilitate circumventing legality, e.g. the *jus cogens* prohibition of the use of force.

7. We must beware of the destruction of language through "narrative managers." Orwell's warnings about newspeak and cognitive dissonance are more relevant than ever. "Human rights," "democracy," and "peace" are words regularly wielded by the mainstream media, but frequently they are used to pursue entirely different ends. Politicians, journalists, academics and even

High Commissioners for Human Rights engage in rhetoric and platitudes, succumbing to pressure and fear of ostracism, while undermining the essence of human dignity.

8. Fake news concerns not only outright lying, but also omitting crucial information. Fake news is disseminated not only by governments, but also by the mainstream media, the so-called "quality press." Censorship by the private sector is no less corrosive to democracy than censorship by government.

9. Authority and credibility is not conferred by a mere title but must be earned by concrete actions. A Secretary-General or High Commission must be judged not only by what he/she says, but by what he/she does, not only by what he/she does, but by what he/she ought to do and doesn't.

10. When the institutions which are tasked with protecting our rights betray their terms of reference—and our trust—it is difficult to rehabilitate them.

PLAN OF ACTION

RECOMMENDATIONS TO STATES

1. Ratify the ten core UN human rights treaties, including the petitions procedures, and incorporate them into national legislation, allowing individuals to invoke the ICCPR and ICESCR before national courts, and giving domestic status to judgments and decisions of UN treaty bodies, thus enabling judges to implement them locally.

2. Recognize peace as a human right and withdraw reservations to Article 20 of the ICCPR, which prohibits both war propaganda and incitement to hatred and violence.

3. Adhere to the International Declaration on the Rights of Indigenous Peoples and take measures to rehabilitate indigenous peoples where they have been subjected to gross violations of human rights, including genocide, exploitation and confiscation

and forced assimilation. Strengthen the Declaration and elevate it to binding treaty status.

4. Grant indigenous peoples a special status in the General Assembly and Human Rights Council with a view to giving them voice and visibility.

5. Adopt concrete measures to implement UNESCO's program for a culture of peace.

6. Commit to the implementation of treaties "in good faith" *pacta sunt servanda* (Article 26, Vienna Convention on the Law of Treaties).

7. Seek win-win solutions. Abandon predatory habits of economic blackmail, unilateral coercive measures and sabre-rattling.

8. Abandon the myth that international criminal law, in particular the International Criminal Court, offers a viable or sufficient solution to violations of human rights. Abandon double standards in the choice of ICC cases. Enable better regional representation on the ICC.

9. Commit to making environmental, health and human rights impact assessments before adopting policies that negatively impact the environment, health and human rights of billions of human beings—and indeed, the very states that enact them.

10. Facilitate the implementation of human rights treaty obligations rather than trying to find ways to escape from the enforcement of treaties or inventing specious loopholes so as to defeat treaties' objectives.

11. Emphasize and display their best practices in implementing human rights at the Human Rights Council and General Assembly.

12. Break down media conglomerates because they hinder the necessary plurality of narratives and hence the proper functioning of democracy.

13. Adopt anti-trust and other appropriate legislation to break down monopolies and other accumulations of undemocratic power.

14. Recognize that every exercise of power and major policy change should be democratically legitimized. Make greater use of referenda.

15. Enact and enforce campaign spending limits to prevent corporations or the super-rich from "buying" elections.

16. Governments must ensure that individuals and transnational corporations are similarly required to observe human rights obligations, rather than "outsourcing" state responsibilities and seeking to utilize the private sector in order to circumvent human rights commitments.

17. Adopt a treaty on corporate social responsibility and abolish the abusive Investor-State Dispute Mechanism, a cynical scam to restrict the regulatory function of States and circumvent the jurisdiction of public, transparent courts.

18. Ensure adequate financing of OHCHR from the general UN budget, so that the Office is not put under pressure by donors who want to dictate the agenda.

19. Strengthen the administration of justice and adopt measures to prevent the political weaponization of the law and the growing use of "lawfare" against political opponents.

20. Strengthen the regional and international human rights courts and tribunals, ensure adequate funding, and adopt mechanisms to prevent their instrumentalization for geopolitical purposes.[3]

RECOMMENDATIONS CONCERNING THE OFFICE OF THE HIGH COMMISSIONER FOR HUMAN RIGHTS

1. Avoid dependence on "voluntary" funding with or without strings attached. Refuse to accept "earmarked" donations, because these compromise the independence of OHCHR and its right to establish priorities.

2. Exercise extreme caution in the selection of High Commissioners with a view to avoiding the growing politicization of the Office. High Commissioners must be committed professionals with a moral compass, the capacity to listen to all points of view, the

readiness to offer advisory services and technical assistance, and the courage to call a spade a spade.

3. Avoid the appointment of former politicians to the role of High Commissioner; choose instead human rights experts with experience in the UN system.

4. Ensure the independence of the High Commissioner by adopting a code of conduct based on General Assembly Resolution 48/141.

5. Protect High Commissioners from mobbing by States, NGOs and media.

6. Establish procedures to assist the High Commissioner in implementing his/her mandate and to avoid *ultra vires* activities.

7. Facilitate the access of Special Procedures mandate holders to the HC.

8. Concentrate on genuine human rights issues and abandon the tendency to join bandwagons promoted by certain countries and lobbies.

9. Treat economic, social, and cultural rights on the same level as civil and political rights.

10. Draft a Global Compact on Education together with UNESCO, emphasizing education for peace and empathy, for adoption by the General Assembly.

RECOMMENDATIONS CONCERNING THE HUMAN RIGHTS COUNCIL

1. Focus on preventive strategies and establish working groups to study the root causes of human rights violations.

2. Create preventive rapporteurships such as a Special Rapporteur on Self-Determination and Prevention of Conflict, a Special Rapporteur on the Right to Peace, a Special Rapporteur on the prevention of incitement to war, hatred and violence with reference to Article 20 ICCPR.

3. Reduce the number of country specific mandates and ensure that there is no overlap or duplication in the work of thematic mandates, country mandates and working groups.

4. Work constructively and not confrontationally. The practice of "naming and shaming" has proven to be largely counterproductive and not yielded improvements in the targeted countries but have instead led to retrenchment and retrogression.

5. Facilitate dialogue within the Council and take procedural measures to prevent the Council from becoming a gladiator arena in which States insult each other and accuse other States, frequently without evidence, of violations of human rights. The Council must be the primary forum for constructive debate, cooperation and solidarity.

6. Improve the system of selection of Special Procedures mandate holders to prevent rapporteurs from "changing hats" and perpetuating themselves.

7. Ensure equitable distribution in the choice of mandate holders. The parameters are not only gender and geographic, but also a better representation of world cultures and religions.

8. Ensure that all legal systems and perspectives are represented in Special Procedures, in particular in Commissions of Inquiry.

9. Establish rules to test the independence and professionalism of mandate holders, who must be strictly held to their code of conduct and be free of related vulnerabilities or conflicts of interest. This should include funding for their time and expenses.

10. Expand the Council's agenda to include the realization of the right of self-determination of peoples as a permanent item (as it was during the Commission on Human Rights).

11. Streamline the Universal Periodic Review procedures addressing the human rights situations in States, so that the UPR is rendered concrete and pragmatic rather than just a diplomatic ritual

12. Establish procedures to prevent mobbing and *ad hominem* attacks on the honour and reputation of independent experts, and enforce penalties upon the perpetrators, if this takes place, nonetheless.

13. Empower the Council to remove NGOs from the Council room when they engage in *ad hominem* attacks against mandate holders or deliberately disseminate fake news and spread evidence-free allegations.

14. Adopt a Code of Conduct applicable to non-governmental organizations, and strip them of consultative status if they repeatedly violate their code of conduct.

15. Adopt a Charter of Whistlebowers Rights that will effectively protect whistleblowers from persecution and prosecution.

16. Strengthen the right to truth and the right to know. Government secrecy is frequently at the source of gross violations of human rights. Citizens have the right to know what governments are doing in their name and must be able to demand accountability. Increase press releases and other publicity surrounding SR reports.

17. Strengthen the Declaration on the Rights of Indigenous Peoples and draft a treaty for adoption by the General Assembly.

18. Grant the representatives of indigenous peoples a special status in the Council so that they can speak as States and observer States.

19. During the Universal Periodic Review and the general debate, the President of the Human Rights Council should address the dangers of war propaganda and demand of all States what, if anything, they are doing to implement the prohibition of war propaganda contained in Article 20 ICCPR.

RECOMMENDATIONS CONCERNING THE GENERAL ASSEMBLY

1. Reaffirm the necessity of multilateralism. Reject any attempt to justify "unilateralism" and "exceptionalism."

2. Reaffirm the vocation of the General Assembly as a forum to advance international justice through dialogue and compromise.

3. Promote "inclusive" policies and reject attempts to divide the world into "good countries" and "bad countries." Facilitate dialogue and reconciliation.

4. Promote constructive debate and provide the President with the tools to initiate change, to draw attention to issues that are deliberately swept under the carpet.

5. Empower the President of the General Assembly to call for international investigation of dubious activities by powerful governments

that attempt to circumvent the UN Charter, in particular when the Security Council is unable to act because of the veto of one of the P5 countries.

6. Prioritize the development of preventive strategies, among them "early warning" procedures to prevent local grievances from developing into a threat of international peace and security.

7. Recognize that the realization of the self-determination of peoples is essential to the prevention of local, regional and international conflicts.

8. Name a Special Advisor to the Secretary General on the Right of Self-Determination. Indeed, since the Second World War there have been hundreds of wars whose origin was the unjust denial of self-determination. Ultimately freedom and democracy are but expressions of the human desire for self-determination.

9. Make use of Article 96 of the UN Charter and elevate more legal questions to the International Court of Justice requesting the necessary clarification of disputed legal issues. It has become necessary to have an authoritative statement by the ICJ to differentiate between laws and geopolitical agendas due to the extent of self-serving "fake law" justifications concocted by governments.

10. Tame the IMF and World Bank and ensure that they work in tandem with the United Nations, in conformity with the UN Charter and the object and purpose of the Organization. These financial institutions must be prevented from facilitating economic neo-colonialist practices and making countries permanently dependent on the rich developed countries' banks and governments by their intermediation in loan provisions, their imposition of "conditionalities," terms, collections and coercive demands for the privatization of public services and utilities.

11. Allow petitions for indigenous groups to be examined by the GA's Committee of 24 (Decolonization Committee). In a very real sense indigenous peoples, e.g. in the U.S., Canada, Chile, were never "decolonized." Their lands were stolen, their natural resources were looted, their populations were decimated. The Committee on the Elimination of Racial Discrimination should channel pertinent petitions to the General Assembly.

12. Grant the representatives of indigenous peoples a special status in the General Assembly so that they can speak under the same conditions as States and observer States.

13. Formally repudiate the "doctrine" of discovery as the Supreme Court in Queensland Australia did and most recently the Vatican. Indeed, Aboriginal lands and indigenous territories were not *terra nullius*, but were inhabited by millions of human beings.[4] Demand restoration and reparation in keeping with Human Rights Council resolution 48/7.

14. Cancel "odious debt" and ensure that developing countries do not become quasi-colonies because of their foreign debt burden, including to the IMF. Reject IMF loan conditionalities that require privatization and restrict the regulatory space of States, unduly interfering in their internal affairs.

RECOMMENDATIONS CONCERNING CIVIL SOCIETY AND NGOS

Civil society deserves to have more space in the UN system. However, it must be quality space and must not be abused. Hence, it is necessary to:

1. Adopt a code of ethics for NGOs, not unlike the code of conduct that exists for Special Procedures mandate holders. The code must be publicized and enforced.

2. Ensure that neither granting or blocking of consultative status to NGOs is subject to undue pressure from powerful countries. Alas, many potential NGOs are blocked by major powers, while unethical NGOs presently enjoying consultative status have been permitted to engage in disinformation, evidence-free allegations, *ad hominem* attacks on rapporteurs, and other disruptive activities both inside the Human Rights Council chamber and on their websites and blogs. It is shocking that these recidivist—and wealthy—NGOs have so much political support that they also enjoy protection in the ECOSOC Committee.

3. Because of their sometimes toxic behaviour, abusive NGOs should be stripped of their consultative status. This requires

urgent ECOSOC reform, including establishing a procedure whereby complaints can be filed and examined considering NGO misconduct.

4. Make the procedure for granting and withdrawing consultative status more transparent and establish a credible system to strip NGOs of that status when it has been established that they have abused their status.

RECOMMENDATIONS WITH REGARD TO UNIVERSITIES, ACADEMIC INSTITUTIONS AND THINK TANKS

1. Push back against corporate redirection of institutions' programs of learning and research to their benefit at the expense of research and development in medical and other branches of learning.

2. Push back against "cancel culture" and defend academic freedom.

3. Push back against the attempt by lobbies to remove tenure, and in particular, to prevent the granting of tenure to competent scholars who challenge the accepted narratives.

4. Promote a plurality of views and a culture of listening to other peoples' opinions.

5. Reject grants from governments whose purpose is to engage universities in military research and make them complicit in the development of lethal weapons.

6. Reject the attempt of governments and corporations to use universities and think tanks as "pens for hire," assigned to write pseudo-academic studies and reports intended only to justify or endorse dubious governmental and corporate policies that frequently violate human rights and human dignity.

RECOMMENDATIONS WITH REGARD TO THE MEDIA

A democracy can only work properly when the population has access to all pertinent information, as required by Article 19 of the International Covenant on Civil and Political Rights. Accordingly:

1. Ensure that democratic societies have access to the facts and to a plurality of views. The enforcement of a "politically correct" matrix is fundamentally undemocratic.

2. Media conglomerates and monopolies must be broken up, so as to assure better reporting and a plurality of interpretations of events.

3. Bearing in mind that governments commit crimes and cover them up, the role of whistleblowers must be recognized as essential to a properly functioning democracy. Whistleblowers are genuine human rights defenders and deserve protection from persecution and prosecution by governments and from defamation and character-assassination by the media. Hence, a Charter of Whistleblower Rights must be adopted.

4. Ensure freedom of the internet and penalize private-sector censorship and the abuse of search engines through algorithnms that either promote or silence certain political goals.

5. Vindicate the "marketplace of ideas" in all platforms online and offline.

CONCLUSION

Ultimately we must understand that the human rights industry is *our* industry and must be the servant of all of humanity.

We resolutely seek to strengthen, not dismantle, the United Nations, the Office of the High Commissioner for Human Rights, the Special Procedures of the Human Rights Council. But we must scrutinize them, reorient them, and recommit all participants in the human rights endeavour to the original task of advancing human dignity and international solidarity, banning war, and eradicating extreme poverty.

Let us use our industry to vindicate human dignity in all corners of the world, to build bridges, not burn them down; to make friends, not rivals; to practice *caritas* toward everything that lives and to respect all humans' right to life and to a healthy environment. Let's harness science and technology for peace, not war, for achieving the 17 Sustainable Development Goals, in the recognition that we are all brothers and sisters and that it is in our hands to pursue our happiness without destroying the happiness of others. Let's learn to forgive others, if we outselves want to be forgiven.

It is my hope that after reading these chapters, the reader will actually feel better than before, rediscovering a modicum of optimism about the future of the human species. Let us rekindle our determination to contribute to the cohesion of the human rights family by returning to the spirituality of the Universal Declaration of Human Rights. We must reaffirm human dignity everyday in every activity we undertake.

As a veteran human rights defender and peace activist, I urge civil society to demand the right priorities from our government officials. Peace is the alpha and omega of human existence and human dignity. Peace is the condition to achieve social justice and human rights. *Si vis pacem, cole justitiam*—if we want peace, we must cultivate justice. This is the simple and straight-forward motto of the International Labour Organization. Thus, let us continue striving for *Pax et Iustitia*—peace and justice—with intelligence and *caritas*. Indeed, let us reformulate our goal: *Si vis pacem, para pacem!* If we want peace, we must prepare the conditions for peace!

To echo the conclusion of Jeffrey Sachs in his book *The End of Poverty:* Our endeavour must be to take those necessary steps, one by one, so that future generations can say of our efforts that we sent forth mighty currents of hope, and that through patience and perseverance we have made it possible to begin healing the world.[5]

Jeff Sachs and Alfred de Zayas in Vienna, September 2022

Endnotes

Preface

1 Joe Silverstein, "Conservatives react to Elon Musk's poll about the World Economic Forum: 'Hell no,'" *Fox News,* January 19, 2023. https://www.foxnews.com/media/conservatives-react-elon-musks-poll-about-world-economic-forum-hell-no

Katarina Bradford, "15 SHOCKING quotes from the World Economic Forum Davos Summit that should deeply trouble you," *Glenn,* January 26, 2023, https://www.glennbeck.com/contributor/15-shocking-quotes-from-the-world-economic-forum-davos-summit-that-should-deeply-trouble-you

2 Terentius, Heauton timorumenos 77.

3 Gudmundur Alfredsson, Jonas Grimheden, Bertrand G. Ramcharan, and Alfred Zayas (eds.), *International Human Rights Monitoring Mechanisms* (Brill, 2009). https://brill.com/view/title/14572

4 "Theo van Boven: A tribute," UNHCR Regional Office for Europe, December 8, 2014. https://europe.ohchr.org/EN/NewsEvents/Pages/DisplayNews.aspx?NewsID=125&LangID=E

5 UN Human Rights Council resolution 5/2, "Code of Conduct for Special Procedures Mandate-holders of the Human Rights Council," June 18, 2007. https://www.ohchr.org/sites/default/files/Documents/Issues/Executions/CodeOfConduct.pdf

6 Iuvenalis, *Satires,* 6, 347–48.

7 "Draft declaration on the right to international solidarity," Annex of report A/HRC/35/35 of the Independent Expert on human rights and international solidarity, Virginia Dandan. https://www.ohchr.org/sites/default/files/Documents/Issues/Solidarity/DraftDeclarationRightInternationalSolidarity.pdf

8 United Nations Department of Economic and Social Affairs, Sustainable Development, "The 17 Goals." https://sdgs.un.org/goals

9 Motto of the Social Forum in Porto Alegre. Norman Solomon, "Letter From Porto Alegre: 'A Different World is Possible,'" *Common Dreams,* January 29, 2001. https://www.commondreams.org/views/2001/01/29/letter-porto-alegre-different-world-possible

John L. Hammond, "Another World Is Possible: Report from Porto Alegre," *Latin American Perspectives 30,* no. 3 (May 2003): 3–11. https://www.jstor.org/stable/3185032

Friends of the Earth, "Building a better world at the Thematic Social Forum in Porto Alegre, Brazil," January 2012. https://foe.org/blog/2012-01-building-a-better-world-at-thethematic-social-forum/

10 *Eleanor Lives! A plan for humanity.* https://www.eleanorlives.org

11 "WSF 2022 Declaration: Building together a common agenda for another urgent and necessary world," *Pressenza,* May 12, 2022. https://www.pressenza.com/2022/05/wsf-2022-declaration-building-together-a-common-agenda-for-another-urgent-and-necessary-world/

"World Social Forum 2022 in Mexico: First two days," *Culture of Peace News Network,* May 2, 2022. https://cpnn-world.org/new/?p=27212

Stiaan van der Merwe, "The 2022 World Social Forum: "A different world is possible"… differently" (a two-part series), Karibu Foundation, May 2022. https://www.karibu.no/newsletter/2022/05/the-2022-world-social-forum-a-different-world-is-possible-differently/

CHAPTER 1

1 See the interview with former Executive Director of the Sustainable Development Index, Calin Georgescu, *Oligarchen besitzen die U.N.* [video, 1:04:22], ICIC-Net, December 25, 2022. https://video.icic-net.com/w/wqc3AJJbm2Gn3HroLxUWdp

2 *Eleanor Lives! A plan for humanity.* https://www.eleanorlives.org

3 Pelle Neroth, "Hans Blix: The engineer of peace," *Engineering and Technology,* July 11, 2022. https://eandt.theiet.org/content/articles/2022/07/hans-blix-the-engineer-of-peace/

Patrick E. Tyler, "US is Pressuring Inspectors in Iraq to Aid Defections," *The New York Times,* December 6, 2022. https://www.nytimes.com/2002/12/06/international/middleeast/us-is-pressuring-inspectors-in-iraq-to-aid.html

4 CNN, "Transcript of ElBaradei's U.N. presentation," March 7, 2002. https://edition.cnn.com/2003/US/03/07/sprj.irq.un.transcript.elbaradei/index.html

Amy Fleming, "Elbaradei: It is Not US Duty to Monitor Iraqi Disarmament," Global Policy Forum, April 1, 2003. https://archive.globalpolicy.org/security/issues/iraq/unmovic/2003/0401elbaradei.htm

5 BBC News, "Iraq war illegal, says Annan," September 16, 2004. http://news.bbc.co.uk/2/hi/middle_east/3661134.stm

Ewen MacAskill and Julian Borger, "Iraq war was illegal and breached UN charter, says Annan," *The Guardian,* September 15, 2004. https://www.theguardian.com/world/2004/sep/16/iraq.iraq

6 Sydney Young, "Depleted Uranium, Devastated Health: Military Operations and Environmental Injustice in the Middle East," *Harvard International Review,* September 22, 2021. https://hir.harvard.edu/depleted-uranium-devastated-health-military-operations-and-environmental-injustice-in-the-middle-east/

7 Allen S. Keller, "Torture in Abu Ghraib," *Perspectives in Biological Medicine 49,* no. 4 (Autumn 2006): 553–69. https://pubmed.ncbi.nlm.nih.gov/17146140/

Maha Hilal, "Abu Ghraib: The legacy of torture in the war on terror" [opinion], *Aljazeera,* October 1, 2017. https://www.aljazeera.com/opinions/2017/10/1/abu-ghraib-the-legacy-of-torture-in-the-war-on-terror/

8 Alfred de Zayas, "The Status of Guantanamo Bay and the Status of the Detainees," *UBC Law Review,* 2004. Alfred de Zayas, "Guantanamo Naval Base," in Max Planck *Encyclopedia of Public International Law* (Oxford, 2012).

9 Larry Siems, *The Torture Report: What the Documents say about America's Post 9/11 Torture* (OR Books, 2012).

10 UN News, "General Assembly resolution demands end to Russian offensive in Ukraine," March 2, 2022. https://news.un.org/en/story/2022/03/1113152

11 "General Assembly adopts resolution on Russian reparations for Ukraine," *Global Issues,* November 14, 2022. https://www.globalissues.org/news/2022/11/14/32411

12 "Russia Dismisses UN Claims That Russian Soldiers Were Given Viagra To Promote "Rape" In Ukraine," *Pindula,* October 17, 2022. https://news.pindula.

co.zw/2022/10/17/russia-dismisses-un-claims-that-russian-soldiers-were-given-viagra-to-promote-rape-in-ukraine/

13 Adam Staten, "Ukraine Official Fired Over Handling of Russian Sexual Assault Claims," *Newsweek,* May 31, 2022. https://www.newsweek.com/lyudmila-denisova-ukraine-commissioner-human-rights-removed-russian-sexual-assault-claims-1711680

Paul Joseph Watson, "Ukrainian Official Admits She Lied About Russians Committing Mass Rape to Convince Countries to Send More Weapons," Ron Paul Institute, June 9, 2022. http://www.ronpaulinstitute.org/archives/peace-and-prosperity/2022/june/09/ukrainian-official-admits-she-lied-about-russians-committing-mass-rape-to-convince-countries-to-send-more-weapons/

14 RT, "RT sends request to UN over rape allegations," November 15, 2022. https://www.rt.com/russia/566592-rt-request-un-rape-allegations/

When asked by the pranksters whether she was provided with any evidence to substantiate these reports, Patten said it was *"not her job"* to conduct investigations, adding that she was just *"sitting in New York"* and providing *"strategic leadership."*

RT, "UN official admits to lack of Ukraine rape evidence in prank call," November 10, 2022:*"It's not my role to go and investigate. It's not the role of my office."* https://www.rt.com/russia/566312-un-rape-claims-vovan-lexus/

15 RT, "Russia responds to UN official's rape claims," October 16, 2022. https://www.rt.com/russia/564788-russia-respond-un-rape-claim/

16 "Noam Chomsky at United Nations: It Would Be Nice if the United States Lived up to International Law," *Democracy Now!,* October 22, 2014. https://www.democracynow.org/2014/10/22/noam_chomsky_at_united_nations_it

17 Thalif Deen, "World's Custodian of Peace Remains Glaringly Irrelevant," Inter Press Service, February 25, 2022. https://www.ipsnews.net/2022/02/worlds-custodian-peace-remains-glaringly-irrelevant/

Nile Gardiner, "The Decline and Fall of the United Nations: Why the U.N. Has Failed and How It Can Be Reformed," The Heritage Foundation, February 7, 2007. https://www.heritage.org/report/the-decline-and-fall-the-united-nations-why-the-un-has-failed-and-how-it-can-be-reformed

Stephane Mahe, "The United Nations: Indispensable or irrelevant?" Foreign Affairs Intelligence Council, September 18, 2020. https://foreignaffairsintelligencecouncil.wordpress.com/2020/09/20/the-united-nations-indispensable-or-irrelevant/

CHAPTER 2

1 Alfred de Zayas "Strengthening the Secretariat," in *Nordic Journal of International Law* 61/62, p. 263 et seq.

2 Theo van Boven, People Matter: Views on International Human Rights Policy, (Amsterdam: Meulenhoff, 1982), reviewed in The British Yearbook of International Law 54, no. 1 (1983), 269. https://doi.org/10.1093/bybil/54.1.269

3 Alfred de Zayas, "Human Rights, United Nations High Commissioner," in Helmut Volger (ed.), A Concise Encyclopedia of the United Nations, second edition (Leiden: Martinus Nijhoff, 2010), 275–284. De Zayas, "United Nations High Commissioner for Human Rights," in R. Bernhardt (ed.), *Encyclopaedia of Public International Law,* vol. 4 (Elsevier, Amsterdam 2000), 1129–1132.

4 Victor Gollancz, *Our Threatened Values* (London, 1947).

5 Alfred de Zayas, *50 Theses on the Expulsion* (London and Berlin: Verlag Inspiration, 2012), 39–40. See also Prof. Dieter Blumenwitz, Dokumentation der Gedenkstunde 50 Jahre Flucht, Deportation, Vertreibung (Bonn, 1995), 4–5. Also Zayas, Heimatrecht ist Menschenrecht, (Munich: Universtas Verlag, 2001), 287–89.

6 Zayas, *50 Theses,* 41–48.

7 OHCHR, "UN Human Rights Chief Türk issues open letter to Twitter's Elon Musk" (press release), November 5, 2022. https://www.ohchr.org/en/press-releases/2022/11/un-human-rights-chief-turk-issues-open-letter-twitters-elon-musk

8 United Nations Ukraine, "UN High Commissioner for Human Rights Volker Türk concludes his official visit to Ukraine" [press release], December 7, 2022. https://ukraine.un.org/en/210494-un-high-commissioner-human-rights-volker-turk-concludes-his-official-visit-ukraine

United Nations, "Ukraine's suffering must not become new normal, declares UN rights chief," *UN News,* December 7, 2022. https://news.un.org/en/story/2022/12/1131447

9 United Nations, "United Nations HC Volker Türk statement on Ukraine to the 52 HRC," video, 4:48, *UN Multimedia Newsroom,* March 31, 2023. https://www.unognewsroom.org/story/en/1735/united-nations-hc-volker-tuerk-statement-on-ukraine-to-the-52-hrc

10 United Nations, "Unanimously Adopting Resolution 2202 (2015), Security Council Calls on Parties to Implement Accords Aimed at Peaceful Settlement in Eastern Ukraine," *UN Meetings Coverage and Press Releases,* February 17, 2015. https://press.un.org/en/2015/sc11785.doc.htm

UN. Security Council (70th year : 2015), "Resolution 2202 (2015) / adopted by the Security Council at its 7384th meeting, on 17 February 2015," *UN Digital Library.* https://digitallibrary.un.org/record/787968

11 "Resolution adopted by the General Assembly: 60/251. Human Rights Council," A/RES/60/251, April 3, 2006. https://www2.ohchr.org/english/bodies/hrcouncil/docs/A.RES.60.251_En.pdf

12 International Progress Organization, "Blueprint for Peace in Ukraine," March 11, 2022. https://i-p-o.org/IPO-nr-UKRAINE-PEACE-11March2022.htm

13 Martin Armstrong, "Merkel Admits Minsk Agreement was to Trick Russia," Armstrong Economics, December 9, 2022. https://www.armstrongeconomics.com/international-news/russia/merkel-admits-minsk-agreement-was-to-trick-russia/

Ana Luisa Brown, "Angela Merkel reveals intention of Minsk agreements," *Prensa Latina,* December 7, 2022. https://www.plenglish.com/news/2022/12/07/angela-merkel-reveals-intention-of-minsk-agreements/

Scott Ritter, "Merkel Reveals West's Duplicity," *Consortium News,* December 5, 2022. https://consortiumnews.com/2022/12/05/scott-ritter-merkel-reveals-wests-duplicity/

14 OHCHR, "Interactive dialogue on oral update on Ukraine," United Nations, December 15, 2022. https://www.ohchr.org/en/statements/2022/01/interactive-dialogue-oral-update-ukraine

But compare the recent analysis of the situation in Crimea by the US journalist Rick Sterling, "Why Zelensky Will NOT Take Back Crimea," *L.A. Progressive,* April 3, 2023. https://www.laprogressive.com/war-and-peace/why-zelensky-will-not-take-back-crimea

15 *John Mearsheimer: The West is playing Russian roulette,* YouTube video, 1:17:12, posted by Unherd, November 29, 2022. https://www.youtube.com/watch?v=HBiV1h7Dm5E

16 Alfred de Zayas, "My two interventions on behalf of IHRAAM at the UN Human Rights Council," *Alfred de Zayas' Human Rights Corner* [blog], December 15, 2022. https://dezayasalfred.wordpress.com/2022/12/15/my-two-interventions-on-behalf-of-ihraam-at-the-un-human-rights-council/

17 António Guterres, "Secretary-General's briefing to the General Assembly on Priorities for 2023," United Nations, February 6, 2023. https://www.un.org/sg/en/content/sg/speeches/2023-02-06/secretary-generals-briefing-the-general-assembly-priorities-for-2023

18 OHCHR, "UN High Commissioner for Human Rights Volker Türk concludes official mission to Venezuela" (statement), January 28, 2023. https://www.ohchr.org/en/statements/2023/01/un-high-commissioner-human-rights-volker-turk-concludes-official-mission

José Luis Granados Ceja, UN Human Rights Chief Calls for Suspension of Sanctions on Venezuela," *Venezuela Analysis,* January 31, 2023. https://venezuelanalysis.com/news/15695

19 Redacción EC, Pedro Castillo solicita audiencia al equipo del Alto Comisionado de la ONU para los DD.HH.," *El Comercio,* January 19, 2023. https://elcomercio.pe/politica/actualidad/pedro-castillo-solicita-audiencia-al-equipo-del-alto-comisionado-de-la-onu-para-los-derechos-humanos-dina-boluarte-noticia/

"Castillo solicita una visita a la cárcel de la delegación del Alto Comisionado de la ONU para DDHH en Perú," *Europa Press International,* January 20, 2023. https://www.europapress.es/internacional/noticia-castillo-solicita-visita-carcel-delegacion-alto-comisionado-onu-ddhh-peru-20230120013722.html

Jonathan Fortuna, "Pedro Castillo solicita audiencia con equipo técnico de la ONU en el penal de Barbadillo – Mundo," *titulares.ar,* January 20, 2023. https://titulares.ar/pedro-castillo-solicita-audiencia-con-equipo-tecnico-de-la-onu-en-el-penal-de-barbadillo-mundo/

"Pedro Castillo solicita visita a la cárcel a delegación de la ONU," *Diario Las Américas,* January 19, 2023. https://www.diariolasamericas.com/america-latina/pedro-castillo-solicita-visita-la-carcel-delegacion-la-onu-n5328769

20 United Nations Dispute Tribunal, Kompass v. Secretary General of the United Nations Dispute Tribunal, Order on an Application for Suspensioin of Action, May 5, 2015. https://www.un.org/en/internaljustice/files/undt/orders/gva-2015-099.pdf

"Anders Kompass Cleared: UN Official Who Reported Child Sexual Abuse by Peacekeepers Speaks Out," Government Accountability Project, January 19, 2016. https://whistleblower.org/uncategorized/anders-kompass-cleared-un-official-who-reported-child-sexual-abuse-by-peacekeepers-speaks-out-5/

21 AP, "U.N. Official Cleared in Leak Inquiry," *The New York Times,* January 19, 2016. https://www.nytimes.com/2016/01/19/world/un-official-cleared-in-leak-inquiry.html

22 "UN whistleblower resigns over French peacekeeper 'child abuse,'" *BBC News,* June 8, 2016. https://www.bbc.com/news/world-africa-36481372

23 OHCHR, "UN High Commissioner for Human Rights Volker Türk concludes official mission to Venezuela" (statement), United Nations, January 28, 2023. https://rwi.lu.se/2021/06/10/the-swedish-national-institute-for-human-rights/

24 United Nations, Countries & Territories: Venezuela (Bolivarian Republic of), https://www.ohchr.org/en/countries/venezuela. See also visit reports by the UN Independent Expert on International Order, https://www.ohchr.org/en/special-procedures/ie-international-order/country-visits, and by the Special Rapporteur on Unilateral Coercive Measures, https://documents-dds-ny.un.org/doc/UNDOC/GEN/G21/269/56/PDF/G2126956.pdf, both of them based on country visits and evaluation of documents and other evidence provided by the Venezuelan government, the opposition, and more than 40 non-governmental organizations. The reports by the rapporteurs question the methodology used by the OHCHR in establishing its own reports without any in-situ visit, and overwhelmingly relying on information provided by the opposition.

25 OHCHR, "UN Human Rights Office issues assessment of human rights concerns in Xinjiang, China" (press release), August 31, 2022. https://www.ohchr.org/en/press-releases/2022/08/un-human-rights-office-issues-assessment-human-rights-concerns-xinjiang

26 OHCHR, "Statement by UN High Commissioner for Human Rights Michelle Bachelet after official visit to China" (statement), United Nations, May 28, 2022. https://www.ohchr.org/en/statements/2022/05/statement-un-high-commissioner-human-rights-michelle-bachelet-after-official

27 But compare the pre-mission mobbing she had to endure. Patrick Wintour and Vincent Ni, "UN human rights commissioner criticised over planned Xinjiang visit," *The Guardian,* May 20, 2022. https://www.theguardian.com/world/2022/may/20/un-human-rights-commissioner-xinjiang-michelle-bachelet-criticised

28 I published the full text of the statement in my book: Alfred de Zayas, *Heimatrecht ist Menschenrecht* (Munich: Universitas, 2001), 278–281. Statement by High Commissioner Ayala Lasso, at the consultation "The Human rights dimensions of Population Transfers" February 17–21, 1997, and is reflected in the Report of Awn Shawkat al Khasawneh to the Sub-Commission, doc. A/CN.4/Sub.2/1997/23.

29 "Russia and the Phony Human Rights Defenders Who Watched My Son Being Taken," *JAR2.com*, December 13, 2020. http://www.jar2.com/Articles/2020/NGO_Evictions.html

30 Alfred de Zayas, Report to UN Human Rights Council, 2014. https://documents-dds-ny.un.org/doc/UNDOC/GEN/G14/087/30/PDF/G1408730.pdf

31 "Video," *Ben Ferencz.org,* https://benferencz.org/video/
Benjamin B. Ferencz, *The Evolution of International Criminal Law – A Personal Account* [lecture], Audiovisual Library of International Law, https://legal.un.org/avl/ls/Ferencz_CLP.html
Benjamin Ferencz, *Planethood: The Key to Your Future* (Vision Books, 1988).

32 John Carey Obituary, *The New York Times,* October 10, 2019. https://www.legacy.com/us/obituaries/nytimes/name/john-carey-obituary?id=14906324

33 OHCHR, "Country visits: Independent Expert on international order," United Nations, https://www.ohchr.org/en/special-procedures/ie-international-order/country-visits

34 Richard Falk, *Public Intellectual* (Clarity Press, 2021), 319.

35 Ricardo Vaz, "Venezuelan Government Slams 'Biased' UN Human Rights Report," *Venezuela Analysis,* July 7, 2019. https://venezuelanalysis.com/news/14575

36 "Statement by UN High Commissioner for Human Rights Michelle Bachelet at the end of her visit to Venezuela," *Hearts of Venezuela,* June 22, 2019. https://www.heartsonvenezuela.com/statement-by-un-high-commissioner-for-human-rights-michelle-bachelet-at-the-end-of-her-visit-to-venezuela/

37 OHCHR, "Country visits: Special Rapporteur on unilateral coercive measures." United Nations. https://www.ohchr.org/en/special-procedures/sr-unilateral-coercive-measures/country-visits

Report of the Special Rapporteur on the negative impact of unilateral coercive measures on the enjoyment of human rights, Alena Douhan - Visit to the Bolivarian Republic of Venezuela (A/HRC/48/59/Add.2) (Advance unedited version), *reliefweb*, September 14, 2021. https://reliefweb.int/report/venezuela-bolivarian-republic/report-special-rapporteur-negative-impact-unilateral-coercive

38 Go ahead and defame with audacity, because always something will stick.

39 United Nations Human Rights Special Procedures, "Statement by Ms. Reem Alsalem, Special Rapporteur on violence against women and girls," November 29, 2022. https://www.ohchr.org/sites/default/files/documents/issues/women/sr/activities/SR-VAWG-statement-response-SRI.pdf

40 "Stories written by Alfred de Zayas," *Inter Press Service*, https://www.ipsnews.net/author/alfred-de-zayas/

Alfred de Zayas, "The Crisis in Venezuela" [op-ed], *Inter Press Service*, March 12, 2019. https://www.ipsnews.net/2019/03/the-crisis-in-venezuela/

41 Alfred de Zayas, "How can Philip Morris sue Uruguay over its tobacco laws" [op-ed], *The Guardian*, November 16, 2015. https://www.theguardian.com/commentisfree/2015/nov/16/philip-morris-uruguay-tobacco-isds-human-rights

42 Alfred de Zayas, "As a former UN special rapporteur, the coup in Venezuela reminds me of the rush to war in Iraq," *Independent*, February 7, 2019. https://www.independent.co.uk/voices/venezuela-crisis-coup-maduro-guaido-us-troops-un-iraq-a8767506.html

43 OHCHR statement, United Nations, February 10, 2023. https://www.ohchr.org/en/statements/2023/02/genuine-solidarity-earthquake-survivors-calls-lifting-sanction-induced

44 United Nations, *Responsibility of States for Internationally Wrongful Acts*, 2001. https://legal.un.org/ilc/texts/instruments/english/draft_articles/9_6_2001.pdf

45 European Commission against Racism and Intolerance (ECRI), "Hate speech and violence," Council of Europe. https://www.coe.int/en/web/european-commission-against-racism-and-intolerance/hate-speech-and-violence/

European Commission, "The EU Code of conduct on countering illegal hate speech online." https://ec.europa.eu/info/policies/justice-and-fundamental-rights/combatting-discrimination/racism-and-xenophobia/eu-code-conduct-countering-illegal-hate-speech-online_en

Council of Europe, "Fighting Disinformation and Hate Speech Online: cooperation with EU," December 11, 2020. https://www.coe.int/en/web/freedom-expression/-/fighting-disinformation-and-hate-speech-online-cooperation-with-eu

46 Grégor Puppinck, "Conflicts of interest at the ECHR: the fight continues!," *European Centre for Law & Justice*, October 20, 2022. https://eclj.org/geopolitics/echr/conflits-dinterets-a-la-cedh--le-combat-continue

47 *Alliance Defending Freedom.* https://adflegal.org/

See also Paul Coleman, *Censored. How European "Hate Speech" laws are threatening freedom of Speech* (Vienna: Kairos Publication, 2016).

ADF International. https://adfinternational.org/

48 Grégor Puppinck, Written observations submitted to the European Court of Human Rights in the case M.L. v. Poland (No. 40119/21), *European Centre for Law & Justice*, http://media.aclj.org/pdf/ECLJ-Written-observations-ML-v.-Poland-21-March-2022.pdf

49 Tahira Mohamedbhai, "Poland constitutional tribunal rejects ECHR decision on legality of judges' appointments," *JURIST,* November 28, 2021. https://www.jurist.org/news/2021/11/poland-constitutional-tribunal-rejects-echr-decision-on-legality-of-judges-appointments/

50 "Lawfare in the Making: Habeas Corpus Denied to President Pedro Castillo in Peru," *Orinoco Tribune,* March 1, 2023. https://orinocotribune.com/lawfare-in-the-making-habeas-corpus-denied-to-president-pedro-castillo-in-peru/

51 "Tenth Anniversary of the Inter-American Democratic Charter," Organization of American States (OAS), https://www.oas.org/en/democratic-charter/

CHAPTER 3

1 United Nations Human Rights Council, "5/2. Code of Conduct for Special Procedures Mandate-holders of the Human Rights Council," https://www.ohchr.org/sites/default/files/Documents/Issues/Executions/CodeOfConduct.pdf

2 United Nations Human Rights Council, *Universal Periodic Review.* https://www.ohchr.org/en/hr-bodies/upr/upr-main

3 United Nations Human Rights Council, *Special sessions.* https://www.ohchr.org/en/hr-bodies/hrc/special-sessions

4 United Nations Human Rights, *Special Procedures of the Human Rights Council,* https://www.ohchr.org/en/special-procedures-human-rights-council

5 United Nations Human Rights Council, *Introduction.* https://www.ohchr.org/en/hr-bodies/chr/commission-on-human-rights

6 *United Nations Declaration on the Rights of Indigenous Peoples* (A/RES/61/295), UN Department of Economic and Social Affairs, Division for Inclusive Social Development (DISD). https://www.un.org/development/desa/indigenouspeoples/declaration-on-the-rights-of-indigenous-peoples.html

7 Document E/CN.4/Sub.2/1997/23. This declaration was adopted by the Commission in 1998, but there was no follow-up, and it was never proclaimed by the General Assembly. See Alfred de Zayas "Forced Population Transfer" in Max Planck Encyclopedia of Public International Law, Vol. IV (Oxford, 2012),.165–175.

8 See "Economic Sanctions Kill," Chapter 12 in Zayas, *Countering Mainstream Narratives,* op.cit.

9 See my report to the Human Rights Council 2016, A/HRC/33/40, especially paragraphs 77–84.

10 United Nations Department of Economic and Social Affairs, Sustainable Development, *Gross National Happiness Index.* https://sdgs.un.org/partnerships/gross-national-happiness-index

11 United Nations, *International Day of Happiness, 20 March.* https://www.un.org/en/observances/happiness-day

12 United Nations Human Rights, *Annual thematic reports: Independent Expert on international order.* https://www.ohchr.org/en/special-procedures/ie-international-order/annual-thematic-reports

13 See Naomi Klein, *The Shock Doctrine,* op.cit. See also Chapter 11, "The Adverse Impact of IMF Policies on Human Rights," in Zayas, Building a Just World Order, op. cit.

14 Glele Ahanhanzo Curriulum Vitae (advanced unedited version). https://www2.ohchr.org/english/bodies/hrc/docs/membersCVs/Mr.MauriceGlele-AhahanzoFrench_.pdf

15 I was P.E.N. president 2006–2009 and again 2014–2017.

16 "Dozens of NGOs call on UN rights chief to resign after China visit," *News24,* June 8, 2022. https://www.news24.com/news24/world/news/dozens-of-ngos-call-on-un-rights-chief-to-resign-after-china-visit-20220608"

17 Amnesty International, "China: UN visit falls short of addressing crimes against humanity in Xinjiang," May 28, 2022 (https://www.amnesty.org/en/latest/news/2022/05/un-xinjiang-china-visit/): "the High Commissioner instead should condemn the ongoing gross human rights violations and seek accountability, truth and justice." This puts the cart ahead of the horse and violates the most fundamental rules of due process. Precisely what the High Commissioner's mission was intending to do, it did, namely to establish a working relationship with China so as to be able to better observe the situation on the ground, and not a priori condemn without having the solid evidence. I experience the same kind of mobbing when I went to Venezuela and did not immediately call for"regime change" against Maduro. It speaks poorly for the "independence" of rapporteurs and High Commissioners.

18 OHCHR, "Statement by UN High Commissioner for Human Rights Michelle Bachelet after official visit to China" (statement), United Nations, May 28, 2022. https://www.ohchr.org/en/statements/2022/05/statement-un-high-commissioner-human-rights-michelle-bachelet-after-official

19 Alfred de Zayas, "The Flaws in the 'Assessment' Report of the Office of the High Commissioner for Human Rights on China," *CounterPunch,* September 6, 2022. https://www.counterpunch.org/2022/09/06/the-flaws-in-the-assessment-report-of-the-office-of-the-high-commissioner-for-human-rights-on-china/

Alfred de Zayas and Richard Falk, "The Unjustified Criticism of High Commissioner Michelle Bachelet's Visit To China," *CounterPunch,* June 13, 2022. https://www.counterpunch.org/2022/06/13/the-unjustified-criticism-of-high-commissioner-michelle-bachelets-visit-to-china/

20 United Nations, "UN rights chief Bachelet holds 'valuable' meeting with China's President Xi," *UN News,* May 25, 2022. https://news.un.org/en/story/2022/05/1118992

Yew Lun Tian and Tony Munroe, "U.N. rights chief says she urged China to review counter-terrorism policies," *Reuters,* May 28, 2022. https://www.reuters.com/world/china/un-rights-chief-says-she-urged-china-review-counter-terrorism-policies-2022-05-28/

21 United Nations, "UN human rights expert urges to lift unilateral sanctions against Venezuela," February 12, 2021. https://www.ohchr.org/en/press-releases/2021/02/un-human-rights-expert-urges-lift-unilateral-sanctions-against-venezuela

22 I could give many examples, but that would consume a considerable number of pages and would well justify a book devoted to assessing those problems. See Zayas, *Countering Mainstream Narratives* (Clarity Press, 2022).

23 UN Mission to Spain, "Report of the Working Group on Enforced or Involuntary Disappearances," Addendum to HRC 27th session, A/HRC/27/49/Add.1. https://docslib.org/Report-of-the-Working-Group-on-Enforced-Or-Involuntary-Disappearances-Mission-to-Spain

24 United Nations OHCHR, *Special Rapporteur on truth, justice and reparation.* https://www.ohchr.org/en/special-procedures/sr-truth-justice-reparation-and-non-recurrence
United Nations General Assembly, "Report of the Special Rapporteur on the promotion of truth, justice, reparation and guarantees of non-recurrence, Pablo de Greiff," July 22, 2014. https://documents-dds-ny.un.org/doc/UNDOC/GEN/G14/090/52/PDF/G1409052.pdf

25 Stanley Payne, *The Spanish Civil War* (Cambridge University Press, 2012). César Vidal, *Paracuellos-Katyn, un ensayo sobre el genocidio de la izquierda* (Barcelona: Random House, 2006). Felix Schlayer, *Matanzas en el Madrid republicano* (Diplomat im roten Madrid) (Editorial Altera, 2006). Ramon Salas Larrazabal, *Pérdidas de la Guerra* (Madrid: Editorial Planeta, 1977).

26 Paul Claudel, "Aux martyrs espagnols morts à cause de leur foi," poem written as a preface to [Catalan] Joan Estelrich, La Persécution religieuse en Espagne (Paris, 1937). César Vidal, Paracuellos-Katyn (Madrid: Libroslibres, 2005).

27 United Nations Human Rights Council, "Visit to Honduras: Report of the Working Group on the issue of discrimination against women in law and in practice," May 8, 2019. https://documents-dds-ny.un.org/doc/UNDOC/GEN/G19/134/30/PDF/G1913430.pdf

28 United Nations Human Rights, *Country visits: Special Rapporteur on violence against women and girls, its causes and consequences,* https://www.ohchr.org/en/special-procedures/sr-violence-against-women/country-visits

29 Alfred de Zayas, "Peace," in William Schabas (ed.), Cambridge Companion to International Criminal Law (Cambridge, 2016).

30 Chapter 3, "Peace as a Human Right," and "Conclusion: Reflections on the Way Forward," in Alfred de Zayas, *Building a Just World Order* (Clarity Press, 2021).

31 See my 2014 report to the Human Rights Council, A/HRC/27/51. See also Chapter 4, "Military Expenditures and Human Rights," in Zayas, *Building a Just World Order,* and the Human Right Committee's General Comment on Article 6, the Right to Life.

32 Bruce Miller, Witness to the Human Rights Tribunals: How the System Fails Indigenous Peoples (Vancouver: UBC Press, 2023). https://www.ubcpress.ca/witness-to-the-human-rights-tribunals

33 Martin Luther King, Jr., *Why We Can't Wait* (1964; Boston: Beacon Press, 2011), 119–20; 141. David Stannard, *American Holocaust* (Oxford 1992). Marcel Grondin, *Moema Viezzer Le genocide des Amériques* (Quebec: Ecosociété, 2022).

34 Alfred de Zayas and Áurea Roldán Martín, "Freedom of Opinion and Freedom of Expression: Some reflections on General Comment No. 34 of the UN Human Rights Committee," *Netherlands International Law Review,* (Cambridge University Press, December 7, 2012). https://www.cambridge.org/core/journals/netherlands-international-law-review/article/abs/freedom-of-opinion-and-freedom-of-expression-some-reflections-on-general-comment-no-34-of-the-un-human-rights-committee/ADCD74F635F688851788E9079E1ABB76

35 Edward Snowden, *Permanent Record* (Metropolitan Books, 2019).

36 United Nations Human Rights, "Ukraine: Joint statement on Russia's invasion and importance of freedom of expression and information," May 4, 2022. https://www.ohchr.org/en/statements-and-speeches/2022/05/ukraine-joint-statement-russias-invasion-and-importance-freedom

37 A search under "Wikipedia disinformation" only shows articles on disinformation by Russia and China, not by the U.S., UK, or EU. This indicates also that the search engine selects for us what the manipulators of public opinion want us to know. Nothing on disinformation by the State Department and Pentagon concerning Nordstream 2, nothing about disinformation campaigns by the US concerning Libya, Syria, etc.

38 Arthur Grimonpont, *Algocratie* (Paris: Actes Sud, 2022).

39 Alfred de Zayas and Aurea Roldan, "Freedom of Opinion and Freedom of Expression," *Netherlands International Law Review* (2012), 425–54. https://www.cambridge.org/core/journals/netherlands-international-law-review/article/abs/freedom-of-opinion-and-freedom-of-expression-some-reflections-on-general-comment-no-34-of-the-un-human-rights-committee/

Norman Lewis, "The EU's censorship regime is about to go global," *Spiked,* March 23, 2023. https://www.spiked-online.com/2023/03/23/the-eus-censorship-regime-is-about-to-go-global/?mc_cid=cbdb02cd73&mc_eid=4be644833e

40 A/HRC/22/52 Framework principles for securing the accountability of public officials for gross or systematic human rights violations committed in the course of States-sanctioned counter-terrorism initiatives.

41 Council of the European Union, "COUNCIL DECISION on identifying the violation of Union restrictive measures as an area of crime that meets the criteria specified in Article 83(1) of the Treaty on the Functioning of the European Union," June 30, 2022. https://data.consilium.europa.eu/doc/document/ST-10287-2022-REV-1/en/pdf

"Article 83(1) TFEU currently does not provide for the establishment of minimum rules concerning the definition of and penalties for the violation of Union restrictive measures, since their violation as such is not yet covered by the areas of crime listed in that Article. The areas of crime currently listed in Article 83(1), second subparagraph, are terrorism, trafficking in human beings, sexual exploitation of women and children, illicit drug trafficking, illicit arms trafficking, money laundering, corruption, counterfeiting of means of payment, computer crime and organised crime. The violation of Union restrictive measures can however in some cases be related to criminal offences covered by some of the listed areas of crime, such as terrorism and money laundering."

42 European Centre for Law & Justice, "The ECLJ alerted the UN on "dark funding" of several U.N. experts - Grégor Puppinck," Video, 1:37, posted on YouTube by *ECLJ Officiel,* October 14, 2022. https://eclj.org/geopolitics/hrc/the-eclj-alerted-the-un-on-dark-funding-of-several-un-experts---gregor-puppinck

European Centre for Law & Justice, *The Financing of UN Experts* [downloadable report]. https://eclj.org/the-financing-of-un-experts-report

43 For more discussion of smear campaigns, lack of honour and "groupthink" in the Human Rights Council, see Chapter 6, "The Rule of Law and the Right to Truth: Information as a Key Element of Democracy," in Zayas, *Building a Just World Order.*

44 Asociación Española para el Derecho Internacional de los Derechos Humanos, *Declaración de Luarca sobre el derecho humano a la paz* (AEDIDH, 2010). http://aedidh.org/es/la-declaracion-de-luarca-sobre-el-derecho-humano-a-la-paz-2/

45 "Declaración de Santiago sobre el derecho humano a la paz," AEDIDH, December 18, 2010. http://aedidh.org/es/2010/12/18/declaracion-de-santiago-sobre-el-derecho-humano-a-la-paz/

46 OHCHR, Documentation for "Expert workshop: The right of peoples to peace" held in Geneva, Switzerland, December 15–16, 2009. https://www2.ohchr.org/english/issues/rule_of_law/workshop/

United Nations Human Rights, "The right to peace," April 4, 2013. https://www.ohchr.org/en/stories/2013/04/right-peace. See William Schabas, "The Human Right to Peace," in Asbjorn Eide, J. Möller and I. Zeimele, *Making Peoples Heard* (Leiden: Martinus Nijhoff, 2011), 43–58; Alfred de Zayas, "Peace as a Human Right," in Eide, op. cit., 27–42; Theo van Boven, "The Right to Peace as an emerging Solidarity Right," in Eva Rieter and Henri de Waele, *Evolving Principles of International Law* (Leiden: Martinus Nijhoff, 2012), 137–48.

47 United Nations Human Rights, *United Nations Forum on Human Rights, Democracy and the Rule of law.* https://www.ohchr.org/en/hrc-subsidiaries/democracy-forum

48 United Nations Human Rights, *United Nations Forum on Business and Human Rights.* https://www.ohchr.org/en/hrc-subsidiary-bodies/united-nations-forum-business-and-human-rights

49 Tweet by Asociación AIDHDES, May 25, 2022: https://twitter.com/aidhdes/status/1596276066615803905 for the Fourth session of the Forum on human rights, democracy and rule of law.

50 Frits Kalshoven, "The International Humanitarian Fact-Finding Commission: A Sleeping Beauty?," *Humanitäres Völkerrecht* (Journal of International Law of Peace and Armed Conflict) no. 4 (April 2002), 213–216. https://www.icrc.org/en/doc/assets/files/other/frits_kalshoven_2.pdf

International Committee of the Red Cross, "The International Humanitarian Fact-Finding Commission – Factsheet," August 31, 2018. https://www.icrc.org/en/document/international-humanitarian-fact-finding-commission-facsheet

51 Resolution A/HRC/RES/S-30/1

52 United Nations Human Rights, "Commission of Inquiry welcomes General Assembly resolution requesting an ICJ Advisory Opinion relating to the Israeli occupation of Palestinian territory" (press release), December 31, 2022. https://www.ohchr.org/en/press-releases/2022/12/commission-inquiry-welcomes-general-assembly-resolution-requesting-icj

53 The first order of the ICJ was issued on February 3, 2023: "Legal Consequences Arising from the Policies and Practices of Israel in the Occupied Palestinian Territory, including East Jerusalem (request for advisory opinion)." https://www.icj-cij.org/public/files/case-related/186/186-20230203-ORD-01-00-EN.pdf. See also the earlier advisory opinion of July 9, 2004, "Legal Consequences of the Construction of a Wall in the Occupied Palestinian Territory." https://www.icj-cij.org/en/case/131

54 "International Commissions of Inquiry, Fact-finding Missions: Americas," *United Nations Research Guides,* https://libraryresources.unog.ch/factfinding/americas

55 United Nations Human Rights Council, *Independent International Fact-Finding Mission on the Bolivarian Republic of Venezuela.* https://www.ohchr.org/en/hr-bodies/hrc/ffmv/index

56 Livingstone Sewanyana and Alfred de Zayas, "Report of the Independent Expert on the Promotion of a Democratic and Equitable International Order on his mission to the Bolivarian Republic of Venezuela and Ecuador : note / by the Secretariat," *United Nations Digital Library,* 2018. https://digitallibrary.un.org/record/1640958

57 Nino Pagliccia, "The Death of the 'Lima Group' and Re-Birth of the Latin American Anti-Imperialist Left," *CounterPunch,* August 17, 2021. https://www.counterpunch.org/2021/08/17/the-death-of-the-lima-group-and-re-birth-of-the-latin-american-anti-imperialist-left/

"Declaración del Grupo de Lima sobre Venezuela," *CNN Español,* February 4, 2019. https://cnnespanol.cnn.com/2019/02/04/declaracion-del-grupo-de-lima-sobre-venezuela/

"Tras dejar el Grupo de Lima, Argentina retiró su apoyo a la demanda contra el régimen de Nicolás Maduro ante la Corte Penal Internacional," *infobae,* May 26, 2021. https://www.infobae.com/america/venezuela/2021/05/26/tras-dejar-el-grupo-de-lima-argentina-retiro-su-apoyo-a-la-demanda-contra-el-regimen-de-nicolas-maduro-ante-la-corte-penal-internacional/

"Venezuela: Grupo de Lima ya está en el basurero de la historia," *HispanTV,* August 10, 2021. https://www.hispantv.com/noticias/venezuela/497125/grupo-lima-maduro

58 On September 27, 2019, the United Nations Human Rights Council established the Independent International Fact-Finding Mission on the Bolivarian Republic of Venezuela by virtue of resolution 42/25 for a period of one year, to assess alleged human rights violations committed since 2014. The mandate of the Fact-Finding Mission was extended by the Council through resolution 45/20 and resolution 51/29, until September 2024.

59 John McEvoy, "UN human rights report on Venezuela 'fundamentally flawed and disappointing,'" *Canary,* July 8, 2019. https://www.thecanary.co/global/world-analysis/2019/07/08/un-human-rights-report-on-venezuela-fundamentally-flawed-and-disappointing/

Alfred de Zayas, "UN Human Rights Council's Report on Venezuela is 'Unbalanced' (1/2)," *The Real News Network,* July 12, 2019. https://therealnews.com/de-zayas-un-human-rights-councils-report-on-venezuela-is-unbalanced-1-2

60 United Nations Human Rights, *Countries & Territories: Nicaragua.* https://www.ohchr.org/en/countries/nicaragua

61 Katherine Hoyt, "Exceptionalism and Nicaragua," *Alliance for Global Justice,* March 25, 2021. https://afgj.org/download/katherine-hoyt-exceptionalism-and-nicaragua

NACLA, "Articles by Katherine Hoyt." https://nacla.org/author/Katherine%20Hoyt

62 International Court of Justice, "Military and Paramilitary Activities in and against Nicaragua (*Nicaragua v. United States of America*)." https://icj-cij.org/case/70

63 United Nations Human Rights, "Nicaragua: Crimes against humanity being committed against civilians for political reasons, investigation says" [press release], March 2, 2023. https://www.ohchr.org/en/press-releases/2023/03/nicaragua-crimes-against-humanity-being-committed-against-civilians

64 United Nations Human Rights Council, Membership of the Human Rights Council. https://www.ohchr.org/en/hr-bodies/hrc/membership

65 At its 2000 conference on Self-Determination IHRAAM called for the creation of the function of a High Commissioner for Self-Determination.

66 Richard Roth, Kate Sullivan, Samantha Beech and Laura Ly, "UN suspends Russia from Human Rights Council," *CNN,* April 7, 2022. https://edition.cnn.com/2022/04/07/politics/un-russia-human-rights/index.html

67 United Nations, "General Assembly Suspends Libya from Human Rights Council" [press release], March 1, 2011. https://press.un.org/en/2011/ga11050.doc.htm

68 "Iraq war illegal, says Annan," *BBC News,* September 16, 2004. http://news.bbc.co.uk/2/hi/middle_east/3661134.stm

69 "Responsibility to protect" goes back to GA Resolution 60/1 of October 24, 2005, which in paragraph 138 speaks about humanitarian intervention. But R2P cannot trump the jus cogens prohibition of the use of force contained in Article 2(4) UN Charter.

See Security Council Resolution 1973 of March 17, 2011. http://unscr.com/en/resolutions/1973

70 United Nations Human Rights, "Khashoggi killing: UN human rights expert says Saudi Arabia is responsible for "premeditated execution" [press release], June 19, 2019. https://www.ohchr.org/en/press-releases/2019/06/khashoggi-killing-un-human-rights-expert-says-saudi-arabia-responsible

PBS Frontline, *The Crown Prince of Saudi Arabia,* video documentary, 1:54:47. https://www.pbs.org/wgbh/frontline/documentary/the-crown-prince-of-saudi-arabia/

71 United Nations Human Rights, "Ukraine / Russia: Prisoners of war" [press briefing], November 5, 2022. https://www.ohchr.org/en/press-briefing-notes/2022/11/ukraine-russia-prisoners-war

Edith M. Lederer, "UN fact-finding mission will probe Ukraine prison killings," *CBS17.com*, August 3, 2022. https://www.cbs17.com/news/un-fact-finding-mission-will-probe-ukraine-prison-killings/

Jack Dutton, "Ukrainian Troops Seen Killing Russian POWs in Video," *Newsweek,* April 7, 2022. https://www.newsweek.com/ukrainian-troops-seen-killing-russian-pows-video-1695896

Nathan Hodge, Eoin McSweeney and Niamh Kennedy, "Video appears to show execution of Russian prisoner by Ukrainian forces," *CNN,* April 8, 2022. https://edition.cnn.com/2022/04/07/europe/ukraine-execution-russian-prisoner-intl/index.html

United Nations Human Rights Council, *Independent International Commission of Inquiry on Ukraine.* https://www.ohchr.org/en/hr-bodies/hrc/iicihr-ukraine/index

72 "US downplays execution of Russian POWs in Ukraine," *RT,* November 21, 2022. https://www.rt.com/news/566961-washington-ukraine-pow-execution/

73 Kit Klarenberg, "British intelligence operative's involvement in Ukraine crisis signals false flag attacks ahead," *The Grayzone,* March 24, 2022: https://thegrayzone.com/2022/03/24/british-intelligence-ukraine-false-flag/

Do we have here yet another false flag operation as we have seen multiple times in Syria, where chemical attacks that could not be confirmed by expert inspectors, whereas there were good arguments that same were staged? Are the dead persons in Bucha civilians or military? See the allegations of the former French soldier Adrien Bocquet.

"Adrien Boke former soldier of the French special forces speaks about Ukraine," *Windows to Russia,* May 12, 2022. https://windowstorussia.com/adrien-boke-former-soldier-of-the-french-special-forces-speaks-about-ukraine.html

"My time in Ukraine: Adrien Bocquet, former French Special Forces," YouTube video, 32:55, streamed live by *PR.E* May 12, 2022. https://www.youtube.com/watch?v=_bALx2tnRYY

Boquet was the subject of an assassination attempt in Istanbul.

"Adrien Bocquet : le Français dans un sale état après avoir été agressé en Turquie," *Lama Faché,* September 27, 2022. https://lamafache.com/actualites/adrien-bocquet-francais-sale-etat-apres-avoir-ete-agresse-turquie

Whether true or false, the allegations about Bucha and the assassination attempt merit investigation. Were the bodies those of Russian soldiers and Ukrainian civilians, victims of artillery bombardment? Bearing in mind that the Ukrainian videos show numerous bodies with white armbands, could these bodies actually be those of dead Russian soldiers or Ukrainian civilians with white armbands trying to signal their peaceful intentions, who were subsequently lynched by Ukrainian extremists for collaboration with the Russians? An international commission of inquiry should, of course, investigate, but that will take time, because the evidence on the ground (to the extent it has not been destroyed) must be evaluated and witnesses on all sides must be heard.

74 Eric Zuesse, "Videos and Photos of the Odessan Massacre," *CounterPunch,* May 9, 2014. https://www.counterpunch.org/2014/05/09/videos-and-photos-of-the-odessan-massacre/

75 Joel Gehrke, "Russia does not 'deserve' UN Security Council seat, US ambassador says," *Washington Examiner,* March 31, 2023. https://www.msn.com/en-us/news/world/russia-does-not-deserve-un-security-council-seat-us-ambassador-says/ar-AA19kvsl

Julian Borger, "'Absurdity to a new level' as Russia takes charge of UN security council," *The Guardian,* March 31, 2023. https://www.theguardian.com/world/2023/mar/31/absurdity-to-a-new-level-as-russia-takes-charge-of-un-security-council

76 OperationMindCrime, "The Odessa Massacre – detailed video analysis – one month later," *Shadowproof,* June 1, 2014. https://shadowproof.com/2014/06/01/the-odessa-massacre-detailed-video-analysis-one-month-later/

77 See *OSCE Special Monitoring Mission to Ukraine (SMM) Daily Report 40/2022 issued on 21 February 2022* by the Organizaton for Security and Co-operation in Europe. https://www.osce.org/special-monitoring-mission-to-ukraine/512683. Russian Foreign Minister Lavrov has pointed out these OSCE reports, but his statements have been largely ignored in the Western press.

78 United Nations Peacekeeping, *UNPROFOR Fact Sheet* [United Nations Protection Force]. https://peacekeeping.un.org/en/mission/unprofor

James Bovard, "America's Forgotten Bullshit Bombing of Serbia," *CounterPunch,* August 20, 2019. https://www.counterpunch.org/2019/08/20/americas-forgotten-bullshit-bombing-of-serbia/

79 United Nations, "Special Meeting of the Human Rights Council (12.11.2015)," video, 49:16, *UN Web TV,* November 12, 2015. https://media.un.org/en/asset/k1b/k1b3e69l3e

80 Carmen Lucía Castaño, "'No se dejen usar': Maduro al Consejo de Derechos Humano," *Panorama,* November 13, 2015. https://panorama.ridh.org/no-se-dejen-usar-maduro-al-consejo-de-derechos-humanos/

81 "Alto Comisionado Zeid pronunció discurso en ocasión de visita de Presidente Maduro al Consejo de Derechos Humanos," *Observatorio Venezolano de Prisiones,* November 13, 2015. https://oveprisiones.com/alto-comisionado-zeid-pronuncio-discurso-en-ocasion-de-visita-de-presidente-maduro-al-consejo-de-derechos-humanos/

82 José Miguel Vivanco, "No debe permitirse que Maduro use el Consejo de Derechos Humanos de la ONU para promover inescrupulosamente sus propios intereses" [op-ed], Human Rights Watch, November 11, 2015. https://www.hrw.org/es/news/2015/11/11/columna-de-opinion-no-debe-permitirse-que-maduro-use-el-consejo-de-derechos-humanos

83 The note verbale reads in part: "El mandato del Alto Comisionado de Naciones Unidas para los Derechos Humanos se fundamenta en los principios de imparcialidad, objetividad y no selectividad, con debido respeto a la soberanía y a la jurisdicción interna de los Estados, en el marco del diálogo constructivo con todos los Gobiernos de la comunidad de naciones, de conformidad con lo dispuesto en la Resolución 48/141, de la Asamblea General."

84 Could this not in fact be the goal of the West, to free itself of the constraints of the UN Charter by pushing its rivals out of the UN? Observers have surmised that the dream of some Western elites is to fully subordinate the UN to their interests, and thereby give a quasi-legalistic stamp of approval to past and future actions that are in fact contrary to the spirit of the Charter.

CHAPTER 4

1 Marjorie Cohn, "ICC Charges Putin With War Crimes While US and Israeli Leaders Enjoy Impunity," *Truthout*, March 25, 2023. https://truthout.org/articles/icc-charges-putin-with-war-crimes-while-us-and-israeli-leaders-enjoy-impunity/

2 See "The Rule of Law Must Evolve Into the Rule of Justice," Chapter 23 in Zayas, *Countering Mainstream Narratives* (Clarity Press, 2022), 165–69.

3 For a discussion of the concepts of law and justice, justice and punishment, see Chapters 24 and 25 of *Countering Mainstream Narratives* (Clarity Press, 2022).

4 Robert H. Jackson, *Opening Statement before the International Military Tribunal,* November 21, 1945, Robert H. Jackson Center, https://www.roberthjackson.org/speech-and-writing/opening-statement-before-the-international-military-tribunal/

5 The International Military Tribunal for Germany (1946-09-30), Judgment of the International Military Tribunal, the Avalon Project, Yale University. https://legal.un.org/ilc/documentation/english/a_cn4_5.pdf

6 See Charles Percy Snow, *Science and Government* (Harvard University, 1960). https://www.hup.harvard.edu/catalog.php?isbn=9780674072374

7 Imperial War Museums, "The Incredible Story Of The Dambusters Raid," *IWM,* https://www.iwm.org.uk/history/the-incredible-story-of-the-dambusters-raid https://ww2db.com/battle_spec.php?battle_id=211

8 Alfred de Zayas, *Nemesis at Potsdam* (London: Routledge, 1977); *A Terrible Revenge* (New York: Macmillan, 1994); *50 Theses on the Expulsion of the Germans* (London and Berlin: Inspiration, 2012).

9 International Criminal Tribunal for the former Yugoslavia, 1993–2017. https://www.icty.org/. See also General Assembly Resolution 47/121.

10 John Cameron, *The Peleus Trial* (London, 1948). See discussion of the case in Zayas, *The Wehrmacht War Crimes Bureau* (Lincoln: University of Nebraska Press, 1989), 259 et seq.

11 Zayas, *The Wehrmacht War Crimes Bureau,* 317. Samuel Eliot Morison, *History of the United States Naval Operations in World War II* (Boston, 1950), 62: "Planes and PTs went about the sickening business of killing survivors in boats, rafts or wreckage. Fighters mercilessly strafed anything on the surface. On March 5, the two PTs which had sunk Oigawa Maru put out to rescue a downed pilot and came on an enemy submarine receiving survivors from three large landing craft. Torpedoes missed as the U-boat crash-dived. The PTs turned their guns on, and hurled depth charges at the three boats—which, with over a hundred men on board, sank. It was a grisly task …"

12 Gustav Gilbert, *Nuremberg Diary* (Farrar, Straus, 1947).

13 Zayas, "An International Criminal Court," *Nordic Journal of International Law 61/62,* 171 et seq.

14 Corbett Daly, "Clinton on Qaddafi: 'We came, we saw, he died,'" *CBS News,* October 20, 2011. https://www.cbsnews.com/news/clinton-on-qaddafi-we-came-we-saw-he-died/

15 Ivan Katchanovski, "The Maidan massacre in Ukraine: revelations from trials and investigations," *MR Online,* December 8, 2021 (udated Dec. 11 by Jordan Russian Center). https://mronline.org/2021/12/11/the-maidan-massacre-in-ukraine/

"The Maidan Massacre in Ukraine: Revelations from Trials and Investigation," *Freedom of Speech,* March 8, 2022. https://fos-sa.org/2022/03/08/the-maidan-massacre-in-ukraine-revelations-from-trials-and-investigation/

Gordon Hahn, "REPORT: The Real Ukrainian 'Snipers' Massacre,' February 20, 2014," *Russian & Eurasia Politics,* March 9, 2016. https://gordonhahn.com/2016/03/09/the-real-snipers-massacre-ukraine-february-2014-updatedrevised-working-paper/

"Reuters investigation exposes 'serious flaws' in Maidan massacre probe," RT, October 10, 2014. https://www.rt.com/news/195004-ukraine-maidan-sniper-investigation/

Stefan Korinth, "Top expert on Maidan's sniper massacre explains fundamental differences between his & Kiev's investigations," *SOTT,* February 25, 2016. https://www.sott.net/article/313028-Top-expert-on-Maidans-sniper-massacre-explains-fundamental-differences-between-his-Kievs-investigations

Ivan Katchanovski, "The Maidan Massacre in Ukraine: Revelations from Trials and Investigation," *SSRN,* March 28, 2022. https://papers.ssrn.com/sol3/papers.cfm?abstract_id=4048494

The Ukrainian-Canadian Professor Ivan Katchanovski of the University of Ottawa presented a paper in October 2014 at the University of Ottawa and a revised version at the American Politican Science Association in San Francisco in September 2015 arguing that leaders of the anti-government movement had successfully pulled a false flag operation, which brought them to power as a result of a massacre organized by their own supporters. This was based on an analysis of video footage, TV and Internet broadcasting, radio intercepts, witness testimonies, and bullet hole locations. The paper argued that "armed groups and the leadership of the far right organizations, such as the Right Sector, Svoboda and oligarchic parties, such as Fatherland, were directly or indirectly involved in various capacities in this massacre of the protesters and the police." See Ivan Katchanovski, "The 'Snipers' Massacre' on the Maidan in Ukraine," September 2015. https://www.researchgate.net/publication/266855828_The_Snipers%27_Massacre_on_the_Maidan_in_Ukraine

16 Alfred de Zayas, "The U.S. Naval Base at Guantánamo: Indefinite Detention, Torture, Belligerent Occupation," Chapter 18, in *Countering Mainstream Narratives* (Clarity Press, 2022).

"Former Guantanamo inmate Sami Elhaj explains why ICRC visits were important to him" (interview), International Committee of the Red Cross, August 25, 2009. https://www.icrc.org/en/doc/resources/documents/interview/guantanamo-interview-250809.htm

"Entretien avec Sami Elhaj, ancien détenu à Guantánamo," *Voltairenet.org,* July 21, 2008. https://www.voltairenet.org/article160923.html

17 See Human Rights Council Resolution No. 48/7 of October 2021.

18 Geko, "Project: Resolution 1469," *Tales of Hawaii* [blog], https://talesofhawaii.net/2020/10/17/5949/

A Call for Review of the Historical Facts Surrounding UNGA Resolution 1469 (xiv) of 1959 Which Recognized Attainment of Self-Government for Hawaii, filed May 9, 2019. https://www.hawaiianperspectives.org/wp-content/uploads/2021/06/Annex-5-A-Call-for-Review-of-the-Historical-Facts-Surrounding-UNGA-Resolution-1469-xiv-of-1959-Which-Recognized-Attainment-of-Self-Government.pdf

19 *Ms Fatou Bensouda, Former Prosecutor,* International Criminal Court. https://www.icc-cpi.int/about/otp/who-s-who/fatou-bensouda

20 International Criminal Court, "Statement of ICC Prosecutor, Fatou Bensouda, following the Appeals Chamber's decision authorising an investigation into the Situation in Afghanistan: 'Today is an important day for the cause of international criminal justice'" [press release], March 5, 2020. https://www.icc-cpi.int/news/statement-icc-prosecutor-fatou-bensouda-following-appeals-chambers-decision-authorising

21 *Karim A. A. Khan KC, Prosecutor,* International Criminal Court. https://www.icc-cpi.int/about/otp/who-s-who/karim-khan

22 "ICC prosecutor leaves US forces out of new Afghanistan probe," *Aljazeera,* September 27, 2021. https://www.aljazeera.com/news/2021/9/27/icc-prosecutor-targets-taliban-isis-k-in-afghanistan-probe

23 "Afghanistan: ICC Prosecutor's statement on Afghanistan jeopardises his Office's legitimacy and future," Amnesty International, October 5, 2021. https://www.amnesty.org/en/documents/ior53/4842/2021/en/

"Statement of the Prosecutor of the International Criminal Court, Karim A. A. Khan QC, following the application for an expedited order under Article 18(2) seeking authorisation to resume investigations in the Situation in Afghanistan," International Criminal Court, September 27, 2021. https://www.icc-cpi.int/news/statement-prosecutor-international-criminal-court-karim-khan-qc-following-application

24 AP, "ICC prosecutor seeks to resume Afghanistan war crimes probe," Courthouse News Service, September 27, 2021. https://apnews.com/article/crime-courts-afghanistan-war-crimes-taliban-a758ac22703e13c37a58322f0c26c3f1

In 2016, before seeking authorization to open a full-scale investigation in Afghanistan, ICC prosecutors said in a report that U.S. troops and the CIA may have tortured and mistreated people in detention facilities in Afghanistan, Poland, Romania, and Lithuania. Also see Alice Speri, "How the U.S. Derailed an Effort to Prosecute Its Crimes in Afghanistan," *The Intercept,* October 5, 2021. https://theintercept.com/2021/10/05/afghanistan-icc-war-crimes/

25 Marjorie Cohn, "ICC Charges Putin With War Crimes While US and Israeli Leaders Enjoy Impunity," *Truthout,* March 25, 2023. https://truthout.org/articles/icc-charges-putin-with-war-crimes-while-us-and-israeli-leaders-enjoy-impunity/

26 Alice Speri, *The Intercept.*

27 "War as Crime of Aggression: Reed Brody on Prosecuting Putin & Probing Western Leaders for Other Wars," *Democracy Now!,* February 6, 2023. https://www.democracynow.org/2023/2/6/ukraine_russia_war_crimes

Reuters, "Germany has evidence of war crimes in Ukraine 'in three-digit range,'" prosecutor says," February 3, 2023. https://www.reuters.com/world/europe/germany-has-evidence-war-crimes-ukraine-in-three-digit-range-prosecutor-2023-02-04/

Beth Van Schaack, "War Crimes and Accountability in Ukraine," Foreign Press Center Briefing, U.S. Department of State, June 15, 2022. https://www.state.gov/briefings-foreign-press-centers/war-crimes-and-accountability-in-ukraine

28 "UN Commission concludes that war crimes have been committed in Ukraine, expresses concern about suffering of civilians" [press release], United Nations Ukraine, September 23, 2022. https://ukraine.un.org/en/200623-un-commission-concludes-war-crimes-have-been-committed-ukraine-expresses-concern-about

"Report on alleged Ukrainian war crimes presented to UN," *RT,* October 18, 2022. https://www.rt.com/russia/564912-ukrainian-war-crimes-report/

"UN condemns executions of Russian POWs by Ukrainians," *RT,* February 10, 2023. https://www.rt.com/russia/571297-un-ukraine-pow-execution/

29 John Whitbeck, "On the ICC, Putin, Netanyahu and Prosecutorial Discretion," *CounterPunch,* March 21, 2023. https://www.counterpunch.org/2023/03/21/on-the-icc-putin-netanyahu-and-prosecutorial-discretion/

George Monbiot, "How many of those calling for Putin's arrest were complicit in the illegal invasion of Iraq?," *The Guardian,* March 20, 2023. https://www.theguardian.com/commentisfree/2023/mar/20/putin-arrest-illegal-invasion-iraq-gordon-brown-condoleezza-rice-alastair-campbell-russia

Marjorie Cohn, "After Undermining International Criminal Court, US Wants It to Charge Russians" [op-ed], *Truthout,* April 17, 2022. https://truthout.org/articles/after-undermining-international-criminal-court-us-wants-it-to-charge-russians/

Carl 'Mpangazitha' Niehaus, "Is the ICC indictment of President Putin an amateurish propaganda gimmick?" [op-ed], *The Star,* March 29, 2023. https://www.msn.com/en-za/news/other/is-the-icc-indictment-of-president-putin-an-amateurish-propaganda-gimmick/ar-AA19dL9z

"After arrest warrant for Putin, Russia opens case against ICC," *Aljazeera,* March 20, 2023. https://www.aljazeera.com/news/2023/3/20/arrest-warrant-for-putin-russia-opens-own-case-against-icc

30 K. P. Fabian, "George Bush Is a War Criminal: Why Didn't the ICC Issue an Arrest Warrant Against Him?" [op-ed], *Madras Courier,* March 20, 2023. https://madrascourier.com/opinion/george-bush-is-a-war-criminal-why-didnt-the-icc-issue-an-arrest-warrant-against-him/

Ahmed Twaij "Bush did what Putin's doing—so why is he getting away?" [op-ed], *Aljazeera,* March 28, 2023. https://www.aljazeera.com/opinions/2023/3/28/putin-should-be-punished-so-must-bush

31 Anthony J. Colangelo, "Germany Used "Universal Jurisdiction" to Convict ex-Syrian Official Who Sent Protestors to Torture Camp," SMU (Southern Methodist University) [op-ed], https://blog.smu.edu/opinions/2022/05/11/germany-used-universal-jurisdiction-to-convict-ex-syrian-official-who-sent-protestors-to-torture-camp/

Andy Beyer, "Where Will Universal Jurisdiction Go from Here?," Berkeley Political Review, March 2, 2022. https://bpr.berkeley.edu/2022/03/01/where-will-universal-jurisdiction-go-from-here/

32 Human Rights Watch, "Sweden: Iran War Crimes Trial Opens," August 9, 2021. https://www.hrw.org/news/2021/08/09/sweden-iran-war-crimes-trial-opens

Center for Human Rights in Iran, "UN Expert Welcomes Historic Verdict in Universal Jurisdiction Case on Iran," July 15, 2022. https://iranhumanrights.org/2022/07/un-expert-welcomes-historic-verdict-in-universal-jurisdiction-case-on-iran/

33 Richard Falk, "Kuala Lumpur tribunal: Bush and Blair guilty" [op-ed], *Aljazeera,* November 28, 2011. https://www.aljazeera.com/opinions/2011/11/28/kuala-lumpur-tribunal-bush-and-blair-guilty/

Yvonne Ridley, "Bush Convicted of War Crimes in Absentia," *Foreign Policy Journal,* May 12, 2012. https://www.foreignpolicyjournal.com/2012/05/12/bush-convicted-of-war-crimes-in-absentia/

34 "Iraq war illegal, says Annan," *BBC News,* September 16, 2004. http://news.bbc.co.uk/1/hi/world/middle_east/3661134.stm

35 "Judgment of the Kuala Lumpur Tribunal Re Israel War Crimes and Genocide," *Covert Geopolitics,* February 16, 2020. https://geopolitics.co/2020/02/16/judgment-of-the-kuala-lumpur-tribunal-re-israel-war-crimes-and-genocide/

36 Permanent People's Tribunal (PPT). http://permanentpeoplestribunal.org/?lang=en

37 Permanent People's Tribunal, *01. Western Sahara (Brussels, 10–11 November 1979).* http://permanentpeoplestribunal.org/sahara-occidentale-bruxelles-10-11-novembre-1979/?lang=en

38 ACLU, *Extraordinary Rendition.* https://www.aclu.org/issues/national-security/torture/extraordinary-rendition

39 ACLU, "A Conversation with Survivors of the CIA's Post-9/11 Torture Program," September 10, 2021. https://www.aclu.org/news/civil-liberties/a-conversation-with-survivors-of-the-cias-post-9-11-torture-program

40 Tim Weiner, *Legacy of Ashes* (Doubleday, 2007).

41 *Charter of the International Military Tribunal,* August 8, 1945. http://www.icls.de/dokumente/imt_statute.pdf

42 Laura Steiner, "Tamil Rights Group takes Fight for Justice to the International Criminal Court," *Toronto Star,* November 18, 2021. https://www.thestar.com/news/canada/2021/11/18/tamil-rights-group-takes-fight-for-justice-to-the-international-criminal-court.html

Tamil Rights Group, "Tamil Rights Group Initiates Global Campaign Seeking Justice for Eelam Tamils at the International Criminal Court," November 9, 2021. https://www.tamilrightsgroup.org/tamil-rights-group-initiates-global-campaign-seeking-justice-for-eelam-tamils-at-the-international-criminal-court/

43 National Security Archive, *Ayotzinapa Investigations* [special exhibit], https://nsarchive.gwu.edu/special-exhibit/ayotzinapa-investigations

"Ayotzinapa: the timeline of a tragedy," *El Universal,* September 26, 2019. https://www.eluniversal.com.mx/english/ayotzinapa-timeline-tragedy

44 SanctionsKill Campaign. https://sanctionskill.org/

Margaret Flowers, "Stop US Sanctions: 'You Don't Feel Them, but They Are Killing Our People,'" *antiwar.blog, Sepember 27, 2021.* https://www.antiwar.com/blog/2021/09/27/stop-us-sanctions-you-dont-feel-them-but-they-are-killing-our-people/

45 John Barber and Andrei Bzeniskevich, *Life and Death in Besieged Leningrad, 1941–44* (New York: Palgrave Macmillan, 2005).

46 Norman Finkelstein, *Gaza* (Oakland: University of California Press, 2018).

47 Mark Leon Goldberg, "War Crimes in Yemen," *UN Dispatch,* September 3, 2019. https://www.undispatch.com/war-crimes-in-yemen/

Tara Sepehri Far, "Biden Doubles Down on a Failed Yemen Policy," Human Rights Watch, February 15, 2022. https://www.hrw.org/news/2022/02/15/biden-doubles-down-failed-yemen-policy

48 Mark Weisbrot and Jeffrey Sachs, *Economic Sanctions as Collective Punishment* (Center for Economic and Policy Research, April 2019). https://cepr.net/images/stories/reports/venezuela-sanctions-2019-04.pdf

49 United Nations Human Rights, *OHCHR and unilateral coercive measures.*
https://www.ohchr.org/en/unilateral-coercive-measures
United Nations Human Rights, *Annual thematic reports: Special Rapporteur on unilateral coercive measures.* https://ohchr.org/EN/Issues/UCM/Pages/Reports.aspx

50 *Human rights and unilateral coercive measures,* UN Commission on Human Rights (56th sess. : 2000 : Geneva), United Nations Digital Library. https://digitallibrary.un.org/record/414237

51 "General Comment 8: The relationship between economic sanctions and respect for economic, social and cultural rights: 12/12/97," *ESCR-Net.* https://www.escr-net.org/resources/general-comment-8

52 United Nations Human Rights, *Reports on unilateral coercive measures from the Office of the UN High Commissioner for Human Rights: OHCHR and unilateral coercive measures,* https://www.ohchr.org/en/unilateral-coercive-measures/reports-unilateral-coercive-measures-office-un-high-commissioner-human-rights

53 United Nations Human Rights, *Professor Alena Douhan, Special Rapporteur on the negative impact of the unilateral coercive measures.* https://www.ohchr.org/en/special-procedures/sr-unilateral-coercive-measures/professor-alena-douhan-special-rapporteur-negative-impact-unilateral-coercive-measures

54 Nils Melzer, *The Trial of Julian Assange* (New York: Verso Books, 2022).

55 Alfred de Zayas, "Amnesty Clause," in Rudolf Bernhardt (ed.), *Encyclopedia of Public International Law,* vol. I (Amsterdam: North Holland, 1992), 148–151.

56 *Treaty of Westphalia,* The Avalon Project, Yale Law School. https://avalon.law.yale.edu/17th_century/westphal.asp

57 Alfred de Zayas, "Westphalia, Peace of" in Bernhardt, *Encyclopedia of Public International Law,* vol. IV (Amsterdam: North Holland, 2000), 1465–1469.

58 William Schabas, *The Trial of the Kaiser* (Oxford, 2019).

59 Alfred de Zayas, "An International Criminal Court," in *Nordic Journal of International Law* (1992–93), 271–277.

60 Cherif Bassiouni and Alfred de Zayas, *The Protection of Human Rights in the Administration of Criminal Justice* (Transnational Publishers, 1994).

CHAPTER 5

1 Aaron Maté, "In moving UN speech, veteran diplomat confronts OPCW 'stonewalling and smear tactics' on Syria," *The Gray Zone,* April 19, 2021. https://thegrayzone.com/2021/04/19/in-un-speech-veteran-diplomat-issues-moving-call-for-action-on-opcws-syria-cover-up/
The GrayZone, "At UN, Aaron Maté debunks OPCW's Syria lies and confronts US, UK on cover-up," *Pushback by Aaron Maté,* YouTube video, 27:21, April 18, 2021. https://www.youtube.com/watch?v=Ge4W9e6YeXQ
Berlin Group 21,"Statement of Concern: The OPCW investigation of alleged chemical weapons use in Douma, Syria." https://berlingroup21.org/

2 David Swanson, "Lies and Consequences in Our Past 15 Wars," *Truthout,* May 28, 2012. https://truthout.org/articles/lies-and-consequences-in-our-past-15-wars/
"Debunking A Century of War Lies," *WanttoKnow.info,* https://www.wanttoknow.info/war/war-lies-century
"A Guide to Mainstream Media 'Fake News' War Propaganda," *21st Century Wire,* February 14, 2017. https://21stcenturywire.com/2017/02/14/fake-news-week-a-guide-to-mainstream-media-fake-news-war-propaganda/

Jack Xiong, "The Fake News in 1990 That Propelled the US into the First Gulf War," *Citizen Truth,* May 7, 2018. https://citizentruth.org/fake-news-1990-that-ignited-gulf-war-sympathy/

"Army Colonel: False Flag 'Gulf of Tonkin Incident' May Be Used to Get US Into War with Iran," *Freedom Outpost,* January 17, 2021. https://investortimes.com/freedomoutpost/army-colonel-false-flag-gulf-of-tonkin-incident-may-be-used-to-get-us-into-war-with-iran/

Taylor Synclair Goethe, "War, Propaganda and Misinformation: The Evolution of Fake News," *Reporter,* April 26, 2019. https://reporter.rit.edu/features/war-propaganda-and-misinformation-evolution-fake-news

3 Homer, *Odyssey,* Virgil, *Aeneid.*

4 Kit Klarenberg, "Network of UK Intel-Linked Operatives Helped Sell Every Alleged Syrian Chemical Weapons Attack," *Consortiuim News,* August 10, 2021. https://consortiumnews.com/2021/08/10/network-of-uk-intel-linked-operatives-helped-sell-every-alleged-syrian-chemical-weapons-attack/

"How the CIA Paid and Threatened Journalists to Do Its Work," *Daily Beast,* October 14, 2016; updated July 12, 2017. https://www.thedailybeast.com/cheats/2016/10/14/how-the-cia-paid-and-threatened-journalists-to-do-its-work

Kara Goldfarb, "Inside Operation Mockingbird — The CIA's Plan To Infiltrate The Media," *All That's Interesting,* December 4, 2021; updated January 21, 2022. https://allthatsinteresting.com/operation-mockingbird

Paul Szoldra, "5 national security-related conspiracy theories that turned out to be true," *Insider,* June 16, 2015. https://www.businessinsider.com/5-conspiracy-theories-that-turned-out-to-be-true-2015-6?op=1&r=US&IR=T

5 Kit Klarenberg, "How a network of UK intel-linked operatives helped sell every alleged Syrian chemical weapons attack," *The Grayzone,* August 4, 2021. https://thegrayzone.com/2021/08/04/network-uk-intel-operatives-syrian-chemical-weapons/

6 Cicero, Statement in defence of Sextus Roscius, §30, 84; also, in Pro Milone 12, 32, and the second Philippica 14, 35.

7 United Nations Office for Disarmament Affairs, *Treaty on the Non-Proliferation of Nuclear Weapons (NPT),* https://www.un.org/disarmament/wmd/nuclear/npt/

United Nations, *Tenth Review Conference of the Parties to the Treaty on the Non-Proliferation of Nuclear Weapons (NPT),* August 1-26, 2022. https://www.un.org/en/conferences/npt2020

8 Scott Ritter, *Disarmament in the Time of Perestroika* (Clarity Press, 2022).

9 Organisation for the Prohibition of Chemical Weapons (OPCW), *Chemical Weapons Convention.* https://www.opcw.org/chemical-weapons-convention

10 CWC Coalition, *The Chemical Weapons Convention.* https://www.cwccoalition.org/what-is-the-cwc/

11 See Organization for Security and Co-operation in Europe, "OSCE Special Monitoring Mission to Ukraine (SMM) Daily Report 40/2022 issued on 21 February 2022," February 21, 2022. https://www.osce.org/special-monitoring-mission-to-ukraine/512683

12 Juvenalis, *Satires,* 6, 347–48.

13 Horatius, *Epistles* 1,2,40. "Have the courage to use your judgment." Immanuel Kant called "sapere aude" the hallmark of the Enlightenment.

14 Vesselin Popoviski, *International Rule of Law and Professional Ethics* (Farnham, England: Ashgate Publishing, 2014), 158–60. Marlise Simmons, "To

Ousted Boss, Arms Watchdog was seen as an Obstacle in Iraq" *The New York Times,* October 13, 2013.

15 "General Wesley Clark: We're going to take out 7 countries in 5 years," *Progressive Truth Seekers,* February 7, 2021, video clip, 2:00. https://www.youtube.com/watch?v=b5UhQ-gqVkg

16 Reuters, "Iraq: U.S. Weapons Inspectors Continue Search as Hans Blix and Mohamed El Baradei Hold Press Conference, Calling for Greater Co-operation," *ScreenOcean,* February 9, 2003, news video, 5:51. https://reuters.screenocean.com/record/334134

17 Mehdi Hasan, "'We know where your kids live': How John Bolton once threatened an International Official," *Information Clearing House,* March 29, 2018. https://www.informationclearinghouse.info/49096.htm.

18 Paul Adams, "Syria 'submits chemical weapons data' to Hague watchdog," *BBC News,* September 20, 2013. https://www.bbc.com/news/world-middle-east-24178830

Julian Borger, "Syria deadline for chemical weapons destruction will be met, says OPCW," *The Guardian,* October 23, 2013. https://www.theguardian.com/world/2013/oct/23/syria-deadline-chemical-weapons-opcw

Alan Rappeport, "Syria's Chemical Arsenal Fully Destroyed, U.S. Says," *The New York Times,* August 18, 2014. https://www.nytimes.com/2014/08/19/world/middleeast/syrias-chemical-arsenal-fully-destroyed-us-says.html

Kounteya Sinha, "UK confirms destruction of Syria's chemical weapons," Flouride Action Network, August 7, 2014. https://fluoridealert.org/news/uk-confirms-destruction-of-syrias-chemical-weapons/

19 Yousra Fazili, Devon Bistarkey, and Amanda Ducasse, "U.S. Meets Milestone in Chemical Weapons Stockpile Destruction," U.S. Department of Defense, May 19, 2022. https://www.defense.gov/News/News-Stories/Article/Article/3036463/us-meets-milestone-in-chemical-weapons-stockpile-destruction/source/us-meets-milestone-in-chemical-weapons-stockpile-destruction/

20 "UN's Del Ponte says evidence Syria rebels 'used sarin,'" *BBC News,* May 6, 2013. https://www.bbc.com/news/world-middle-east-22424188

"Syria: the rebels battling for Assad's chemical weapons," *4 News,* May 6, 2013. https://www.channel4.com/news/syria-chemical-weapons-rebels-al-nusra-defence-factories-un

Peter Bergen, "Al Qaeda's track record with chemical weapons" [op-ed], *CNN,* May 6, 2013. https://edition.cnn.com/2013/05/06/opinion/bergen-chemical-weapons-syria/index.html

21 Alan Rappeport, "Syria's Chemical Arsenal Fully Destroyed, U.S. Says," *The New York Times,* August 19, 2014. https://www.nytimes.com/2014/08/19/world/middleeast/syrias-chemical-arsenal-fully-destroyed-us-says.html

22 Organisation for the Prohibition of Chemical Weapons, "OPCW Issues Fact-Finding Mission Report on Chemical Weapons Use Allegation in Douma, Syria, in 2018," March 1, 2019. https://www.opcw.org/media-centre/news/2019/03/opcw-issues-fact-finding-mission-report-chemical-weapons-use-allegation

23 Brandon Turbeville, "BBC Producer Admits Douma "Chemical Attack" Was "Staged;" Confirms Independent Media Reporting," *Activist Post,* February 20, 2019. https://www.activistpost.com/2019/02/bbc-producer-admits-douma-chemical-attack-staged-confirms-independent-media.html

"Douma Chemical Attack Was Staged: This Short Video Proves it," *Signs of the Times,* April 17, 2018. https://www.sott.net/article/383167-Douma-Chemical-Attack-Was-Staged-This-Short-Video-Proves-it

Aaron Maté, "The Grayzone's Aaron Maté testifies at UN on OPCW Syria cover-up," *The Grayzone,* September 29, 2020. https://thegrayzone.com/2020/09/29/grayzones-aaron-mate-testifies-at-un-on-opcw-syria-cover-up/

24 "Statement of Concern: The OPCW investigation of alleged chemical weapons use in Douma, Syria," *The Transnational TFF,* April 6, 2021. https://transnational.live/2021/04/06/statement-of-concern-the-opcw-investigation-of-alleged-chemical-weapons-use-in-douma-syria/

25 United Nations Human Rights, *Special Rapporteur on truth, justice and reparation.* https://www.ohchr.org/en/special-procedures/sr-truth-justice-reparation-and-non-recurrence

26 Mark Siegal, "Former UN official says sanctions against Iraq amount to 'genocide,'" *Cornell Chronicle,* September 30, 1999. https://news.cornell.edu/stories/1999/09/former-un-official-says-sanctions-against-iraq-amount-genocide

27 H. C. von Sponeck, A Different Kind of War: The UN Sanctions Regime in Iraq (Oxford, 2005; Berghahn Books 2006).

CHAPTER 6

1 Charles Stewart Mott Foundation, "From the Mott Archives: Nelson Mandela interview with Mott staff," December 10, 2013. https://www.mott.org/news/articles/from-the-mott-archives-nelson-mandela-interview-with-mott-staff/

2 Erica-Irene Daes, *Special Rapporteur of the Sub-Commission, Freedom of the Individual under Law, a study under Article 29 of the UDHR* (New York: United Nations, 1990). See also *Human rights and human responsibilities: final report of the Special Rapporteur, Miguel Alfonso Martínez, on the study requested by the Commission in its resolution 2000/63, and submitted pursuant to Economic and Social Council decision 2002/277.* https://digitallibrary.un.org/record/491708

3 Gospel according to St. Matthew, Chapters V-VII.

4 Nikolas Barry-Shaw, Yves Engler, and Dru Oja Jay, *Paved With Good Intentions: Canada's Development NGOs from Idealism to Imperialism* (Halifax, Nova Scotia: Fernwood Publishing, 2012).

5 Kristin Christman, "The National Endowment for 'Democracy': A Second CIA," *Counter Currents,* May 30, 2022. https://countercurrents.org/2022/05/the-national-endowment-for-democracy-a-second-cia/

Robert Parry, "CIA's Hidden Hand in 'Democracy' Groups," *Consortium News,* January 8, 2015. https://consortiumnews.com/2015/01/08/cias-hidden-hand-in-democracy-groups/

6 David Ainsworth, "Amnesty issues public apology over golden handshakes," *Third Sector,* March 1, 2011. https://www.thirdsector.co.uk/amnesty-issues-public-apology-golden-handshakes/communications/article/1057803

7 Juvenalis, *Satires* (*Satire VI,* lines 347–48).

8 International Peace Bureau, *Who we are.* https://www.ipb.org/who-we-are/

International Peace Bureau, "International Appeal for a Christmastime Peace in Ukraine," *Christmas Peace Appeal,* https://www.christmasappeal.ipb.org/

9 Women's International League for Peace and Freedom. https://www.wilpf.org/

10 Asociación Española para el Derecho Internacional de los Derechos Humanos (AEDIDH), *Quiénes somos.* http://aedidh.org/es/quienes-somos-2/

11 PEN International. https://pen-international.org/

12 www.i-p-o.org

13 *Eleanor Lives! A plan for humanity.* https://www.eleanorlives.org

14 William Engdahl, private email communication, February 27, 2023.

15 Africa 101 Las Tribes: *Bubi.* https://www.101lasttribes.com/tribes/bubi.html OHCHR, "El Pueblo Indigena Bubi de la Isla de Bioko." https://www.ohchr.org/sites/default/files/Documents/Issues/IPeoples/EMRIP/FPIC/PuebloBubi.pdf

16 Carol C. Ngang," Self-Determination and the Southern Cameroons Quest for Sovereign Statehood," *African Journal of International and Comparative Law 29,* no. 2 (March 2021):288–308. https://www.researchgate.net/publication/349733626_Self-Determination_and_the_Southern_Cameroons_Quest_for_Sovereign_Statehood

17 "Self determination as vital as right to life: Speakers," *Kashmir Media Service,* October 5, 2020. https://kmsnews.org/news/2020/10/05/self-determination-as-vital-as-right-to-life-speakers/

18 Erik Jensen, *Western Sahara: Anatomy of a Stalemate?* (International Peace Studies, 2005).

19 Nicos Panayiotides, "The Kurds' enduring struggle for self-determination," *Asia Times,* July 18, 2018. https://asiatimes.com/2018/07/the-kurds-enduring-struggle-for-self-determination/

20 Kelvin Ebiri, "MOSOP restates call for Ogoni self-rule," *The Guardian,* September 29, 2017. https://guardian.ng/news/mosop-restates-call-for-ogoni-self-rule/

21 "Eelam Tamils rally for self-determination and call justice for Sri Lanka's genocide against Tamils," *Tamil Genocide Memorial,* March 5, 2022. https://tamilgenocide.com/news/press-releases/eelam-tamils-rally-for-self-determination-and-call-justice-for-sri-lankas-genocide-against-tamils/

22 Peace for Okinawa Coalition, *Ryukyu Independence Movement.* https://www.peaceforokinawa.org/ryukyu-independence-restoration-movement.html

23 "West Papua and the Right to Self Determination under International Law,: Legal analysis by human rights lawyer Melinda Janki" Free West Papua Campaign, https://www.freewestpapua.org/info/legal-basis-for-self-determination/

24 Nicolas Nevrat, Sandrina Atunes, Guillaume Tusseau, and Paul Williams, *Catalonia's Legitimate Right to Decide:Paths to Self-determination.* https://www.academia.edu/71670889/A_Report_by_a_Commission_of_International_Experts_Catalonias_Legitimate_Right_to_Decide_Paths_to_Self_Determination

25 United Nations Human Rights, *Mr. Alfred-Maurice de Zayas, former Independent Expert (2012-2018).* https://www.ohchr.org/en/special-procedures/ie-international-order/mr-alfred-maurice-de-zayas-former-independent-expert-2012-2018

United Nations Human Rights, "UN expert calls for concrete protection to support civil society voices, including 'whistleblowers'" [press release], September 11, 2013. https://www.ohchr.org/en/press-releases/2013/09/un-expert-calls-concrete-protection-support-civil-society-voices-including

United Nations, "UN expert calls on countries to strengthen protection of civil society voices, whistleblowers," *UN News,* September 11, 2013. https://news.un.org/en/story/2013/09/448712

United Nations Human Rights, "Statement by Alfred de Zayas Independent Expert on the promotion of a democratic and equitable international order at the 24th session of the Human Rights Council," September 10, 2013. https://newsarchive. ohchr.org/en/NewsEvents/Pages/DisplayNews.aspx?NewsID=13699

26 Alfred de Zayas, "Expert meeting on the Human Right to Peace: Around the World, Across the Generations," AEDIDH, June 22, 2018. http://aedidh.org/es/tag/ alfred-de-zayas/

27 Fondation GIPRI, *Cahiers.* https://gipri.ch/publications/cahiers/

28 International Human Rights Association of American Minorities, *Human Rights Council.* https://ihraam.org/un-activities/human-rights-council/

29 Internationale Gesellschaft für Menschenrechte (IGFM). https://www.igfm. de. See its activities for persecuted Christians in the Middle East, for indigenous populations of South America, the Chaco indigenous of Paraguay, against blasphemy laws, against female genital mutilation, etc.

30 See my articles in the *Encyclopedia of Human Rights* (David Forsythe, ed., Oxford, 2009), including my entries on Aryeh Neier, Kenneth Roth, Simon Wiesenthal Centre, P.E.N. and Human Rights. See also my entries in the *Encyclopedia of Genocide and Crimes Against Humanity* (Dinah Shelton, ed., Macmillan), including Nelson Mandela.

31 Reporters Without Borders, "#FreeAssange: sign this petition opposing Julian Assange's extradition to the United States!" [petition], https://rsf.org/en/ petition/freeassange-sign-petition-opposing-julian-assanges-extradition-united-states

32 Reporters Without Borders, "Pardon Jeffrey Sterling, CIA Whistleblower," *PopularResistance.org,* February 18, 2016. https://popularresistance.org/pardon-cia-whistleblower-jeffrey-sterling/

33 Diana Barahona and Jeb Sprague, "Oui, Reporters sans Frontières est bien payé par la CIA," *Investi'Action,* August 5, 2006. https://www.investigaction.net/fr/ Oui-Reporters-sans-Frontieres-est/

F. William Engdahl, "Reporters Without Borders seems to have a geopolitical agenda," *Voltairenet.org,* May 5, 2010. https://www.voltairenet.org/article165297. html

34 Brandon Turbeville, "Reporters Without Borders Tries to Shut Down Independent Press Event Discussing White Helmets," *Activist Post,* November 28, 2017. https://www.transcend.org/tms/2017/12/reporters-without-borders-tries-to-shut-down-independent-press-event-discussing-white-helmets/

35 Reporters Without Borders, "Reporters Without Borders keeps UNESCO consultative status, condemns disinformation" March 13, 2012; updated January 25, 2016. https://rsf.org/en/reporters-without-borders-keeps-unesco-consultative-status-condemns-disinformation

36 Reporters Without Borders, "Listed as a 'foreign agent,' Russia's most popular independent website risks disappearing," May 5, 2021. https://rsf.org/en/news/listed-foreign-agent-russias-most-popular-independent-website-risks-disappearing

Radio Free Europe/Radio Liberty, "Reporters Without Borders Slams Russia's 'Foreign Agent' Listing For Meduza," *RFE/RL,* May 5, 2021. https://www.rferl.org/a/ russia-meduza-rsf-slams-foreign-agent-label/31239476.html

Radio Free Europe/Radio Liberty, "Journalism Watchdog Warns That Russia Is 'Killing Off' Independent Media," *RFE/RL,* June 16, 2021. https://www.rferl.org/a/ russia-independent-media-foreign-agents-rsf/31311354.html

Lajme nga Bota, "Reporters Without Borders: Russia is killing independent media," *TiranaPost,* June 16, 2021. https://tiranapost.al/english/lajme-nga-bota/reporteret-pa-kufij-rusia-po-i-vret-mediat-e-pavarura-i499499

37 RT, "Reporters Without Borders seeks to cancel press event critical of White Helmets," *Aletho News,* November 28, 2017. https://alethonews.com/2017/11/28/reporters-without-borders-seeks-to-cancel-press-event-critical-of-white-helmets/

"VIDEO: Why is Reporters Without Borders trying to cancel panel on White Helmets?" *Off Guardian,* December 1, 2017. https://off-guardian.org/2017/12/01/video-why-is-reporters-without-borders-trying-to-cancel-panel-on-white-helmets/

38 Rick Sterling, "The 'White Helmets' Controversy," *Consotrium News,* July 22, 2018. https://consortiumnews.com/2018/07/22/the-white-helmets-controversy/

Ben Norton, "White Helmets corruption scandal deepens: Dutch gov't investigated parent org for fraud, but covered it up," *The Grayzone,* May 7, 2021. https://thegrayzone.com/2021/05/07/syria-white-helmets-mayday-fraud-netherlands/

21st Century Wire, "White Helmets Implicated in Cash Embezzlement and Fraud Scandal," *SGT Report,* July 20, 2020. https://www.sgtreport.com/2020/07/white-helmets-implicated-in-cash-embezzlement-and-fraud-scandal/

Vanessa Beeley, "White Helmets: The 'Old Etonian" Cartel Protection Racket," *21st Century Wire,* July 5, 2018. https://21stcenturywire.com/2018/07/05/white-helmets-the-eton-mess/

39 I wrote the entries "Kenneth Roth" and "Aryeh Neier" of the Open Society Institute for the *Encyclopedia of Human Rights* edited by Prof. David Forsythe (Oxford, 2009). https://www.oxfordreference.com/display/10.1093/acref/9780195334029.001.0001/acref-9780195334029;jsessionid=3A9542EE14A80A72FBAD794C5974AD39

I also penned an op-ed critical of HRW and Kenneth Roth. See Idriss Jazairy and Alfred de Zayas, "Human Rights Watch disappoints on Human Rights," *Inter Press Service,* July 25, 2019. https://www.ipsnews.net/2019/07/human-rights-watch-disappoints-human-rights/

40 The Nobel Prize 1997: Press Release. https://www.nobelprize.org/prizes/peace/1997/press-release/

41 Human Rights Watch, *History.* https://www.hrw.org/about/about-us/history

42 Human Rights Watch, *Israel and Palestine: Events of 2021.* https://www.hrw.org/world-report/2022/country-chapters/israel/palestine

Human Rights Watch, *A Threshold Crossed: Israeli Authorities and the Crimes of Apartheid and Persecution,* April 27, 2021. https://www.hrw.org/report/2021/04/27/threshold-crossed/israeli-authorities-and-crimes-apartheid-and-persecution

Omar Shakir, "A Threshold Crossed," *Zenith,* July 19, 2021. https://magazine.zenith.me/en/society/israeli-policies-palestinians-and-apartheid

Linah Alsaafin, "Israel uses 'apartheid' to subjugate Palestinians: HRW," *Aljazeera,* April 27, 2021. https://www.aljazeera.com/news/2021/4/27/israel-uses-apartheid-to-subjugate-palestinians-hrw-report

Phyllis Bennis, "Why Human Rights Watch Designating Israel's Crimes as Apartheid Is a Very Big Deal," *Common Dreams,* May 5, 2021. https://www.commondreams.org/views/2021/05/05/why-human-rights-watch-designating-israels-crimes-apartheid-very-big-deal

See in this connection Jimmy Carter, *Palestine: Peace, Not Apartheid*, (New York: Simon & Schuster, 2006).

43 United Natioins Human Rights, "Richard J. Goldstone Appointed to Lead Human Rights Council Fact-finding Mission on Gaza Conflict" [press release], April 3, 2009. https://www.ohchr.org/en/press-releases/2009/10/richard-j-goldstone-appointed-lead-human-rights-council-fact-finding-mission

Human Rights Watch, "UN: US, EU Undermine Justice for Gaza Conflict," September 30, 2009. https://www.hrw.org/news/2009/09/30/un-us-eu-undermine-justice-gaza-conflict

Steven Stotsky, "Goldstone Retracts, Human Rights Watch Attacks," *CAMERA* (Committee for Accuracy in Middle East Reporting and Analysis), April 6, 2021. https://www.camera.org/article/goldstone-retracts-human-rights-watch-attacks/

44 Human Rights Watch, "Human Rights Consensus Around Crime of Apartheid" [statement], March 25, 2022. https://www.hrw.org/news/2022/03/25/human-rights-consensus-around-crime-apartheid

45 Branco Marcetic, "If Even Ken Roth Can't Criticize Israel, No One Can," *Jacobin,* January 13, 2023. https://jacobin.com/2023/01/ken-roth-human-rights-watch-israel-palestine-apartheid-harvard-kennedy

46 "HRW 'concerned' after ex-director loses Harvard offer" *The New Arab,* January 11, 2023.

47 Chris McGreal, "Harvard reverses decision on role for Israel critic after outcry," *The Guardian,* January 19, 2023. https://www.theguardian.com/education/2023/jan/19/harvard-kenneth-roth-fellowship-israel-criticism

48 Afrah Nasser, "US Assistance to Saudi-Led Coalition Risks Complicity in War Crimes," Human Rights Watch, April 7, 2022. https://www.hrw.org/news/2022/04/07/us-assistance-saudi-led-coalition-risks-complicity-war-crimes

Andrea Prassow, "U.S. War Crimes in Yemen: Stop Looking the Other Way," Human Rights Watch, September 21, 2020. https://www.hrw.org/news/2020/09/21/us-war-crimes-yemen-stop-looking-other-way

49 Human Rights Watch, "Singapore: Events of 2020," *World Report 2021.* https://www.hrw.org/world-report/2021/country-chapters/singapore

50 Human Rights Watch, "Lebanon: Abolish Kafala (Sponsorship) System," July 27, 2020. https://www.hrw.org/news/2020/07/27/lebanon-abolish-kafala-sponsorship-system

51 Patrick Rak, "Modern Day Slavery: the Kafala System in Lebanon," *Harvard International Review,* December 21, 2020. https://hir.harvard.edu/modern-day-slavery-the-kafala-system-in-lebanon/

United Nations Human Rights, *Special Rapporteur on contemporary forms of slavery.* https://www.ohchr.org/en/special-procedures/sr-slavery

52 "Human Rights Watch is Roundly Criticized By… Human Rights Activists," Mrs. Mairead Maguire's segment, audio clip via uprisingradio.com, 14:59, *World Summit of Nobel Peace Laureates,* http://www.nobelpeacesummit.com/human-rights-watch-is-roundly-criticized-by-human-rights-activists/

Belén Fernández, "Human Rights Watch's Revolving Door," *Jacobin,* June 8, 2014. https://jacobin.com/2014/06/human-rights-watchs-revolving-door/

"Nobel Peace Laureates to Human Rights Watch: Close Your Revolving Door to U.S. Government," AlterNet, May 8, 2014. https://www.alternet.org/2014/05/nobel-peace-laureates-human-rights-watch-close-your-revolving-door-us-government

"Debate: Is Human Rights Watch Too Close to U.S. Gov't to Criticize Its Foreign Policy?," *Democracy Now!,* June 11, 2014. https://www.democracynow.org/2014/6/11/debate_is_human_rights_watch_too

53 Tirana Hassan has been the Acting Executive Director since 2022. Human Rights Watch, *Tiarna Hassan, Executive Director.* https://www.hrw.org/about/people/tirana-hassan

54 Javier Sethness, "The Structural Genocide That Is Capitalism" [review], *Truthout,* June 16, 2013. https://truthout.org/articles/the-structural-genocide-that-is-capitalism/

55 Gary Leech, "The Bias of Human Rights Watch," *CLT* (Critical Legal Thinking), March 21, 2013. https://criticallegalthinking.com/2013/03/21/the-bias-of-human-rights-watch/

56 Ewen MacAskill and Julian Borger, "Iraq war was illegal and breached UN charter, says Annan," *The Guardian,* September 15, 2004. https://www.theguardian.com/world/2004/sep/16/iraq.iraq

Patrick E. Tyler, "Annan Says Iraq War Was Illegal," *The New York Times,* September 16, 2004. https://www.nytimes.com/2004/09/16/international/annan-says-iraq-war-was-illegal.html

57 "U.S.: Hundreds of Civilian Deaths in Iraq Were Preventable," Human Rights Watch, December 12, 2003. https://www.hrw.org/news/2003/12/12/us-hundreds-civilian-deaths-iraq-were-preventable

58 Ibid.

59 Human Rights Watch, "Acronyms," *Off Target: The Conduct of the War and Civilian Casualties in Iraq,* December 11, 2003. https://www.hrw.org/report/2003/12/11/target/conduct-war-and-civilian-casualties-iraq

60 Jonathan Cook, "Human Rights Watch: Still Missing the Point," *CounterPunch,* September 25, 2006. https://www.counterpunch.org/2006/09/25/human-rights-watch-still-missing-the-point/

61 Glen Ford, "'Human Rights' Warriors for Empire," Black Agenda Report, February 16, 2012. https://blackagendareport.com/content/%E2%80%9Chuman-rights%E2%80%9D-warriors-empire

Mohandeer, "'Human Rights' Front Groups ('Humanitarian Interventionalists') Warring on Syria," *Worldtruth* [blog], February 21, 2016. https://mohandeer.wordpress.com/2016/02/21/human-rights-front-groups-humanitarian-interventionalists-warring-on-syria/

62 See the discussion in my 2018 report to the Human Rights Council: https://documents-dds-ny.un.org/doc/UNDOC/GEN/G18/018/46/PDF/G1801846.pdf

63 Ben Norton, "Billionaire-backed Human Rights Watch lobbies for lethal US sanctions on leftist governments as Covid crisis rages," *The Grayzone,* April 8, 2020. https://thegrayzone.com/2020/04/08/billionaire-human-rights-watch-sanctions-nicaragua-venezuela/

64 United Nations Human Rights, *Country Visits: Independent Expert on international order,* https://www.ohchr.org/en/special-procedures/ie-international-order/country-visits

65 U.S. Department of the Treasury, Office of Foreign Assets Control, *Sanctions Programs and Country Information.* https://home.treasury.gov/policy-issues/financial-sanctions/sanctions-programs-and-country-information

"Countries the United States Has Sanctions and Embargoes Against," *World Atlas,* https://www.worldatlas.com/articles/countries-the-united-states-has-sanctions-and-embargoes-against.html

66 See Marc Weisbrot and Jeffrey Sachs, "Economic Sanctions as Collective Punishment: The Case of Venezuela," *CEPR* (Center for Economic and Policy

Research), April 25, 2019. https://cepr.net/report/economic-sanctions-as-collective-punishment-the-case-of-venezuela/

Andrew Buncombe, "US sanctions on Venezuela responsible for 'tens of thousands' of deaths, claims new report," *Independent,* April 26, 2019. https://www.independent.co.uk/news/world/americas/venezuela-sanctions-us-excess-death-toll-economy-oil-trump-maduro-juan-guaido-jeffrey-sachs-a8888516.html

67 UN doc. A/HRC/19/33.

68 Mausi Segun, "Burundi's Vicious Crackdown Never Ended," Human Rights Watch, February 8, 2022. https://www.hrw.org/news/2022/02/08/burundis-vicious-crackdown-never-ended

69 Mark Weisbrot and Jeffrey Sachs, *Economic Sanctions as Collective Punishment: The Case of Venezuela* (Center for Economic and Policy Research, April 2019). https://cepr.net/images/stories/reports/venezuela-sanctions-2019-04.pdf

70 Alan MacLeod, "Human Rights Watch supports US-backed far-right coup in Bolivia, whitewashes massacre of indigenous protesters," *The Grayzone,* November 20, 2019. https://thegrayzone.com/2019/11/20/human-rights-watch-bolivia-coup-massacre/

71 Council on Hemispheric Affairs, "Taking Human Rights Watch to Task on the Question of Venezuela's Purported Abuse of Human Rights: Over 100 U.S. and Foreign Scholars Take Issue with the head of HRW's Latin American Division," December 18, 2008. https://www.coha.org/taking-human-rights-watch-to-task/

For a more detailed but still not exhaustive account of the HRW report's exaggerations, errors, and omissions, see Gregory Wilpert, "Smoke and Mirrors: An Analysis of Human Rights Watch's Report on Venezuela," *Venezuelanalysis.com* October 17, 2008. http://www.venezuelanalysis.com/analysis/3882

72 United Nations Human Rights, *Country visits: Independent Expert on international order.* https://www.ohchr.org/en/special-procedures/ie-international-order/country-visits

73 United Nations Human Rights, A/HRC/48/59/Add.2: "Visit to the Bolivarian Republic of Venezuela – Report of the Special Rapporteur on the negative impact of unilateral coercive measures on the enjoyment of human rights, Alena Douhan," October 4, 2021. https://www.ohchr.org/en/documents/country-reports/ahrc4859add2-visit-bolivarian-republic-venezuela-report-special

74 Ibid.

75 During the Trump administration. But it is hardly different under Biden.

76 Human Rights Watch, "Nicaragua: Events of 2021," *World Report 2022.* https://www.hrw.org/world-report/2022/country-chapters/nicaragua

Human Rights Watch, *Nicaragua.* https://www.hrw.org/americas/nicaragua

77 Roger Stoll, "The Revolution Won't Be Stopped: Nicaragua Advances Despite US Unconventional Warfare," *Orinoco Tribune,* April 8, 2021. https://orinocotribune.com/the-revolution-wont-be-stopped-nicaragua-advances-despite-us-unconventional-warfare/

See also Max Blumenthal and Ben Norton, "How US govt-funded media fueled a violent coup in Nicaragua," *The Grayzone,* June 12, 2021. https://thegrayzone.com/2021/06/12/coup-nicaragua-cpj-100-noticias/

78 See my article with Prof. Richard Falk, "Reflections on Genocide as the Ultimate Crime," *CounterPunch,* April 23, 2021. https://www.counterpunch.org/2021/04/23/reflections-on-genocide-as-the-ultimate-crime/

Also see Jeff Sachs and William Schabas, "The Xinjiang Genocide Allegations Are Unjustified," *Project Syndicate,* April 20, 2021. https://www.project-syndicate. org/commentary/biden-should-withdraw-unjustified-xinjiang-genocide-allegation-by-jeffrey-d-sachs-and-william-schabas-2021-04

79 Amnesty International, "USA must drop charges against Julian Assange" [petition]. https://www.amnesty.org/en/petition/julian-assange-usa-justice/

Julia Hall, "Julian Assange extradition hearing: Punishing the publisher," Amnesty International, September 10, 2022. https://www.amnesty.org/en/latest/ news/2020/09/julian-assange-extradition-hearing-punishing-the-publisher/

"The US diplomatic assurances are inherently unreliable. Julian Assange must be released," Amnesty International, July 26, 2021. https://www.amnesty.org/en/ latest/news/2021/07/the-us-diplomatic-assurances-are-inherently-unreliable-julian-assange-must-be-released/

80 Amnesty International, "Singapore Failing to Respect Civil Rights" – Amnesty International Submission to the UN Universal Periodic Review, May 2011 (Amnesty International, 2011), p. 7.

81 Ibid.

82 Amnesty International, "Afghanistan: ICC Prosecutor's statement on Afghanistan jeopardises his Office's legitimacy and future," October 5, 2021. https:// www.amnesty.org/en/documents/ior53/4842/2021/en/

83 Amnesty International, "Fidel Castro's human rights legacy: A tale of two worlds," November 26, 2016. https://www.amnesty.org/en/latest/news/2016/11/fidel-castro-s-human-rights-legacy-a-tale-of-two-worlds/

84 United Nations Human Rights, *Country visits: Independent Expert on human rights and international solidarity.* https://www.ohchr.org/en/special-procedures/ie-international-solidarity/country-visits

85 United Nations Human Rights, "A/HRC/48/59/Add.2: Visit to the Bolivarian Republic of Venezela – Report of the Special Rapporteur on the negative impact of unilateral coercive measures on the enjoyment of human rights, Alena Douhan," October 4, 2021. https://www.ohchr.org/en/documents/country-reports/ ahrc4859add2-visit-bolivarian-republic-venezuela-report-special

United Nations, "UN human rights expert urges to lift unilateral sanctions against Venezuela" [press release], February 12, 2021. https://www.ohchr.org/en/ press-releases/2021/02/un-human-rights-expert-urges-lift-unilateral-sanctions-against-venezuela

Andreína Chávez Alava, "UN Expert Releases Full Report on Impact of US-led Sanctions Against Venezuela," *Venezuelanalysis,* September 18 2021. https:// venezuelanalysis.com/news/15323

86 Alfred de Zayas, "Economic Sanctions Kill," *CounterPunch,* March 18, 2022. https://www.counterpunch.org/2022/03/18/economic-sanctions-kill/

87 Amnesty International, *Open letter to the UN High Commissioner for Human Rights, Volker Türk, in the context of his visit to Venezuela,* January 26, 2023. https:// www.amnesty.org/es/wp-content/uploads/2023/01/AMR5363712023ENGLISH.pdf

88 Vanessa Beeley, "The Secret History Of How British Intelligence Created Amnesty International," *The Wall Will Fall,* October 5, 2020. https://thewallwillfall. org/2020/10/05/the-secret-history-of-how-british-intelligence-created-amnesty-international/

89 WikiSpooks, *Brian Berletic.* https://www.wikispooks.com/wiki/Brian_ Berletic

90 Tony Cartalucci, "Amnesty International is US State Department Propaganda," *Land Destroyer Report,* August 22, 2012. https://landdestroyer. blogspot.com/2012/08/amnesty-international-is-us-state.html

91 Brian Berletic, "Why is Amnesty International FINALLY Reporting on Kiev's War Crimes Months Later?" *TheAltWorld,* August 16, 2022. https://thealtworld.com/ anthony_cartalucci/why-is-amnesty-international-finally-reporting-on-kievs-war-crimes-months-later

92 Great Game India, "The Secret History Of How British Intelligence Created Amnesty International," September 29, 2020, published by Vanessa Beeley on *The Wall Will Fall,* October 5, 2020. https://thewallwillfall.org/2020/10/05/the-secret-history-of-how-british-intelligence-created-amnesty-international/

93 John Perry and Rick Sterling, "How Can Some Progressives Get Basic Information about Nicaragua So Wrong?," *L.A. Progressive,* December 20, 2021. https://www.laprogressive.com/latin-america-2/slandered-election

94 Giorgi Lomsadze, "Far from FARA? Georgia's foreign agent law controversy," *Eurasianet,* March 6, 2023. https://eurasianet.org/far-from-fara-georgias-foreign-agent-law-controversy

Reuters, "Parliament in Georgia Gives Initial Approval to 'Foreign Agents' Law," *VOA,* March 7, 2023. https://www.voanews.com/a/parliament-in-georgia-gives-initial-approval-to-foreign-agents-law/6994450.html

Martin Russell, "European Parliament, 'Foreign agents' and 'undesirables': Russian civil society in danger of extinction?" [briefing], EPRS (European Parliamentary Research Service), March 2022. https://www.europarl.europa.eu/RegData/etudes/BRIE/2022/729297/EPRS_BRI(2022)729297_EN.pdf

Congressional Research Service, "Foreign Agents Registration Act: An Overview," *In Focus,* updated March 7, 2019. https://crsreports.congress.gov/product/pdf/IF/IF10499

Maria Katamadze, "Georgia's 'foreign agent' bill undermines EU hopes," *DW,* March 7, 2023. https://www.dw.com/en/georgias-foreign-agent-bill-undermines-eu-hopes/a-64908879

European Federation of Journalists, "Bulgaria: 'Foreign agent' bill threatens media freedom," November 17, 2022. https://europeanjournalists.org/blog/2022/11/17/bulgaria-foreign-agent-bill-threatens-media-freedom/

U.S. Department of State, U.S. Embassy in Sarajevo, "Statement on the Proposed Republika Srpska Legislation" [press release], March 10, 2023. https://ba.usembassy.gov/statement-on-the-proposed-republika-srpska-legislation/

95 Sophiko Megrelidze, "Georgia drops foreign agents law after massive protests," *ABC News,* March 10, 2023. https://abcnews.go.com/International/wireStory/georgia-drops-foreign-agents-law-after-massive-protests-97763776

96 Tania Mason, "Charity Commission has 'no jurisdiction' over board member's payment from Amnesty," *civilsociety.co.uk,* February 21, 2011.

97 "Amnesty's pay-offs spark outrage," *The Sunday Times* (London), February 20, 2011.

98 Niki May Young, "Paying off Khan was 'least-worst option' according to Amnesty's IEC chair," *Civil Society,* March 1, 2011. https://www.civilsociety.co.uk/news/paying-off-khan-was--least-worst-option--according-to-amnesty-s-iec-chair.html

"Revealed: Amnesty International's £800,000 payoffs to two bosses," *Daily Mail Online,* February 18, 2011. https://www.dailymail.co.uk/news/article-1358537/Revealed-Amnesty-Internationals-800-000-pay-offs-bosses.html

NGO Monitor, "The Irene Khan Affair," December 30, 2015. https://www.ngo-monitor.org/reports/the_irene_khan_affair/

99 Westminster News, "Amnesty boss gets secret £1/2m pay-off," *Conservatives,* February 19, 2011. https://www.philip-davies.org.uk/news/amnesty-boss-gets-secret-ps12m-pay

100 Women's International League for Peace and Freedom (WILPF), *Vision, Values and Approach.* https://www.wilpf.org/vision/

101 The Nobel Peace Prize, *Nomination.* https://www.nobelpeaceprize.org/nobel-peace-prize/nomination/

102 Fredrik Heffermehl, Alfred Nobel, 2006.

103 Doc A/HRC/27/51. https://documents-dds-ny.un.org/doc/UNDOC/GEN/G14/087/30/PDF/G1408730.pdf

104 Celtic Thunder, *Christmas 1915,* video, 3:45, posted on October 23, 2014. https://www.youtube.com/watch?v=JG3l-OBdcPI

105 In 1875 *The Arbitrator,* a journal that espoused pacifism, wrote: "War does not decide who is right or who is wrong but simply who is strongest." *The Arbitrator: A Journal Established to Promote the Principles of the Workmen's Peace Association,* no. 40 (London: William Randal Cremer, 1975), p. 11 (col. 1). In 1946 the *Rotarian* printed a variant that replaced "war" with "atom bomb": "The atom bomb, some grim wit has said, will never determine who is right—only who is left." *The Rotarian* (Rotary International, December 1946), p. 64 (col. 1).

106 NGO Monitor, "International Progress Organization: Analysis," March 30, 2006.   https://www.ngo-monitor.org/reports/international_progress_organization_analysis/

UIA Global Civil Society Database, *International Progress Organization (IPO)* https://uia.org/s/or/en/1100009049

107 IPO, *Dialogue among civilizations.* http://www.i-p-o.org/civilizational_dialogue-roster.htm

108 IPO, *Papers and Resolutions on United Nations Reform and the Advancement of International Law,* http://www.i-p-o.org/unref.htm

Hans Köchler, *The Voting Procedure in the United Nations Security Council: Examining a Normative Contradiction in the UN Charter and its Consequences on International Relations* (Hans Köchler, 1991). http://www.i-p-o.org/Koechler-Voting_Procedure-UN_Security_Council.pdf

109 I.P.O. Information Service, "Blueprint for Peace in Ukraine," March 11, 2022. http://i-p-o.org/IPO-nr-UKRAINE-PEACE-11March2022.htm

110 International Human Rights Association of American Minorities (iHRAAM). https://ihraam.org/

111 iHRAAM, *African Americans.* https://ihraam.org/situations/african-americans/

iHRAAM, *Borinken (Puerto Rico),* "Proclamation/ Declaration of Freedom and Sovereignty of the Natioinal Sovereign State of Borinken." https://ihraam.org/situations/boricuas-situation-borinken-puerto-rico/

iHRAAM, *Lil'wat.* https://ihraam.org/situations/lilwat/

112 Fondation GIPRI. https://gipri.ch

113 Fondation GIPRI, *Multimédia* [conference], October 15, 2022. https://gipri.ch/evenements/conferences/conference-quelle-paix-pour-quel-ordre-du-monde/multimedia-2/

Alexandre Berenstein and Zidane Meriboute, "Geneva International Peace Research Institute (GIPRI) Colloquium on 'Nuclear Arms and International Law,' held during 1-3 February 1984 in Geneva, Switzerland," *Environmental Conservation, 11,* no. 2 (1984), 186-87; at *RERO doc Digital Library.* https://doc.rero.ch/record/295333

114 Alexandre Berenstein and Zidane Meriboute, *Geneva International Peace Research Institute (GIPRI) Colloquium on 'Nuclear Arms and International Law', held during 1–3 February 1984 in Geneva, Switzerland* (Cambridge University Press, August 24, 2009). https://www.cambridge.org/core/journals/environmental-conservation/article/abs/geneva-international-peace-research-institute-gipri-colloquium-on-nuclear-arms-and-international-law-held-during-13-february-1984-in-geneva-switzerland/D0637DFE887191F8D012908A9961104C

115 Fondation GIPRI, *Fondation.* https://gipri.ch/institut/fondation/

116 PEN International. https://www.pen-international.org/

117 PEN International, *Bled Manifesto of the Writers for Peace Committee,* https://static1.squarespace.com/static/628f9ae10b12c8255bd8814d/t/63e63b2624e8f95619f61434/1676032811096/Bled+Manifesto+of+the+Writers+for+Peace.pdf

I am the delegate of PEN Centre Suisse romand to the Writers for Peace Committee.

118 PEN International, "US/UK: Decision to extradite Julian Assange to the United States condemned," June 17, 2022. https://www.pen-international.org/news/usuk-decision-to-extradite-julian-assange-to-the-united-states-condemned?rq=.

See also the commemorative book issued to celebrate PEN's years.

119 Stefan Simanowitz, "How the US pursuit of Julian Assange is a distraction from impunity for war crimes," Amnesty International, October 26, 2021. https://www.amnesty.org/en/latest/news/2021/10/how-the-us-pursuit-of-julian-assange-is-a-distraction-from-impunity-for-war-crimes/

"UK: Refusal by Supreme Court to grant Assange right to appeal is "a blow for justice"," Amnesty International, March 14, 2022. https://www.amnesty.org/en/latest/news/2022/03/uk-refusal-by-supreme-court-to-grant-assange-right-to-appeal-is-a-blow-for-justice/

120 Amnesty International, *USA must drop charges against Julian Assange* [petition]. https://www.amnesty.org/en/petition/julian-assange-usa-justice/

121 Human Rights Watch, *Coalition Letter to US Department of Justice: Drop Assange Prosecution,* February 8, 2021. https://www.hrw.org/news/2021/02/08/coalition-letter-us-department-justice-drop-assange-prosecution

See also Dinah PoKempner, "UK Should Reject Extraditing Julian Assange to US," Human Rights Watch, June 19, 2018. https://www.hrw.org/news/2018/06/19/uk-should-reject-extraditing-julian-assange-us

Dinah PoKempner, "New Assange Charges Threaten Investigative Journalism," Human Rights Watch, May 24, 2019. https://www.hrw.org/news/2019/05/24/new-assange-charges-threaten-investigative-journalism

122 *Who Is Hrant Dink?* https://hrantdink.org/en/hrant-dink/3565-who-is-hrant-dink

123 See my book, *The Genocide against the Armenians and the Relevance of the 1948 Genocide Convention* (Beirut: Haigazian University Press, 2010).

124 *United Nations International Covenant on Civil and Political Rights,* "General comment No. 34 – Article 19: Freedoms of opinion and expression," Human Rights Committee 102nd session, September 12, 2011. https://www2.ohchr.org/english/bodies/hrc/docs/GC34.pdf

125 "Appel de Blois," *Liberté pour l'histoire;* archived at The Wayback Machine, August 28, 2008. https://web.archive.org/web/20081111031740/http://www.lph-asso.fr/actualites/42.html

126 *Eleanor Lives! A Plan for Humanity.* https://eleanorlives.org/

127 *Eleanor Lives!* Blog. https://eleanorlives.org/daily-planet-blog/

128 The Nobel Peace Prize 1968: *René Cassin—Facts.* https://www.nobelprize.org/prizes/peace/1968/cassin/facts/

129 African Court on Human and Peoples' Rights. https://www.african-court.org/wpafc/

130 Alfred de Zayas, An International Court of Human Rights," *Nordic Journal of International Law* 61 (1–4):267, April 16, 2014. https://www.deepdyve.com/lp/brill/an-international-court-of-human-rights-N0d0HxEk8H

131 AEDIDH. http://aedidh.org/es/
Carmelo Faleh Pérez, "En defensa del derecho internacional," *La Provincia,* March 27, 2022. http://aedidh.org/wp-content/uploads/2022/03/En-defensa-del-derecho-internacional-La-Provinci_220327_104845.pdf

AEDIDH, "Sáhara Occidental: una carta que nunca se debió escribir," March 22, 2022. http://aedidh.org/es/2022/03/22/sahara-occidental-una-carta-que-nunca-se-debio-escribir/

AEDIDH, "Ucrania: la paz debe ser respetada urgentemente, la legalidad internacional respetada y los derechos humanos protegidos," February 26, 2022. http://aedidh.org/es/2022/02/26/ucrania-la-paz-debe-ser-respetada-urgentemente-la-legalidad-internacional-respetada-y-los-derechos-humanos-protegidos/

Matiangai Sirleaf, AEDIDH, *Report on the Regional Expert Meeting on the Human Right to Peace,* South African Human Rights Commission, Johannesburg, South Africa, April 17, 2009. http://www.aedidh.org/sites/default/files/Report-of-SA.pdf

Federico Mayor Zaragoza, Carmelo Faleh Pérez and Carlos Villan Duan, *Hacia la Paz desde los derechos humanos* (UNESCO, 2008).

132 AEDIDH, *Publicaciones AEDIDH.* http://aedidh.org/es/publicaciones/

133 Carmen R. Rueda y Carlos Villán (eds.), *La Declaración de Luarca sobre el Derecho Humano a la Paz,* Edición parcialmente trilingüe (castellano/inglés/francés) (Madú, 2007 y 2008). http://aedidh.org/es/la-declaracion-de-luarca-sobre-el-derecho-humano-a-la-paz/

134 *Declaración de Bilbao sobre el Derecho Humano a la Paz.* https://fund-culturadepaz.org/wp-content/uploads/2021/02/Declaracion-Bilbao_DerechoHumanoPaz.pdf

135 *Declaración de Santiago Sobre el Derecho Humano a La Paz.* http://www.aedidh.org/sites/default/files/DS%20pdf%2024%20marzo%2011.pdf

136 AEDIDH, Resultados de buscar: "zayas." http://aedidh.org/es/?s=zayas

137 Adama Dieng (ed.), "The follow-up procedure of the Human Rights Committee," *ICJ review* no. 47, December 1991.

138 Beirut: Haigazian University Press, 2010.

139 Wikipedia, *Jacqueline Berenstein-Wavre.* https://en.wikipedia.org/wiki/Jacqueline_Berenstein-Wavre

140 Alexandre Berenstein, *Labour Law in Switzerland* 3rd edition (Wolters Kluwer; January 30, 2018). https://www.amazon.com/Labour-Law-Switzerland-Alexandre-Berenstein/dp/9041199608

141 Zeki Ergas, *In Search of a Better World* (Geneva 2007).

CHAPTER 7

1 Unistica, *Fourth power – the role of the media in modern society.* https://en.unistica.com/fourth-power-the-role-of-the-media-in-modern-society/

2 Kieran Davies, "What is the Fourth Estate and where does the term for the media come from?," *The Sun,* January 17, 2023. https://www.thesun.co.uk/news/6600872/fourth-estate-media-fourth-estate-term/

3 United Nations Human Rights, "UN expert calls for democratization of the media: A Day for Democracy" [press release], September 15, 2017. https://www.ohchr.org/en/press-releases/2017/09/un-expert-calls-democratization-media

4 Fredrik Heffermehl, *The Nobel Peace Prize: What Nobel Really Wanted* (Praeger, 2010). In 1948 the selection of members of the Nobel Committee was delegated by the Norwegian Parliament (contrary to what Nobel prescribed) to the major political parties. According to Heffermehl, committee membership is deemed recognition for political services, instead of non-partisan peace activism.

5 "The Ministry of Truth (had) three slogans: WAR IS PEACE, FREEDOM IS SLAVERY and IGNORANCE IS STRENGTH." "Sampler From the Book," *The New York Times,* January 18, 1984. https://www.nytimes.com/1984/01/18/arts/ministry-truth-had-three-slogans-war-peace-freedom-slavery-ignorance-strength.html

Natalie Frank, "The Meaning of War Is Peace, Freedom Is Slavery, and Ignorance Is Strength in Orwell's '1984,'" *Owlcation,* June 30, 2022. https://owlcation.com/humanities/The-Meaning-of-War-is-Peace-Freedom-is-Slavery-and-Ignorance-is-Strength-in-Orwells-1984

6 See my 2015 and 2016 reports to the UN Human Rights Council and General Assembly – https://www.ohchr.org/en/special-procedures/ie-international-order/annual-thematic-reports – and my November 16, 2015 op-ed in the *Guardian,* "How can Philip Morris sue Uruguay over its tobacco laws?" https://www.theguardian.com/commentisfree/2015/nov/16/philip-morris-uruguay-tobacco-isds-human-rights

7 Naomi Klein, *The Shock Doctrine: The Rise of Disaster Capitalism* (Picador, 2008.) See also my 2017 report to the General Assembly on IMF misconduct: https://www.ohchr.org/en/special-procedures/ie-international-order/annual-thematic-reports

8 Walter Lippmann, *Public Opinion* (New York: Macmillan, 1922; reprinted by Martino Fine Books, 2012), 226.

9 Edward Bernays, *The Edward Bernays Reader: From Propaganda to the Engineering of Consent* (New York: Ig Publishing, New York 2021).

10 Malcolm X, born Malcolm Litte in Nebraska, was assassinated in New York in 1965 at the age of 39.

11 See JFK's commencement address at American University in Washington, D.C., of June 10, 1963. https://www.jfklibrary.org/archives/other-resources/john-f-kennedy-speeches/american-university-19630610

Rick Sterling, "JFK and the Strategy of Peace," *Mint Press News,* January 27, 2021. https://www.mintpressnews.com/jfk-foreign-policy-strategy-of-peace/274787/

12 Robert F. Kennedy, "Tribute to John F. Kennedy at the Democratic National Convention, Atlantic City, New Jersey, August 27, 1964," JFK Presidential Library and Museum. https://www.jfklibrary.org/learn/about-jfk/the-kennedy-family/robert-f-kennedy/robert-f-kennedy-speeches/tribute-to-john-f-kennedy-at-the-democratic-national-convention-atlantic-city-new-jersey-august-27

13 See "Military-Industrial Complex Speech, Dwight D. Eisenhower, 1961," Yale Law School Lillian Goldman Law Library. https://avalon.law.yale.edu/20th_century/eisenhower001.asp

14 The date of Eisenhower's address at West Point is June 3, 1947. https://www.quotescosmos.com/quotes/Dwight-D.-Eisenhower-quote-8.html

15 Multiple clips of Albright's remark on *YouTube:* https://duckduckgo.com/?q=madelein+albright+the+indispensable+country&atb=v314-1&iax=videos&ia=videos&iai=https%3A%2F%2Fwww.youtube.com%2Fwatch%3Fv%3D-0AF4cyRFJo

William Danvers, "Madeleine Albright: The indispensable American" [op-ed], *The Hill,* March 24, 2022. https://thehill.com/opinion/national-security/599570-madeleine-albright-the-indispensable-american/

16 First published in 1964; later Beacon Press edition, 2010.

17 "Scott Ritter: US Domination On Russia Failed, Western Media Nonsensical Talk On Using Nuclear Weapon," video, 12:14, posted by *Finance Mail,* December 20, 2022. https://www.youtube.com/watch?v=zuv4PAlKIrA

Amit Sengupta, "Angela Merkel's revelation on Minsk Agreements | MINSK Explained | Russia Ukraine war," *Geopolitics,* video, 16:44, December 14, 2022. https://www.youtube.com/watch?v=0-57KOwG9co

18 "Chomsky says US is world's biggest terrorist," *Euronews,* April 17, 2015. https://www.euronews.com/2015/04/17/chomsky-says-us-is-world-s-biggest-terrorist

Noam Chomsky, "The Leading Terrorist State" [op-ed], *Truthout,* November 3, 2014. https://truthout.org/articles/the-leading-terrorist-state/

19 Brett Wilkins, "Jimmy Carter: US 'Most Warlike Nation in History of the World,'" *CounterPunch,* April 19, 2019. https://www.counterpunch.org/2019/04/19/jimmy-carter-us-most-warlike-nation-in-history-of-the-world/

20 "The Stages of Grief: What Do You Need to Know?," *Healthline.* https://www.healthline.com/health/stages-of-grief

21 Chris Hedges provides us with many useful analyses of the Ukraine war. See, for example, "The Chris Hedges Report: Ukraine and the crisis of media censorship," video, 36:00, *The Real News Network,* September 2, 2022. https://www.youtube.com/watch?v=N0H7PIJcEP0.

For German views see also:

Alice Schwarzer und Sahra Wagenknecht, "Manifest für Frieden" [petition] at *Change.org.* https://www.change.org/p/manifestfuerfrieden-aufstandfuerfrieden.

Stefanie Hildebrant, "Frauen 'für den Frieden': Alice Schwarzer und Sahra Wagenknecht veröffentlichen Manifest," *Berliner Kurier,* February 10, 2022. https://www.berliner-kurier.de/berlin/frauen-fuer-den-frieden-alice-schwarzer-und-sarah-wagenknecht-veroeffentlichen-manifest-li.316329.

Alice Weigel, Member of Parliament, before the Bundestag, "Alice Weidel's Speech on Ukraine Crisis (eng subs)," video clip, 2:59, posted by *The Truth Seeker,* March 10, 2022. https://www.youtube.com/watch?v=OyspXX4ikWc.

Klaus von Dohnanyi, *Nationale Interessen. Orientierung für deutsche und europäische Politik in Zeiten globaler Umbrüche* (Siedler Verlag, 2022).

22 Roger L. Simon, "Who's Worse—Julian Assange or the New York Times and Washington Post?," *PJ Media,* April 11, 2019. https://pjmedia.com/rogerlsimon/2019/04/11/whos-worse-julian-assange-or-the-ny-times-and-washington-post-n218877

23 See A.B. Abrams, *Atrocity Fabrication and Its Consequences: How Fake News Shapes World Order* (Clarity Press, 2023). https://www.claritypress.com/book-author/a-b-abrams/

24 The Daily Take Team, The Thom Hartmann Show, "How the Media Fueled the War in Iraq" [op-ed], Truthout, March 20, 2013. https://truthout.org/articles/how-the-media-fueled-the-war-in-iraq/

Alan MacLeod, *Propaganda in the Information Age* (Routledge, 2021).

Jeremy R. Hammond, "The Lies that Led to the Iraq War and the Persistent Myth of 'Intelligence Failure,'" *Foreign Policy Journal,* September 8, 2012. https://www.foreignpolicyjournal.com/2012/09/08/the-lies-that-led-to-the-iraq-war-and-the-persistent-myth-of-intelligence-failure/

Anup Shah, "Iraq War Media Reporting, Journalism and Propaganda," *Global Issues,* August 1, 2007. https://www.globalissues.org/article/461/media-reporting-journalism-and-propaganda

Alan MacLeod, "Humanitarian imperialism: How the media exploits liberals' empathy to sell them war," *Salon,* March 7, 2021. https://www.salon.com/2021/03/07/humanitarian-imperialism-how-the-media-exploits-liberals-empathy-to-sell-them-war_partner/

25 "'Nearly Every War Has Been The Result Of Media Lies': Julian Assange, State-Corporate Media And Ukraine," *Media Lens,* December 14, 2022. https://www.medialens.org/2022/nearly-every-war-has-been-the-result-of-media-lies-julian-assange-state-corporate-media-and-ukraine/

26 "The Great Iraq War Fraud," *Media Lens,* July 13, 2016. https://www.medialens.org/2016/the-great-iraq-war-fraud/

Anup Shah, op. cit. https://www.globalissues.org/article/461/media-reporting-journalism-and-propaganda

Christopher Bedford, "Media Coverage of Iraq Is A Case Study of Ignorance and Manipulation," *The Federalist,* January 7, 2020. https://thefederalist.com/2020/01/07/media-coverage-of-iraq-is-a-case-study-of-ignorance-and-manipulation/

27 Wesley Morgan, "Pentagon looks to restart top-secret programs in Ukraine," *Washington Post,* February 10, 2023. https://www.washingtonpost.com/national-security/2023/02/10/us-special-operations-ukraine-surrogate-program/, also Caitlin Johnstone in Melbourne, Australia.

28 Guy Mettan, *Creating Russophobia* (Clarity Press, 2017); *Europe's Existential Dilemma* (Clarity Press, 2021).

29 Verso Books, New York, 2022.

30 Elizabeth Nix, "What Was the Dreyfus Affair?" *History,* January 14, 2015; updated August 23, 2018. https://www.history.com/news/what-was-the-dreyfus-affair

31 Daniel Ellsberg, former United States military analyst, blew the whistle on U.S. Government crimes during the Vietnam War by leaking the "Pentagon Papers," which revealed revealed that, early on, the government had knowledge that the war as then resourced could most likely not be won. Ellsberg was charged under the U.S. Espionage Act of 1917, carrying a total maximum sentence of 115 years. Due to governmental misconduct and illegal evidence gathering, the charges were later dropped. Ellsberg's disclosures are credited as a major factor in ending the war. See National Whistleblower Center, *Daniel Ellsberg: National Security Whistleblower.* https://www.whistleblowers.org/whistleblowers/daniel-ellsberg/

32 A.B. Abrams, *World War in Syria: Global Conflict on Middle Eastern Battlefields* (Clarity Press, 2021). https://www.claritypress.com/product/world-war-in-syria-global-conflict-on-middle-eastern-battlefields/

33 Syrian Observatory for Human Rights (SOHR). https://www.syriahr.com/en/

34 Chloe Hadjimatheou, "Mayday: How the White Helmets and James Le Mesurier got pulled into a deadly battle for truth," *BBC News,* February 27, 2021. https://www.bbc.com/news/stories-56126016

"James Le Mesurier: White Helmets co-founder died from fall, Turkey says," *BBC News,* December 16, 2019. https://www.bbc.com/news/world-europe-50808180

"BBC Radio 4 launches major new podcast Mayday: Investigating The Life And Death Of James Le Mesurier," *BBC Media Center,* November 4, 2020. https://www.bbc.co.uk/mediacentre/latestnews/2020/radio4-podcast-mayday

35 Michael Safi, "British founder of White Helmets found dead in Istanbul," *The Guardian,* November 11, 2019. https://www.theguardian.com/world/2019/nov/11/british-founder-of-white-helmets-found-dead-in-istanbul-james-le-mesurier

36 "The White Helmets | FULL FEATURE," Netflix video, 40:01, April 17, 2020. https://www.youtube.com/watch?v=fQM6t1oSQkE

37 Ben Norton, "White Helmets corruption scandal deepens: Dutch gov't investigated parent org for fraud, but covered it up," *The Grayzone,* May 7, 2021. https://thegrayzone.com/2021/05/07/syria-white-helmets-mayday-fraud-netherlands/

Aaron Maté, "Chain of corruption: how the White Helmets compromised OPCW investigations in Syria," *The Greyzone,* September 9, 2022. https://thegrayzone.com/2022/09/09/syrian-white-helmets-opcw/

Rick Sterling, "The 'White Helmets' Controversy," *Constorium News,* July 22, 2018. https://consortiumnews.com/2018/07/22/the-white-helmets-controversy/

38 Kit Klarenberg, "Questions about BBC producer's ties to UK intelligence follow 'Mayday' White Helmets whitewash," *The Grayzone,* April 7, 2021. https://thegrayzone.com/2021/04/07/bbc-white-helmets-mayday-uk-intelligence/

39 Rick Sterling, "The 'White Helmets' Controversy," *Constorium News,* July 22, 2018. https://consortiumnews.com/2018/07/22/the-white-helmets-controversy/

40 Crescent International, Authors: Eva Bartlett. https://crescent.icit-digital.org/authors/eva-bartlett

PV Vancouver Bureau, "Eva Bartlett Dismantles Media Lies about Venezuela and Syria," Community Party of BC, May 2019. http://cpcbc.ca/?p=666

41 "UN Press Conference on Syria Aleppo - Eva Bartlett Exposes Media LIES - 09-12-2016," video, 22:27, posted by *UKIP Debate,* December 14, 2016. https://www.youtube.com/watch?v=4Ap1_4Ak2WA

42 Carl Bunderson, "Carmelite nun from Syria describes pain of civil war," *Catholic News Agency,* November 21, 2013. https://www.catholicnewsagency.com/news/28499/carmelite-nun-from-syria-describes-pain-of-civil-war

Monica Clark, "Controversial nun speaks out on war in Syria," *National Catholic Reporter,* November 14, 2013. https://www.ncronline.org/news/world/controversial-nun-speaks-out-war-syria

43 "Mother Agnes-Mariam: 'Assad's nun' or peace activist?," *CBC News,* December 2, 2013. https://www.cbc.ca/news/world/mother-agnes-mariam-assad-s-nun-or-peace-activist-1.2448458

44 Dave DeCamp, "OPCW Tries To Discredit Whistleblowers in Response to Douma Leaks," *Activist Post,* February 10, 2020. https://www.activistpost.com/2020/02/opcw-tries-to-discredit-whistleblowers-in-response-to-douma-leaks.html

45 Aaron Maté, "OPCW Syria whistleblower and ex-director attacked by US, UK, France at UN. *The Grayzone,* October 7, 2020. https://thegrayzone.com/2020/10/07/opcw-syria-whistleblower-and-ex-opcw-chief-attacked-by-us-uk-french-at-un/

Ben Norton, "OPCW investigator testifies at UN that no chemical attack took place in Douma, Syria," *The Grayzone,* January 22, 2020. https://thegrayzone.com/2020/01/22/ian-henderson-opcw-whistleblower-un-no-chemical-attack-douma-syria/

"Was 'gas attack' in Douma, Syria staged? OPCW inspector speaks out at UN," video, 2:19, posted by *The Grayzone,* January 22, 2020. https://www.youtube.com/watch?v=_2QQml9S52g

Aaron Maté, "New Leaks Shatter OPCW's Attacks on Douma Whistleblowers," *Consotrium News,* February 11, 2020. https://consortiumnews.com/2020/02/11/new-leaks-shatter-opcws-attacks-on-douma-whistleblowers/

Dave DeCamp, "Syria Chemical Attack: Douma Whistleblowers Respond to OPCW's Attempts to Discredit Them," *Global Research,* March 10, 2020. https://www.globalresearch.ca/douma-whistleblowers-respond-opcw-attacks/5706111

46 https://www.bellingcat.com/

47 Bellingcat Investigation Team, "The OPCW Douma Leaks Part 2: We Need To Talk About Henderson" *Bellingcat,* January 17, 2020. https://www.bellingcat.com/news/mena/2020/01/17/the-opcw-douma-leaks-part-2-we-need-to-talk-about-henderson/

48 Aaron Maté, "Chain of corruption: How the White Helmets compromised OPCW investigations in Syria," *The Grayzone,* September 9, 2022. https://thegrayzone.com/2022/09/09/syrian-white-helmets-opcw/

49 Mehdi Hasan, "'We Know Where Your Kids Live': How John Bolton Once Threatened an International Official," *The Intercept,* March 29, 2018. https://theintercept.com/2018/03/29/john-bolton-trump-bush-bustani-kids-opcw/

Michal Kranz, "'We know where your kids live': Trump's new national security adviser reportedly made an implicit threat against the family of a retired Brazilian diplomat in 2002," *Business Insider,* March 29, 2018. https://www.businessinsider.com/john-bolton-threatened-family-of-brazilian-diplomat-iraq-war-2002-2018-3?op=1&r=US&IR=T

50 Rick Sterling, "Biased Reporting on Syria in the Service of War," *CounterPunch,* April 20, 2015. https://www.counterpunch.org/2015/04/20/biased-reporting-on-syria-in-the-service-of-war/

51 Alan MacLeod is author of *Bad News From Venezuela: 20 Years of Fake News and Misreporting* (Routledge, 2018). His latest book, *Propaganda in the Information Age: Still Manufacturing Consent,* was published by Routledge in May 2019.

52 Alan MacLeod, "How Bellingcat Launders National Security State Talking Points into the Press," *Mint Press News,* April 9, 2021. https://www.mintpressnews.com/bellingcat-intelligence-agencies-launders-talking-points-media/276603

"'It May Be In No One's Interest To Reveal More': Cancelling Facts That Challenge Establishment Power," *Media Lens,* April 18, 2023. https://www.medialens.org/2023/it-may-be-in-no-ones-interest-to-reveal-more-cancelling-facts-that-challenge-establishment-power//

53 Ibid.

54 Jon Jackson, "Navalny Dying by Illness May be Putin's End Game: Professor," *Newsweek,* January 9, 2023. https://www.msn.com/en-us/news/world/navalny-dying-by-illness-may-be-putins-end-game-professor/ar-AA169031

"Russia Navalny: Poisoned opposition leader held after flying home," *BBC News,* January 17, 2021. https://www.bbc.com/news/world-europe-55694598

Haroon Siddique, "Muslim employee sues Amnesty over sacking after Alexei Navalny objections," *The Guardian,* February 8, 2023. https://www.theguardian.com/world/2023/feb/08/amnesty-international-employee-sacked-alexei-navalny

55 "Russian spy poisoning: What we know so far," *BBC News,* October 8, 2018. https://www.bbc.com/news/uk-43315636

56 The Complete Works of George Orwell: *1984* Part 2, Chapter 9. http://george-orwell.org/1984/16.html

57 "She's exposing the TRUTH in Ukraine and they don't like it | Redacted Conversation with Eva Bartlett," video, 3:17, posted by *Redacted* on May 1, 2022. https://www.youtube.com/watch?v=OzMLPSXb7RU

"Eva Bartlett: What's really going on in Ukraine | Right Now | Ickonic," video, 4:45, posted by *Ickonic* on March 4, 2022. https://www.youtube.com/watch?v=hZgEjNp6DSc

"Eva Bartlett Reports from Mariupol: 'Ukraine Forces Used Scorched Earth Tactics,'" *Internationalist 360°*, April 28, 2022. https://mronline.org/2022/04/28/eva-bartlett-reports-from-mariupol/

"Eva Bartlett: Western Silence As Ukraine Targets Civilians in Donbass," video, 7:06, posted by *Shiller Institute* on December 23, 2022. https://www.youtube.com/watch?v=Pg_AxQqqj0w

"Eva Bartlett: 'Ukraine Has a Kill List, and I'm On It,'" *21st Century Wire*, June 12, 2022. https://21stcenturywire.com/2022/06/12/eva-bartlett-ukraine-has-a-kill-list-and-im-on-it/

Pam Barker, "Ukraine Army War Crimes, Which We're Not Supposed to Know About," *Europe Reloaded*, October 25, 2022. https://www.europereloaded.com/ukraine-army-war-crimes/

58 Eva Bartlett, "The West is silent as Ukraine targets civilians in Donetsk using banned 'butterfly' mines," *MR Online*, August 18, 2022. https://mronline.org/2022/08/18/eva-bartlett-the-west-is-silent-as-ukraine-targets-civilians-in-donetsk-using-banned-butterfly-mines/

59 Referred to as a "sham" tribunal by CBC: Justin Ling, "In Russia, a 'sham tribunal' investigates what it says are Ukraine's war crime," *CBC News*, July 17, 2022. https://www.cbc.ca/news/world/russia-tribunal-ukraine-1.6512853

60 Sonja Van den Ende, "Eye-Witness Report from Donbass: How the War Looks from the Russian Side," *CovertAction*, April 7, 2022.

61 Freddie Sayers, "Jeffrey Sachs: Who really blew up the Nord Stream 2 pipeline?," video, 43:32, interview on *UnHerd*, February 15, 2023. https://www.youtube.com/watch?v=_Fv_nKyF_5g

62 Alind Chauhan, "US bombed Nord Stream gas pipelines, says top investigative journalist. What happened under the Baltic Sea last year?," *The Indian Express*, February 10, 2023. https://indianexpress.com/article/explained/explained-global/us-bombed-nord-stream-gas-pipelines-journalist-claims-8434423/

George Koo, "Nord Stream explosions hard to cover up," *Asia Times*, February 15, 2023. https://asiatimes.com/2023/02/nord-stream-explosions-hard-to-cover-up/

Wang Qi, "US urged to explain Nord Stream blasts after Pulitzer winner's probe," *Global Times*, February 9, 2023. https://www.globaltimes.cn/page/202302/1285165.shtml

63 Alex Blair, "Columbia professor Jeffrey Sachs yanked off air after accusing US of sabotaging Nord Stream pipeline," *New York Post*, October 4, 2022. https://nypost.com/2022/10/04/jeffrey-sachs-yanked-off-air-after-accusing-us-of-sabotaging-nord-stream/

Jeffrey Sachs yanked off air after accusing US of sabotaging Nord Stream," *Daily Bank News*, October 6, 2022. https://thebank.news/2022/10/06/jeffrey-sachs-yanked-off-air-after-accusing-us-of-sabotaging-nord-stream/

64 Jacob J, "US Bombed Russia's Nord Stream Gas Pipeline After Months-Long Planning by White House – Seymour Hersh," *International Business Times,* February 10, 2023. https://www.ibtimes.sg/us-bombed-russias-nord-stream-gas-pipeline-after-months-long-planning-by-white-house-seymour-68965

Caitlin Doornbos and Samuel Chamberlain, "Pulitzer winner Seymour Hersh claims US Navy behind Nord Stream 2 pipeline explosion," *New York Post,* February 8, 2023. https://nypost.com/2023/02/08/seymour-hersh-claims-us-navy-behind-nord-stream-2-pipeline-explosion/

Jake Johnson, "Seymour Hersh Report Alleges US Was Behind Nord Stream Pipeline Sabotage," *Common Dreams,* February 8, 2023. https://www.commondreams.org/news/seymour-hersh-nord-stream

Leah Barkoukis, "Bombshell Report Alleges US Behind Sabotage of Nord Stream Pipeline," *Townhall,* February 9, 2023. https://townhall.com/tipsheet/leahbarkoukis/2023/02/09/nord-stream-report-n2619370

Andre Damon, "Seymour Hersh's exposure of the Nord Stream bombing: A lesson and a warning," *Defend Democracy Press,* February 12, 2023. https://www.defenddemocracy.press/seymour-hershs-exposure-of-the-nord-stream-bombing-a-lesson-and-a-warning/

65 "Sweden shuns formal joint investigation of Nord Stream leak, citing national security," *Reuters,* October 14, 2022. https://www.reuters.com/world/europe/sweden-shuns-formal-joint-investigation-nord-stream-leak-citing-national-2022-10-14/

Charlie Duxbury, "Nord Stream investigation tests EU intelligence sharing around the Baltic," *Politico,* October 28, 2022. https://www.politico.eu/article/sweden-denmark-germany-nord-stream-investigation-tests-eu-intelligence-sharing-around-the-baltic/

66 Jan Oberg, *About and CV,* https://janoberg.me/om/

67 Jan Oberg, "Of course, Nordstream was blown up by the US and NATO allies: A US economic war on submissive allies." *The Transnational TFF,* February 12, 2023. https://transnational.live/2023/02/12/of-course-nordstream-was-blown-up-by-the-us-and-nato-allies-a-us-economic-war-on-submissive-allies/

68 Jan Oberg, "Why NATO is not defensive, but outdated and should be dissolved," *Transnational TFF,* April 14, 2022. https://transnational.live/2022/04/14/why-nato-is-not-defensive-but-outdated-and-should-be-dissolved/

69 "U.S. blowing up Nord Stream pipelines 'economic war' against EU allies: Swedish expert," *CGTN,* February 14, 2023. https://news.cgtn.com/news/2023-02-14/U-S-blew-up-Nord-Stream-pipelines-in-economic-war-with-EU-Expert-1hq83gjpLl6/index.html

70 Jan Oberg, "How stupid do they think we are? A small pro-Ukrainian group in a yacht did whaaaat?," *Jan Oberg* [blog], March 8, 2023. https://janoberg.me/2023/03/08/how-stupid-do-they-think-we-are-a-small-pro-ukrainian-group-in-a-yacht-did-whaaaat/

71 Bradley K. Martin, "Did US raise a false flag on Nord Stream blasts?," *Asia Times,* March 9, 2023. https://asiatimes.com/2023/03/did-us-raise-a-false-flag-on-nordstream-blasts/

72 Glenn Greenwald, "How Covert Agents Infiltrate the Internet to Manipulate, Deceive, and Destroy Reputations," *The Intercept,* February 24, 2014. https://theintercept.com/2014/02/24/jtrig-manipulation/

73 Caitlin Johnstone, "Destroying Western Values To Defend Western Values," *Caitlin's Newsletter,* November 1, 2022. https://caitlinjohnstone.substack.com/p/destroying-western-values-to-defend

74 "How the CIA Paid and Threatened Journalists to Do Its Work," *Daily Beast,* October 14, 2016, updated July 12, 2017. https://www.thedailybeast.com/cheats/2016/10/14/how-the-cia-paid-and-threatened-journalists-to-do-its-work

Kara Goldfarb, "Inside Operation Mockingbird — The CIA's Plan To Infiltrate The Media," *All That's Interesting,* December 4, 2021, updated January 21, 2022. https://allthatsinteresting.com/operation-mockingbird

Paul Szoldra, "5 US national security-related conspiracy theories that turned out to be true," *Insider,* June 16, 2015. https://www.businessinsider.com/5-conspiracy-theories-that-turned-out-to-be-true-2015-6?op=1&r=US&IR=T

75 "CNN ends contract with contributor Mark Lamont Hill after speech on Israel," *The Guardian,* November 29, 2018. https://www.theguardian.com/media/2018/nov/29/cnn-marc-lamont-hill-israel

76 Russia in Global Affairs, *Authors.* https://eng.globalaffairs.ru/authors/glenn-diesen/

77 Øystein Bogen, "Professor beskyldes for å drive russisk propaganda fra norsk universitet," *TV2* The Netherlands, February 5, 2021.

Igor Kuznetsov, "Norwegian Professor Faces Propaganda Accusations Over Collaboration With Russian Media," *Sputnik International,* Feburary 10, 2021.

78 Russia in Global Affairs, *Authors: Glenn Diesen.* https://eng.globalaffairs.ru/authors/glenn-diesen/

79 Glenn Diesen, "War with Russia?" [review], *Russia in Global Affairs,* March 28, 2019. https://eng.globalaffairs.ru/articles/war-with-russia/

80 Vaclav Klaus and Glenn Diesen, "'The EU in its current form is a tragic mistake of the European history,'" *Russia in Global Affairs,* October 10, 2019. https://eng.globalaffairs.ru/articles/the-eu-in-its-current-form-is-a-tragic-mistake-of-the-european-history/

81 Palki Sharma, "Putin and Zelenski were ready to talk in March 2022, but NATO leaders had other plans and refused," *The Transnational TFF,* February 10, 2023. https://transnational.live/2023/02/10/putin-and-zelenski-were-ready-to-talk-in-march-2022-but-nato-leaders-had-other-plans-and-refused/

82 Matthew Vernon Whalan, "An Interview with Norman Finkelstein: 'I'm Not Betraying the Legacy of My Parents in Order to Make Myself Palatable.'" *CounterPunch,* May 17, 2018. https://www.counterpunch.org/2018/05/17/an-interview-with-norman-finkelstein-im-not-betraying-the-legacy-of-my-parents-in-order-to-make-myself-palatable/

83 "'The Holocaust Industry' by Norman G. Finkelstein" [book review and author interview], *Salon,* https://www.salon.com/2000/09/05/finkelstein_4/

But the preeminent Holocaust Historian Raul Hillberg wrote: "He is a well-trained political scientist, has the ability to do the research, did it carefully, and has come up with the right results. I am by no means the only one who, in the coming months or years, will totally agree with Finkelstein's breakthrough" [Jon Wiener, "Giving Chutzpah New Meaning," *The Nation,* June 23, 2005]. See also Raul Hilberg interviews on the Holocaust Industry at *NormanFinkelstein.com.*

84 AP, "DePaul denies tenure to controversial professor," *NBC News,* June 10, 2007. https://www.nbcnews.com/id/wbna19158376

Ron Grossman, "Controversial professor denied tenure at DePaul," *Chicago Tribune,* June 10, 2007. https://www.chicagotribune.com/news/ct-xpm-2007-06-10-0706090462-story.html

85 "The Holocaust Industry – by Norman Finkelstein," book-related article by Finkelstein posted by KSamman, UC Riverside, May 20, 2001. https://wsarch.ucr.edu/wsnmail/2001/msg00838.html

86 Wikipedia, *Michel Chossudovsky.* https://en.wikipedia.org/wiki/Michel_Chossudovsky#Centre_for_Research_on_Globalization

87 Rachel Gordon, "Study finds Wikipedia influences judicial," *MIT News,* July 27, 2022. https://news.mit.edu/2022/study-finds-wikipedia-influences-judicial-behavior-0727

88 Sometimes referred to as the "puppet master": "Leaked: George Soros 'Puppet Master' Behind Ukrainian Regime, Trails Of Corruption Revealed," *Mint Press News,* June 15, 2015. https://www.mintpressnews.com/leaked-george-soros-puppet-master-behind-ukrainian-regime/206574/

See also Alexander Rubinstein, "Billionaire political meddlers, disinformation agents launch 'Good Information Inc.' to fight disinformation," *The Grayzone,* October 27, 2021. https://thegrayzone.com/2021/10/27/billionaire-political-meddlers-disinformation-agents-launch-good-information-inc-to-fight-disinformation/

89 Federal Election Commission, *Citizens United v. FEC.* https://www.fec.gov/legal-resources/court-cases/citizens-united-v-fec/

90 MRC NewsBusters, *George Soros.* https://www.newsbusters.org/non-journalists/george-soros

91 Joseph Vazquez and Dan Schneider, "George Soros: Propaganda Powerhouse," MRC NewsBusters, January 31, 2023. https://www.newsbusters.org/blogs/business/joseph-vazquez/2023/01/31/george-soros-propaganda-powerhouse

See also *Business Leaders: George Soros* / "India FM Jaishankar says Soros dangerous, debate needed on democracy," *MarketScreener,* February 18, 2023. https://www.marketscreener.com/business-leaders/George-Soros-56/news/India-FM-Jaishankar-says-Soros-dangerous-debate-needed-on-democracy--43023321/

"India's foreign minister accused Soros of trying to 'determine how the whole world works," *The Eastern Herald,* February 18, 2023. https://www.easternherald.com/2023/02/18/indias-foreign-minister-accused-soros-of-trying-to-determine-how-the-whole-world-works/

92 Ajit Singh, ""Wipe out China!" US-funded Uyghur activists train as gun-toting foot soldiers for empire," *The Grayzone,* March 31, 2021. https://thegrayzone.com/2021/03/31/china-uyghur-gun-soldiers-empire/

93 Malcolm Moore, "Wikileaks: No bloodshed inside Tiananmen Square, cables claim," *The Telegraph,* June 4, 2011. https://www.telegraph.co.uk/news/worldnews/wikileaks/8555142/Wikileaks-no-bloodshed-inside-Tiananmen-Square-cables-claim.html

94 "Wikileaks: no bloodshed inside Tiananmen Square," *The Mystery of Ephraim* [blog], June 26, 2019. https://wulfstein.org/2019/06/26/wikileaks-no-bloodshed-inside-tiananmen-square/

[…] In 2009, James Miles, who was the BBC correspondent in Beijing at the time, admitted that he had "conveyed the wrong impression" and that "there was no massacre on Tiananmen Square. Protesters who were still in the square when the army reached it were allowed to leave after negotiations with martial law troops…"

95 Alfred de Zayas, "International Day of Democracy – Friday 15 September 2017: UN expert calls for democratization of the media," *Alfred de Zayas' Human Rights Corner* [blog], September 15, 2017. https://dezayasalfred.wordpress.com/2017/09/15/international-day-of-democracy-friday-15-september-2017-un-expert-calls-for-democratization-of-the-media/

For further elucidation on the lack of correlation between the will of the people and the policies that affect them, see Martin Gilens and Benjamin I. Page, "Testing Theories of American Politics: Elites, Interest Groups, and Average Citizens," *Perspectives on Politics 12,* no. 3 (American Political Science Association, 2014). https://scholar.princeton.edu/sites/default/files/mgilens/files/gilens_and_ page_2014_-testing_theories_of_american_politics.doc.pdf

CHAPTER 8

1 Bertrand Russell, "The Triumph of Stupidity" (May 10, 1933), in *Mortals and Others* (Routledge Classics, 2009), 204. https://quoteinvestigator.com/2015/03/04/ self-doubt/.

2 W. B. Yeats, "The Second Coming." https://poets.org/poem/second-coming

3 See my books: *Nemesis at Potsdam* (Routledge 1977), reviewed by Ben Ferencz in the *American Journal of International Law* (AJIL); *The Wehrmacht War Crimes Bureau, 1939–1945* (University of Nebraska Press, 1989), reviewed by Ben Ferencz in AJIL; *Völkermord als Staatsgeheimnis* (Olzog, 2011), reviewed in *Genocide Prevention Now* (Jerusalem: Hebrew University, Winter 2011).

4 A list of states adhering to the Rome Statute can be found at International Criminal Court, *The States Parties to the Rome Statute:* https://asp.icc-cpi.int/states-parties

5 Ibid.

6 The U.S. has disregarded 30 resolutions by the General Assembly calling for the lifting of the U.S. embargo against Cuba.

7 United Nations Department of Economic and Social Affairs, Sustainable Development, *Gross National Happiness Index.* https://sdgs.un.org/partnerships/ gross-national-happiness-index

8 UN General Assembly Documentation, *Voting in the General Assembly.* https://research.un.org/en/docs/ga/voting

9 A/RES/39/11: Resolution adopted by the General Assembly, *39/11. Right of peoples to peace,* November 12, 1984. http://www.un-documents.net/a39r11.htm

10 Mike Stone, "Ukraine war spurs European demand for U.S. arms, but not big-ticket items," *Reuters,* February 17, 2023. https://www.reuters.com/world/europe/ ukraine-war-spurs-european-demand-us-arms-not-big-ticket-items-2023-02-17/

11 United Nations Human Rights Council, *Right to Peace.* https://www.ohchr. org/en/hr-bodies/hrc/advisory-committee/right-to-peace

12 United Nations Human Rights Council, *Open-ended intergovernmental working group on a draft United Nations declaration on the right to peace.* https:// www.ohchr.org/en/hr-bodies/hrc/right-peace/wg-draft-un-declarationonthe-rightto-peace

13 See Chapter 3, "Peace is a Human Right," in Zayas, *Building a Just World Order* (Clarity Press 2021).

14 United Nations Human Rights, "The right to peace," April 4, 2013. https:// www.ohchr.org/en/stories/2013/04/right-peace

15 Christian Guillermet Fernández and David Fernández Puyana [Inter Press Service–IPS], "The UN Human Rights Council Adopts the Declaration on the Right to Peace," *Transcend Media Service,* August 1, 2016. https://www.transcend.org/ tms/2016/08/the-un-human-rights-council-adopts-the-declaration-on-the-right-to-peace/

16 A/HRC/RES/32/28 2: Resolution adopted by the Human Rights Council *Declaration on the Right to Peace,* July 1, 2016, United Nations Digital Library. https://digitallibrary.un.org/record/845647

17 Declaration on the Right to Peace: Resolution adopted by the UN General Assembly, 2017 (71st sess. : 2016-2017). UN Digital Library. https://digitallibrary. un.org/record/858594?ln=en

18 Alfred de Zayas, "UN and unilateral coercive measures," *New Age,* February 1, 2023. https://www.newagebd.net/article/193203/un-and-unilateral-coercive-measures

Peoples Dispatch, "UN Human Rights Council Condemns Impact of Sanctions," *Consortium News,* April 6, 2023.

19 United Nations Human Rights, "Intervention by Alfred de Zayas - Unilateral sanctions," May 23, 2014. https://www.ohchr.org/en/2014/05/intervention-alfred-de-zayas-unilateral-sanctions

20 On April 4, 2023, the 52nd session of the Council adopted a similar resolution condemning UCMs by a vote of 33 in favour, 13 against and 1 abstention.

21 General Assembly resolution 77/7 of November 3, 2022.

22 Alfred de Zayas, "The United Nations and Unilateral Coercive Measures," *Swiss Standpoint,* February 7, 2023. https://schweizer-standpunkt.ch/news-detailansicht-en-recht/the-united-nations-and-unilateral-coercive-measures.html

23 Craig Murray, "US & Ukraine at UN Refuse to Condemn Nazism," *Consortium News,* December 23, 2021. https://consortiumnews.com/2021/12/23/us-ukraine-refuse-to-condemn-nazism-at-un/

24 United Nations, "General Assembly Emergency Session Overwhelmingly Demands Israel's Compliance with International Court of Justice Advisory Opinion" [press release], July 20, 2004.https://press.un.org/en/2004/ga10248.doc.htm

25 International Court of Justice, *Legal Consequences of the Construction of a Wall in the Occupied Palestinian Territory.* https://www.icj-cij.org/en/case/131

26 The interior notes for this document can be accessed on the pdf at https://documents-dds-ny.un.org/doc/UNDOC/GEN/N22/756/93/PDF/N2275693.pdf?OpenElement

27 Ben Norton, "West opposes rest of world in UN votes for fairer economic system, equality, sustainable development," Geo Political Economy, *G/E,* December 22, 2022. https://geopoliticaleconomy.com/2022/12/22/west-un-vote-economic-system-equality/

28 United Nations, "General Assembly Takes Up Second Committee Reports, Adopting 38 Resolutions, 2 Decisions" [press release], December 14, 2022. https://press.un.org/en/2022/ga12482.doc.htm

29 United Nations General Assembly, *Resolutions of the 77th Session.* https://www.un.org/en/ga/77/resolutions.shtml

30 For example, on September 28, 2022. See video archive: "UNHRC Panel on the Legacies of Colonialism," *UNPFIP Network,* October 5, 2022. https://unpfip.blogspot.com/2022/10/blog-post.html

31 "Spinoza's Political Philosophy," *Stanford Encyclopedia of Philosophy,* April 21, 2008, updated April 15, 2019. https://plato.stanford.edu/entries/spinoza-political/

32 In his *Tractatus Politicus* (Political Treatise), written 1675–76 and published after his death, Spinoza asserts: "For peace is not mere absence of war but is a virtue that springs from force of character." This definition of peace anticipates later expositions that see peace as a virtue. See "Philosophy of Peace," *Internet Encyclopedia of Philosophy,* https://iep.utm.edu/peace/

CONCLUSION & RECOMMENDATIONS

1 See "A Culture of Cheating," Chapter 20 in Zayas, *Countering Mainstream Narratives* (Clarity Press, 2022).

2 President John F. Kennedy, "Commencement Address at American University, Washington, D.C., June 10, 1963," JFK Library, https://www.jfklibrary.org/archives/other-resources/john-f-kennedy-speeches/american-university-19630610

3 See the proposals of the San Francisco NGO, Eleanor Lives! https://www.eleanorlives.org

4 "Vatican formally rejects 'Doctrine of Discovery' after Indigenous calls," *PBS News Hour,* March 30, 2023. https://www.pbs.org/newshour/politics/vatican-formally-rejects-doctrine-of-discovery-after-indigenous-calls

AIATSIS, "Case summary: *Mabo v Queensland."* https://aiatsis.gov.au/publication/35464

5 Jeffrey Sachs, *The End of Poverty: Economic Possibilities for Our Time* (Penguin 2005), 368.

INDEX